As a Minister, Parliamensed his decades in the House — service to his constituents and creativ...

Long before many others ... understood the crucial and informed connection that has to be made between science and technology and political decision-making. No-one has ever campaigned more diligently and intelligently for making that connection a coherent and central feature of accountable modern government. Some of his initiatives, including the Office of Science and Technology and the present Select Committee on Science and Technology, provide tangible continuing testimony of the value of Jeremy's work. But the broader counsel that he offered on research, on education, and on industrial and government responsibility for the discovery and use of scientific potential is still not applied with the necessary energy, even in the new century. It needs to be. As Jeremy Bray has always argued, the protection and prosperity of humanity depend upon it.

Rt Hon Neil Kinnock
Leader of the Labour party 1983-92 Vice-President of the European Commission.

THE CONSTITUENCY MEMBER OF PARLIAMENT

I have love for that guy and a great deal of respect. He was our friend. Many Lanarkshire steelworkers came to share my gratitude for Jeremy the academic's genuine sustained hard work and concern. My lasting memory is of George Quinn, Craft Convenor, and myself leaving Jeremy's office at 2.30 in the morning, while he finished his work on a report on the steel industry.

Tommy Brennan
Convenor of the Ravenscraig Shop Stewards.

To me, Jeremy Bray's finest performance in the Chamber was in April 1990 when, still recuperating from a life-saving heart bypass operation, he determinedly turned up to speak in defence of his constituency steelworks at Ravenscraig. The steelworks had a fiercely proud and efficient work force who prided themselves on their steel-making expertise. Steel suffered death by a thousand cuts. To his great credit, Jeremy fought against every cut along the way. It is an honour and privilege to be his successor.

Jeremy's successor, Frank Roy, Member of Parliament for Motherwell and Wishaw, in his maiden speech, 2 July 1997.

OVERLEAF: COMMENDATIONS FROM

Professor Berc Rustem
(Department of Computing, Imperial College, London).
Professor John Ziman FRS
(Formerly Chairman, Science Policy Support Group; Convenor Epistemology Group).
Professor Duncan B. Forrester
(Emeritus Professor of Theology & Public Issues, University of Edinburgh).

THE PIONEER IN ECONOMIC MODELLING AND OPTIMISATION

Jeremy Bray spanned science, economics and politics with insight, skill and wisdom. He was one of the pioneers of modelling dynamic economic systems, forecasting and policy. Throughout his political career, and even into retirement, he kept an up-to-date research agenda in these areas. He played a key role in encouraging HM Treasury in the early development of the Treasury model; his amendment of the 1975 Industry Act resulted in the Committee on Policy Optimisation and ensured the general availability of the HM Treasury model of the UK economy. Both actions opened major discussions on macroeconomic models. He had wide ranging interests. He demanded effective research results from scientists in forecasting and policy design, and high standards of decision making from his colleagues in politics. He himself could do both quite easily.

Professor Berc Rustem
Department of Computing, Imperial College, London.

THE OPPOSITION SPOKESMAN FOR SCIENCE AND TECHNOLOGY

The research system frequently brings working scientists and scholars into active contact with elected politicians. Most are inclined to be helpful, but Jeremy Bray was almost alone as a senior political figure who also understood the true nature of modern science. This was not just because, as this book explains, he had early professional experience of it from the inside. It was because he was truly interested in how it really works, and continued to read and think, listen and talk, about this enigmatic subject, throughout a busy and socially creative life. It was always highly pleasurable and instructive to converse with him on such matters. Alas, no more. But we can still appreciate the wisdom of that fine, thoughtful man as he speaks out from these pages.

Professor John Ziman FRS
formerly Chairman, Science Policy Support Group; Convenor Epistemology Group.

THE THINKER

Jeremy Bray played a quiet but informed and influential role in British politics for some forty years, spanning a time of fundamental changes in almost every area of life. His insistence that science and technology were of the greatest importance for the future well-being of society has left a lasting imprint on British politics. And his undogmatic concern that government should take economic and social research with the greatest seriousness was another contribution of one noted for his personal integrity and care for the weak and vulnerable in our society, and indeed in the world. For him politics was a vocation from God, and his faith shaped his whole life in public as in private.

Duncan B. Forrester
Emeritus Professor of Theology & Public Issues, the University of Edinburgh.

Standing on the Shoulders of Giants

*Science, politics and trust:
A parliamentary life*

STANDING ON THE SHOULDERS OF GIANTS

Science, politics and trust
A parliamentary life

Jeremy Bray

Edited by
Elizabeth Bray

EB

Published by Elizabeth Bray
21 Horn Lane, Linton, Cambridge CB1 6HT

2004

First published in 2004

Published by Elizabeth Bray
21 Horn Lane, Linton,
Cambridge CB1 6HT, UK
elizabeth_bray@tiscali.co.uk

© 2004 by Jeremy Bray & Elizabeth Bray

All rights reserved.

No part of this publication may be reproduced,
stored in a retrieval system or transmitted,
in any form or by any means, electronic,
mechanical, photocopying, recording or otherwise,
without the prior permission of the publisher.

ISBN 0-95469220-0-9

British Library Cataloguing-in-Publication Data
A CIP catalogue record for this book is available from the British Library

Printed and bound by
E & E Plumridge Ltd
41 High Street, Linton, Cambridge CB1 6HS

 **THE ROYAL SOCIETY**

Foreword
Lord May of Oxford
President of the Royal Society

I knew Jeremy before I moved to Britain in 1988. For many, many years he was notable among Members of the House of Commons as a person who was influential in shaping Labour Party policies, while at the same time having a deep and wide interest not only in economic theory but across the sweep of the physical and biological sciences. This, indeed, is how I made his acquaintance while still a member of the Biological Faculty at Princeton University.

I had many discussions with him after I moved to Britain as a Royal Society Research Professor. He was the originator of the idea of creating an Office of Science and Technology within the Cabinet Office. This was part of the Labour Party manifesto in the 1992 election which John Major won, and Major was characteristically wise enough to borrow the idea. I subsequently became the head of the OST for five years.

Jeremy was, in my opinion, possibly too reflective and intellectual a character ever to have emerged at the very top of the political tumble. But as an influential thinker in Westminster, he was at the centre of much of the formulation of policy, and even more in thinking wider thoughts, through important decades in the latter half of the Twentieth Century. Jeremy has always been noted for the breadth and originality of his thinking – unusual for a person who was so active in politics itself. He was always aware of new developments in economic theory and more generally. It was, for example, in the early days of Chaos Theory, of which I am one of the early principal figures, that we first met.

I am sure that this book will have a substantial readership – and a substantial impact – both among academic students of political science and among practitioners of politics and I warmly commend it.

Robert M. May

In gratitude to
our four beloved daughters
Margaret, Bridget, Teresa & Beatrice
who did their best to keep me human
JWB

Left to right:
Bridget, Jeremy, Elizabeth, Tess & Margaret
Front: Beatrice & Honey (the dog)
This photo was taken on the occasion of our Silver Wedding 1978

Photograph courtesy of Ronnie Weir Dick, Helensburgh.

Author's Preface

My life in politics spanned the second half of the twentieth century. Throughout I was principally concerned with the application of science to politics and government: that is to say, the application of the patterns, strategies and models of science to the major questions of politics today: how we manage our economy, how we use science in framing policies, how we prepare to face the future, how – in other words – we optimise, making the best decisions in an imperfect world, given our own fallibility and limitations.

None of us can know the future. It is hidden from our eyes. Indeed, at any and every time, there are many possible futures. But that does not absolve politics from the inescapable duty of taking action and changing lives. True, policy decisions are made on the basis of very partial knowledge. There are huge uncertainties. But you are more likely to make good decisions, or, at least, more likely not to make very bad decisions, if you are prepared to listen to what science (and history) has to say, and to learn how to use and evaluate the available evidence and structures.

Parliament was an immensely privileged position from which to view a rapidly changing world, and to play my small part in shaping it. I will be trying in this book to describe what happened in my life so readers can learn for themselves. Some conclusions may emerge. I try to recognise my own limitations – limitations of understanding, of skills, of powers of persuasion, of personality, of political appeal. Where does that leave me? It leaves me at bottom a cheerful man. For the brilliant intellectual success of science in exploring the world in which we live has been impressive. Living as we do at a time of great discovery and scientific fertility, we are standing on the shoulders of giants.

I am conscious that remarkable advances are taking place in medicine, physics, astronomy, chemistry, mathematics and biology with ever increasing rapidity. Economic and social research have been contributing to understanding the responses needed to the massive changes in society. Over the past fifty years there has been a growing recognition of the great benefits science can bring to improving the quality of our lives with technologies that can address our needs and aspirations. True, not all that science offers is conducive to the well-being of humanity, and we need more than science to help us make intelligent, well-informed and humane choices about the value, or otherwise, of particular technologies. But, far from being untrustworthy, science on the whole has proved remarkably reliable within its sphere of relevance.

Unsurprisingly, science and technology now have a key role in every aspect of government policy: science shapes the way our economy develops, and science, technology and innovation are the key to industrial success and the provision of the infrastructure - transport, the health service, education and much more. Of particular interest to me was science as a powerful source of ideas – the patterns, strategies, and models that can help us better to describe, and to react to, practical social and political problems.

The key role of science is far clearer today than it was when I was growing up in the 1930s and 1940s, and being taught mathematics, computer science and control theory at Cambridge, Harvard and MIT in the early 1950s. At that time you could count on one hand the total number of computers in Britain. They were clumsy, primitive machines. Circuitry which can now be packed onto a chip smaller than a postage stamp was then hand-wired on to a panel the size of a door. Most households today have more computers, and more computing power, under one roof than there were in the whole of Britain when I graduated. By the end of my parliamentary life I was able to run a copy of the Treasury's own model of the national economy on my desktop computer at the House of Commons.

Yet the wider interpretation of science policy still awaits development. Science policy remains in limbo. Decisions lack coherence. By and large ministers (and the media) have a blind spot when it comes to science. Few if any cabinet ministers have a grounding in science. Despite the major constitutional changes initiated by the Blair governments of 1997 and 2001 (reform of the House of Lords, devolution, and much else), the fundamental questions about the role of science and technology, and its place in the machinery of government, have not been addressed. It is a grave defect and limits our ability to handle vital questions.

Why did I devote so much of my life to these concerns? Because they mattered. Like so many MPs I entered politics because I hoped and prayed I might be able to change things for the better. And I continued in this hope until the end of my political career.

Author's Preface ♦ xi

Denied ministerial office, but free-lancing within a parliamentary framework, I was able to take the long view. My concerns with science and technology and economics, and their interaction, spanned some fifty years from the 1950s to today. These concerns developed simultaneously, but in this book I will discuss them in sequence within the context of my own political life. Furthermore they are unfinished business and will always remain so. So the narratives will verge into forward views and wider horizons. Out of them will emerge conclusions for politics and society. I think I reach strong conclusions on major issues, but the reader must judge and I hope improve on them.

Science, in the broadest sense, may be the key to managing the economy and public policy competently, efficiently and effectively. But in itself it is not enough.

In my concluding chapters I step back and seek clues from the history and philosophy of science that may help us to see the interaction of science, politics and our value systems, principally value systems based on religion. Here too we stand upon the shoulders of giants.

We have to ask how science works, how, in effect, we know. The inadequacy of the approach of the economists to modelling behaviour lies not so much in its over-elaboration as in its narrowness in the choice of activity modelled. We need to introduce the concepts of stewardship, co-operation and transparency. We have to ponder the giving and withholding of trust or belief. We have to consider the different attitudes of different kinds of people, of scientists and lay people, of the secular and the religious, of the uneducated and the highly educated, in America, Europe and the rest of the world. I take these up in my final chapters.

Many of my insights owe much to those whom I have met in my pilgrimage through life: my family and friends; my colleagues in parliament; my constituents; my neighbours; and in particular the many distinguished scientists and economists, academics and religious leaders, whom I have met over the course of years, or whose works I have read. To them all, my grateful thanks.

Jeremy Bray
31 May 2002

Jeremy and Elizabeth Bray during the 1992 General Election campaign

Acknowledgements

Jeremy would have wished to acknowledge the help and advice
of his many colleagues and correspondents.

Elizabeth acknowledges the help and encouragement of friends including
Lord May, Neil Kinnock, Professor Berc Rustem, Professor John Ziman,
Tommy Brennan and Frank Roy MP;
also Beverley Hough and Mary Ryecroft for proof reading,
and Ronnie Weir Dick, Helensburgh, for the cover and other photos.

She also wishes to acknowledge the kind permissions of copyright holders:
acknowledgement of sources is made wherever possible. In some cases the
copyright holder was untraceable. She would be grateful if any such copyright
holder would contact her at the address given on the title page.

Editor's note

My husband, Jeremy, died at home, suddenly but peacefully, on the evening of 31st May 2002. We both knew he had not long to live, a fact he faced courageously. Earlier that day we had discussed his book, which, despite his long illness, he had just completed in draft. He asked me to prepare it for publication. 'I haven't the strength left to do it,' he said. I am neither a scientist nor an economist. But we had worked collaboratively for over fifty years, and I had worked in Jeremy's parliamentary office at Westminster for the last fourteen years of his life as an MP.

So I agreed to edit the book. We discussed in some detail the changes necessary. During the remainder of the day, he prepared the book for me to work on. It was a sunny day, and we had tea together in the garden. He died an hour or two after he had printed out the last chapter.

As far as it lies in me, I have undertaken the editing in the spirit he requested. The principal changes I have made are as follows:

We agreed that the book needed to be more accessible to the general reader. So although about 97% of the book is in his words, I have added some explanatory material, and I have occasionally sketched in the background more fully – who's who, and the sequence of political events, for example.

The book was over-long. We had talked this through. Most books are improved by judicious cuts. So I have made cuts, some – but not all – of which we had discussed; I have also précised parts where the argument needed to be tightened up.

Sometimes I have re-ordered the material to make it easier to navigate within the book. I have occasionally used extracts from Jeremy's published and unpublished writings to clarify the argument. But essentially this is his valediction to a life in science and politics, informed by his faith in science, in the political process, in humanity and in God.

Elizabeth Bray

Note: Jeremy Bray's original text is archived along with his other papers in Churchill College, Cambridge. Access can be arranged with the College archivist.

Contents

♦ PART ONE ♦ 1
BEGINNINGS

INTRODUCTION TO PART ONE 2

1. Formative years 1930-1956 5
2. Industrial and practical experience 1956-1962 21
3. By-election victor 37

♦ PART TWO ♦ 47
A PARLIAMENTARY APPRENTICESHIP

INTRODUCTION TO PART TWO 48

4. A first spell in parliament 1962-1966 51
5. A taste of office 1966-1969 67
6. *Decision in Government* and resignation 1969 77
7. Wilderness Years 1970-1974 87
8. Member for Motherwell and Wishaw 1974-1997 94

♦ PART THREE ♦ 107
OPTIMISATION & THE BRITISH ECONOMY

INTRODUCTION TO PART THREE 108

9. Policy optimisation 1970-1983 116
10. Open government and the Industry Bill 1975 126
11. The IMF loan and the abandonment of Keynesian demand management 1976 132
12. Monetary Policy: Treasury Select Committee Report 1981 137
13. International Monetary Arrangements: Treasury Select Committee Report 1983 149
14. Opening up access to the Treasury model 1983-1993 156
15. New Labour's economic strategy as it emerged 1992-97 165

♦ PART FOUR ♦   179
SPOKESMAN FOR SCIENCE & TECHNOLOGY

INTRODUCTION TO PART FOUR   180

16	Opposition Spokesman for Science & Technology 1983-1992	184
17	Science policy as an election issue in 1987 and 1992 …	194
18	The Science and Technology Select Committee 1992-1997	204
19	Science in parliament and government … … … …	211
20	Farewell to parliament 1997 … … … … … … …	221

♦ PART FIVE ♦   229
ON TRUST

INTRODUCTION TO PART FIVE   230

21	Ground on which to stand … … … … … …	236
22	Politics, science and crystal balls … … … … …	249
23	The ethos of a covenant … … … … … … …	266
24	The moral and ethical foundations of society … … …	277
25	A climate of trust … … … … … … … …	287

INDEX OF NAMES   299

Abbreviations

BSE	Bovine Spongiform Encephalopathy
CSO	[The British government's] Central Statistical Office
DES	Department of Education & Skills
DTI	Department of Trade and Industry
EDM	Early Day Motion
EMU	European Monetary Union
ERM	Exchange Rate Mechanism
ESRC	Economic and Social Research Council
EU	European Union
Fed	The Federal Reserve Board, USA
FT	Financial Times
FRS	Fellow of the Royal Society
GDP	Gross Domestic Product
HMSO	Her Majesty's Stationery Office
ICI	Imperial Chemical Industries
IMF	International Monetary Fund
LBS	London Business School
LSE	London School of Economics
MinTech	Ministry of Technology
MIT	Massachusetts Institute of Technology
MP	Member of Parliament
NEDO	National Economic Development Office
NATO	North Atlantic Treaty Organisation
NIESR	National Institute of Economic & Social Research
OECD	Organisation for Economic Cooperation and Development
OPEC	Organization of Petroleum Exporting Countries
OST	Office of Science and Technology
PLP	Parliamentary Labour Party
PM	Prime Minister
PPS	Parliamentary Private Secretary [a ministerial aide]
PREM	Programme for Research into Econometric Methods
PROPE	Programme for Research into Optimal Policy Evaluation
QC	Queen's Counsel
R&D	Research and Development
SCM	Student Christian Movement
SSRC	Social Science Research Council
T&GWU	Transport and General Workers' Union (also TGWU)
TUC	Trades Union Congress
UMIST	University of Manchester Institute of Science & Technology
VAT	Value Added Tax

Part One
BEGINNINGS

In a Chinese temple. Photograph: Arthur Bray c. 1930

Introduction to Part One

BEGINNINGS

I owe much to my parents – my interest in science and technology, and in mathematics, and, not least, a sense of vocation, a commitment to public service, and a grounding in faith. They were serving as Christian missionaries in China at the time of my birth and I spent my early years in China. Fortunately we returned to Britain in 1939 as China was being overrun by invading Japanese armies. So I was educated at John Wesley's foundation, Kingswood School, Bath. From there I won a scholarship to study mathematics at Cambridge.

It was in Cambridge that I fell in love with my wife-to-be, Elizabeth. We met through the Student Christian Movement. It was the start of a life-long partnership for which I am eternally grateful.

Mathematics may seem an unlikely choice for an aspiring politician – a dry unattractive subject in the general view. Yet mathematicians would claim it is the most beautiful subject in science, and the key to much of science. My mentors at Cambridge and Harvard in the early 1950s found my interest in what we now call computer science and control theory decidedly odd. Who then could have imagined that the two or three machines people were beginning to call 'computers' were destined to become essential tools in every sphere?

My working life began in industry in ICI where we were pioneering the new tools for modelling systems. With computers still in their infancy, we were only just beginning to develop key concepts and applications not only in industrial processes but also in guiding economic and social policy. These concepts were to remain relevant throughout my parliamentary career.

PART ONE

BEGINNINGS

1   **FORMATIVE YEARS**   4
    My childhood in China ~ Schooldays in Britain ~ University
    life and falling in love ~ .... and mathematics ~ Graduation
    and marriage ~ Yet more mathematics ~ The beginnings of
    computer science ~ Harvard and the Massachusetts Institute
    of Technology

2   **INDUSTRIAL AND PRACTICAL EXPERIENCE**   21
    Laying the foundations for a political career ~ A
    mathematician among chemists ~ The origins of computer
    control and automation in ICI ~ The relevance of my
    industrial experience ~ Handling other operational problems
    ~ Putting down roots on Teesside ~ ICI in its local context
    ~ A launch pad for politics

3   **BY ELECTION VICTOR 1962**   37
    The rough and tumble of politics ~ Victory is in sight ~ The
    first Labour by-election win for over a decade ~ My debt to
    my constituents in Middlesbrough & Thornaby

4 ♦ STANDING ON THE SHOULDERS OF GIANTS

Above: Pagoda. Photograph by Arthur Bray c. 1925

Above: Jeremy's parents: Muriel Bray (neé Campbell) & Arthur Bray
Probably taken at the time of their wedding in 1921

1

Formative years
1930-1956

The abiding impression my parents left on me was one of vocation. They felt called by God to be Christian missionaries in China, just as they felt all people are called to some occupation. To them I owe my grounding in faith.

My childhood in China

My mother, Muriel Campbell, graduated and took an M.Sc. in physics at Queen's University, Belfast. She was born in 1892 in Tralee, in the south western corner of Ireland, a daughter of Joseph Campbell, a Methodist minister, who was to become the President of the highly regarded school, Methodist College, Belfast, and President of the Irish Methodist Conference. She must have been capable. There were not many women M.Sc. physicists before the First World War. She taught mathematics at Methody (the Methodist College) to Ernest Walton, another son of the Irish Methodist manse who later, with John Cockcroft at Cambridge, shared a Nobel Prize for splitting the atom. But she gave up her science to go out to China as a missionary teacher. There she met my father, a Methodist missionary. She never spoke to us about her science: when we sought her help with our homework thirty years later she explained that the mathematics used even at school had changed completely. If mathematical ability is a heritable trait, I owe it to my mother.

My father, Arthur Bray, was born in 1886, the younger son of Thomas Bray who kept the shoe shop in Ledbury, Herefordshire. He graduated at Durham University in classics and studied at Didsbury Methodist Theological College, Manchester, where he became an assistant tutor. Ordained as a minister, he went out to China as a missionary in 1914, and it was in China he met and married my mother, a calm and rather beautiful woman.

Above: View from Cheung Chow ~ an island near Hong Kong, where the Bray family used to holiday in the 1930s. Note the Chinese junks and fishing vessels.

*Below: Fun on the beach at Cheung Chow :
Left to right: Eleanor (3), Jeremy (5), Denis (9) & Barbara (7) Both photos: Arthur Bray*

My father retained a lifelong interest in theology, and a deep personal commitment. But he was also very interested in China and warmed to its people. Both my parents spoke fluent Cantonese, the dialect in south China and Hong Kong (and this was my first language as a small child). My father studied the *Analects of Confucius*, and I have to this day his copy[1], with the Chinese and English text side by side. His annotations, often of the Chinese characters, show his interest in Chinese culture.

Above all, he loved building – and building up – institutions: churches, schools and hospitals. In Hong Kong and Foshan in the Guangdong province, despite wars and revolutions, they flourish to this day.

He was a fine craftsman – perhaps those shoe-making forebears passed down their skills – and he admired traditional Chinese crafts. But soon after the First World War he had the boys in the Wa Ying High School (now the Number One High School in Foshan), learning western engineering and using machine tools in a major departure from the Mandarin tradition of education, which did not encourage scholars to dirty their hands with manual work.

My own family were fortunate to survive unharmed the real enough hazards we faced in China during the Japanese invasion of China in 1937, as the crowds of refugees from Canton fled past us in Foshan, pursued by a Japanese army looting and killing as they went. We escaped on the ancient hospital launch down the long winding muddy creeks to Canton and the Pearl River – a long, tedious and perilous journey – and with difficulty were hauled aboard the river steamer waiting to collect us and evacuate us to Hong Kong. The dangers were not trivial, and my father, usually so good natured, was almost incandescent with rage and anxiety when we nearly missed the rescue boat. I was seven at the time, and my youngest sister five.

My elder brother, Denis, has published a vivid description of our childhood[2]. Like Denis, and my elder sister, Barbara, I was sent soon after my seventh birthday to a China Inland Mission boarding school at Chefoo in northern China. In Chefoo, already under Japanese occupation, I remember seeing Chinese prisoners being marched to their execution under armed guards. The voyage up the coast from Hong Kong to our school on the Shandong peninsular (not far from Beijing) took over a week. A few years earlier a boatload of children had been captured by pirates. We still heard their stories. The child passengers were rescued, but

---

[1] Confucius, *Analects of Confucius*, Ed Soothill, William Edward (1910) Fukuin Printing Company, Yokohama
[2] Bray, Denis, (2001) *Hong Kong Metamorphosis*, Hong Kong: Hong Kong University Press

the chief officer was killed. Because of the length of the voyage, Chefoo pupils spent the spring and summer holidays at school, only returning to our families once a year, for the two month winter break. Although the staff were dedicated, for a small child this absence of ten months from home and family was an emotional deprivation. Tears, home-sickness and even signs of affection between brothers were seen as 'sissy'. I sometimes think I would have been a better father to my own children – more fun, more openly affectionate and more relaxed and sympathetic – if my childhood experiences had been different.

Fortunately, as my father was due to retire, the family returned to England in 1939 – my parents, elder brother Denis (13) and elder sister Barbara (11), myself (aged nine) and our youngest sister Eleanor (seven). So we were spared the fate of many other families, of being split up and interned in different Japanese camps in World War 2.

Schooldays in Britain

During World War 2, my father was the minister in the English Methodist church in Aberystwyth, where there was a large student congregation from the evacuated University College of London, as well as the University College of Wales, an RAF Initial Training Wing and an anti-aircraft training regiment. I met at home leading preachers of the day whom my father had invited to speak to the students. I remember particularly C.S.Lewis and W.F.Howard, the Johannine scholar. Then, and later at Kingswood School, Bath, which John Wesley had founded in the eighteenth century for the sons of his itinerant preachers, theologians were the most impressive people I met, not I think because they had the greatest power in our little world, but because of their eloquence and learning. It was not at the cost of science: John Wesley himself had made sure the Kingswood School library had the *Philosophical Transactions of the Royal Society*, and that was in the middle of the eighteenth century.

That school library also had the dry but analytic *Grammar of Politics*, by Harold Laski, the London School of Economics political scientist and Labour Party activist, which persuaded me to become a socialist. LSE was a seedbed of radical ideas. Beveridge, a former Director of LSE, had produced the Beveridge Plan which helped to cement the wartime coalition. I was in my early teens, and only dimly aware of the dynamic ideas being propounded: socialism, Keynsian economics, a welfare state, the nationalisation of swathes of industry, and – the jewel in the crown – a National Health Service. I was just fifteen years old when Labour swept into power in 1945. It was a time of high expectations and great excitement. Despite the grim austerity of the post-war years, all these things came to pass.

Kingswood School, under its remarkable headmaster, A.B.Sackett, and its chaplain, the Lutheran scholar, Rupert Davies, offered as good a model as I have seen of an unreservedly Christian education, engaged in the world, and loving learning. I shall dwell on it a little because it seemed to offer more in the way of a Christian education than anything, I am ashamed to say, that I or my generation in politics have provided for our children.

Sackett belonged to the same remarkable generation as Harold Macmillan (the future Prime Minister but then, in the 1940s, just a junior minister). Like Macmillan he had survived the trenches of the First World War. He had lost only a leg, and found it good to be alive.

Rupert Davies set out in the teaching and life of the school an attitude to Christian education and what is in effect a simple modern synthesis of all knowledge. He later summarised his ideas in the introductory chapter to *An Approach to Christian Education*[3], a symposium with contributions by Charles Coulson, the mathematical physicist; Gordon Rupp and Herbert Butterfield, the historians; Basil Willey, the English scholar, and others.

I can recall Davies arguing that Christians at least are committed to the view that we live in a universe, not in a fortuitous conglomeration of individual existences, for they believe in one Creator of all things. So a synthesis of its apparently contradictory and certainly very diverse elements must be at least theoretically possible. To leave the attempt at a synthesis aside, and accept single things, such as democracy, or freedom, or justice, or culture, as having truth and value separately, in and by themselves, is to acquiesce in a lazy pluralism. Such a synthesis had a strong appeal to me as I began to think what I should try to do in life.

For Davies, the co-ordinating principle in such a synthesis was the knowledge of God which comes to us through Christ, in whom God makes himself known to man and is approached in faith and obedience by man – approached by man in all his conditions, not only by the sophisticated theologian and philosopher, but also by the child and by the unlearned too in their own way. While he was developing this epistemology Davies was at the time undoubtedly influenced by Karl Barth.

---

[3] Davies, Rupert (ed.) (1956) *An Approach to Christian Education* London: Epworth Press

Davies did not put knowledge of God through Christ on a level with other forms of knowledge, but in a unique and unapproachable relation to all other knowledges. Science, art, history and non-Christian religions and philosophies, he argued, can give us information about God which cannot be derived from any other source. But they need to be taught objectively. There is, he would say, no such thing as 'Christian history' (although there is a history of Christianity) nor 'Christian mathematics'; there is just history and mathematics. But those who have both the necessary skills and insights, and who accept the Christian synthesis, will (he would argue) teach them better. It was a natural step for me as a boy to go on to suppose that what is true about teaching must also be true about the practice of what is taught, and life outside the classroom.

This ambitious approach was an enormously attractive perspective for a young person. For me, that synthesis took root and grew throughout my life. But there was no magic formula about it: some of my friends who went through the same experience at the same time, did not continue as practising Christians in later life. Fifty years ago, for better or worse, Christianity was a greater influence than any other single faith. Today there is a widespread ignorance of what religion is, and how it works, whether Christian or not. That ignorance may be shared by the unlearned school child of the inner city, and the sophisticated humanist of postmodernity. A century of scepticism does not seem to have left many people secure in their own beliefs. It is a situation which I think many people accept, without being happy about it: it leads to a general sense of *annuie* or normlessness, but that still exists alongside what Barth spoke of as 'that moral perception which dwells in all its simplicity in the midst of the rough and tumble of human life'.

University life …. and falling in love

On going up to Cambridge in 1949, I found a continuity with the ideas I had found so stimulating at school. By this time my parents were back in Hong Kong, launched on a new task. My father was over sixty.

Undergraduate life was fun. Being at Jesus College, I rowed of course, though badly. I flew Tiger Moths and Chipmunks in the University Air Squadron until the instructors were forced to admit that the RAF had been right in failing me in the pilot aptitude tests during my national service. Later, as a research student, I founded a college student art collection, which still has the Henry Moore leaf figure bronze and the Ivon Hitchens oil painting we bought.

More important to me, I was active in the then large university Student Christian Movement. Here I met and fell deeply in love with Elizabeth Trowell, who was reading English at Girton College. Her parents, like mine, were abroad. Her father, Hugh Trowell, was a doctor working in Uganda's leading African hospital and the medical school; her mother, Peggy Trowell, was the founder and head of the School of Art at Makerere College (later university). They turned out to be delightful, if eccentric and formidable, parents-in-law. Elizabeth and I were to marry in 1953. Religion and mainstream Christian beliefs have been a part of life for us ever since, not conflicting with other aspects of life, but helpfully and constructively illuminating them all in ways that have continued to develop.

The Student Christian Movement, to which we both owed much, was an ecumenical movement, well organised in the universities since our parents' day. In those days it enjoyed wider support in Cambridge than any of the political parties. It delighted in learning, ancient and modern, religious and secular, and enjoyed the support of church leaders. It was the Christian establishment of the next generation, and we made many life-long friends through the Cambridge SCM. I became the President of the SCM branch in Cambridge, and Elizabeth the Secretary, so we learnt to work as a team before we were wife and husband.

At the time, the SCM was deeply committed to an engagement with the world – with industry, with politics, with welfare issues and overseas development, with science and medicine, art and music. So it made sense for me to see public service and politics as Christian vocations. It was all encompassed in the phrase, 'Christianity and ...', which owed much to the inspiration of William Temple, the Archbishop of Canterbury.

The influences that mattered to students at Cambridge were primarily the interests and attitudes of other students, not just those of the staff. Lectures and supervisions were formally important – you produced a weekly essay or (in the case of mathematicians) worked through a past exam paper each week. However, many of the staff exerted their influence mainly through their social relations with students, and as the tutors, and, for those so inclined, as the deans and chaplains of college chapels.

One such was John Robinson, later to become the Bishop of Woolwich and the author of the best seller *Honest to God*[4]. He was then the Dean of Clare College. He had been President of the Cambridge SCM in 1942-43 while an undergraduate at Jesus, and I was succeeding him as President in 1951-52. On the recommendation of my father, I had read his first book *In*

---

[4] Robinson, John (1963) *Honest to God* London: SCM Press

the End God...: a study of the Christian doctrine of the last things[5]. He was ready to advise, but not to impose. For example, there had been a tradition for Christian groups from Cambridge going out to some urban or industrial community and conducting a mission, usually for a week or so. I proposed to the SCM that we should do this in Batley, Yorkshire, with which I was in touch. We were not sure about the strength of our vocation to do this, and the executive committee delegated me to consult Michael Ramsey, then Regius Professor of Divinity, and later to be such an impressive Archbishop of Canterbury. He listened carefully, and in the end advised against this plan. I learnt much from him.

Elizabeth and I kept in touch with John and Ruth Robinson, and they invited us all as a family to stay with them when he was Bishop of Woolwich in 1962, and I was taking my seat in parliament for Middlesbrough West. At that time, John's book *Honest to God* was in the press. Through all that, and all the palaver over his evidence at the *Lady Chatterley's Lover* trial in 1960, I felt there was no contradiction between John's Christianity, even his churchmanship, and his dealing with practical issues in the world and in politics.

Much later, in 1983, I visited him in Addenbrooke's Hospital, Cambridge, where he was being treated for terminal cancer. No talk then from John about the Last Things! He lectured me on the iniquity of the Labour Party not accepting proportional representation at Westminster! Two years before, speaking at the funeral of a 16-year-old girl at his home in Arncliffe, Yorkshire, he had said God was to be found in the cancer from which she died, as much as in the sunset. Just weeks before his own death, I heard him say, in his last sermon in Trinity College, that that was an intellectual statement: now he had to ask if he could say it of himself.

My involvement in the Student Christian Movement (and with Elizabeth) was all so much more powerful and so much more fun than the university student Labour Club or the Union, with which I should have persisted for the good of my political soul.

By this time – the early 1950s – Labour was in the doldrums: gone was the momentum and idealism of the 1945-51 Labour post-war government, ideals that had fired my imagination and won my allegiance. But now the newly launched welfare state and the National Health Service were imperilled by an economy exhausted by war. The nation was facing the very real threat of the Cold War, and the dilemmas about the possibility of

---

[5] Robinson, John (1949) *In the End God ...: a study of the Christian doctrine of the last things* London: SCM Press

nuclear defence. This did not feature prominently in Union debates, and to me, student politics seemed a pretty trivial make-believe by contrast with the real issues, and the concerns of student friends from former colonial territories in Asia and Africa, where hope of independence burned brightly.

...and mathematics

My interest in mathematics and science had taken shape before I went to university.

At the age of fifteen in 1945, like everyone else in my generation of English schoolchildren who got that far, I was having to choose between doing arts or science in the sixth form. When the atom bombs were dropped on Hiroshima and Nagasaki I made up my mind. I decided that some at least of those active in community affairs, if not specifically in politics, in the next generation should understand how the bombs worked, and how such power could be controlled, and put to other use.

As a bright boy, such were the conventions of the time, in the sixth form I was offered classics, or other humanities, or science. I was committed to science.

Within science, the most difficult, challenging and (some would say) most beautiful subject is mathematics. It is the key to much of science. So I did mathematics: I was a good enough mathematician to attempt this, and enjoyed the intellectual rigour, the thrill of the pursuit of a solution and the hard graft of problem solving. The use of mathematics has been extraordinarily exciting and fruitful in particle physics, in astronomy and cosmology, and in many aspects of engineering, from telecommunications to the design of structures. More controversially, it has played an important role in the provision of concepts and techniques in the social sciences, particularly economics and business. This has been complicated by the differing aptitudes and interests of technicians and general readers, raising questions about trust, to which I shall return after describing my practical experience in the field.

I was not a 'natural' – nor even a particularly good – mathematician in the way that for example some of my contemporaries were, like the brilliant mathematician Michael Atiyah, a Fields Medallist (equivalent in mathematics to a Nobel Prize), and in due course both Master of Trinity College, Cambridge, and President of the Royal Society. But I won a major open scholarship in natural sciences on entrance to Jesus College, Cambridge. I gained a double first in maths, and won the annual college Keller Prize on graduation, beating, I am glad to say, my contemporaries in the college, Patrick Jenkin and John Biffen, both of whom were to rise to senior cabinet posts in the Thatcher government in the 1980s. It only shows how limited a performance predictor is academic grading. Sam Brittan, later Economic Editor of *The Financial Times*, won the Keller Prize a few years after me. He would cross swords with me many years later.

Graduation and marriage

At the end of our undergraduate days, I went on to take Part III of the maths tripos (a postgraduate degree) in preparation for research, while Elizabeth spent a year at Bristol University training as a teacher.

We married in the summer of 1953. It was the best thing I ever did. We were both just twenty three years old. In those days young people married first and then lived together – a quaintly old fashioned idea in today's culture, but one which in its time proved a firm foundation for many loyal, faithful, committed and loving relationships.

Yet more mathematics

I started out on my postgraduate research career with the vague feeling that classical mathematical analysis, which I understood, was the best way into the philosophical underpinnings of mathematics, which I really wanted to understand. My first supervisor was the Russian mathematician, A.S. Besicovitch. He was interested in such gems as the now important, and much applied, fractional dimension sets or fractals. However, Besicovitch went off to the United States on a sabbatical after one term, and Professor J.E.Littlewood kindly took me on.

I was the last and least distinguished of Littlewood's research students. Littlewood (1885-1977) was, with his colleague and collaborator, G.H.Hardy, the leading British pure mathematician of his day. Reflecting the consensus among mathematicians, C.P.Snow, in his Foreword to G.H.Hardy's *A Mathematician's Apology*[6], said,

> The Hardy-Littlewood researches dominated English pure mathematics, and much of world pure mathematics for a generation... Hardy's judgement was that Littlewood was the more powerful mathematician of the two[7].

---

[6] Hardy, G.H. (1940) *A Mathematician's Apology* Cambridge: Cambridge University Press
[7] Snow, C.P., Foreword to Hardy, G.H. (1940) *A Mathematician's Apology* Cambridge: Cambridge University Press

1 : Formative years 1930~1956 ♦ 15

Above: Elizabeth 1953

Right: Jeremy & Elizabeth outside the Senate House, Cambridge, on the day they both graduated in June 1952

Right: Jeremy & Elizabeth on their wedding day 26 August 1953 at All Saints' Church, Wytham, Oxford

Below: Jeremy with baby Margaret 1954

A flavour of the Hardy-Littlewood partnership is given by comparing Hardy's *A Mathematician's Apology* with Littlewood's *A Mathematician's Miscellany*[8], edited with a Foreword by Bela Bollobas[9], who quotes a memoir by Henry Dale for the Royal Society in 1943:

> Littlewood, on Hardy's own estimate, is the finest mathematician he has ever known. He was the man most likely to storm and smash a really deep and formidable problem; there was no one else who could command such a combination of insight, technique and power.

In his prime, as a Senior Fellow of Trinity College, Cambridge, Littlewood was the life and soul of the Combination Room after dinner in hall. His contemporaries, students and associates in mathematics in Cambridge had been a pioneering lot. Among the best known were the philosophers Bertrand Russell and Alfred North Whitehead, and the pioneering economist John Maynard Keynes. R.E.A.C.Paley was Littlewood's outstanding student, but he died young. The two associates of Littlewood whose work made the greatest impression on me were Norbert Wiener and Alan Turing. Wiener wrote about and was credited with developing the idea of cybernetics or automation, which was to have an immense influence on developments in engineering and space technology, the investigation of climate change, and much else. Alan Turing, who spent the 1939-45 war at Bletchley, was responsible, with others, for breaking the famous 'Enigma' code, a crucial intelligence battle which gave the Allies information on German strategies and tactics. Turing established both the theory of computers and the application of mathematics to biological structures. Both Weiner and Turing spoke to my own interest and motivation in mathematics and science, and indeed the interests they pursued have moulded and are still moulding the modern world.

Littlewood used to maintain a list of unsolved mathematical problems for his students and colleagues, in manuscript on one side of foolscap. The problems ranged from three star problems including the great unsolved problems of number theory, to one star problems. Hardy once described the one star problems as 'Problems which any old fool can solve in three months'. Littlewood asked him to define 'any old fool'. Hardy replied, 'A

---

[8] Littlewood, J.E. (1953) *A Mathematician's Miscellany* Cambridge: Cambridge University Press
[9] Bollobas, Bela ed. (1986) Foreword to a new edition of *Littlewood's Miscellany* Cambridge: Cambridge University Press

mathematician with a first class honours degree and five years' research experience.'

I qualified as one such 'old fool'. It took me two years to solve my one star problem, and then only in a restricted case. I did not think it worth publishing, but after some years Littlewood[10] published my results himself, with of course due acknowledgement. It was one of his last papers on new mathematics. The Editors of *Collected Papers of J.E.Littlewood*, appointed by the London Mathematical Society, made a comment on this paper saying

> As Littlewood says, this work is exciting, hard and still uncompleted. In some sense it is an outgrowth of ideas from 1954. It should be read in conjunction with the sections on rearrangements in *Inequalities* by Hardy, Littlewood and Polya[11] and the work by Beckenbach and Bellman.

More to the point was Littlewood's advice once when I said I was interested in the philosophical foundations of mathematics. He said, 'I know the feeling. If you lie down quietly, it will soon go away.' (He did not claim originality for such a banal and untypical remark!)

Mainstream Hardy-Littlewood analysis dealt with workaday real and complex variables. Wiener, and Littlewood's former student Paley, had worked with differential equations with random variable terms. Littlewood said to me he thought it was a strange concept, and he thought Quennouille's pioneering book on stochastic variables strange. Bollobas[12], writing twenty years later in his Foreword to *Littlewood's Miscellany*, said Littlewood had never heard about Martingales, a form of stochastic process, but was keen to learn about them. I got the impression that Littlewood thought abstract spaces a bit of a gimmick. As for computer scientists, Littlewood said Hardy had once said they were 'fellows of another college', which, whatever else it meant, said they were not Trinity mathematicians!

The beginnings of computer science

In 1954, while working on my PhD at Cambridge, I began learning to programme on EDSAC, one of the very earliest computers in Britain.

---

[10] Littlewood, J.E. (1967) 'Some New Inequalities and Unsolved Problems' in *Collected Papers of J.E.Littlewood* Oxford: Oxford University Press.[Ch 1]
[11] Hardy, G.H., Littlewood, J.E. and Polya, G. (1934) *Inequalities* Cambridge: Cambridge University Press
[12] Bollobas, Bela (1986) Ed. with a Foreword *Littlewood's Miscellany* Cambridge: Cambridge University Press

18 ♦ STANDING ON THE SHOULDERS OF GIANTS

EDSAC 1, Cambridge, in about 1950. EDSAC, with its hand built, floor-to-ceiling panels, had less computing power than any personal computer today. Reproduced courtesy of University of Cambridge Computing Services

The EDSAC course must have been the first, or almost the first, postgraduate programming course in Britain. The operating system and software were as primitive as the hardware, so to use the computer you had to write your own programs. There were other problems too. EDSAC was so expensive, and consumed so much electrical power, that doomsday soothsayers declared we could probably only afford three such machines in the whole of Britain, given the scarcity of fuel in the post war years, and the frequency of power cuts. I remember my wife querying my decision to learn how to program this rarity. It seemed unlikely to have much of a future.

EDSAC was housed in the embryonic Mathematical Laboratory at the back of the Cavendish Laboratory in Cambridge. In Cambridge mathematics, we were rather smugly used to the idea of standing on the shoulders of giants, so we did not talk much about it. Few of us working on EDSAC then could have envisaged the widespread and immensely powerful applications of computers today, from the management of the economy to programming washing machines, from launching space craft to crafting computer games, from forecasting climate change and global warming to modelling the functions of the heart, and operating the Internet.

When in 1992, forty years later, I revisited the Department of Applied Mathematics and Theoretical Physics at Cambridge as a member of the new House of Commons Select Committee on Science and Technology, an eager Tory member wished to demonstrate his practical mindedness and asked David Crighton, head of the department, what practical applications had come from his department's work. I could not resist interjecting, 'Would you like to start with gravitation, or electricity and magnetism?'

Harvard and the Massachusetts Institute of Technology

My last year in academia, 1955-56, was spent at Harvard as Choate Fellow, and the summer of 1956 at Chicago University. But I found most stimulus at MIT (Massachusetts Institute of Technology). There I attended Claud Shannon's pioneering Information Theory seminar in the Electrical Engineering Department, where he and his students, including Oliver Selfridge and Marvin Minsky, explored many of the problems which have preoccupied the computing world ever since. I remember driving up with Marvin to see Don Hebb, the neuro-physiologist at Montreal, to hear about his work on brain modelling. Sharing the driving, and unused to the automatic drive on Marvin's Buick, I gently bumped the car in front, and lost much of our chrome. Far from getting mad, Marvin said it had too much chrome anyway. He had and still has a marvellous grasp of essentials. At Princeton as an undergraduate, he had never taken a degree: as von Neumann's student he had been too busy. Von Neumann of course was one of the original designers of the modern computer and the inventor of game theory.

At about that time, Professor Herman Bondi, the cosmologist, interviewing me for a job at an overseas university, asked, 'Are you a real mathematician?' I replied, 'Define real mathematician.' He replied, 'A person who if wrecked on a desert island would start doing mathematics in the sand.' I said, 'In that case, I am not a real mathematician.' However, having since been wrecked on a number of desert islands, mathematically speaking, including ICI's vast Wilton Works on Teesside, and the House of Commons, and having ended up doing mathematics in the sand, I am no longer sure.

My plan had been to continue with mathematical research until I was no longer playing in the top league, and then gain some industrial experience before seeking a political career. I applied for a research fellowship in my own college, Jesus College, Cambridge, but was not elected. It was only years later, when I was an MP, that Littlewood told me that as my research supervisor he had not received the request from Jesus College for the essential reference. That summer he had been with me in Chicago, visiting Zygmund, the Fourier series analyst. The request had not been forwarded to him from Trinity until it was too late. I never reproached him. But I wondered whether Littlewood's unusual step of publishing my work – an indifferent student's PhD thesis – years later – was by way of an apology.

If everybody gave up academic pursuits on failing to get the first research fellowship for which they applied, many a fine research career would have been nipped in the bud. Even in politics, an Oxbridge fellowship would have had its uses as an accolade: these things contributed to that effortless sense of superiority enjoyed by the likes of Dick Crossman, Tony Crosland, Roy Jenkins, and Bryan Gould among my parliamentary contemporaries, which had its uses in politics. But the denial of a fellowship sent me out into industry at an exciting and as it turned out a seminal time, with a background which I have never exhausted, and perhaps with a modicum of self-doubt that did me no harm.

I had demonstrated a serviceable mathematical competence and learned how to sculpt in diamond hard material, which is the nature of mathematical research: the shape is in the diamond if you can find it. But my leaving pure mathematical research would not deny the world the services of a mathematical genius. Clearly I was feeling it was time for me to move on.

Margaret, aged 2, aboard the Queen Mary homeward bound from the United States 1956

2

Industrial and practical experience
1956-1962

On leaving academic mathematics in 1956 my first choice was to go into a tough industrial situation as a manual worker, with a view eventually to entering parliament. I had been in the States at the time of the 1955 General Election, when the Conservatives, under the brief leadership of Sir Anthony Eden, increased their majority from 17 to 60. They were to hold power, first under Prime Minister Harold Macmillan and later under Sir Alec Douglas-Home, until 1964. Labour, exhausted by wartime responsibilities and the pace of creating the welfare state in the post-war government, was in a state of disarray. Hugh Gaitskell, who had succeeded Prime Minister Clement Attlee as Leader of the Labour Party, was under constant pressure. But I believed the tide would turn.

Laying the foundations for a political career

Seeking work as a manual worker made sense in terms of Labour Party politics at the time. But I realise now that I was extraordinarily naïve, in political terms. There was no family background or tradition of political involvement, either in local government or trade union membership. I had no background in law, then as now favoured by many ambitious would-be politicians who see legislation as the prime concern of politics. I was never to be much good at jockeying for advancement and had avoided student politics. The currently popular (but to my mind suspect) option of work experience on the fringes of politics, perhaps as a researcher for an MP or political party, did not then exist, as MPs did not receive any office allowance or expenses.

I was attracted by the priest-worker concept in France. There ordained priests lived and worked with ordinary manual workers, identifying themselves with them in their home and working environment. As a variant, Simone Weil, the radical young French woman philosopher and mystic, who was not ordained, nor even a practising Catholic, had worked in a car factory. More earthily in Britain, 'Bevin boys' doing their National Service had worked in the pits in the 1940s and early 1950s – not as a vocation, but because the pits were chronically short of miners. Industrial chaplains were well established in Britain.

So I signed up as a trainee coal face worker outside Doncaster in the Yorkshire field. It was a crazy, idealistic plan. My wife valiantly went along with the idea, despite misgivings on behalf of our two-year-old toddler, Margaret. Our parents had done equally crazy things in their youth as the world judges these things, mine in China and Elizabeth's in Africa. There was also an element of careerist political entryism; Yorkshire was fertile Labour Party territory, with a large number of Labour seats. But I was failed on the first medical, with a double hernia which would require surgery. Perhaps it was just as well. I did not have a future as an Arthur Scargill in the South Yorkshire coalfield.

So I switched to trying to make full use of such qualifications and experience as I had. The choice was between the aircraft, electronics, nuclear and chemical industries. The aircraft, electronics and nuclear industries were still too defence-orientated to give a fair view of civil industry. So I went for chemicals. ICI was then the leading science-based firm in Britain. I applied for and was accepted as a Work Study Officer at ICI Wilton. Neither ICI nor I had very much idea of what to do with an inexperienced pure mathematician. I suspect that Nial Charlton, the finance director at Wilton, himself a classicist and an Oxford Greats graduate, thought a Cambridge Wrangler would be a complement: he was also a kindly old-fashioned Tory, who thought it a good idea to educate young socialists in the facts of life.

A mathematician among chemists

Wilton was ICI's new south Teesside site with major post-World War II developments supplying each other with intermediate products and services. It was at the time hailed as the showpiece for British industry. As a job applicant I had arrived in the dark, by train, via Darlington. You went past the iron furnaces and foundries of the first industrial revolution in Middlesbrough, Cargo Fleet and South Bank works, with the dust and smoke bellowing out over the yellow and red flows of molten iron and steel. Then, just before Redcar, you came upon the dazzling technological city of Wilton, with its brilliantly lit, gleaming, stainless steel towers and distillation columns. These separated the mixture of products from the oil crackers: hydrogen and methane gases off the top and the petrol and tar off the bottom, from the olefines, ethylene, propylene and butadiene, in the middle. The olefines were then compressed at up to 1500 atmospheres or otherwise processed into the polymers and plastics of the modern world, some of them discovered over the Pennines in the old ICI plants in Cheshire.

At that time about 8,000 of us were operating the dozen or so plants at Wilton, and another 10,000 were constructing new plants. The site was so vast you never saw large numbers of people. The staff had high ambitions for the success of the enterprise, which was at the forefront of innovation. This striving for excellence in no way conflicted with the works motto which was emblazoned on the coat of arms: 'Not for ourselves, but for all', it read.

In theory the Work Study officers like myself had the freedom to work anywhere on the site provided the plant management were prepared to tolerate us. In fact, the operating divisions were all-powerful. I was initially put into the time office in the Olefine Works, probably the only place where Nial Charlton had the authority to place me. Here I assisted Tommy, the time clerk, thus gaining early useful grass roots experience of the fictional element in productivity statistics. Tommy, a typical cloth-capped diminutive Yorkshireman, had made himself indispensable. He kept the clocking cards in random order in the racks, entering the card of a new employee wherever there was a vacant slot. So only Tommy and the worker knew where his card was in the rack. And Tommy had to be there to put the cards back in the racks every day after they had been checked, or there would have been a riot.

Soon I was sharing an office with the ebullient John Harvey-Jones, who later became chairman of ICI (and eventually a TV pundit on productivity)[1]. The Wilton management had no more idea of how to employ a Russian-speaking former naval intelligence officer like John than a Ph.D. pure mathematician. While John went off to measure the work of lorry drivers in the noble cause of finding some excuse for paying them more within the company's wages policy, I ended up looking at how the basic oil crackers were operated.

It was a major feat of human organisation to build and operate a petro-chemical complex combining the very diverse science, engineering, craft and human skills and experience of some thousands of men and a few women. It not only constituted a fair model of an economy in miniature, but was itself a fair-sized slice of the national economy.

---

[1] Harvey-Jones, John (1991) *Getting it together: Memoirs of a troubleshooter* London: Heinneman

*Above: No. 3 Olefines Plant. Below: Wilton works by moonlight.
Photographs: Courtesy of ICI*

Wilton was an exciting place to work, and I admired the skills and competence of my colleagues. I remember a meeting to consider an intractable problem on the butadiene plant. The plant consisted of a couple of towers, with associated plumbing, and the regular shift teams each numbering three or four people. The plant was not achieving its design output. At that meeting I counted seventeen different kinds of scientist and engineer, from eight or nine departments, gathered to consider every conceivable possibility, from the fitter having left his cap inside a vessel at the maintenance shut down, to unknown features of the chemistry, or an obscure non-linear feature of the control dynamics.

The chemists were the kings, the real managers of ICI plants, with the engineers having fought for and won due recognition. Chemical engineers, physicists and mathematicians did not come into the picture, but they existed in various staff departments, and were expected to be able to tackle the difficult problems that baffled the chemists and engineers.

The chemists were expected to give a lead, and they did. When the flare on the 150 foot high flare stack on Number 1 Olefine Plant had to be re-lit in the middle of a gale, Ron Thomson, the Plant Manager, did not order an expert rigger with a professional's head for heights to do it: he climbed the stack and lit it himself. Ron Whiteley, the manager on Number 2 Olefine Plant, was the only person I ever saw on the plant getting out his slide rule to check the heat and mass transfers assumed on the designer's flow sheets. Ken Gee, the Olefine Works Manager, did the most difficult job with such a team in keeping things simple, so that the plant could be operated safely by process workers who not long before had been bus drivers.

It was with a sense of excitement and challenge that we went in to work on a Monday morning. No individual could achieve anything on his own on such plants. But I will describe a handful of situations in which I was involved, because they taught me lessons that had wider application and would shape my contribution to politics.

I went in once in the middle of the night to check an experimental set up. The olefine plants were working at reduced rates: I was told a 'customer' polythene plant (the plant to which the Olefine Plant sent ethylene) was 'down'. This often happened. So I went over to the polythene plant (the 'customer') and found the operators having an extended midnight tea break. They told me an olefine plant was down. It had been, but by now was repaired. Next morning there was hell to pay.

A few days later I produced a set of interlocking decision trees which embraced the transport system of tankers to customer works as well as operations at Wilton itself. Ken Gee, the Olefine Works Manager, said it was impossibly complicated, and would screw things up. But he argued it through with me to turn it into a practicable scheme.

At that time, the two olefine plants were connected to the main customer Polythene Works by a single three inch pipeline. This carried the ethylene gas to the Polythene Works which compressed the gas to 1500 atmospheres and polymerised it into the solid plastic polythene. The only buffering intermediate storage of the gas was a 20 metre Horton sphere attached to the pipeline. This could store only 20 minutes' production of ethylene. ICI being a cooperatively minded company, the ethylene-producing Heavy Organic Chemicals Division and the ethylene-consuming Plastics Division set up a joint working party to define an agreed operating level. A report was duly produced recommending that the Horton sphere should be kept half full, thus effectively forfeiting all the intermediate storage!

Ken Gee and I argued it out. We concluded that there should be no agreed operating level or rate: the supplying works should try to keep the storage full, and the customer works should try to keep it empty. And it worked. It was a good lesson for a socialist to find that a competitive solution was the best one. Ron Whiteley, the manager on Number 2 Olefine Plant, then found a spare vessel that would store a full day's production of liquid ethylene. The HOC Board refused the modest capital expenditure to connect it up because a new Olefine Plant was planned which would provide plenty of ethylene capacity and intermediate storage would be irrelevant. Storage, they argued, did not produce chemicals. Later, after I had been elected to parliament and was safely off the site, the HOC Board created storage for three months' production of liquid ethylene in underground caverns at Wilton in the salt strata, with big savings.

The mathematical analysis of the problem was minimal. It was the politics that was unmanageable. I was not an employee of HOC Division: they did not have a mathematician. I was naïve and inexperienced, but not a goof, political or otherwise. Had the problem been solved by a complicated piece of mathematics that no self-respecting chemist could be expected to do for himself there would have been no problem. Or at least so I thought.

The origins of computer control and automation in ICI

Perhaps to show goodwill, I was quietly allowed to get on with an experiment on the optimal cracking conditions on Number 2 Olefine Plant.

In a cracker, the feedstock naphtha, a fraction of oil like a low grade petrol, is injected into the 'soakers', 10 cm diameter pipes in a furnace, where the oil is hit by superheated steam. The reactions splitting up the oil molecules are over in a fraction of a second. It is however impossible to measure accurately what has been achieved until the various products, from liquid tar to methane and hydrogen gas, have been separated out; this process only occurs a long way down the sequence of distillation columns. What we wanted to know was how the temperature and flow rates of the steam and the naphtha affected the composition of the product mixture: the controlling of them is a complicated task. The plant configuration, and the composition of the feedstock, was changing all the time too, as heavy compressors and other plant units came on and off line, changing the efficiencies of the various stages of separation. The accuracy with which inputs and outputs could be measured was poor. But it was a valuable business, important for company profitability.

By the late 1950s, the cybernetics or control engineering literature, which I had seen at MIT, covered multi-variable systems extensively. Norbert Wiener of MIT and others had contributed to the mathematical theory and methods of solution, usually in the form of maximising the profit, while maintaining the stability of the system. Most of the practical experience and mathematical methods were for electrical and mechanical processes like telecommunications and rockets, with quite rapid fluctuations of many cycles per second in the system, and in its controls. For such systems, it was natural to measure the frequency and amplitude of variations. You could observe thousands of cycles, and use standard control engineering methods to design control systems, generally combinations of single variable feedback control loops, much as you could control water levels and temperature in a bath without a plug by adjusting the hot and cold taps to control the inflow.

At Wilton we were faced with a new situation. The relevant processes had periodic variations of hours or days, and they operated continuously. There were few cycles to observe before the plant changed in uncontrollable ways. In the old kind of high frequency problem with mechanical and electrical systems, there was no time to do any complicated calculations within the cycle. In the new process plants with longer cycle times of up to a few hours, and with the possibility of using fast electronic computers, we should be able to make a series of measurements and do much calculation within the cycle, and thus to optimise within the cycle.

In the late 1950s ICI ordered a Ferranti Mercury computer to go on the Wilton site, to serve the whole of ICI.

Computers were enormous in those days – what is now packed into a desktop 'tower' then filled a sizeable room. There were freestanding panels the size of wardrobe doors, all intricately hand-wired with reels of tape and flashing light bulbs. The Ferranti was the first reliable transistor machine, with sizeable magnetic drum storage. This made it practicable to consider continuous on-line use, or at least use for some hours at a time. Furthermore it had Tony Brooker's high level Basic-like user programming language Autocode. All this transformed the possibilities of practicable operation on plants. The computer was owned and operated by the Central Instrument Laboratory of ICI, with a data logger in a caravan to hitch it up to plant instruments: it was up to any ICI division to propose applications. Dick Beeching was then the main board Technical Director of ICI (and later to be the Chairman of British Rail); he had ruled that plants using the computer would be expected to pay.

I had no budget.

Undaunted, I suggested an application optimising the operation of the oil crackers, to maximise the output of ethylene. There were no other such proposals to use the new computer. Another part of the Central Instrument Laboratory was building a pilot plant in their laboratory at Pangborne to try out a dedicated process control computer. I asked, 'Why not tackle a problem on an already operating plant?' They said, you cannot experiment on the operating plant. But, I replied, there is a lot of information generated by the uncontrollable variations on the plant; with the right mathematics you can sort out what is due to the plant, and what to the random variations. (I was later to make the same point with those who argued that you cannot experiment on the economy.) There were endless arguments. But as the expenditure on the computer was already committed, permission was given for the experiment to go ahead.

In the months that we were waiting for the delivery of our Mercury computer, I used the nearest available machine – the prototype Ferranti Mercury in the University of Manchester. Carefully carrying the data from our plant data logger, we would travel by train from Teesside to Manchester, and then use the computer in all-night sessions to get long uninterrupted runs. I wrote a general programme baptised Dynamic Regression Analysis (DRA), for learning the dynamic characteristics of a plant, linked to an optimisation programme, Guidance of Networks (GON), constituting a package with the acronym DRAGON. The intention was that the plant operator in the control room could look at computer generated graphs of performance and select preferred control settings to optimise the process. There was no suggestion of putting the plant under the control of a computer: the plant was already operating under a fairly primitive automatic control setting – there was no operator sitting with his hand on a joy stick or steering wheel. I found the standard errors of plant coefficients and the 'noise levels' (random variations) were very high, but the broad operating characteristics shown were consistent with some of the accepted plant operating wisdom.

I wrote up the DRAGON exercise, warts and all. The operating management were quite pleased because the results could be taken as confirming their perceptions. The fun began with the experts. Being a technically competent, well-organised company, ICI had a Statistical Methods Panel. The panel had published two useful hand books on statistical methods edited, before my time, by O.L. Davies[2]. The work had been further developed by George Box, a creative statistician in the Dyestuffs Division, with the encouragement of George Barnard, Professor of Statistics at Imperial College, London and a consultant to ICI. Box had developed an approach to experimental design in which he moved the area of experiment to follow the optimum, and keep track of its movement[3]. Unfortunately he had left ICI and emigrated to Canada shortly before I arrived. Until he left ICI all his work had been directed at batch processes and static data, rather than continuous time series data. It was only later that Box, working with Gwylim Jenkins (of Imperial College), produced the highly regarded 'Box-Jenkins' time series analysis[4]. This would address precisely the problem of using plant and other operating time series data that I was tackling some years earlier. Their methods were superior to mine, and I shall describe their application to economics in later chapters. They made the first economic applications of their work in the discussion of a paper I read to the Royal Statistical Society in 1971[5].

Yet again, company politics intervened. My work applying DRAGON on the Number 2 Olefine Plant had not been proposed or sponsored by the ICI Statistical Methods Panel. The Central Instrument Laboratory had collaborated fully in providing computer facilities. But a chairman of the

---

[2] Davies, O.L. (ed.)(1954) *The Design and Analysis of Industrial Experiments* London: Oliver & Boyd
Davies, O.L. (1957) *Statistical Methods in Research and Production*, London: Oliver & Boyd
[3] Box, G.E.P.(1957) Evolutionary operation: a method of increasing industrial productivity, *Applied Statistics*, 2, 81-101, 1957
[4] Box, G.E.P. and G.M. Jenkins (1970) *Time Series Analysis, Forecasting and Control* San Francisco: Holden Day
[5] Bray, Jeremy (1971) 'Dynamic Equations for Economic Forecasting with the G.D.P.-Unemployment Relation and the Growth of G.D.P. in the United Kingdom as an Example' *Journal* of the *Royal Statistical Society* Series A, 134 (2)

Statistical Methods Panel had been appointed who was an ICI veteran, and not a statistician. He seemed to regard my work as a personal challenge to himself. I wrote my work up in an internal report describing fully both the opportunities it offered and the difficulties, including some reservations about the exercise. I intended it to be as useful a guide as possible to future workers in the field. He did his best to rubbish my work, somewhat to the embarrassment of his statistician colleagues. I was an easy target: I had fought the 1959 General Election as the Labour candidate in a safe Tory seat, and it was clear that I was not likely to stay in ICI for ever. However, the availability of powerful computers was enabling statisticians, mathematicians, systems engineers, and computer scientists throughout ICI to make increasing contributions to company operations and profitability. Later, in 1966, the Statistical Methods Panel was succeeded by a Mathematical Applications Advisory Committee under the chairmanship of a statistician, Philip Youle, in which the statisticians were joined by mathematicians, operational research workers and systems engineers.

The applicability of the methods I was developing was not confined to the chemical industry. Among outside researchers who took an interest in my work and advised were new control engineering teams at Cambridge under John Coales, at Imperial College under John Westcott, and at the University of Manchester Institute of Science and Technology (UMIST) under Howard Rosenbrock. These were all key pioneers.

I was encouraged by ICI to learn what I could from these and other outsiders, and I was sent to the first congress of the International Federation of Automatic Control in Moscow in 1961. Basking in the credit for the world's first space craft – the sputnik – were the powerful Russian teams; across the table were their rivals, the American teams. It was not always easy, with so much research, defence and commercial secrecy and professional lifemanship, to distinguish what was theory, and what had entered into practical operations. Rudi Kalman of the 'Kalman Filter' reminded me years later that I had contributed to the discussion of his announcement at that congress of his results with his pioneering state space methods.

The relevance of my industrial experience

My early experience in automatic control and computer modelling stood me in good stead in the 1970s and later in modelling the economy – a cause I was to pursue throughout my parliamentary career until I retired in 1997.

The established engineering control systems methods in the 1960s handled inputs and outputs described simply as waves of which only the average frequency and amplitude were measurable, but where many thousands of cycles were available for measurement. By contrast on chemical and process plant, cycles of many minutes and hours could be measured minute by minute, and computations carried out within the cycle. It is this slow and measurable feature in process plant that makes its mathematics relevant to macroeconomic problems. In the early days, old fashioned economists argued that human agents, with their capacity to reason, made it impossible to treat economic variables in this way. They were anticipating the sophisticated modern problem of how economic agents learn rational expectations, to which I shall return in Chapters 9-15.

My experience also taught me decision makers can benefit from direct experience of the application of science. Politicians rightly, when dealing with technical issues, whether scientific, legal or otherwise esoteric, seek advice from the experts. Choosing and structuring scientific advice is an expertise in itself. Robert May as Chief Scientific Adviser, set out guidelines for departments and agencies in *The Use of Scientific Advice in Policy Making*[6]. Lord May is now President of the Royal Society, a powerhouse for providing disinterested scientific advice to governments. Evaluating such advice, and acting on it, may come more readily to politicians with a scientific background.

Handling other operational problems

In 1961 I was asked to look at a classic operational problem: what sizes, colours and shapes of perspex sheet should be supplied from the production plant at Wilton? The question had been examined twice before, once by Dick Beeching (who later, as Chairman of British Rail, closed all those railway lines) and once by Maurice Hodgson, who later became chairman of ICI. In 1961 they were respectively Technical Director and Technical General Manager of ICI, dealing with company strategy. Dick Beeching's conclusion for the perspex plant, if I remember rightly, had been that any size of Perspex sheet should be sold provided it was 4 feet by 8 feet; and Maurice Hodgson's that any colour should be sold, provided it was black, white or clear. Or it may have been the other way round. My own solution was that any size, colour or shape could be sold provided it was profitable to do so. It was premature. Only later, with the advent of

---

[6] May, Robert (1994) *The Use of Scientific Advice in Policy Making* London: HMSO Office of Science and Technology

computers, did such a solution become operable. There was a probably apocryphal story about an ICI salesman in New York who had found himself stuck with yellow, triangular shapes cut off the corners of the square sheets from which Shell filling station signs were moulded. So he equipped New York Yellow Cabs with their characteristic roof signs.

Another moral tale was more puzzling. ICI had long before closed the plant that made beta-naphthylamine, a dyestuffs intermediate, because it was carcinogenic. While I was at Wilton it was operating a new plant making alpha-naphthylamine, an isomer with no known carcinogenic effects. A conscientious employer, ICI imposed a draconian precautionary practice of requiring workers, and anyone visiting the plant, to shower and change all clothing on leaving the plant. Furthermore every person on every shift had to provide a urine sample for a Papanicolou test by the local health service pathologists. It is a difficult test even now, and it takes a long time to train the pathologists who can do the test reliably. At the time in 1961 cancer screening using the Papanicolou test on cervical smears was just being introduced, and Harold Evans, the distinguished future editor of *The Times* and *The Sunday Times*, and then editor of the local daily newspaper *The Northern Echo*, was conducting a campaign for its speedy development. But ICI was pre-empting all the Papanicolou testing capacity available in the North of England. Concerned, ICI asked me to look at the accumulated test results. I could not find one test indicating cancer. Not a single worker had developed cancer. This expensive, and unnecessary, testing was denying others access to a service. Cervical screening was an issue I later followed up as a newly elected MP, and the national screening system was introduced as a result of Harold Evans' remarkable and energetic campaign, with immense benefit to thousands of women.

There were many other lessons I learned in ICI. I acted as secretary to a joint working party with trade union representatives comparing local employers' pension schemes including the electricity, gas, coal and railway nationalised industries, central and local government, steel companies, and banks. The ICI scheme was incomparably the best, and it showed in the local pensioners' standard of living. I tried to persuade the trade unions to take some interest in the ICI workers' profit sharing scheme. On its old formula, it would have become a gold mine for employees as capital intensity increased and employment fell: but the unions cold shouldered it. I recall management finding the stalwart local engineering union convenor Paddy Toombes a pain in the neck. So I went to see him in his mushroom growing Nissen hut at Lazenby, and thought he could be engaged in sensible negotiation. But then my mother was Irish too.

Putting down roots on Teesside

As a family we settled well in Nunthorpe on Teesside. Bridget and Tess, younger sisters for Margaret, were born there, and it was here at the local village school that the two elder girls began their schooling. We enjoyed rambling and camping in the nearby Cleveland Hills and the Yorkshire Dales – beautiful uncrowded countryside. In the 1959 General Election I stood as Labour candidate in the nearby rural seat of Thirsk and Malton. I lost, of course. Was I being unfair on my wife and young children in dreaming of a political career? Probably, yes. And yet ... and yet ...

Our daughters (left to right) Bridget, Margaret and baby Teresa. 1962
(Photograph courtesy of the Middlesbrough Evening Gazette)

Most of our friends and neighbours worked in ICI and other industries on Teesside. They were fellow parents, people we met in local churches, trade unions and political activities, and in the evening classes in which I taught mathematics in Constantine College, the local further education college. Engineering firms like Head Wrightson, Ashmore, Benson and Pease, and Parson Reyrolle on Tyneside, were enterprising and capable. Parson's established International Research and Development under Monty Finniston, who was brought in from AEA Harwell, where he was Chief Metallurgist. He was eventually to become Chairman of British Steel.

Shipbuilding on the Tees was a graveyard. Dorman Long was the dominant steel company in Middlesbrough, and South Durham was not far away in West Hartlepool. I was only able to trace two graduates, engineers or any other kind, who worked in Dorman Long. One of them, Ted Judge, became its chairman, and later the chairman of the steel makers with whom we managed an orderly handover of the industry when Labour re-nationalised it in 1967. Elsewhere, in United Steel, the Steel Company of Wales, and Richard, Thomas and Baldwin, the industry was in better shape, but it was nowhere near able to finance its own modernisation plan (the Benson Report) which recommended concentrating production on five major coastal sites. I was to meet with no political problems with Labour's proposals to re-nationalise the steel industry.

ICI in its local context

ICI was far from perfect. But for me it provided a basic standard on which I thought it possible for a nationalised industry to improve. Although a private enterprise, ICI encouraged us to think of the public good. We took care of the environment - there were wide lawns along the avenues which carried the services, high flare stacks which burned the minimal waste products; and careful monitoring of the health of employees, air quality and dust deposition – most of which came from the neighbouring Dorman Long steel mill. We had the best pension and profit sharing arrangements in Britain. Trade unions were recognised, and works councils had worker representatives. We published handbooks and textbooks of industrial technology. We cooperated freely with academics and other industries in research. We licensed new products and processes we invented, and used those of others, at home and abroad. We recognised the advantages we had inherited from the enlightened policies of our predecessors, and we were ready to learn. Our management were ready to help out wherever asked - nationally in nuclear power, running the railways, or teaching in local schools. There were no problems about joining in political activity, locally and nationally.

However, I would not have been content to stay in my job at Wilton. I had no career line and no prospects of promotion. I was constantly applying for other jobs. I had already stood in the 1959 General Election as Labour candidate in nearby Thirsk and Malton, a rock-solid north Yorkshire Tory seat. The Conservative government, under the nonchalant Prime Minister Harold Macmillan, had increased its majority to 100 under the slogan, 'You never had it so good!'

In later years my diplomatic parliamentary colleague and neighbour, Arthur Bottomley – later Lord Bottomley – used to tell a story that when he asked ICI directors at Wilton how they managed to pay me when I was spending all that time on politics, the no less diplomatic ICI directors told him that I saved them so much money on Monday mornings that they could pay me for the rest of the week. Utterly fictitious! I took no time off beyond my entitlements to annual leave and holidays. It was my young family, not my work, which paid the price.

A launch pad for politics

While I had sought experience in matters I believed would be useful in politics, that was not the criterion by which I set objectives and made career choices. I set objectives which I thought were worthwhile in themselves, and the criteria I set in career choices were those which anyone might apply: I tackled problems which I thought I was equipped to handle, found interesting, and were ripe for consideration.

Looking back now at my working life I do not think I could have made a better choice than ICI. It was an extraordinarily fruitful period and we were pioneering developments in science, in information technology, and in economics. But I could certainly have pursued my objectives more productively. I should have built more alliances, worked better with other people, and played the politics of organisations better.

Although I was working with a practical view of the operating realities of big industry, including steps needed for its reform, it was not a widely shared view, and I was suspect for having a view at all. It would have been an immense help had I had a mentor, or belonged to some like-minded group.

Years later in the 1980s when I was in parliament and Labour spokesman on science and technology and John Harvey-Jones had become chairman of ICI, the two of us were talking to Duncan Davies. Duncan was an ebullient chemist: he had written a sensible book on industrial economics, and had been head of the ICI Central Research Laboratory, and later General Manager, Research and Development. In the late 1970s he had left the company and had subsequently been appointed Keith Joseph's Chief Scientific Adviser and Engineer in the Department of Trade and Industry (the DTI). It was he who persuaded Keith Joseph, then Secretary of State for Industry, and through him Margaret Thatcher, that government had to pay for basic scientific research because industry did not have adequate incentives to do so. Since then the science budget has been a relatively protected area of public expenditure. John Harvey-Jones said it was a fault of ICI that it did not offer career paths to people like Duncan and myself. I rather think Duncan and I were not the only ones.

However, being an ICI employee had one advantage. ICI was, as far as I know, the only company to have a clause in its standard contract of employment allowing any employee, staff or payroll, leave with pay to fight any parliamentary election. The clause had been there since the company was formed in 1926: Alfred Mond, the first chairman of ICI, was himself an MP at the time. The result was that almost always there were in parliament more MPs who had been in ICI than any other company. They included David Price, who had been personal assistant to Alexander Fleck, the chairman of ICI; Ted Garrett, a Tyneside engineer; John Garrett, a management consultant who did much of the work on civil service reform for the Fulton Committee; Edmund Dell, who had been on the commercial side of ICI and was with me in the Ministry of Technology; and Michael Clark, who had been at Wilton with me. There were generally rather more Labour than Tory MPs among the ICI alumni. Shortly after my by-election, Patrick Jenkin, who had been my contemporary at Jesus College, Cambridge, asked me how I had managed to stand, because he, as company secretary of a Distiller's owned subsidiary, was having difficulties, even as a Tory candidate. Patrick much later became Secretary of State for Trade and Industry under Ted Heath.

All I needed was a seat – preferably a safe seat (many a promising parliamentary career comes to grief on winning, and then losing, a marginal seat). I had applied fruitlessly for many such seats before and after the 1959 General Election. Would my luck ever change?

Then in 1962 a series of by-elections took place on Teesside: Middlesbrough East, Stockton-on-Tees, and Middlesbrough West. I put my name forward for each in turn. I was the only local candidate. The nomination for Middlesbrough East, a rock-solid Labour seat, went to Arthur Bottomley, a Labour stalwart and former Secretary for Overseas Trade in the Attlee government. Stockton-on-Tees, a safe Labour seat, went to young Bill Rodgers, a former General Secretary of the Fabian Society (and later one of the Gang of Four founding members of the Social Democrats in the 1980s).

That left only Middlesbrough West. With its 9000 Tory majority it was virtually unwinnable. Still, it would be good experience. At the selection conference I beat Roy Hattersley, another young hopeful, to become Labour candidate in the Middlesbrough West by-election.

3

By election victor
1962

By-elections in those days were run not by spin doctors but by the local candidate, and his local agent (in my case, the stalwart Charlie Shopland in Middlesbrough). It was all very amateurish, but perhaps better rooted in the local community. I wrote my own election address, and my wife designed the layout. My main duty was pounding streets, accompanied by my wife. (Yes, we kissed babies, shook hands and walked up to ten or twelve miles every day!) We were accompanied by an elderly jeep, moving at walking pace and belting out the campaign song from a loud speaker lashed to the roof. I addressed well-attended public meetings every evening.

However Labour Party headquarters did despatch Percy Clarke, their sole Press Officer and a colourful character, as my minder. He drove up to Middlesbrough with his caravan, parked it in a local car park, and slept, lived and worked in it for the three week duration of the campaign. Percy brought with him a level of expertise with which we locals were unfamiliar: an example is the 'Election Special' he brought out in the closing week of the campaign. (See next page.) Percy ensured that the candidate's voice was heard, rather than that of the party machine or Transport House (the Labour Party's London headquarters). An army of voluntary workers delivered a copy of the 'Election Special' to every single household.

There were daily press conferences for the local evening paper, and later for the Fleet Street nationals who hurried north as opinion polls began to suggest the possibility of first a Liberal and then (shock!) a Labour victory. I learnt a lot about how to handle the press from Percy.

Charles Shopland ran a superb local machine. On election night, using the old fashioned Reading system, we had a record of every household – For, Against, Won't say (meaning, No). Party workers would be knock knocking on every single 'Yes' voter's door, twice or thrice if need be. We would need every vote.

The rough and tumble of politics

As I was an ICI employee, inevitably the question would be raised in my by-election campaign in 1962 as to whether Labour would nationalise ICI. So I asked Hugh Gaitskell, by now firmly in control of the Labour party, what I should say. He said, 'Say Labour has no plans to nationalise ICI.' It was my first experience of that useful phrase, 'has no plans', I have heard so many times since. It does say something, but not very much. In fact since 1962 the nationalisation of ICI has never been a serious possibility. But ICI has suffered much from private sector mergers, de-mergers, acquisitions and disposals.

The major move at the time was the ICI bid for Courtaulds in 1961, with the ICI bid led by its chairman, Paul Chambers, and the Courtaulds resistance by a rising young director, Frank Kearton (whom I would meet again later). There was genuine local interest and concern. The bid was to fail. I suspect ICI would not have made a good job of all the viscose and downstream activities of Courtaulds, although it supplied these products. Roy Jenkins, already an MP with ministerial experience (and a future Chancellor of the Exchequer 1967-70), came out with a dramatic and very readable account of the bid as a two part feature in *The Observer*. As a young by-election candidate I was keen to seek Roy's views. I wrote to him. Roy very kindly asked me to lunch at the House of Commons, and I was immensely flattered. But he seemed very little interested in the appropriate structure of the fibre and textiles industry. I was disappointed, and a little shocked.

The other big question locally concerned the future of the steel industry. Nationalised by the post-war Labour government, it had been privatised by the succeeding Conservative government. My experience of big corporations had started in ICI. Against that background, I had not the least difficulty in advocating the re-nationalisation of our neighbouring steel industry. It was a different industry with its own traditions. It had major problems which needed resolution. Nationalisation was one way – an expensive way as it turned out. But it worked, and produced one of the most efficient steel industries in the world.

However, like all by-elections, mine was much more concerned about bread and butter issues. It was in the middle of a potato shortage, and I remember the stalwart Bessie Braddock, from the heart of Old Labour, coming to Middlesbrough and attacking the Tories for the price of potatoes. 'Fish 1/6. Chips hire purchase terms arranged!' That, she told us, was the cry in her Liverpool constituency.

Below: the top half of the front page of Jeremy Bray's 'Election News', late May 1962.
The opinion polls were beginning to move in Bray's favour.
Could Labour overturn a Tory majority of 8,710 votes?

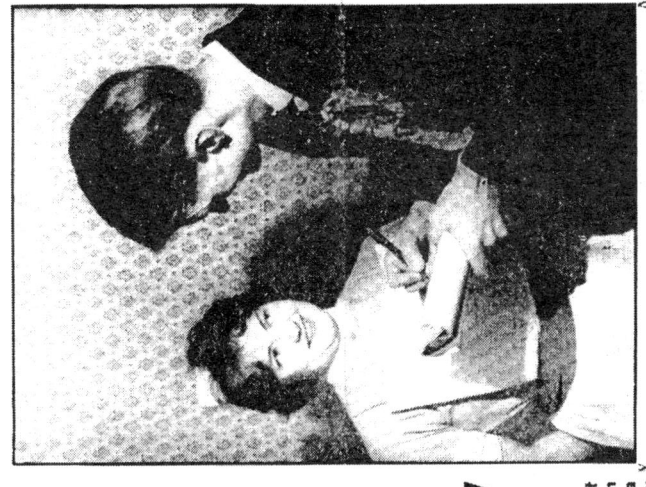

JEREMY BRAY'S ELECTION NEWS

We said it —now the Gallup Poll

VICTORY IS IN SIGHT FOR DR. BRAY

A GALLUP POLL published as this edition goes to press says that Labour is in the lead in the Middlesbrough West by-election. An earlier national opinion poll had shown the Tories holding the seat by a very narrow majority, but that was before Labour's Dr. Jeremy Bray had made his personal impact on the electors.

THIRD MAN

Both polls agree that the Liberals must come third. All this means that the contest in Middlesbrough West is the keenest in any British by-election for many years. Every single vote will count. Every Labour vote must be polled

It would set the trend for the next General Election.

POSITIVE

BUT a vote for Jeremy Bray is not just a protest vote against the Tory government, it is a vote for a young, keen local scientist who believes that only Labour's positive policies can push Britain ahead in the space age.

MINISTERING ANGELS IN REVOLT

Tees-side nurses are up in arms against the Tory Chancellor's meanness in their wages claim. One of Dr. Bray's nomination papers was signed entirely by nurses and many nurses are warmly supporting his campaign. "Labour founded the national health service," says Dr. Bray, "and we mean to see the nurses get a fair deal."

40 ♦ STANDING ON THE SHOULDERS OF GIANTS

*The upper half of the back page of Labour's election newssheet.
Note the emphasis on pay and prices.*

JEREMY BRAY'S ELECTION NEWS

TAKE HOME PAY—IT DEPENDS ON WHO YOU ARE

WHAT has happened to your "take home pay", wages and salaries stated in £s per week and £s per year? What has been happening to the money left on fixed incomes after P.A.Y.E., national insurance and so on?

GONE DOWN

Under Labour rule, "take home pay" went up, but under the Tories "take home pay" for the lowest-paid workers has actually gone down. "Take home pay" for most workers (and for people like doctors and plant managers) has remained almost stationary, but "take home pay" for the big boys, directors of giant combines and others, has zoomed skywards.

The story of "take home pay" under the Tories is told in the chart at the foot of this column. Of couse if, like Dr. Beeching, you get £450 a week, you are one of the lucky ones.

LABOUR PLANS

Why has this happened and why is it so different from things under Labour rule? Because the Tories look after the interests of

Continued next page

TALKING OF PRICES

Many hundreds of housewives in Middlesbrough and Thornaby have talked with Dr. Jeremy Bray during their shopping expeditions during the past few weeks. Most of them have complained about prices which have rocketed

*The lower half of the back page of Labour's election newssheet.
Note the graph on pay (a typical Bray touch).*

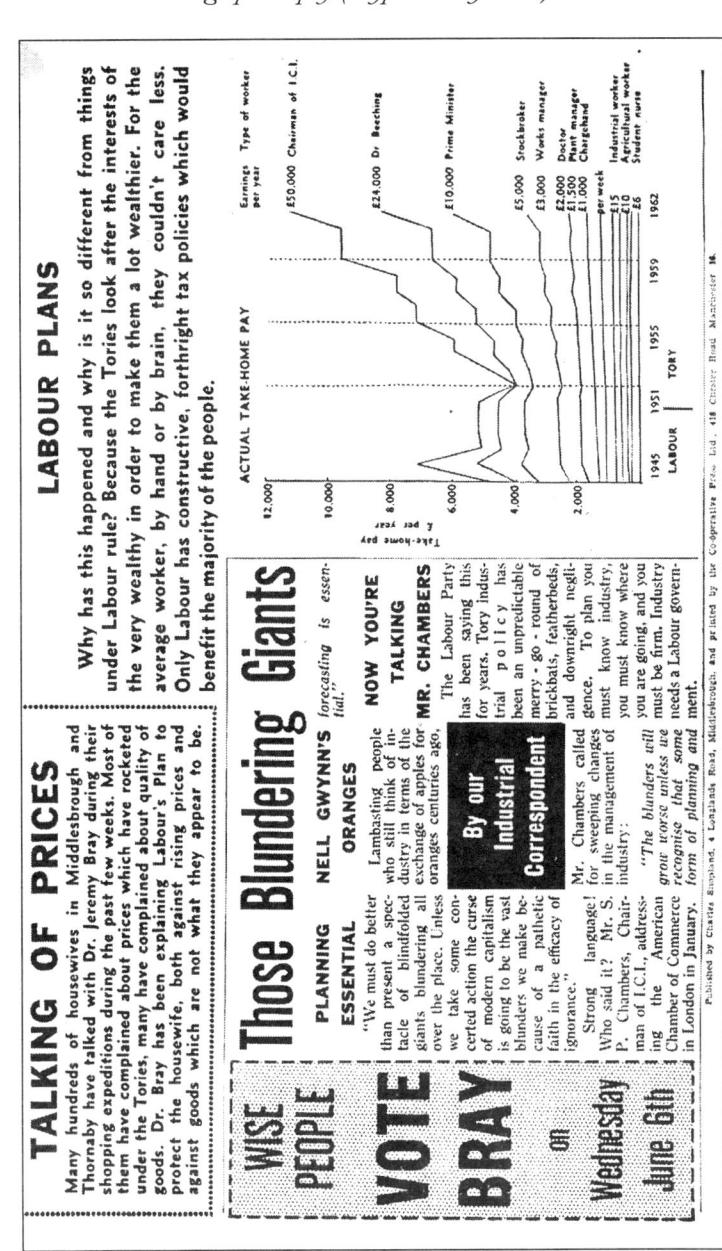

TALKING OF PRICES

Many hundreds of housewives in Middlesbrough and Thornaby have talked with Dr. Jeremy Bray during their shopping expeditions during the past few weeks. Most of them have complained about prices which have rocketed under the Tories, many have complained about quality of goods. Dr. Bray has been explaining Labour's Plan to protect the housewife, both against rising prices and against goods which are not what they appear to be.

Those Blundering Giants

PLANNING ESSENTIAL

NELL GWYNN'S ORANGES

Lambasting people who still think of industry in terms of the exchange of apples for oranges centuries ago,

By our Industrial Correspondent

Mr. Chambers called for sweeping changes in the management of industry:

"The blunders will grow worse unless we recognise that some form of planning and

NOW YOU'RE TALKING MR. CHAMBERS

The Labour Party has been saying this for years. Tory industrial policy has been an unpredictable merry-go-round of brickbats, featherbeds, and downright negligence. To plan you must know industry, you must know where you are going, and you must be firm. Industry needs a Labour government.

forecasting is essential."

"We must do better than present a spectacle of blindfolded giants blundering all over the place. Unless we take some concerted action the curse of modern capitalism is going to be the vast blunders we make because of a pathetic faith in the efficacy of ignorance."

Strong language! Who said it? Mr. S. P. Chambers, Chairman of I.C.I., addressing the American Chamber of Commerce in London in January.

LABOUR PLANS

Why has this happened and why is it so different from things under Labour rule? Because the Tories look after the interests of the very wealthy in order to make them a lot wealthier. For the average worker, by hand or by brain, they couldn't care less. Only Labour has constructive, forthright tax policies which would benefit the majority of the people.

ACTUAL TAKE-HOME PAY

Earnings per year	Type of worker
£50,000	Chairman of I.C.I.
£24,000	Dr Beeching
£10,000	Prime Minister
£5,000	Stockbroker
£3,000	Works manager
£2,000	Doctor / Plant manager
£1,500	Chargehand
per week	
£15	Industrial worker
£10	Agricultural worker
£6	Student nurse

1945 — 1951 — 1955 — 1959 — 1962
LABOUR | TORY

WISE PEOPLE VOTE BRAY

on Wednesday June 6th

Published by Charles Simpfend, 4 Longlands Road, Middlesbrough, and printed by the Co-operative Press Ltd., 418 Chester Road, Manchester 16.

Continued from previous page

Victory is in sight

The party machine was beginning to scent victory. Volunteers flocked in. Jim Callaghan, then Shadow Chancellor, spoke in the open air in Thornaby on a parking lot using my idiosyncratic loudspeaker system. Home-going workmen still in their overalls and industrial boots, and housewives in their pinnies, crowded around.

Not to be out done, George Brown, the Deputy Leader of the Labour Party, played truant, and came up to speak on Budget Day when he should have been in the House of Commons. He survived my fetching him from Darlington Station in my elderly Ford Popular, sitting there smiling, wreathed in the exhaust fumes coming up through the floor boards. Quite a change from his own preferred Jaguar.

We needed a large turnout to win. We got it: a 71% poll. Labour won with a majority of 2,270 votes (39.7% in a three cornered fight).

A famous victory. And a very unsafe foundation for a parliamentary career.

The first Labour by-election win for over a decade

The Middlesbrough West result was sensational. It was Labour's first by-election triumph over the Conservatives since the late 1940s. Labour, having narrowly lost power in 1951, had lost decisively in the 1955 and 1959 General Elections: in 1955 it had gained only one Conservative seat (and lost ten); in 1959 Labour captured five seats (but lost twenty eight).

In those days party leaders kept clear of the actual by-election campaign, but Hugh Gaitskell, who was party leader, came up to Middlesbrough with Dora, his wife, for the celebration party afterwards. Gaitskell had watched the BBC by-election TV Special with incredulity: in a three cornered fight Labour had overturned the 1959 Tory majority of 8,710. For Gaitskell, then at the height of his powers, it must have seemed like a harbinger of a Labour revival. He did not live to see this: he was to die after a brief illness in January 1963.

Opposite: Top:
Jeremy on the town hall balcony thanking his cheering supporters after the announcement of his victory 6th June 1962

Bottom:
Hugh Gaitskell, with Dora, his wife, congratulating Jeremy (and Elizabeth) at the local party's victory celebration.
(Both photographs courtesy of the Middlesbrough Evening Gazette.)

3 : By election victor 1962   ♦   43

My debt to my constituents

You owe your seat to your constituents. Middlesbrough West was never going to be an easy seat to hold. The margin was too narrow. I was to hold it – just – in the 1964 and 1966 General Elections.

On the face of it the Yorkshire seat of Middlesbrough West, which I represented from 1962 to 1970, and Motherwell and Wishaw, my seat in the Scottish central industrial belt from 1974 to 1997, are very similar. Both started as nineteenth century steel and heavy engineering communities which attracted people from Ireland and a rural hinterland, with iron ore and coal deposits to feed the first industrial revolution.

In the 1960s the increasing capital intensity of steel, oil, chemical and other heavy industry was already making its impact on Teesside, making capital subsidies very inefficient incentives to local industrial development and job creation. As the local MP I maintained my working links with industry, including local industries, though I decided against actually working for ICI, the principal employers in the constituency. I needed to be seen as independent.

The lack of higher educational and research institutions was, in both constituencies, an adverse influence on the local economy. On Teesside I convened a university promotion committee from local authorities and industry. It was led enthusiastically by Tony Challis from ICI Billingham Research Department, and we campaigned energetically and ambitiously for an establishment to match Imperial College, London, the University of Manchester Institute of Science and Technology, and Strathclyde University in Glasgow. We had no success even with the Labour governments of 1964 and 1966, despite Labour's manifesto promises in the 1964 General Election of a 'programme of massive expansion in higher, further and university education', with similar (though less bombastic) promises in 1966.

I fought this and other constituency issues vigorously.

This however is not the time or place to write more about my responsibilities as a constituency MP, since I am concerned in this book principally with the application of science to politics and government.

I will say only that I have a deep and abiding respect for the immense courage and grace of the ordinary people who came, often with severe and painful problems, to my surgeries seeking help. I would also like to pay tribute to all those who sought to make life better for their local communities – councillors and local government officials, priests and ministers of religion, doctors and social workers, business leaders and shop-keepers, trades unionists and youth workers, play group leaders and the women who took round meals-on-wheels, voluntary workers and teachers, and the unsung multitude of ordinary people who were good neighbours one to the other.

I felt privileged to be asked to help with launching new initiatives, supporting efforts which were under stress, or sorting out what seemed at times intractable problems. As an MP you can sometimes unlock doors, and purses, and hearts. I hope and pray that I was of service to these good people, and to their communities.

Part Two

A PARLIAMENTARY APPRENTICESHIP

Jeremy takes his seat at Westminster, 26 June 1962.
George Brown, Deputy Leader of the Labour Party (centre),
greets the two new MPs, Jeremy (left) and Tam Dalyell,
the victors in the Middlesbrough West and West Lothian by elections.

Photograph: PA Photos with kind permission.

Introduction to Part Two

A PARLIAMENTARY APPRENTICESHIP

I entered parliament in 1962: the first Labour gain for many years. My by-election in Middlesbrough West was the harbinger for Labour's narrow victory in the 1964 General Election. Billed as the first working scientist to enter parliament for decades, I was hopeful about the applicability of science to government. You can learn how I fared as a backbencher, very soon working on key parliamentary committees whose reports were to have a significant impact on government policy.

I then had a relatively brief experience of ministerial responsibility. As a very junior minister I found myself frustrated in my efforts to introduce more system into government. The central problem of the relationship between micro-economic industrial policy, and macro-economic policy, was highly relevant to the economic crises which doomed the Labour governments of 1964-66 and 1966-70.

So I wrote a book entitled *Decision in Government*. When however in 1969 I sought permission as a minister to publish, Harold Wilson refused. Foolishly, I felt I had no alternative but to resign. It was a turning point in my life: I would never again become a minister.

It looks a simple story. Here was a one track, mathematical minded technocrat, a naïve enthusiast, hopelessly overselling the power of modelling in applications beyond his power to influence, let alone control.

Yet over the following decades, economics, the core discipline of politics, was to become more and more mathematical, and more and more useful, as I had predicted. Unfortunately, established politicians felt this as

Introduction to Part Two

a threat to their capacity as politicians to shape, or even to follow, the arguments.

When the Tory party, under Edward Heath, won the General Election of 1970, I, like so many other Labour members, lost my seat. It was a humiliating experience, and, with no severance pay then, made life precarious for my dear family. I could not know whether this would simply interrupt my parliamentary career, or terminate it. I sought nomination in a number of safe seats, but with no success.

In the end, when the job I had in London in the electronics industry folded, I took up an academic post and we moved to Scotland. I had no expectations of a return to parliament.

However, my luck was to change dramatically.

You can read how I became a Scottish MP in the last chapter in this section.

PART TWO

A PARLIAMENTARY APPRENTICESHIP

4 **A FIRST SPELL IN PARLIAMENT 1962-66**   51

Labour in the 1960s ~ The white heat of the scientific revolution ~ A backbencher in opposition ~ A first brush with economic policy ~ Manifesto promises before the 1964 General Election ~ The need for statistical reform of our national accounts ~ Labour returned 1964 ~ My apprenticeship as a PPS ~ Wilson sends in his MPs ~ Making the case for civil service reform ~ Reform of government statistics

5 **A TASTE OF OFFICE 1966-69**   67

Ministry of Power, & fuel policy 1966-67 ~ Steel nationalisation ~ The 1967 ministerial reshuffle ~ Ministry of Technology 1967-69 ~ The beginnings of the Treasury model

6 ***DECISION IN GOVERNMENT*** **AND RESIGNATION 1969**   77

Publish and be damned ~ Press reaction ~ The cost of resignation ~ Appraisal of reform ~ Can analysis improve policies ~ Undefeated

7 **WILDERNESS YEARS 1970-1974**   87

The global environment and sustainable development ~ A spell in electronics 1970-73 ~ We move to Scotland

8 **MEMBER FOR MOTHERWELL & WISHAW 1974-1997**   94

Member for Motherwell and Wishaw ~ My debt to my constituents ~ Scottish politics ~ The steel-makers ~ Ravenscraig Steel Works ~ Why had I bothered so much about steel?

4

A first spell in parliament
1962-66

Winning a key by-election is to enter parliament on the crest of a wave. You are a bringer of good tidings. You are not lost in the crowd of new MPs at a General Election. You are known to your party leaders who have been up to speak in your by-election. I was thirty two years of age.

It was a time of disenchantment with politics. The three by-elections on Teesside were symptomatic – all three were caused by sitting MPs resigning their safe seats. Entering the Parliamentary Labour Party in 1962 was like walking on to a battlefield still strewn with the dead and wounded after the Bevanite battles of the 1950s.

Labour, after six brief years in government under Prime Minister Attlee – six years that transformed the political agenda with the creation of the Welfare State – had lost power to the Conservatives in 1951. The 1955 and 1959 General Elections had consolidated the Tory grip on power. When I entered parliament in 1962 Prime Minister Macmillan's one hundred seat majority seemed unassailable. Just months before my by-election triumph, a Liberal win in Orpington had transfixed the press, which (as ever) dreamed of a Liberal revival. Orpington's Eric Lubbock was the media darling for several months. No other seats fell to the Liberals, but a handful to Labour.

When I arrived, the first Labour MP to capture a Tory seat in a by-election for a decade, I was astonished to find many Labour members were still not on speaking terms with each other. Past feuds echoed on, although Aneurin Bevan, that dynamic and controversial Welsh heavyweight, had been dead for two years. The animosity was far greater even than in the ructions within the Labour Party in the 1980s. But here I had arrived, a by-election winner, with a freshly picked olive leaf: the Tory waters were subsiding from the earth outside the Westminster ark. No wonder my colleagues welcomed me – most lastingly Tam Dalyell, whose by-election in

West Lothian coincided with my own, and who took his seat on the same day.

Tam is now – forty years later – Father of the House, the longest serving MP: idiosyncratic, principled, determined to argue his case. Unusually for an MP, Tam has thought deeply about science, as his own books[1] and his long running column in the *New Scientist* bears witness. Tam had one great advantage over me: he has a safe seat.

Our by-election victories triggered Prime Minister Macmillan's 'night of the long knives' when he purged half his cabinet. As that gave way to strange stories of the Russian military attaché sharing a girl friend with the Rt Hon John Profumo, the Secretary of State for War, I wondered what kind of a bear pit I had strayed into.

Labour in the 60s

In 1962 the Parliamentary Labour Party was still shaped by the war of 1939-45, the formative experience of that generation of Labour leaders, including Hugh Gaitskell, Aneurin Bevan, Harold Wilson, George Brown, James Callaghan, Barbara Castle, Douglas Jay, Roy Jenkins, Tony Crosland and Denis Healey. They had experienced the depression in the 1930s, but they had heard and done things in the war that had taught them that there was another way. The market was not the Philosopher's Stone that turned everything to gold; the business man was but one operator among others who included soldiers, scientists, and academics from new disciplines, above all economists.

I came in a later wave, where planning, Keynes and the welfare state were at best partial solutions. My generation of scientists created the computer, automation and globalisation. It discovered molecular biology. And with all these developments came a new range of sciences, technologies and problems. I will let the questions, answers and false trails emerge from my narration to follow, because others will draw different conclusions.

The white heat of the scientific revolution

By 1963 and the Labour Party conference at Scarborough, I was a young Labour MP, from Teesside, Labour's first gain in a by-election since before 1951 – a bonus for Harold Wilson, Labour's new leader (Hugh Gaitskell,

---

[1] Dalyell, Tam (1983) *Science policy in Britain* London: FT Pharmaceuticals

4 : A first spell in parliament

his predecessor, had died in January 1963). I had been employed at ICI Wilton, the largest and most modern chemical complex in Britain. I had been pioneering the development of automation and computing on lines I had picked up from their sources at Cambridge and MIT. We were changing the nature of industry, not only in Britain but throughout the world.

The Labour Party policy statement *Labour and the Scientific Revolution*[2], and Harold Wilson's 'white heat of the scientific revolution' speech introducing it, were very much a personal statement. Wilson by now was well on his way to becoming a brilliant Leader of the Opposition and perhaps a great Prime Minister: a promise unfulfilled when he became PM. But for now the ideas came tumbling out, and went far wider than Labour's established line. Harold enthused about the opportunities offered by automation and computers. 'These facts, these inescapable facts, put a whole new argument about industry and economics and Socialism in a new perspective.'

Daringly he proposed a 'university of the air' which was to become the Open University, equipped with all that TV and radio and state-sponsored correspondence courses could provide. (Michael Young, later Lord Young of Dartington, was the original proposer of this inspiring idea.) The proposal was derided, but it came to pass.

Wilson threw his net wide. He cited the health income generated by a new drug, cephalosporin, the product of the National Research and Development Corporation (for which Wilson, as President of the Board of Trade in 1947, had once been responsible). 'We are re-defining and we are re-stating our Socialism in terms of a scientific revolution,' he declared. 'But that revolution cannot become a reality unless we are prepared to make far-reaching changes in economic and social attitudes which permeate our whole system of society.' The 'white heat of the scientific revolution' was not just a spin-doctor's initiative. He believed in it.

In my by-election campaign I had been presented as an embodiment of the 'scientific revolution' that Harold Wilson, once leader, would espouse with such enthusiasm. But like all Members of Parliament, I soon had to settle down to the practical business of being an MP, which is sobering after a spell as the party's latest publicity gimmick.

So I maintained my working links with industry, though I had decided against working for ICI, the principal employers in the constituency. MPs were not well paid in those days and had to pay all their office expenses

---

[2] Labour Party (1963), *Labour and the Scientific Revolution* London: The Labour Party

including a secretary's salary, and even their postage, out of their own pocket. (For financial reasons throughout the 1960s our family holidays were under canvas, in Yorkshire's Cleveland Hills or in Dorset: hotels were out of our reach!) So I continued working on control theory and optimisation at practical level, first with Elliott-Automation on the bench scale water gas shift reactor they built at the DSIR Warren Spring Laboratory, and, later, Rio Tinto Zinc's subsidiary, the Imperial Smelting Company.

A backbencher in opposition

My job in ICI had simply been to put forward ideas for tackling practical problems. In parliament I represented a heavy industry area with chemicals prone to the trade cycle, and steel still more so with the amplifying effect of the stock cycle. So, thought I, what more practical than to make my maiden speech proposing an amendment on the Report Stage of the Finance Bill, that sink of iniquitous Tory special pleading. It was scarcely the stage for the maiden speech of an ambitious new Labour member. My proposal was for an anti-cyclical treatment of tax allowances for inventories. From the Labour front bench Dick Mitchison, the kindly old veteran QC, the husband of Naomi Mitchison (who was the sister of J.B.S. Haldane – of whom more later), and Edward Boyle, then a Tory Treasury minister, somehow got the clerks to find my amendment in order.

Having gone straight from underneath the power station boilers at ICI Wilton, to the party front bench cabals which carve up the timing and votes on the Finance Bill, I felt the doors were open. In 1962, with two years to go before a general election, I was almost immediately put on to the Select Committee on Nationalised Industries, where we were looking at the electricity supply industry, and the power cuts that were plaguing the country that winter.

We questioned the senior executives - Ronnie Edwards, chairman of the Electricity Council, Stanley Brown, chairman of the Generating Board, Denis Rooke from the gas boards and Alf Robens, chairman of the National Coal Board - about their forecasting and planning methods, and the Ministry of Power and the Treasury, about how they responded. The industries, particularly Ronnie Edwards, were happy to discuss the problems with me informally, back in their headquarters where we could go into more technical detail than the committee wished to pursue. Ronnie Edwards was an advocate of the private finance initiative for nationalised industries thirty years ahead of his time. He had been an economics professor at LSE.

In 1962 the Nationalised Industries Select Committee was under the control of Tory MPs: Dick Nugent, the chairman, Donald Kaberry, a Leeds solicitor, and Henry d'Avigdor-Goldsmid, a bullion broker – as good a trio of knights of the shires as could be found: none however was a large country landowner. But like most Select Committee members they gave evidence its due weight, and let reports reflect the strength of the arguments. I learned a lot from them.

First brush with economic policy 1962-64

I had had a first contact with serious operational national economic policy-making in my ICI days when, in 1961, I responded to a letter Richard Stone wrote to *The Times*. As a result, Stone (who in due course became a Cambridge professor) invited me to his first presentation of the pioneering Cambridge Growth Project, an input-output model of the UK economy. ICI gave me leave to attend: I had found that increases in ICI Perspex sales seemed to be related to increases in investment in distributive trades (there was extensive use of Perspex in shop fitting), so I wanted to forecast investment by sectors, and to describe the dynamics.

Dick Stone, whom I got to know quite well, had been personal assistant to Maynard Keynes and he was Keynes's choice as the first Director of the Department of Applied Economics at Cambridge. With James Meade he had produced the first national income and expenditure accounts in Churchill's Cabinet Office, for use in managing the wartime economy. Stone's presentation was attended among others by Alec Cairncross, Chief Economic Adviser to the Government, Sir Donald MacDougall, who later produced George Brown's National Plan, and, of my own generation, John Boreham, who was then producing the National Accounts in the Central Statistical Office and made the CSO contributions to the current Treasury forecast. (He rose to be head of the CSO and deservedly earned a knighthood.)

The objective in Dick Stone's Growth Project was to get at the causes of Britain's disastrously poor growth performance. This it sought to do by presenting the input-output relations between different industries and different goods and services, from investment goods and education, to consumer goods and health. Dick and his team were having difficulty in getting solutions from their model on the Cambridge computer. Given the state of the art in computing at that time, that was entirely understandable.

Dick's methods were technically more ambitious than anything then being attempted in the Treasury and Cabinet Office, but even Stone gave no treatment at that time of the dynamics, such as I had been using on large models in ICI.

The problems I saw in the sceptical reactions of the government economists to the work of Dick and his young assistants were similar to those that I was encountering in ICI. But on becoming an MP in 1962 I was quite unprepared by my research training at Cambridge or my industrial experience in ICI for the politics and scale of the issues at national level.

Soon after my by-election I talked to Peter Shore (then the Research Secretary of the Labour Party), and to Shirley Williams, who was then General Secretary of the Fabian Society. Neither of them was yet in parliament, though both were eventually to hold high office. I remember asking them, 'Given the widespread feeling that the British economy is not achieving its potential, is the party prepared to think afresh about economic policy?'

The Federation of British Industries had persuaded Harold Macmillan, the Prime Minister, and Selwyn Lloyd, the Tory Chancellor of the Exchequer, to set up the National Economic Development Council to introduce French style indicative planning: a public agency that would prepare forecasts of investment and demand, at industry level, to guide firms in the increased investment required to achieve faster economic growth. Peter and Shirley took up my suggestion. Harold Wilson (by 1963 party leader), George Brown (deputy leader of the party) and Jim Callaghan approved, and the Labour Party and the Fabian Society organised the two Bonnington Hotel conferences in 1963. A wide range of politically sympathetic economists, scientists and industrialists were invited. The conferences were successful in creating a timely impression of policy dynamism. They gave me an opportunity of putting faces to mythical creatures like the twin Hungarian economists, Nicky Kaldor and Tommy Balogh (described by Hugh Dalton – Chancellor in the post-war Labour government – as Buddha and Pest, the one so named because of his girth, and the other because of his behaviour), and Richard Kahn, of whom Keynes had made such generous acknowledgement in his preface to *The General Theory of Employment, Interest and Money*[3]. But the conferences did not produce specific initiatives, still less agreement on such sensitive issues as

---

[3] Keynes, John Maynard (1936) *The General Theory of Employment, Interest and Money* Macmillan: London

the exchange rate. They simply gave a general endorsement of NEDC-French type indicative planning.

Manifesto promises before the 1964 General Election

The institutional implementation of the modernisation of the economy, with Harold Wilson's vision of the re-building of socialism in his 1963 Scarborough speech, was set out in Labour's proposals in the 1964 General Election. Expectations were high – mine included. Wilson's performance as Leader of the Opposition since succeeding the late Hugh Gaitskill had been little short of brilliant. He had an impressive record both as a wartime civil servant in key economic departments and as an up and coming Minister in the Attlee government. By the age of thirty one he was President of the Board and a Cabinet Minister. In opposition he had been Shadow Chancellor and then Shadow Foreign Secretary. With these credentials, surely he would handle the big economic questions competently. And yet, and yet ... I remember Wilson mocking Sir Alec Douglas-Home (who had succeeded Macmillan as Prime Minister in October 1963 after the Profumo debacle) during an election rally. Sir Alec, Wilson jeered, used matchsticks to make calculations about the economy, while he (Wilson) claimed he used a slide rule (the most advanced hand-held calculator before the modern calculator). I was for some reason sitting just behind Wilson on the platform, when he made this claim. I whipped my slide rule out and handed it to the maestro. It was manifestly clear that he had not handled a slide rule for decades.

The 1964 Labour Manifesto's big idea was a proposal to establish a Ministry of Economic Affairs which would formulate a national economic plan with both sides of industry. This would set out what was expected of each industry in terms of exports, investment, production and employment. An industrial and economic transformation was promised, with a Ministry of Technology to guide and stimulate a major national effort to bring advanced technology and new processes into industry. However within the Labour Party and the trade unions, at grass roots level, or more widely in industry, there was no evidence of urgency comparable with, for example, the dynamic of the Big Bang in the liberalisation of the City under Margaret Thatcher in the 1980s.

As a novice in economic policy, I had been impressed during the run-up to the election by the high powered economists who were involved. I had eavesdropped on economics lectures at Cambridge as a mathematics research student, having read, or struggled to read, key expositions by

Keynes and Alfred Marshall[4] as an undergraduate. I accepted the discursive and allusive style of argument by some economists, and assumed the gaps in their argument could be filled by lesser labourers in the economic vineyard. I supposed that, although I could not understand all that was said, there must be a rationale there. However one thing was obvious: if the rationale was to work it needed a stronger statistical foundation than the sources, official and unofficial, then available. I cannot recall anyone mentioning Arrow and Debreu, the pioneers of the neo-classical microeconomics. Yet their work was already appearing in the journals in America, and was to have a major impact in the 1970s. Neither figured in the standard political texts of the day such as Tony Crosland's *The Future of Socialism*[5].

The need for statistical reform in our national accounts

I had picked up from Dick Stone the general direction of statistical reform we needed. Dick had been an adviser to the United Nations on their Standard System of National Accounts, and knew what was going on elsewhere in the world. He knew too that, without reliable statistics, the dream of reliable forecasts was a fantasy.

I remember discussing with him the practice in Britain where, perversely, the strong departmental basis of power was reflected in the collection of statistics. Each firm was required to report its employment to the Ministry of Labour, its exports and imports to Customs and Excise, its production to the Board of Trade, its investment in new buildings to the Ministry of Works, and so on. The collecting department would aggregate the returns on a particular activity from the individual firms; the identity of the firm was deliberately hidden, with a rule that no published statistical total should be composed of activities of less than three firms. Each Department had its own register of firms and would decide to which industry to classify a firm, so industry breakdowns in different departments did not match. Mistakes were inevitable. In one year investment in the chemical industry in Wiltshire suddenly shot up, because the Ministry of Works attributed ICI's investment at Wilton on Teesside to Wilton, a small village in rural Wiltshire. Since all information about the firm was lost, it was not possible to produce composite estimates, like the productivity or profitability of a firm, by putting together returns from the one firm to

---

[4] Marshall, Alfred (1st Edition 1890, 8th 1920; my own copy is a 1946 reprint of the 8th edition) *Principles of Economics* London: Macmillan
[5] Crosland, C.A.R. (1956) *The Future of Socialism* London: Jonathan Cape

4 : A first spell in parliament

different ministries, or sometimes even two different returns to the same ministry. The 1947 Statistics of Trade Act allowed government statisticians to treat their particular set of statistical returns as virtually their own private property.

What was needed was a common business register used by all departments, and a single channel of communication for the firm, which would report all aspects of its operations to a single office. Problems of commercial confidentiality could then be addressed specifically.

I outlined this to Harold Wilson before the 1964 election, and suggested a small working party might work out the detail. I suggested Dick Stone, and also Robin Marris who was writing on the corporate economy[6] even before Professor J.F. Galbraith, the author whose works will be familiar to a whole generation of economists. Harold, himself a statistician, accepted the ideas and the names I suggested, adding only Teddy Jackson, (the Director of the Oxford Institute of Economics and Statistics). Harold told me that he and Teddy were contemporaries at Oxford before the war. Teddy had done him the signal service of taking the difficult statistical theory paper in Philosophy, Politics and Economics finals, thus allowing Harold, who took a softer option, to beat him into first place in the aggregate examination marks. Robin Marris and I went to see Pierre Massé, the Director General of the Plan, in Paris, to see how they produced the French Plan.

Though Harold had accepted my proposal, it did not go into any Labour Party policy document before the 1964 General Election, nor on to any ministerial priority list for the incoming Labour government. Nor was there any treatment of how the medium term, industry level projections of output and investment in the National Plan, could be related to the imperatives of the short term management of national demand in the Treasury. Yet this was vitally important to safeguard the exchange rate of the pound. The exchange rate, as was customary under the Bretton Woods agreement which controlled international exchange rates, was of course fixed. Woe betide the nation whose economic performance failed to support its fixed exchange rate. Devaluation – a much feared fate – would become inevitable. I assumed such high strategy was managed in exalted circles to which I had no access.

I had however stimulated the UK Automation Council, the British Computer Society, and the Operational Research Society to organise a

---

[6] Marris, Robin and Wood, Adrian (1971) *The Corporate Economy* London: Macmillan

conference on Computable Models in Decision Making. The date chosen well in advance was 14 October 1964.

My aim was to acquaint my political colleagues with what was going on in the brave new world of computers. Invitations were sent to key ministers and opinion formers. Most accepted. Papers were to be given on forecasting demand for transient life products, consumer durables, and steel; on planning production of public buildings, oil refineries, and machines; on manpower and organisational planning; and on economic planning as perceived in France, and for Britain, in the Treasury, in the National Economic Development Council, and in the social accounting matrix work of Richard Stone's at Cambridge. The meeting was chaired by J.F. Coales, and speakers included professional or executive heads of government departments, firms, public utilities, advertising and market research agencies, and academics: the roll call included Dr Beeching (of British rail), Alec Cairncross, Basil de Ferranti, Professor Sir Willis Jackson, Claus Moser (then a Professor at LSE), Professor Patrick Rivett, Professor Richard Stone. It all went splendidly ...

But unfortunately not a single politician – the intended and invited audience – came to the conference. As luck would have it, polling day had been fixed for the following day, 15 October! Though the proceedings were published as *Models for Decision*[7] in 1965, the impact was lost.

Labour returned 1964

Labour, under Harold Wilson's dynamic leadership, swept into power in 1964 – with a majority of three. It was an undeniable feat: Labour had overturned a Tory majority of around 100. Wilson's success owed much to his personal dynamism, but the reputation of the Tory government had been tarnished by the Suez debacle under Sir Anthony Eden (1956/57), to be followed by the Profumo scandal which led to Harold Macmillan's downfall in 1963 and the Tories' choice of that rather unlikely successor, Sir Alec Douglas-Home (as he became on renouncing his peerage) as Prime Minister.

On achieving office, Wilson promised one hundred days of action, modelled on President John Kennedy's inauguration. We were at the dawn of a new era. His slender majority however did not auger well, and Britain's precarious balance of payments position, and our failure to achieve serious economic growth, were to prove our undoing.

---

[7] Berners-Lee, C.M. (Editor) (1965) *Models for Decision* London: English University Press

My apprenticeship as a Parliamentary Private Secretary (PPS)

Harold Wilson did not make me a minister when he formed his first Labour government after the 1964 election. An incoming prime minister has a lot of debts. A number of younger MPs might have expected to become junior ministers, including Peter Shore, David Ennals, Shirley Williams, and Merlyn Rees: all were to achieve high office, but not one of us was made minister straightaway.

Novices would be well-advised to hitch their wagons to rising stars. Harold Wilson made Peter Shore his PPS – Parliamentary Private Secretary. Jim Callaghan, as Chancellor of the Exchequer, appointed Merlyn Rees as his PPS; and I (unwisely) took the short straw and became George Brown's PPS. George held the newly created and ill fated office of First Secretary of State and Minister for Economic Affairs. (In some ways George's position was analogous to the specially-created posts John Prescott has held, as Deputy to the Prime Minister, since 1997; but George Brown's volcanic temperament, fuelled by alcohol, made him dangerously unreliable.)

The Parliamentary Private Secretary is the lowest form of parliamentary life, not even a minister and unpaid, but often said to be the first rung of the ministerial ladder. It had its hair raising moments in the first few days of the 1964 government, in the mini-run on sterling. George spent the first morning of the run lacing his tea from a bottle of Scotch in his desk, demanding of the Bank of England how many millions they had lost in the past half hour, and then blasting Dr Blessing of the Bundesbank on the phone for selling his sterling holdings. Not a nice introduction to international finance for a prissy young innocent like myself.

George had taken up various people I suggested, such as Fred Catherwood, the chief industrial adviser, whom I had met working with Jim Callaghan's Treasury team. So I now suggested using Dick Stone, from whom I had wrung an agreement to help in working out a methodological basis for statistics and the National Plan. George referred this to Eric Roll (the Permanent Under Secretary), Douglas Allen (the Deputy Secretary), and Donald MacDougall, who had come from NEDO (the National Economic Development Office) to work on the Plan. They turned down the suggestion.

I suspect that senior civil servants, who knew Dick well from war time Cabinet Office days, felt his contribution would only complicate and delay matters that would have to be decided on cruder arguments. The National Plan duly collapsed at the first challenge from the imperatives of short term demand management in the July 1967 measures, not because of any malice from the Treasury, but because of the methodological inadequacies of the National Plan itself.

Dick Stone – later, Sir Richard Stone – would deservedly win the Nobel Prize in 1984 for his outstanding contribution to the development of systems of national accounting. I like to think that maybe I was instrumental in bringing this talented man more closely into public service. Alas, pioneers initially often get short shrift from governments desperately in need of their originality and skill.

I did not remain PPS for George Brown for very long. As First Secretary of State and Minister for Economic Affairs he had, perhaps, an impossible task, and certainly lacked the competence, stability and application required. I decided that I did not wish to be associated with the policies he was putting forward. We parted without acrimony, and I liked to think that my resignation was not held against me.

In career terms however it might have been wiser never to have served as George Brown's PPS.

Wilson sends in his MPs

More favourable to my career, perhaps, than my mis-spent time with George Brown, was a minor escapade. In January 1966 three of us – my fellow MPs David Ennals and Chris Rowland, and I – went out to Southern Rhodesia. Our mission was to attempt to persuade the electorate (then, of course, entirely white) that their Prime Minister, Ian Smith, was wrong in making his Unilateral Declaration of Independence (UDI) a few months earlier. We had the tacit approval of my next-door neighbour, Middlesbrough East MP, Arthur Bottomley. Arthur was by then the Colonial Secretary. (Southern Rhodesia was still a British colony.)

Not surprisingly, when we tried to address a large and rather overheated audience of whites we were attacked, dragged from the platform and pinned on the floor as some louts put the boot in. The police stood by, approvingly. Trog's cartoon (opposite) captures the scene pretty accurately.

We were deported. Wilson was said to have remarked to the press, 'I may not have sent in troops, but, by God, I've sent some of my MPs'.

Our visit accomplished nothing. But nor did the Prime Minister's attempts to dissuade Ian Smith.

The country descended gradually into civil war and chaos, before achieving official independence in 1980. Renamed Zimbabwe, it has been ruled ruthlessly by President Robert Mugabe ever since.

Cartoon by Trog, first published in the Observer, 16 January 1966
Jeremy is on the floor, hands warding off blows to his head. His briefcase (centre) bears his name.
Source: University of Kent. Reproduced by kind permission of Wally Fawkes ('Trog')

Making the case for civil service reform

My resignation from the post of George Brown's PPS had freed me to return to Select Committee work. I saw one way of putting in my pennyworth on the methods of government in the Estimates Committee (a precursor of today's departmental select committees), where I became chairman in 1964 of the general sub-committee, with the freedom to range over issues for public expenditure as a whole.

Talk of civil service reform was in the air, as there always is when a party has been in opposition for years. There was criticism of the reliance on generalists in the senior administrative grades of the civil service, with little employment of specialists and in particular, economists, scientists and engineers technically experienced in particular industries. Also a disproportionately large proportion came from private schools, via Oxford and Cambridge.

The general reform of the civil service was too large a project for a Select Committee sub-committee. But an inquiry into recruitment would make it possible to explore expertise, training, and social bias, and open the door for a wider government inquiry. Shirley Williams (then an up and coming new young MP) and Sir Edward Boyle (a former Conservative cabinet minister) happily served as members of the general sub-committee.

During our inquiry I met Lawrence Helsby, the Head of the Civil Service, to find out how much reform the government and the civil service would stomach. He was ready to accommodate the government's wish to review structure and staffing. I myself wrote the 'Chairman's Draft Report'. Our clerk assumed that that was his prerogative to write this, until advised by his senior colleagues that I was procedurally, if misguidedly, within my rights.

Our principal recommendation was a government inquiry.

This gave Harold Wilson a prompt to set up the Fulton Committee on civil service reform in 1965 under his old Oxford friend, John Fulton (later Lord Fulton), with Shirley Williams and Edward Boyle serving as members of it. Shirley was later replaced by Bob Sheldon, a stalwart Labour MP. The Fulton Committee reported in 1968, with recommendations that broadly fulfilled our expectations, and most of these were gradually implemented.

Reform of government statistics

My next aim was for the sub-committee to tackle something bearing upon mainstream economic policy making. We inquired into the reform of government statistics, where I had a position worked out and a report ready written. I knew from my ICI experience that without reliable statistical data, it is impossible to plan ahead. Yet the statistics on which the government was basing its budgets and policies were, as I have already explained, more than a bit ramshackle.

I wanted to appoint as adviser to the committee someone who knew the field, and sympathised with my position. Graham Pyatt, one of Professor Richard Stone's bright young research staff at Cambridge, was willing to serve. But there was no provision in those days for select committees to have advisers. However procedurally all that was required was that Graham should be allowed to see papers and attend meetings of the Committee. The accommodating clerk found that people who had given evidence to the Committee were permitted to attend further meetings. So Graham was, formally, simply our first witness. The Acton Society Trust kindly paid him a modest fee for his assistance to the impecunious mother of parliaments, as its first select committee adviser in modern times. In preparing briefs for the Committee, Graham and I worked as a team, with no distinction as to which was the politician, which the expert – a distinction which I personally have never observed.

As with our civil service inquiry the year before, I saw the official in charge. I found Harry Campion, the veteran founding Director General of the Central Statistical Office (the CSO), wholly in sympathy with the idea of a common register and the centralised collection of business statistics. He of course knew the idea came from Dick Stone and had the Prime Minister's support.

The 1966 General Election came before we had completed our inquiry. However, our successor Committee in the new parliament chose to complete the inquiry, on, as I thought, the right lines.

The newly re-elected government's response was to put statistical reform in the hands of an unusual joint ministerial-official Cabinet committee, the Statistical Policy Committee, chaired by Peter Shore in the Department of Economic Affairs. Its membership included several junior ministers, including myself (I became a junior minister after the 1966 election), and permanent secretaries, who turned up conscientiously because sensitive issues of departmental powers would arise. The Business Statistics Office was created, the Common Register launched, and the Office of Population Censuses and Surveys replaced the old Social Survey and the General Register Office. Claus Moser was appointed the new Director General of the CSO – an excellent appointment, for he was perhaps the most distinguished statistician of his generation. Practical arrangements were made for a modern statistical service for government and outside users, which lasted for the next thirty years.

Civil service and statistical reforms were narrow fields of a technical and (largely) non-political character, but they persuaded me that the constitutional methods were there to handle more difficult problems like the management of the economy, social security, and even family law, if approached in the right way.

It had taken three bites of the cherry to formulate and implement statistical reform. First came the unofficial paper prepared in Opposition for Harold Wilson by Dick Stone, Robin Marris, Teddy Jackson and myself; second the Select Committee Report on its inquiry into government statistics in 1966-67, which I had chaired; and third the Cabinet Committee on statistical reform on which I served.

It was clumsy and laborious, but it worked, and became something of a model for me of how constitutional and machinery of government reforms could be initiated in parliament and implemented in government.

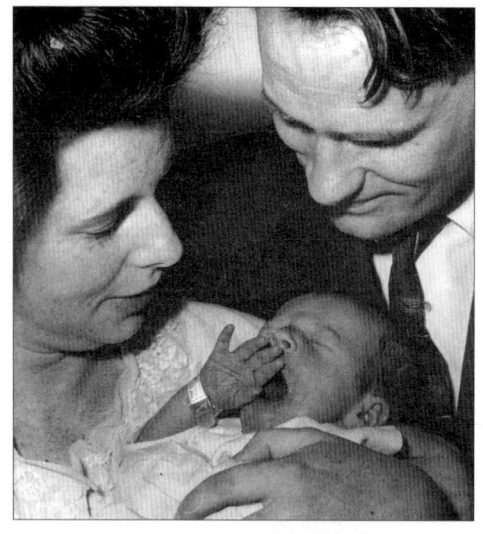

There's more to life than politics!

Our youngest daughter, Beatrice, was born in 1965. Sensibly at even only a few hours old she did not take her father's concerns too seriously.

Mr Speaker King, after attending her baptism in the House of Commons chapel, asked one of her sisters,

'How many girls are there in your family now?'

'Five counting my Mum.'

'And how many boys?'

'Two.'

'Two?'

'Yes. The hamster. And my Daddy.'

The family leaving the House of Commons Chapel of St Stephen's. Photographs: Source untraced.

5

A taste of office
1966-1969

The 1966 General Election at last gave Labour a substantial majority (363 seats out of 630), compared with the knife edge majority of three in the previous parliament. The way ahead seemed clear. But Britain's poor economic performance was to haunt the government, and lead eventually to its downfall.

Ministry of Power – fuel policy 1966-67

After the 1966 election Wilson made a clean sweep of the top levels of a number of the ministries. At the Ministry of Power, a new Minister, Dick Marsh (later Lord Marsh) replaced Fred Lee; the new Permanent Secretary was David Pitblado from the Cabinet Office, with Robert Marshall, from the Ministry of Aviation, as the new Deputy Secretary. I occupied the bottom rung, as Parliamentary Secretary. The new economic adviser was, at my suggestion, Michael Posner. (Michael was to have a distinguished career, and now sits in the House of Lords.) Michael was a former student of Tommy Balogh, the abrasive Oxford economist who had the Prime Minister's ear. (Balogh had been largely responsible for the ill-fated idea of the Department of Economic Affairs.) Michael however did not necessarily agree with his former mentor.

On entering the Ministry of Power I soon had a surprise. I asked to see the working papers underlying the government's 1965 White Paper Fuel Policy[1], which had been published just before the election. It contained estimates of the future production and consumption of the different energy sources - coal, oil, gas, nuclear and renewables (wind power, solar power and so on). What, I wanted to know, was the basis of these estimates? The

---
[1] Power, Ministry of (1965) *Fuel Policy* London: HMSO, Cmnd. 2798

figures would determine whether there would again be frequent power cuts in the next winter, how many and what kind of power stations we should build, and whether we needed to recruit more coal miners. But there was nothing in the file except earlier drafts of the recently published White Paper. There were no working papers. The estimates seemed to be plucked out of the air. If government was going to approve major capital expenditure in energy, it needed to have models of demand and relative costs from the different industries.

I took the matter to Dick Marsh, my Minister. Dick had risen fast. First elected in 1959, his only previous ministerial experience was as a junior minister in the ministries of Technology and of Labour. He usually greeted new ideas with scorn: 'Rubbish. What nonsense!' But he acted. Soon after I raised the question of the new developments in energy supplies, I was summoned unexpectedly to a meeting in the Minister's office, where I found the senior officials of the Ministry of Power assembled. I had said to Dick that although politically the difficult job we were being reported as facing was the re-nationalisation of steel, the most important job was fuel policy, for which the recent White Paper was a totally inadequate guide.

Dick asked me in front of the officials why I thought we needed another review.

I explained. Since the 1965 review, I said, gas has been discovered in the North Sea, and there is the prospect of oil. Nuclear power now looked like becoming cheaper than coal for electricity generation. And miners were voting with their feet, leaving efficient pits like those in the East Midlands at the rate of 1000 men a week.

Now look at the figures, I continued. I jotted them down on the back of an envelope. The 1960 review had forecast that we would need 197 million tons of coal a year by 1970. By 1964 the forecasted demand for 1970 was only 184 million tons. The 1965 Industrial Inquiry had projected that demand for coal in 1970 would decline to 175 million tons. But these were figures plucked from the air. There were *no* working papers.

So another review was conceded.

Revised estimates in the subsequent White Paper on Fuel Policy[2] put demand for coal in 1970 at 139 million tons. This seemed to me unrealistic. If anything went wrong with the price of oil, we would need to increase supply to 142 million tons. (This was a clairvoyant anticipation of the sharp

---

[2] Power, Ministry of (1967) *Fuel Policy* London: HMSO Cmnd. 3438

rise in the price of oil in the early 1970s, though I did not foresee the explosion in oil prices associated with the Yom Kippur war 1973-74.) In the event, coal demand (consumption) in 1970 was 157 million tons (not the 139 forecast in the White Paper). However, a long term decline in consumption was inevitable. By 1990 consumption was to fall to 108 million tons, and in 2000 to 59 million tons. Such was the measure of the challenge of structural change which the economy was about to face in the next thirty years, leaving many ex-miners and mining areas desolated.

I was only arguing what was already becoming obvious.

Where I differed was on the practicality of producing a more robust strategy. I argued for systematic modelling which could respond robustly to events if, and when, they departed from the expected course. I also argued that the separate industries (coal, gas, oil, nuclear power, etc) should themselves produce their own models including the latest information on their position and capabilities.

This was readily accepted in spirit, not only by the nationalised gas and electricity generation and supply organisations, but also by the oil companies, which were used to the disclosure requirements in the United States. But it was resisted by the nationalised National Coal Board on the instructions of the chairman, Alf Robens, a former Labour Minister of Labour. This was rank insubordination by Alf Robens trying out the muscle of the minister, the young Dick Marsh, and the wily Harold Wilson.

It succeeded.

The Prime Minister and Marsh avoided a confrontation. Robens insisted on vetting all the information given to the Ministry of Power about the performance and potential of the pits. I was told by officials that the total information sent to the Ministry about the fixed and marginal cost and employment requirements of all the pits in Britain was cut down to one side of paper. This obscurantism continued to harm the mining industry for a long time by hiding its true position.

... and steel nationalisation

The Labour Party and the Labour government were committed to the re-nationalisation of steel as an almost totemic act in the settlement of the Bevanite, left-right feuds of the 1950s. But there was a straightforward managerial case for it. The steel industry had been nationalised in 1951 just before Labour lost office, and then largely de-nationalised by the Tories. It had one of the most highly developed trade associations – the British Iron and Steel Federation – which kept an eye on iron ore supplies and investment. The British Iron and Steel Federation had produced the Benson report recommending a rationalisation of steel production into five coastal sites, with a great deal of investment in new plant. But it was unable to generate the managerial will or raise the capital needed to carry out the plan. This incapacity was attributed to the political uncertainty that had hung over the industry.

But for me as a young ex-ICI technocratic Labour candidate in 1962 in a steel constituency on Teesside, there was no doubt about the case. Dorman Long, the steel works neighbouring ICI on Teesside, was middle ranking in terms of its plant and productivity in the 1960s. But its state was pitiable compared with that of ICI next door. There was no sign of the depth of managerial capacity that ICI had gone about creating after its merger in 1926, a capacity that not only invented new products, like polythene and polyesters, new industries like nuclear power, and new techniques like automation, but invested in them. Had voters on Teesside been given the choice they would have said, 'Let steel be run like ICI'. And if that meant creating a national corporation to run it, so be it.

(ICI's own problems, incidentally, which had begun to appear after its abortive bid for Courtauld's in the early 1960s, were not then pressing. The de-merger of its pharmaceutical division to form Zeneca in the 1990s would prove its undoing. Both moves were stock-exchange driven rather than market or technology driven moves.)

While nationalisation was still under debate, I interested the Steel Company of Wales in participating in a computer control project John Westcott and his team at Imperial College had developed for a cold strip mill. I could see, with my experience of control theory, the possibility of a powerful application. Monty Finniston, then the technical man on the steel organising committee we had set up to prepare for nationalisation, came along with me to persuade Harold Lever in the Treasury to finance it. It was a success and became a world standard. A young British Steel engineer who worked on it was John Bryant, who decades later became the first chief executive of Corus, the renamed combination of British Steel and Hoogovens.

I left the Ministry of Power in 1967, before the steel nationalisation bill became law. I was to become entangled with the industry again in the 1980s during and after privatisation, when, for admittedly Scottish and constituency reasons, I sought a more competitive structure.

The 1967 ministerial reshuffle

In the Prime Minister's 1967 reshuffle, George Brown was finally ousted from the ill-fated Department of Economic Affairs – he became Foreign Secretary – and Peter Shore, long a Wilson protégé, was promoted to become Secretary of State at DEA. Wilson himself was thereby assuming the reins of power and ultimate control of our economic destiny.

The reshuffle followed hard on the heels of a series of economic crises. Wilson, who had so dazzled the country with his promise of an economic and industrial transformation, had been forced into a humiliating devaluation. Though he assured the British public that devaluation did not mean that 'the pound in your pocket is worth less than it was', his reputation for economic competence was severely tarnished and never really recovered.

For a brilliant and detailed history of these events, readers would be well advised to consult Peter Hennessy's *The Prime Minister: The Office and its Holders since 1945*[3] published in 2000. Hennessy, drawing on recently available cabinet minutes and other privileged sources, makes the confusion and incoherence at the heart of government painfully clear. Lowly underlings like myself could only sense this. I could not know at that time that, for example, the key ministerial committee on economic strategy SCEP (Steering Committee and Economic Policy) was denied access to the Treasury's economic forecasts, and that the job of Wilson's Inner Cabinet or 'Management Committee' (Wilson's preferred name) was not concerned with long-term strategy policy formation, but instead, in Wilson's own words, with 'political strategy, including Parliamentary strategy'.

In the 1967 reshuffle I too was moved – from the Ministry of Power to the Ministry of Technology.

Ministry of Technology: 1967-69

My move to the Ministry of Technology was a challenge.

Min Tech, as it had become known, had been set up in 1964 as the embodiment of Harold Wilson's 1993 party conference speech at Scarborough on the 'white heat of technology' – except that is not what he had said: he spoke of the 'scientific revolution'.

Tony Benn, the Minister of Technology, was an enthusiast. And now he was in charge of what was seen as the powerhouse which would forge

---

[3] Hennessey, Peter, (2000) *The Prime Ministers* London: Penguin

Britain's economic recovery. This Ministry of Technology would in due course take over the Ministries of Aviation (1967) and Power (1969).

When I presented Tony with new ideas, he would respond, 'Marvellous! Go ahead!' But all too often there would be no follow-up, no contacts initiated with other departments – contacts only a minister could make. And Benn was in a strong position to make such contacts. He was at various times part of Wilson's 'Inner Cabinet' and on the key committees I mention above.

Benn had succeeded the ineffectual Frank Cousins, the former General Secretary of the Transport and General Workers' Union (the T&GWU), in 1966. Harold's appointment of Frank as his first Minister of Technology in 1964 had been made presumably on the basis of his membership of the Board of the old Department of Scientific and Industrial Research. It was also to keep him out of mischief by bringing him into government. Frank Cousins only entered parliament early in 1965, in a by-election. He was intensely uncomfortable in parliament. He had asked me to be his PPS, but by then I was already committed to George Brown, Frank's deadliest enemy from old TGWU days. Within the Ministry Frank had been well handled by officials. Otto (Sir Richard) Clarke, the permanent secretary when I arrived, was the inventor of the current art of public expenditure control, and the father of Charles Clarke (by now – in May 2002 – Chairman of the Labour Party[4]). Otto was accomplished in the mandarin art of flattery, and a lot else besides. 'Money? Money!' he used to exclaim, when I inquired whether we had the resources to finance a project. 'There is never a problem about money!' Then he would explain sympathetically in the loo that junior ministers were just the public relations officers of the Ministry in parliament, and had nothing to do with policy.

As one of the two parliamentary secretaries – the other was Edmund Dell (later Lord Dell) – I had succeeded Peter Shore (who had just been promoted Secretary of State for Economic Affairs). Before Peter, my office on the 11th floor of Millbank Tower had been occupied by C.P. Snow, the novelist and Cambridge don, from whom all that I inherited were the dust marks round the edges of his huge Sydney Nolan paintings.

Patrick Blackett, the President of the Royal Society, served as Chief Scientist in the Ministry, and Euan Maddock as Chief Engineer, fresh from making Britain's H-bomb. Euan used to complain, 'If I had to put a bomb under it I would know what to do, but in Whitehall I don't know.'

---

[4] Charles Clarke became Secretary of State for Education in late 2002.

5 : A taste of office 1966-1969

I remember once when we were all waiting for a massive technical report on something, Patrick poked his head round the door five minutes after the copies were put on our desks, and asked what I thought of it. I said, 'Patrick, I have only had it five minutes.' He said 'Yes, but all that ever matters is Figure 1', as if it were a letter in *Nature*, the science magazine.

By the time I got to the Ministry of Technology in 1967 it had settled down comfortably, if that is the word, under Tony Benn, and was engaged on generally sensible interventionist policies in the conventional wisdom of the time. It promoted the rationalisation of the electrical engineering industry round GEC (General Electric), the motor industry around British Leyland, of computers around ICL (International Computers), and of shipbuilding. Tony Benn and Otto Clarke kept the handling of the main issues to themselves. While they were prepared for me to put the spotlight on future product designs of computers in ICL and GEC, and so unblock the log jam in serious merger negotiations, they were not prepared to bring me in on the negotiations themselves.

Edmund Dell, the other parliamentary secretary, was given intractable problems like shipbuilding and motors, and I picked up the issues and interests that were left unsolved in high technology.

Ferranti had a good line in application specific integrated circuits at Gem Mill that GEC wanted to solve with a sledge hammer programme. Theo Williamson was wanting to develop System 24, a computer controlled and integrated set of machine tools. Ian Barron from Elliott-Automation had developed a minicomputer Modular One, which was popular with engineers and scientists; he was asking, not for support, but to be allowed to fight his corner in a free market that was not rigged in favour of Ferranti or Elliott-Automation. I opened his first factory. Ian went on to found INMOS of transputer fame, Britain's last bid at establishing a national integrated circuit producer. If, when you bought your computer, you recognised the words 'Pentium Intel', you are a beneficiary.

Even in the mid-1960s it was already clear that the dominant technology in computing was going to be software and not hardware. I convened a small advisory group on software composed of Alex D'Agapeyeff, the founder of CAP, on commercial software, Stanley Gill on scientific software, and officials like Murray Laver and Ron Aylward from the excellent group we had in the Ministry. I am afraid we did not scoop Bill Gates on a disk operating system, but I think we did something to set the UK off to a good start on specific applications and systems integration, ranging from baggage and freight handling at London Airport, to software suites for systems from computer assisted engineering design, to the Met Office weather forecasting which John Mason was building up.

I was not, however, allowed to speak on Concorde, because during the debates in 1964, I had raised the question of the acceptability of supersonic bangs over land. Concorde, of course, was being built in Bristol, where Tony Benn had constituency interests.

In due course the Cabinet considered the question of supersonic bangs. The RAF had been testing public reactions over air shows and finding none. A random set of bangs from explosives were arranged in Essex where all public reactions could be systematically recorded and considered. Sure enough the cabbages grew bigger, the babies bonnier, and everybody slept the more soundly. To clinch the matter a supersonic bang was arranged over Whitehall one morning when the Cabinet would be in session. With extraordinary courage the Cabinet waited with gritted teeth for the windows to be blown in. In the event the bang sounded like a backfire from a car, scarcely rattling the windows: the Cabinet laughed nervously. The upshot has been that Concorde has been allowed to fly supersonically – but only over the sea, transporting the super-rich so greedy over their time as to ignore its environmental effects on the atmosphere. The Cabinet is not at its best considering scientific and technological questions, nor even public reactions to them.

The beginnings of the Treasury Model

I felt that, despite the constructive work at Min Tech, our contribution to Britain's economic performance was insufficient to make a significant impact. The government had come into office in 1964 with a clear set of objectives. The economic health of the nation had to be restored. The balance of payments had to be corrected and steady economic growth achieved. On entering office in 1964, the Labour government had decided not to devalue the pound. Successive runs on the pound had only been withstood with the support of massive international loans. But the balance of payments remained increasingly precarious, and our sluggish economic performance offered no relief. The pound was devalued in November 1967. The National Plan was abandoned. There was grave concern over the performance and the management of the economy as a whole.

Throughout these disasters I had been observing as closely as possible from my very junior position the process of economic policy making.

When first elected in 1962 I had had no London base, and so initially I had stayed with friends. One such was John Boreham whom I had met at

Dick Stone's presentation of the growth model at Cambridge. He was a government statistician, the Central Statistical Office member of the triumvirate who co-ordinated (that is, made) the Treasury's economic forecast, on which the operation of the government's economic policy was based. The other two at that time were the Treasury economists, Pat Brown and Wynn Godley. John arranged for us to have lunch together, and we talked about economic forecasting methods, with of course no mention of specific numbers or even directions. A lunch date of this kind – a recently elected junior backbencher lunching with a triumvirate of boffins whose work was at the heart of economic policy making in the Treasury – would scarcely be possible in these days of open government! The forecast, I learned, was made formally by an Official (as distinct from a Ministerial) Cabinet Committee EF(O), in which representatives of different departments would contribute forecasts of their variables (the Department of Trade on trade, Employment on unemployment and prices, and so on). These would be put together by the triumvirate and reconciled and approved by a further meeting of the EF(O) Committee.

When I became a minister I asked to see these papers. The Ministerial versions were written at the level of a newspaper article. The Official versions had more numbers, but were little less discursive. As a Minister, and with my hat on as responsible for computer applications, I suggested to the Treasury that they might ask Jim Ball, of the London Business School, to model the effect of a proposed tax change. With Lawrie Klein, Ball had produced the first model of the UK economy; Terry Burns meanwhile had been producing forecasts with a quarterly econometric model[5] at the London Business School from 1966. (Lawrie Klein, Dick Stone and James Meade were later all awarded Nobel prizes for economics, while Ball rose to be a professor and had a very distinguished career.) Jim Ball was invited to sit in on a round of Treasury meetings estimating the effect of a tax change. That led, in about 1969, to the beginning of the Treasury model which was to become an indispensable tool in the making of economic policy.

With our deteriorating economic situation it was painfully obvious that we needed better ways of forecasting. It was forecasts by the EF(O) Committee of a horrendous trade deficit that had precipitated a humiliating devaluation. Yet, as I was to show in a Cabinet Committee meeting after

---

[5] Burns, Terry (1986) 'The interpretation and use of economic predictions' *Proceedings of the Royal.Society* A407, 103-125 London

the event, that alarming forecast deficit was misleading. The actual deficit was in fact far smaller than the forecast deficit!

It could be argued that the devaluation, or at least the scale of the devaluation, was misguided and based on very shaky evidence. I argued that anything that might improve the accuracy of forecasting was worth examining.

Among those who spoke at that same Cabinet Committee meeting was Alec Cairncross who, as Chief Economic Adviser to the Government, was in charge of forecasting. Later Cairncross devoted his presidential address to the Royal Economic Society in 1969 to economic forecasting[6]. The greater turbulence in the economy in the 1970s was to make our economic problems more acute, and the need for better forecasting more pressing.

Editing Cabinet Committee minutes is a Number 10 prerogative. I remember at one meeting Jack Diamond, as Chief Secretary to the Treasury, took a strong line. I thought, and said, he was mistaken. Jack insisted it was in his brief. A decision was reached, based on his argument. However when the Minutes came out, Jack Diamond's advice and the consequent decision reached were reported quite differently. I told this story at a private conference years later. The civil servant in the Cabinet Office who had written the minute was there, and admitted to me privately that he had indeed altered the decision. Jack Diamond had either misread official advice from the Treasury, or failed to read it at all! I tell this story, not to show malpractice in the Cabinet Office, but how the ramblings of even the shrewdest of ministers can be reduced to sense in the minutes by a loyal and intelligent civil service: but future historians should note that the official record is not always in the narrow sense correct.

My concern at the lack of direction in economic policy making increased with my experience as a junior minister, and eventually I began to commit to paper my sense of where the government was getting to and how far it was able to grapple effectively with the problems thrown up by a modern technological society.

The result was my book, *Decision in Government* – a book which was to precipitate my resignation.

---

[6] Cairncross, Alec (1969) 'Economic Forecasting' *Economic Journal* LXXIX (316) December 797-812

6

Decision in Government & resignation
1969

In 1969, in the introduction to my book, *Decision in Government*[1], I wrote:

> By mid-term in the life of the government much had been done but success was elusive. On entering office the government had decided not to devalue the pound.... Successive runs on the pound were withstood with the support of major international loans. But the balance of payments failed to respond adequately. ... Faced with a forecast deficit for the following year as well, the government after three years in office devalued in November 1967. . . . . . .
>
> During these four years of balance of payments crises the government was making major changes in the structure of the economy. The Corporation Tax, the Capital Gains Tax, and the Selective Employment Taxes were introduced ... [and] investment grants, redundancy payments, higher social security benefits, increased training levies, increased support for local authority housing and very high average interest rates. ... Changes were being made in different parts of the economy. The steel industry was nationalised; oil, natural gas and nuclear power took markets from coal; the rationalisation of large companies and whole industries was accelerated, with major mergers in electrical engineering, motors, shipbuilding and computers.
>
> Yet this flood of change was watched over by the same methods of the management of demand ... which had ... proved themselves inadequate even in the milder changes of the fifties and early sixties. It was small wonder that by 1967 from one quarter to the next the Chancellor of the Exchequer was having to revise totally his view of the prospects for the coming year. ...   *Continued*

---

[1] Bray, Jeremy (1970) *Decision in Government* London: Gollancz

The need for improved methods of economic management had been appreciated. There was a vast elaboration of institutional arrangements with new departments in Whitehall and new methods of consultation between government and industry. Furthermore it was appreciated that institutions are not enough and what matters are the arguments they embody. ... The National Plan was produced as a synoptic argument to bring all the developments together. But it offered little help, and in the end therefore the former methods of economic management were left in control.

... Applied economics had not yet advanced to the point where ready-made techniques were available, accepted and waiting to be applied. Most economists felt that there was a fundamental disequilibrium in the balance of payments which had to be put right by devaluation. Their attention was diverted by this single large problem in the foreground from the underlying technical problems of the management of an economy with a rapidly changing structure.

There was a tendency to look for the grand solution especially perhaps among economists whose formative intellectual experience was the brilliant success of the Keynesian revolution. They hankered for the return of an economic Messiah. Mr Maxwell Stamp, by no means a left wing economist, expressed a common attitude when he wrote:

> We need some new breakthrough - some new way of reconciling our aims of full employment, stabilising of prices and growth - similar to the revolution in economic thinking which enabled the unemployment of the thirties to be banished from the scene.

And Sir Eric Roll, Permanent Under Secretary of the Department of Economic Affairs has said since:

> The first economist who develops a general theory from the indications in Keynes of how to make these - sometimes massive - changes in the pattern of resource allocation ... in an environment in which the democratic process makes sole reliance on market forces impossible, even if it were desirable, will indeed deserve a great prize.

As will be clear from the above quotation, in *Decision in Government*, I was setting out on developing an argument which sought to measure 'the pressure of demand', not just in the economy, but in individual enterprises and establishments, which were aggregatable up to the regional, industry and national levels.

All this was thirty years before the days of Internet and the Web, and two decades before the advent of personal computers and the easy use of spread sheets were to make it possible to call for firms to draw their data directly from sources, and to supply models describing their own prospects and performance. That (perhaps unrealistically) I sought to do in the 1970s and 1980s. Today my plea is not for the use of a particular methodology in communicating within and between firms, markets, government and people. My plea is to develop the systems thinking to see how they should work, and to what end.

A striking question today is to ask why New Labour, with all those task forces and advisers, not to mention MPs and ministers, has no group working on systems that would be recognised as such in any top class economics or business graduate school. Why has no one in New Labour re-written *Decision in Government?*

Publish and be damned

I had intended my book as a well meaning contribution from a candid friend and committed supporter of the government. That is not how Harold Wilson took it. In my inexperience and trust I hoped that Harold would take it in the spirit of his Scarborough speech when he had declared:

> We are re-stating our Socialism in terms of the scientific revolution. … The Britain that is going to be forged in the white heat of this revolution will be no place for restrictive practices or for outdated methods on either side of industry.

Indeed when in 1968 the International Federation of Automatic Control held a conference in London I had suggested that they should ask Harold Wilson to open the conference. I provided him with a draft outlining the problem of managing the economy in terms the control engineers in his audience might use about managing any complex system. He took up the idea enthusiastically and embellished it with the blood and guts of politics. But that is not how he reacted to my book when as a junior minister I sought permission to publish.

What Harold, or indeed anyone else, could have said to me at the time, was:

> 'Well done, Bray. The difficulty is that the press will present the book as an attack on the government. Wait a couple of years and

publish it after the election. Meanwhile we will see what can go into the manifesto.'

Harold would have had me eating out of his hand. I would have been wise to take this line myself.

Instead Harold said to me, 'No minister can publish and continue to hold office. The constitution forbids it.' (This, as I was later to discover, was patently untrue. The constitution had not prevented Wilson's own Chancellor of the Exchequer from publishing a book only two years earlier. How naïve I was to take Wilson at his word.)

He added, 'You will never be able to publish this book, inside or outside the government. If you do publish, you will never again hold office.'

That forced me to resign.

Wilson was true to his word. I would never again go through the shiny black door of No. 10 to be offered a job.

Press reaction

My resignation briefly made the headlines on television and in the papers, and merited a few sharp cartoons.

Osbert Lancaster, in the *Observer*, has a worried Prime Minister asking, on the phone, an assistant to check up on whether Roy Jenkins, the Chancellor of the Exchequer, had a new book 'on the stocks'. Roy, of course, was a prolific author. He had not hesitated to criticise aspects of a former Labour government in which Wilson had served[2]. In 1967, shortly before my tussle with Wilson, he had published a volume of essays and speeches[3]. Sacking me fired a warning shot across the Chancellor of the Exchequer's bows.

Emmwood, in the *Daily Mail*, has a grinning Mr Heath, the Leader of the Opposition, standing outside the Brighton venue of Labour's Annual Conference. He is hawking books, and the bill board he is wearing proclaims: DECISION IN GOVERNMENT *AS BANNED BY THE PRIME MINISTER*. Wilson sneaks past, puffing on his pipe. The clouds of smoke show what he is thinking: Maybe he (Wilson) should have waited until after the conference to sack Bray.

---

[2] Jenkins, Roy (1953) *The pursuit of progress: a critical analysis of the achievement and prospect of the Labour Party*
[3] Jenkins, Roy, Ed Anthony Lester (1967) *Essays and Speeches* London

6 : 'Decision in Government' & resignation 1969 ♦ 81

'TALKING OF DECISION IN GOVERNMENT — YOU'RE FIRED!'

Above: Garland in the Telegraph and (below) John Jensen in the Sunday Telegraph.
Source: University of Kent, Cartoon Library. Published with kind permission of the Telegraph.

"Nothing personal, Jeremy – it's just that I'm surrounded by too many damn authors!"

The publicity was undoubtedly a boon to my publisher, Gollancz. The left wing publishing house had been prepared to take on a work by junior minister, or even a junior ex-minister, despite its technical content. However, my seat was among the most marginal in the country. If I lost my seat, publication could not be guaranteed. The General Election was due, at the latest, in October 1971. Time enough to bring the book out, or so Gollancz hoped. In fact, Wilson went to the country in June 1970.

On the eve of the publication of my book, in 1970, the gossip column (headed 'Inside Page') in one newspaper anticipated Harold Wilson's reaction more accurately than I had:

> There is an undertone running through the entire book suggesting that the government has failed to grapple effectively with the problems thrown up by a modern technological society. Mr Wilson probably felt that there was by implication a criticism of him having failed to live up to that famous Scarborough speech of 1963 ... .
>
> The essence of Bray's well argued case really amounts to a judgement on the Labour Government's failure (probably through no fault of its own) to live up to that Wilson speech of 1963. ...
>
> The Bray thesis is that society in Britain is changing rapidly under the stress of almost revolutionary forces from technology and education, and the aspirations of young people. He believes that neither government nor industry nor even the trade unions have yet recognised the great potential in these revolutionary forces[4].

That was the view I took in 1968. Although I say so myself, re-reading the book now, over thirty years later, I still think it was a good book: sound analysis, realistic and achievable methods and objectives. But I have to say it attracted very little comment in parliament or the press. It was too technical to find readers among MPs and in the media.

The cost of resignation

I paid dearly for this. Resignation and publication was a foolish move by a young and inexperienced politician, with no tradition of political *savoir faire* in his family, education or background. My minister, Tony Benn, argued vehemently with me, pointing out how ill-advised was my decision;

---

[4] Editor's note: Source uncertain. Jeremy had pasted this newspaper cutting headed 'The Inside Page' into his personal copy of *Decision in Government*, but failed to note the source and date.

I later learned he had argued with equal vehemence with Harold on my behalf.

I realised with hindsight I might have been wiser in career terms to bide my time, since an election was due shortly – and elections can change events and attitudes. But on the other hand, if delayed the book might never have seen the light of day.

I had earned the undying enmity of Wilson. Rather vindictively, when it came to the General Election in June 1970, Wilson decided to campaign in every single marginal seat but mine – and this was a seat he had to win to return to power.

But was I right to resign? I would have had a much more conventional political career had I not resigned. The action took me down ways that I would not have followed otherwise, and that others have not explored.

Appraisal of reform

A pattern begins to emerge in the frustrations encountered by my efforts to introduce more system into government. To begin with, all went well: Wilson accepted the civil service reforms advocated by the Estimates Committee Report (produced under my chairmanship in 1965), and acted with enthusiasm on the recommendations of the Fulton Committee which he appointed to look into these reforms. The report on Government Statistics (likewise produced by a select committee under my chairmanship) bore fruit, and led to the Dick Stone reforms of government statistics in 1966. Both were put forward as a result of my activities on Select Committees as a backbencher. In 1966 Marsh and Wilson had accepted the need for a systematic cost minimisation approach to fuel policy. But then things began to get stuck. Senior civil servants like Donald MacDougall and Douglas Allen had blocked the introduction of Stone's integration of the meso (industry) level and the macro (large scale, overarching) level in national economic planning in 1964. So, when the National Plan collapsed in 1966, there was nothing to replace it. Benn and Wilson in 1968-9 were just not interested in the industry level tracking of demand.

It looks a simple story. Here I stood, a one track mathematical-minded technocrat, hopelessly overselling the power of modelling in applications beyond my power to influence, let alone control.

But as the years were to prove, Harold Wilson, and his generation of politicians, were to find the economic crises of the 1970s even more intractable than those of the 1960s. They lost their way, and the trust and support of the people. Governments – the Heath government of 1970-74, the Wilson governments of 1974-76, and the Callaghan government (1976-79) – lurched from one economic crisis to another, as did the Thatcher governments in the 1980s (contrary to the myth).

To the consternation of many of the older generation – Wilson's generation – economics, the core discipline of politics, was set to become more and more mathematical. Wilson, remember, was appointed in 1940, at the age of twenty four, as economic assistant to the War Cabinet Secretariat. By 1945 he was the director of economics and statistics at the Ministry of Fuel. First elected to parliament in 1945, he rose rapidly to become President of the Board of Trade by 1947. In 1951 he resigned over a dispute over Labour's budgetary policy. So he knew all about managing the economy. Or thought he did. And here I was, a young whippersnapper, apparently calling into question his capacity and competence.

Can analysis improve policies?

There were two straws in the wind which encouraged me to persist. By 1969 people were getting fed up with incomes policy. Two very able economists, Lipsey and Parkin[5], sent me a paper in which they had sought to measure the effectiveness of the incomes policy by statistically analysing the effects on the rate of inflation, comparing periods when the policy was 'on', and when it was 'off'. They thought it might be relevant to the current policy debate and that I would not be put off by the modest amount of mathematics they had used. By then I was no longer a minister. So I wrote it up in a feature in *The Times*[6] and found it was quoted independently by the Prime Minister Harold Wilson and the Chancellor, Roy Jenkins, and their Conservative shadows, within a week. Everyone was looking for an excuse to be rid of incomes policy.

That experience taught me that a little bit more analysis than usual could help to improve policies. I thought the analytical methods used by Lipsey and Parkin, which took no account of the dynamics, could be improved. I started looking at the literature. It seemed to me that economists at that time were using some very odd treatments of lags.

So I carried out an exercise on the GDP-Unemployment relation, using the time series methods that I had used in DRAGON in ICI ten years

---

[5] Lipsey, R.G. and Parkin, J.M. (August 1969) *Incomes policy: a reappraisal* University of Essex Economics Discussion Paper 10

[6] *The Times*, 1969, exact date uncertain.

earlier, and submitted it to the Royal Statistical Society. The Royal Statistical Society invited me to read it at an open meeting with a distinguished audience[7]. It attracted a good discussion. Discussants included Denis Sargan (the econometrician), John Westcott (the control engineer), Gwylim Jenkins and George Box (the time series analysts), Jim Shepherd, Brian Henry and J.P.Hutton (economists from the Treasury), A.R.Thatcher (the statistician from the Department of Employment), and Peter Young (the control engineer from Cambridge).

It was the first occasion on which an economic audience and I had heard an exposition of results using the Box-Jenkins methods of time series analysis[8] from the authors, and the related methods of Astrom[9] and Bohlin. It was an eye opener. I at once acknowledged that their methods were more general and powerful than my own.

But there was a problem. The discussants were all serious professionals with their own work and research commitments. I was a moonlighting amateur. I could join in – but not as an equal. And they would not do work for me, for I was an MP. The ace that I held was the knowledge that as an MP I was thereby closer to policy and closer to getting things applied.

It was however clear that if I wanted work done I would have to do the research myself or pay others to do it myself. Either solution was problematic. In those days MPs paid all their own expenses – their secretary's salary, office machinery, even postage – out of their own modest salary. I could not afford a researcher. The desktop computer was a thing of the future. My wife worked part-time for me from home, for free, but only on constituency correspondence. She had, after all, the care of our four young daughters. Like most backbenchers, my workspace in parliament was any vacant place at a table in one of the corridors, and (if memory serves) a coin-in-the-slot public telephone. Many MPs wrote all their own letters by hand while sitting in the Chamber. All very amateurish.

Undefeated

I have tried to describe what actually happened so that readers can judge for themselves. The nature of the problem of the scientist seeking to contribute to the wider political process was already becoming clear.

---

[7] Proceedings of the Royal Statistical Society c. 1970
[8] Box, G.E.P. and G.M. Jenkins (1970) *Time Series Analysis, Forecasting and Control* San Francisco: Holden Day
[9] Astrom, Karl J. (1970) *Introduction to Stochastic Control Theory* New York: Academic Press

The problem in any practical matter is reaching a conclusion on the best available evidence. Yet even in the basics of macro-economic policy, the technical assessment of the evidence takes the argument beyond the capacity of the lay politician, let alone the lay voter. The political process has to be pursued at a secondary level. So the building and manoeuvring of alliances within the scientific community, and within the wider political community, and in the relations between them, becomes the nature of the game. If that is the nature of the game, then strategies need to be sought that can win.

As I will argue in the closing chapters of this book, an open and liberal society is the natural habitat of science. But I do not accept the implication that it is simply he who has the most and the most powerful political allies that wins. The strength of the argument matters too.

So where did this experience leave me?

My position in parliament was inevitably rather lonely. Resignation forced me to face up to my own limitations – limitations of understanding, of skills, of political know-how; limitations of powers of persuasion, of personality, of political appeal. For all that, it left me in 1969, in this crisis in my life, wounded but undefeated. I felt I was still pursuing a meaningful path through the dilemmas that surrounded us. And I knew I was not alone. There were others within the parliamentary Labour party concerned by our failure to get to grips with running the government machine and the economy; and others, including many of the most able and distinguished scientists and economists of my generation, working on these problems but with more resources, more expertise, and more collegiate support, than I could muster.

And, as I told myself, if I could just hold on to my seat ....

7

Wilderness Years
1970-1974

The swing to Labour by which we had won the 1962 by-election in Middlesbrough West was more than I could hold against the national swing when Labour lost office in 1970. I lost my seat by 388 votes. For my family it was a devastating blow. I had four young daughters. There was no severance pay in those days, and MPs were not paid for the duration of the month long campaign. MPs were (strangely) self employed, so I had no entitlement to unemployment pay. But I was determined to get back into parliament because it still seemed to me to offer the best way to pursue the causes in which I was interested.

I was to be out of parliament for the four years of the Heath government (1970-74). In terms of a parliamentary career, these were vital years: chairing a select committee, or better still, making your mark as an opposition front bench spokesman, lays the foundations for a ministerial career. Not only had I blighted my career by my untimely resignation, but I could not repair the damage over a period in opposition. I spent a frustrating four years seeking to return to the Commons.

I maintained some political links, which were important in making allies. Like many of my Labour colleagues I was a member of a trade union (the T&GWU), the Fabian Society (of which I was chairman in 1970-71), and various party groups, mostly on economics and science. I was able to launch an econometrics research project – more of this in Chapter 9 – and maintained my interest in the application of science to policy-making. None of these prospered my career.

The global environment and sustainable development

Soon after I had lost my seat I was invited to the inaugural meeting of the Club of Rome in Bern in August 1970 by Hugo Thiemann, Director of the Battelle Laboratory in Geneva. The group had been collected by

Aurelio Peccei, head of Italconsult, to examine the global environmental 'problem'. This was pioneering work at that time.

The Club of Rome was an interesting group which included Saburo Okita, head of the Japan Economic Research Centre; Thor Heyerdahl of Kon Tiki fame; Alex King, Director General of Scientific Affairs in OECD; C.H. Waddington, the biologist; Bertrand de Jouvenal, the French political philosopher; Edouard Pestel, principal of a German technical university, and Jay Forrester, the system dynamicist of the Sloane School, MIT.

Peccei had Hasan Ozbekhan in tow, with a view to asking him to direct a study of the global problem. Was this just a passing fad? Or would the global environment and pollution, globalisation, the global economy and sustainable development, one day be important concerns? I was intrigued.

Ozbekhan was an OECD futurologist who produced lovely diagrams of 'Continuing Critical Problem' clouds labelled population, pollution, resources, poverty, crime and so on, joined together by broad arrows in every direction. By the end of the morning it was quite clear that he would not produce the kind of project Peccei was looking for. The day was saved by Jay Forrester, who said, 'I invented the magnetic core memory. I designed DEWLINE, the missile early warning system that protects the US. I developed system dynamics described in my book, *Industrial Dynamics*[1]. I solved the urban problems of Boston in my next book, *Urban Dynamics*[2]. Come along to MIT (Massachusetts Institute of Technology) in a fortnight and I will show you the solution of the global problem.'

I think I was the only person there who had any hands-on experience of economic modelling. I had read Jay's books. I was in sympathy with his wish to get at the interactions and dynamics of complex systems, but I said it was not quite as easy as that: the work would be panned by the economic and scientific establishments if it lacked a sound empirical basis. But they did go to MIT and within the fortnight Jay showed them the guts of what became his book, *Global Dynamics*[3]. I was not able to go because I was still looking for a job.

Jay Forrester's global dynamics work was followed up by an enterprising, socially conscious young couple, Dennis and Donella Meadows. Dennis was the inventory control man in the Sloane School, the business school of MIT. On a sabbatical he and his wife had gone to look

---
[1] Forrester, Jay W. (1961) *Industrial Dynamics* Massachusetts: MIT Press
[2] Forrester Jay W. (1969) *Urban Dynamics* Massachusetts: MIT Press
[3] Forrester , Jay W. (1971) *Global Dynamics* Cambridge Mass: Wright-Allen Press

at the development problems of India. They started off with the idea that there was nothing that could not be solved by extra doses of birth control and fertilisers. With commendable thoroughness, they bought a Jeep and visited many Indian villages, ending up with the conclusion that no amount of birth control or agricultural fertilisers could help. They came back and produced *The Limits to Growth*[4] for the Club of Rome, with its beguiling graphs soaring and plunging the world into disaster.

John Maddox, the writer and broadcaster, and already at that date the editor of the leading science journal, *Nature*, asked me to review it. I could not recommend it, and it was panned by many other economists and scientists. But that did not mean that our planet's future was unimportant.

I was out of the House and unable to follow up global issues in parliament. However, as Deputy Chairman of Christian Aid from 1972-1984 I found myself campaigning on poverty issues and the north/south divide both within Christian Aid and from public platforms and church pulpits. Disaster relief, I argued, was not enough. We should be campaigning for governments to take the problems – and the solutions – seriously. We should be prepared if necessary to reduce the barriers to trade – the tariff walls, the hidden subsidies for agriculture – even if it cost votes and marginally reduced living standards in Western countries.

In 1972 I produced a Fabian tract entitled *The Politics of the Environment*[5]. It was praised warmly by Tony Crosland, the then opposition spokesman on the environment. (Tony was to become Secretary of State for the Environment in 1974. His early death deprived a generation of Labour politicians of a seminal thinker, though he had little time for, or interest in, the technical demands of economic management.)

It is unfortunate that Jay Forrester's over-ambitious and eccentric book and the Club of Rome's *Limits to Growth* set back serious attention to the problems of modelling global environmental problems by twenty years. It was not until the 1990s that the general circulation models of the oceans and atmosphere began to prove their usefulness. By then the effects of climate change were already fairly advanced, and remedial work was seriously overdue.

It took another decade for politicians to begin to realise the implications. Even now, President Bush is stalling. Perhaps fatally.

---

[4] Meadows, Donella H., Meadows, Dennis L., Randers, Jo rgen, and Behrens III, William W. (1972) *The limits to growth: Report for the Club of Rome's Project on the Predicament of Mankind* New York: A Potomac Associates Book: Universe Books

[5] Bray, Jeremy (1972) *Politics of the Environment* London: Fabian Tract 412

A spell in electronics 1970-73

In the real world, when I lost my seat in the 1970 election, I had a worrying period of a couple of months with no job, no income, and a family to support. Then Frank Jones offered me a job in Mullard, the UK electronic component subsidiary of Philips, and I was glad to take it. The job was as personnel and corporate planning director, a designation which Frank supported. I was attracted because it gave me useful experience across the activities of this major group throughout Europe.

When Frank retired in 1973 I had to look for fresh employment. Hugo Thiemann, of the Battelle Laboratory in Geneva, agreed to work with me on testing the market for a game-playing set of multi-country economic models. The concept was ahead of its time. Without government support, it needed a publishing outlet or an academic base, or both, and I had neither. It did not offer a way forward, or a source of income.

We move to Scotland

Throughout this period I had been applying steadily for safe seats but without success. By the end of 1973 I had decided to accept that my way back into parliament seemed to be blocked. I decided, with Elizabeth's support, to undertake work I would be content to stay with for the rest of my life. I was unable to get a good job in macro-economics where I had been doing stimulating fresh work. So I accepted a research job in development economics at Strathclyde University in Glasgow in January 1974, and the family moved to Scotland.

Our home in Helensburgh, on the Firth of Clyde, proved an excellent choice: we made many friends. We enjoyed hill walking (Loch Lomond was only a few miles away), and, even more important to us, we sailed on the Clyde and to the West Coast and the Hebrides: beautiful, remote sailing waters. We shared ownership of *Fingal*, a Hunter Sonata, with Bill Carlaw – a superb helmsman and a great name in racing circles on the Clyde. Elizabeth, already an experienced sailor, enjoyed cruising[6] and was particularly good at handling the boat under sail in tricky situations. Our eldest daughter, Margaret, was already at Cambridge. Bridget, our second born, stayed on in London to complete her GCEs then moved up to the local school. The two younger ones, Tess and Beatrice, flourished.

In career terms too, as things turned out, it was a canny move.

---

[6] See too: Bray, Elizabeth (1986) *The Discovery of the Hebrides: Voyages to the Western Isles 1745-1883* Glasgow: Collins (2nd edition 1996 Edinburgh: Birlinn)

7 : *Wilderness Years 1970-1974* ♦ 91

Racing on the Clyde: 'Fingal', our Hunter Sonata, (sail no 725) leads the fleet. Skipper: Bill Carlaw.

92 ♦ STANDING ON THE SHOULDERS OF GIANTS

Above: Our Hunter Sonate, 'Fingal', sailing past Fingal's Cave, Island of Staffa.
Below: Jeremy at the tiller, passing through the Dorus Mor, Sound Of Luing

7 : *Wilderness Years 1970-1974* ♦ 93

Above: 'Fingal' at anchor, by Kismul Castle, Barra, in the Outer Hebrides
Below: Elizabeth at the helm. Background: the Cullins of Skye.

8

Member for Motherwell & Wishaw
1974-1997

We moved to Scotland in February 1974. Snow was falling. The house had no central heating. On election night that bitterly cold February we lay abed listening as the results came in over the radio. For the past fifteen years I had been a parliamentary candidate, in the centre of the rough and tumble of counting the votes, then standing there on the platform, with my wife at my side, to hear the declaration of the poll. In the dark night hours of that long night I ran through in my head past election campaigns: my apprenticeship as a Labour candidate in a hopeless seat in north Yorkshire in the 1959 general election; the excitement of snatching victory in the Middlesbrough West by-election in 1962; the battle to hold Middlesbrough West by perilously reducing majorities in 1964 and 1966; my final defeat in 1970 by a few hundred votes. Now I had no role.

The night hours passed. By noon the following day it was clear that we had a hung parliament. No party had won outright. Labour, with 37.2% of the popular vote, was marginally behind the Tories' 38.2%. But Labour held 301 seats to the Conservative tally of 297 (which included the Speaker). If Edward Heath, the Tory PM, could build a coalition with the fourteen Liberals, he would remain prime minister. Days of negotiation ended in failure.

Wilson meanwhile was wooing the Liberals with greater success. Eventually it was he who rode to the Palace to meet the Queen. But his position was extremely precarious. He could not survive. It was clear that another election was only months away. As a stranger in a strange land I could not expect to be involved.

Yet in the spring of 1974 I was asked by the Scottish Labour Party staff, and Jim Foley and Hutcheson Sneddon from the constituency, if I was interested in the Motherwell and Wishaw constituency: George

Lawson, the then Labour MP and a government Whip, had decided to stand down in the second 1974 election. In the same week I was offered a chair in the Department of Economics at Strathclyde University.

For better or for worse I chose the parliamentary seat rather than the professorial chair.

Member for Motherwell and Wishaw 1974-1997

So began twenty three years of what I found a happy and rewarding association with Motherwell and Wishaw, which lies some miles south east of Glasgow, in Scotland's industrialised central belt. I became deeply attached to my constituency. I came to respect profoundly the sterling qualities of so many of my constituents, as they shared with me their aspirations and concerns. Many came to my surgeries for help in coping with life's challenges and problems, troubles and joys.

As a Methodist I was on equally good terms with the Church of Scotland and the Catholics: that counted in a town where probably half the people still went to church. I served regularly as a Methodist local preacher in local churches in the constituency until I retired in 1997. I also found myself called upon to read the lesson or speak at special services in other denominations.

When my own children had completed their schooling my wife and I moved to Motherwell, and were glad to be part of the community.

It is the privilege of an MP who has a long association with his or her constituency to see youngsters he met at the school gates or the lads who helped to distribute election literature grow into parents themselves. As the years pass, too, he will join the mourners at the graveside when a loved and respected friend is laid to rest.

The people of Motherwell and Wishaw (like many towns in Scotland) have a strong sense of belonging. Many of the local professionals and community leaders and opinion formers were born and raised here, and had deep roots. Very often it took only a few minutes of genial conversation for two apparent strangers to work out that their great grandmas had been at the same school, or that they were in fact distant related. 'Och, aye, I ken ye the noo!' one would exclaim. 'You'll be Old Archie McDonald's grandbairn – he that used to live in Ladywell (or Craigneuk or wherever), and it was his sister, Isa, that was wed to our Uncle Jimmy.' This made it the more remarkable that my wife and I, both so clearly incomers, were made so welcome.

96 ♦ STANDING ON THE SHOULDERS OF GIANTS

On the campaign trail in Motherwell & Wishaw

8 : Member for Motherwell & Wishaw 1974-1997   ♦   97

My debt to my consituents

It would be invidious to name individually the scores of close friends I made in the constituency and to whom I owe a debt of gratitude – local councillors and party stalwarts from the Provosts who held office to the dear lady who kept the public conveniences so sparkling clean (and entertained the clientele with her gossip!), ministers of religion and parish priests, local industrialists and trade union members, doctors, teachers and dinner ladies, journalists on the local papers and the kind souls who opened their doors and their hearts. To them all, and especially those who worked so hard for me in the five elections I fought as their candidate, my thanks.

Scottish politics

Scottish politics looks monolithic from outside, but it is very diverse within. Lanarkshire generally was not dominated by the fiefdoms of Glasgow wards, the politicking of Edinburgh city, nor the manipulation by powerful unions. So it was able to make open selections for parliament.

We tended to get capable MPs, such as Peggy Herbison and Judith Hart. I well remember those two feisty women as parliamentary colleagues. Judith, the member for nearby Lanark, was a few years my senior, and held various ministerial offices; she was on the Labour Party National Executive, and had succeeded Peggy Herbison. Peggy, born in 1907, had been first elected for North Lanark in 1945, and, although retired by the time I was selected, still held sway in the Scottish Labour party.

My immediate parliamentary neighbours at various times were John Smith (an extremely able lawyer who would briefly succeed to the Labour Party leadership in 1992), George Robertson (now, as Lord Robertson, Secretary General of NATO) and John Reid (by now Secretary of State for Northern Ireland – a challenging post[1]).

The Scottish group within the Parliamentary Labour Party would in due course come to include such heavyweights as Gordon Brown (the future Chancellor), Donald Dewar (founding father of the Scottish Assembly), Robin Cook (one day to be Foreign Secretary and then Leader of the House) and Tam Dalyell (now Father of the House), to name but a few. I am grateful to my colleagues in the Scottish Group for their ready acceptance of myself.

---

[1] The positions described are those held in May 2002 at the time of Jeremy Bray's death..

8 : *Member for Motherwell & Wishaw 1974-1997* ♦ 99

Peggy Herbison (seated centre) with Ken Collins MEP, and (standing left to right) local MPs Jeremy Bray, Willie McKelvie, John Reid, John Smith, Tommy McEvoy, Tom Clarke, Adam Ingram and George Robertson. 8 May 1984.
Photograph with permission of Contrast Photography, Glasgow.

The steel makers

Motherwell, with its four steel works – Craigneuk, Lanarkshire, Dalziel and Ravenscraig – was the heavy industry heart of Lanarkshire. Steel was the largest employer in the constituency in 1974. As a former minister I had had a hand in nationalising steel. I knew the business and technology of steel-making, and as a minister had visited Ravenscraig in the 1960s.

Our highly skilled steelworkers had a fierce pride in their work. By 1974 the new technologies of steel making were achieving far higher productivity, but higher productivity meant a declining the work force. British Steel decided that they needed only two integrated hot strip mills, and they had three: Port Talbot and Llanwern, both in South Wales and Ravenscraig in Scotland. Ravenscraig was the smallest and the one they wanted to close. The plan was attributed to 'Black Bob' Scholey, successively chief executive, and then deputy chairman.

Above: Jeremy with three Ravenscraig Shop Stewards.
Below: Steel making at Ravenscraig: Charging of liquid iron into a basic oxygen steel making vessel. From a British Steel brochure.

The Member for Ravenscraig?

I identified closely with local industry, both management and the workforce, and it sometimes felt as if I was the member for Ravenscraig steel works, an issue which dominated local politics and working lives.

I maintained throughout, with the support of the Ravenscraig shop stewards, ably led by Tommy Brennan and George Quinn, that the alternative plans we were putting forward were economically viable. We got most Scottish opinion rallied behind us.

In Motherwell, I knew that however successful we were in producing steel, the future of the Scottish economy lay elsewhere. Off shore oil rigs, electronics, and highly automated engineering design and production would be the directions for future manufacturing growth in Scotland, but the major growth would be in service industries.

I campaigned, unsuccessfully, for a local science park. But I succeeded in persuading Ferranti, the electronics firm, to come to Motherwell.

But from 1974, when I was first elected, until my retirement in 1997, I fought too for the survival of Ravenscraig Works, the heart of steel-making in Motherwell and Wishaw. I made the case for Ravenscraig as a technologically advanced, profit-making industry – and these were not empty slogans. Careful economic studies I initiated showed that this was a viable industry, of which the community could be justly proud.

In 1978, however, Donald Dewar, fighting a high profile by-election in the Glasgow Garscadden constituency, put only the social case against closure. I objected. John Smith, then Secretary of State for Trade, got Donald Dewar, Tommy Brennan and myself together, and gave me a dressing down in true West of Scotland style. We capitulated. I realised that while my colleagues could make political and social judgements I could not expect them to make economic judgements. It was a crippling limitation in handling nationalised industries.

With the Tory victory in 1979 the pressures on steel increased. Manufacturing was collapsing, and nowhere faster than in Scotland. I persuaded Patrick Jenkin, who was Secretary of State for Industry from 1981 to 1983, that the bottom of a recession was not a good time to decide the capacity needed in the steel industry by the act of closing Ravenscraig. Like me, Patrick had a heavy industry background. But I realised that Ravenscraig was vulnerable. Any excuse, and British Steel would close it.

In the miners' strike in 1984/85, the miners made a dead set at major steel works. Ravenscraig's coal and iron ore came by rail, and the railwaymen were supporting the miners. Deprive a blast furnace of its charge of coke and iron ore, and it solidifies, ending the life of the furnace lining. If this happened, Ravenscraig was doomed. Polkemmet, the nearby pit devoted to the supply of coking coal for Ravenscraig, flooded. The miners refused to keep the pumps going. They lost their pit for ever.

The miners were picketing the gates of Ravenscraig, but the lorries carrying coal and iron ore from bulk carriers at Hunterston on the Clyde got through with T&GWU drivers. It was touch and go whether Ravenscraig could survive. I was in the Works Manager's office at Ravenscraig with the shop stewards and local BSC management when they agreed a deal with ASLEF (the engine drivers union), and Mick McGahey, leader of the NUM (National Union of Miners) in Scotland.

Ravenscraig lived on.

British Steel was wanting to introduce a rationalised pay structure, to improve productivity. Eventually Port Talbot and Llanwern agreed but Ravenscraig was sticking out. Our older steel works in the town, like the Lanarkshire, Dalzell, and Craigneuk Works, were manned by long serving steelworkers. The newer Ravenscraig Works had been manned by ex-miners, agricultural workers and labourers, often regarded by the older steelworkers in other plants as cowboys.

One week I devoted my weekly column in the local papers to explaining why Ravenscraig had to improve its productivity. The community was rife with stories of absenteeism, men coming off the plant in the middle of a shift for a drink at the local, and so on. I said, 'Ravenscraig is not a holiday camp'. The *Scottish Daily Express* picked up my column and made it its front page lead. That created uproar at Ravenscraig. The coke oven workers, who had a hell of a job sweeping up flaming coal on top of the hot coke ovens, came out on strike – a strike not against British Steel, but against their own Labour MP. Jimmy Allison from the Scottish Labour Party rang me up to say that I was a traitor. Tommy Brennan, the convenor of the shop stewards, rang me up quietly. I agreed to meet the shop stewards. Tommy had not been convenor for long. He had the reputation of being a firebrand. But he was an ex-naval petty officer, and he understood the meaning of discipline. He told the stewards that they should listen to me quietly, and then say what they wanted. They did, with dignity and restraint. The stewards went on to negotiate a deal with British Steel, and stuck to it. In the ensuing Works Burns Supper, Tommy told the lads there should be no cat-calling when I came in as one of the guests, and there was none. Gradually the atmosphere improved. At my last Burns' Supper in 1997 they very generously presented me with a fine oil painting of the Falls of the Clyde, a noted local beauty spot, by a local artist.

Ian McGregor, the Scottish-born American whom Keith Joseph (Secretary of State for Industry from 1979 to 1981) had brought in as chairman of British Steel, conceived the idea of closing the hot and cold strip mills at Ravenscraig and Gartcosh (another Scottish works). Ravenscraig would simply produce high quality slabs for the Fairless Works of United Steel in Pennsylvania (whose steel making plant was obsolete). I went over to see the United Steel Workers at Fairless and in Washington, and found they were as opposed as the Ravenscraig men. The Washington Labour Lobby made British lobbying on the issue look tame. The plan foundered.

Privatising British Steel had not been specifically included in the Tory June 1987 election manifesto. But then, in December 1987, the Thatcher government announced its intention to privatise steel. Ravenscraig and Dalzell were specifically mentioned. I persuaded Motherwell District Council to commission the consultants Arthur Young to produce a strategy report. They employed a number of former British Steel accountants, and we had the support of the Ravenscraig shop stewards who had their own access to current operating costs, which showed that BSC profits from closing Ravenscraig and Dalzell would be around £100 million per annum, compared with 'one off' closure and redundancy costs of £50 million. There would be a loss of around 11,000 jobs in Scotland, with a loss of income in Scotland of around £100 million per annum. One British Steel director thanked me for doing their corporate planning for them.

Our consultants' Report showed that an alternative competitive structure, retaining steel making at Ravenscraig, with the plate mill at the adjoining Dalzell Works and the cold mill and coated strip plant at Shotton, would make a well balanced and profitable flat products company, to compete with the rest of British Steel. If a larger group was needed partners could be found across the channel (as has since been arranged with Hooghovens in Holland, to form Corus). John Smith, then the industry spokesman for the Labour Party and MP for neighbouring Monklands East, helped by actively lobbying.

The Tory government refused to listen. The Scottish industrial establishment accepted the BSC line, refusing mulishly to see that it would lead to the closure of Ravenscraig.

Meanwhile soaring productivity records at Ravenscraig were continuing to be broken. The works survived the catastrophic loss of its electricity supply in the middle of one winter's night, by the skills and commitment of its workers, who very expertly ran down the plant manually.

Then the handful of T&GWU dockers at Hunterston, the terminal through which the Craig's iron ore and coal was imported, went on strike, threatening to strangle Ravenscraig. With the support of the Ravenscraig stewards, I asked John Prescott up to sort things out with the dockers. With insights dating from his time in the merchant navy, he settled the dispute, and Britain was saved from another national dock strike.

As Ravenscraig went on turning out productivity records, Bob Scholey started saying they had decided to close the wrong works. But its fate was sealed. For years the other works had been getting new investment, and Ravenscraig none. When Bob Scholey retired he spent his last day in BSC at Ravenscraig.

In 1990, the closure of Ravenscraig was announced in the Commons. I was still recovering from a very recent coronary by-pass. After the minister and our own front bench spokesman had spoken, I rose unsteadily to my feet. A hush fell on the House. Despite the microphone, my voice was weak, but (I was told) just audible. I spoke with a passion I genuinely felt, based on my deep respect for the steelworkers of Lanarkshire.

Later, when I had recovered sufficiently and with the clock ticking to closure, I thought there might be a way of continuing steelmaking in Scotland by introducing new technology. I attempted to interest Nucor, a very innovative and highly profitable American firm. But in the end the plan failed, despite my visits to Nucor's mini-mill at Crawfordsville, Indiana, to see continuous casting of coil less than 10 mm thick. I was extremely impressed by the chairman, Kenneth Iverson, whom I visited in the US. He arranged to visit us in Scotland.

Unfortunately BSC said they would not sell at any price to someone who proposed to produce steel in Britain. The Tory government were showing no signs that they would get tough with British Steel, and compel them to sell. So Nucor packed up. That was the end of any prospect of continuing the manufacture of bulk steel in Scotland, the cradle of the industrial revolution. But it was not the end of British Steel's interest in Nucor, because they became interested in Ken Iverson's management methods.

Ravenscraig was closed, ending bulk steelmaking in Scotland after 120 years, in June 1992. For the next five years the empty shell of the workshops and cooling towers would dominate the skyline.

Why had I bothered so much about steel?

The modern minded scientist, engineer or businessman should have been concerned with the future, I was told by people who were cave dwellers by comparison with my own track record on new technology. The reason was I felt it important that the steelworkers themselves, the people of Scotland, and the Scottish industrial tradition that they produced, should be proud of their achievements, as skilled, responsible workers. It was on this that the future economic strength of Scotland would depend, whatever happened to steel. And I think it worked.

But there was a wider reason for not regretting my involvement first in ICI, and then politically with steel. There has been a tendency to dismiss the smoke stack industries as old fashioned by comparison with the glamorous new industries like electronics, pharmaceuticals and genetic engineering, and the dot.com enterprises of telecommunications and even the mass media and public relations. But the needs of mankind and the environment that we will have to cope with depend heavily on meeting our needs for fresh water, clean air, transport, drainage, and waste disposal a lot more efficiently than we do today, with all the re-engineering and updating of capital investment that will be required, both in the industrial and the developing world.

That will pose major political challenges, as recent problems with transport and flooding have reminded us. A political system with capital markets attuned to short term profitability is liable to make a mess of the construction and management of modern complex systems, even if such systems go no further than the information handling stage, and barely engage with the physical and natural world. We have seen such problems, for example, in the difficulties in handling air traffic control, and the computerisation of the stock exchange and social security systems. It will be much more difficult to cope with the way complex systems engage with the physical and material world and with human beings. For example, transport poses multifaceted problems ranging from the implications for global warming of our use of fuels to the impact on the lives and work of users and the shape of communities. The challenges still posed by the old smoke stack industries have offered us relatively simple challenges on which to learn politically in recent years, and the lessons remain relevant.

There is, as far as I can see, not a single minister in the New Labour government who is at home in science and technology, and has worked in such industries at the sharp end.

Part Three

OPTIMISATION & THE BRITISH ECONOMY

Jeremy, on the terrace of the House of Commons c. 1983

Introduction to Part Three

OPTIMISATION & THE BRITISH ECONOMY

In 1974 I returned to parliament as member for Motherwell and Wishaw in Scotland as Labour, by the narrowest of margins, regained office. However, neither Wilson nor Callaghan, his successor as Prime Minister, offered me ministerial office. So I spent the next two decades – through the premierships of Wilson and Callaghan (Labour 1974-79) and the first Thatcher government (Conservative 1979-1983) – as a backbencher. This however gave me the welcome freedom to work on the application of control theory to the optimisation of economic policy with national economy models, which eventually led to all the UK models installing policy optimisation facilities. I was able to propagate these ideas by working through the select committee system and by publishing a series of research papers. Among our advisers were world-class economists.

This all sounds dauntingly technical and indeed, in some of the following chapters I confess I am writing mainly for those professionals involved in the game of managing the economy.

But before you switch off, may I suggest you at least read this Introduction where I shall be explaining briefly why the concepts of 'modelling' and 'optimisation' offer such powerful tools.

Mankind's earliest models

Ancient civilisations were made possible by (among other things) an imaginative leap: the realisation that the barter of goods – a sack of wheat for a lamb, say – could be represented symbolically by the use of metal disks (coins, usually of gold, silver or baser metals).

We have here the earliest model – the earliest mathematical model – of the economy. The coinage or currency, usually validated by a ruler, provided a model of the relative values of, say, a day's labour, or a goat, or the materials to build a house, or the value of a piece of land. Currency systems, by facilitating trade, allow individuals and communities to create and transmit wealth within and across boundaries and generations. Governments emerged which, by taxation, built up an infrastructure – roads, ports, irrigation systems, defences, places of learning, law courts.

We still use this four thousand year old model of the economy – a currency – although it has become immensely more sophisticated as refinements of the system led to banks, and, facilitated by computers, virtual money – your credit card, your on-line bank account, the transactions of international finance, and the workings of the nation's economy and the global economy.

The model most of us (myself included) use for personal decisions is still often a back-of-an-envelope calculation. But whether you have all the figures at your finger tips (or on your computer), or just a few jottings on a sheet of A4, the data in any model keeps changing – house prices rise or fall, the stock market crashes or soars, one's circumstances change. In other words, life being what it is, the 'model' of your personal finances is never static. It has moving parts. It is subject to external, random events. Times, and priorities, keep changing. This is particularly true when we are faced with the difficult 'What if ....?' questions. What if we were to start a family? Buy a house? Change jobs? Take early retirement? What if things go wrong? I lose my job? The stock market crashes? I become too ill or disabled to work? Without any model, we are completely at sea.

Optimisation – making the best of your situation

A model – even that back-of-an-envelope calculation or a bank statement – gives us a better chance of keeping some control over our destiny. It enables you to optimise, that is, to make the best of your situation. You can attempt to balance your priorities, both in the short term with bread-and-butter issues (housekeeping, keeping a roof over your head, purchasing a new car, or having a holiday) and the long term (saving for retirement, saving up to help your sons and daughters through university, or paying off the mortgage). Optimisation also gives guidance on the 'how' – the strategies you could use to achieve these targets – incomplete guidance, sometimes fallible, but better than nothing.

I use the word 'optimise' advisedly. It's not just about money. What we really want to do is to make the best possible decisions not only for ourselves, but above all for those whom we love and those whose welfare depends upon us. To 'optimise' is not to be unreasonably optimistic. In an uncertain world, where events – sometimes dire – can deal heavy blows, we must use our intelligence and our experience of life to make the best of things (the Latin word is 'optimum'). However incomplete our model (whether it is a back-of-the-envelope calculation or a spreadsheet), it is an essential tool.

When it comes to running a nation's economy, the problems – and the possible consequences – are formidable. When I entered parliament in 1962 the nation's accounts were still kept more or less on the back of an envelope. The data – the figures – were collected and entered manually, and the addition and subtraction was done either in the head or using those old fashioned mechanical calculators where you turned a handle.

With my background in the use of the first generation of computers in the control of chemical plants, it was apparent to me that Britain's poor economic performance was due, in no small measure, to poor economic management by a succession of post-war governments. Competence matters. So does attention to detail. Over the long term, optimising our economic performance by raising growth from, say, 2% per annum to a steady 3% can in the long run make a significant difference.

To achieve such improvements the government needs adequate and reliable data, and the ability to handle it so that policy decisions are evidence-based, and subject to outside scrutiny.

So I argued for robust but flexible methods of forecasting and management which would 'optimise' performance, given life's challenges, crises and opportunities. What is more, I was prepared to use mathematics and computer-based technologies to explore the potential of these arguments, and to open up this process to outside researchers, able to advise and criticise.

Now most people, certainly most politicians, can use verbal models with some confidence. It is a peculiarity of our political systems that by and large only verbal models are used by politicians because, for historic reasons, parliamentary democracies are based on the cut and thrust of the debating chamber. Yet today's computer technology could give unparalleled access to the models on which policy decisions should be based.

Why we need models

The power of models – models based on reliable data and using reliable software – lies in their ability to provide information on past trends, and predict future trends.

- They can suggest possible answers to the important 'What if ...?' policy questions.
- They can make accessible expert advice.
- They present both the pros and the cons.
- They can rehearse certain scenarios – what the short and medium term consequences might be if we were to raise (or lower) taxes, or increase or cut public expenditure, or change interest rates.
- They can be used to evaluate verbal models: given a new economic theory about the relationship of (say) interest rates to inflation, do the numbers add up?

Yet to the best of my knowledge, I have been the only MP ever to have run the Treasury model of the economy on my desktop computer at the House of Commons. And vital debates on, for example, the budget, or the economic consequences of, say, a Middle Eastern war, continue to be discussed at the simplest of levels, and are reported in the media simply in terms of personal income tax liabilities or petrol prices at the pump.

The beginnings of computer models of the economy

From the early 1960s, economists were beginning to build models that included economic relationships, and to give estimates of the accuracy of forecasting. This had previously only been argued about verbally. With the new mathematical models, it became evident that uncertainties were large – too large for political comfort (and media comprehension). The question frequently asked by politicians, some economists, and the media was whether models could, or should, offer guidance on policy on adjustments taxation, public expenditure and interest rates, to avoid inflation and imbalances of trade, growth and employment.

Yet the mathematics of control theory had been developed for handling just such forecasting errors in simultaneous dynamic systems in engineering. Beginning in the 1960s and gathering momentum in the 1970s, control theory was being adapted to the different configurations of the problem in economics.

Many outstanding economists worked in this area. I had the privilege of involvement in this process.

Neither the Wilson nor the Callaghan governments of the 1960s and 1970s made the least use of this newly developing technology. It was, after all, in its infancy. Both Prime Ministers, and their Chancellors, relied instead on verbal models and flawed forecasts which were often labelled as 'scientific'. Their fatal mishandling of the economy resulted in Labour losing the mandate to govern for eighteen years. I would not claim that, had the models then available been used, the outcome of the 1970 or 1979 elections (when Labour lost power) would have been markedly different. But the economy might have been in rather better shape.

The same would be true of the Thatcher governments of the 1980s, as unemployment and inflation soared and interest rates yo-yoed. Unfortunately, politicians striving to balance the wayward economy sought the advice of theorists whose unreliable hypotheses about the economy were often based on the flimsiest evidence. The results could be dire.

We have since the early to mid 1990s enjoyed a period of unparalleled stability, with inflation well controlled and low interest rates. This may be simply a cyclical effect of the economy, but I would like to believe it is due to improved and prudent management of national economies (particularly in the US and UK) sustained in part by a sounder understanding.

However, as I write in the spring of 2002, war clouds are gathering on the horizon. President Bush's neo-conservative economic policies, including substantial tax cuts for the very rich, threaten to destabilise the US economy. The omens are not good.

The search for a sounder way of life

The search for a sounder way of managing the economy was conducted both at a technical level (with the development of more reliable models of the economy) and a political level. I was privileged to be involved in both processes.

The background to this work was the failure of governments throughout the 1960s, 1970s and 1980s to achieve stable management of the economy. In a turbulent world various economic gurus offered governments conflicting advice, advice based on theories that appealed to the instincts and prejudices of their political masters but lacked sound foundations.

Introduction to Part Three

In Chapter 9 I will be discussing the technical side – the development of policy optimisation and model building from 1970 onwards which, as the statistical data improved, and computer models were developed to handle the necessary analysis, offered a way forward.

I then turn to the role of parliament, and parliamentary lobbying. I describe in Chapter 10 how the Treasury model was opened up to public scrutiny as a result of an amendment I made to a government bill (the Industry Act 1975).

In the succeeding chapters I go on to trace the effect of parliamentary lobbying through the Treasury Select Committee, on which I served from 1979 to 1984. This gives not only an interesting insight into the way Select Committees can work, but also a blow by blow account of the way a government's key policy (in this case, Thatcherite monetarism) can be subjected to rigorous investigation by a parliamentary committee.

The resulting technical developments in economic management have been imperfectly understood by both Tory and Labour front benches, by parliament in general, and by journalists. But their gradual adoption within government underlies the improvements in economic performance since the mid-1990s. They offer hope that we may be better able to steer a wiser course in the troubled days which lie ahead. For the stability of the world's economies continues to be at risk. Treasury ministers will need cool heads, the courage to take a long view, and the best technical advice available.

PART THREE

OPTIMISATION &
THE BRITISH ECONOMY

9   **POLICY OPTIMISATION FROM 1970 ONWARDS**   116
    The application of control theory to the management of the economy ~ Economics: the make-or-break issue for governments ~ Launching PROPE (the Programme for Research into Optimal Policy Evaluation) ~ Flourishing and floundering ~ The economy: a complex abstraction of human behaviour ~ The uses and limitations of models

10 **OPEN GOVERNMENT AND THE INDUSTRY ACT 1975**   126
    My amendment to the Industry Bill 1975 ~ Policy optimisation and the Ball Committee ~ Open government

11 **THE IMF LOAN & THE ABANDONMENT OF KEYNSIAN DEMAND MANAGEMENT 1976**   132
    Negotiations on the IMF loan: a side show ~ The acquiescence to monetary targeting

Introduction to Part Three ♦ 115

12 MONETARY POLICY: THE TREASURY SELECT 137
    COMMITTEE REPORT 1981
    Launch of the Treasury Select Committee ~ Monetary
    policy and the Lucas critique ~ The scope of the Select
    Committee's work ~ The Treasury Select Committee's
    working methods ~ The Committee's conclusions ~ Press
    comment on the Monetary Policy Report ~ Was the
    judgement of the Committee broadly correct? ~ And the
    future?

13 INTERNATIONAL MONETARY ARRANGEMENTS: THE 149
    TREASURY SELECT COMMITTEE REPORT 1982
    Learning rational expectations ~ The Committee's Reports
    on International Monetary Arrangements ~ Scuppered? ~
    The Chairman's draft

14 OPENING UP ACCESS TO THE TREASURY MODEL 1983- 156
    1993
    The ESRC Macroeconomic Modelling Bureau at Warwick
    University ~ Running the Treasury Model on a desktop
    computer ~ Making sense of policy optimisation ~ Do we
    still need the Treasury model? ~ The Treasury model: a
    tribute

15 NEW LABOUR'S MACROECONOMIC POLICY AS IT 165
    EMERGED 1992-1997
    The run-up to the 1997: Lessons from America ~ US
    macroeconomic policy-making ~ The role of the Federal
    Reserves Board ~ President Clinton's advisers .... and
    Gordon Brown's ~ The 'Golden Rule' ~ New Labour at the
    helm: the Bank of England ~ The Golden Rule in practice
    ~ The Public Private Finance Initiative ~ The emergence of
    the 'Taylor rule' ~ Targeting forecast-inflation in the UK (a
    Taylor-type rule) ~ The exchange rate again – and the
    balance of trade

9

Policy optimisation
from 1970 onwards

Optimisation is central to decision making, and in particular to policy decision on the way governments manage the national economy. So, despite losing my seat in parliament in 1970, I had been determined to make a systematic attempt here in Britain to apply control theory to the management of the national economy.

The application of control theory to the management of the national economy

Fortunately Robin Matthews, then chairman of the recently founded Social Science Research Council, was prepared to receive an application for a research grant, but it had to go to an academic for research costs and not for the remuneration of the initiator and principal investigator (for the early years, myself), as I was just a private individual doing a day-time job in Phillips (See Chapter 7). However I found Maurice Peston, the economist at Queen Mary College, London University, and John Westcott, the control theorist at Imperial College, were prepared to have a go. So together we established what was originally called the Programme for Research into Econometric Methods (PREM) at Queen Mary College. Later the unit was relocated at Imperial College and more aptly renamed the Programme for Research into Optimal Policy Evaluation (PROPE). Professor John Westcott was in due course to be elected a Fellow of the Royal Society, in recognition of his work. Professor Maurice Peston is now a life peer.

Over its life time of some twenty years, the optimisation methods PROPE produced, or similar methods, were adopted by all the main UK modelling teams, including those of the Treasury and the Bank of England. I believe the methods have contributed significantly to the recent relative stability of the economy under Labour (I am writing in May 2002). They will be needed if we are to survive the turbulence which I foresee, given present international turmoil.

Optimisation had been appropriately described by Professor Berc Rustem (one of my erstwhile colleagues and collaborators in PROPE, and still, as I write, at Imperial College) in the following terms:

> Optimisation is the expression of the longing for the best. It studies how to describe and attain the best, once we know how to measure, and alter, the good or bad. As optimisation involves the best way of doing things, it has obvious applications in mathematical and physical sciences, engineering, economics and administration. Often in the practical world small gains in efficiency can change failure into success; optimisation is an important tool in securing such gains, in transmuting possible failure into success[1].

Optimisation is relevant to anything from quite small projects – your central heating programmer, with its timer and thermostats, optimises performance – to complex, large scale, multiplayer systems such as telecommunications where millions of calls, including calls accessing the internet, are routed across the globe (and if you think the performance here could be optimised, you are not alone).

Now I am a practical mud-on-the boots kind of optimiser. We are all conditioned by the circumstances and problems in which we first encountered a new intellectual discipline. It was my good fortune to work on the application of optimisation with giants whose experience came from many related fields.

For me working in control engineering, it was the optimisation and control of petro-chemical plant in ICI Wilton, with the first large transistor-based computer to go into an industrial plant for on-line use in the late 1950s. It had seemed to me sensible to tackle the optimisation of the profitability of the plant as a whole (see Chapter 2). At ICI Wilton we had the algorithmic experience of George Box and Gwylim Jenkins, John Coales and John Westcott, and Howard Rosenbrock, to draw on[2]. This was an outstanding bunch, almost all of them to earn a well-deserved FRS in due course. George Box had moved to the USA in 1960 to become Professor of Statistics at Wisconsin-Madison; John Coales was Professor of Engineering at Cambridge; John Westcott, Professor at Imperial College;

---

[1] Rustem, Berc (1998) Inaugural Lecture by Professor Berc Rustem, at Imperial College, London, 24 February.
[2] Bray, Jeremy (1998) Speech at the Inauguration of Professor Berc Rustem at Imperial College, London, 24 February.

and Howard Rosenbrock, Professor of Control Engineering and later Vice Chancellor at the University of Manchester Institute of Science and Technology.

Since my 1955-56 year as a graduate student at Harvard, eavesdropping on a number of subjects there and at MIT, I had a healthy respect for American prowess and achievements, and kept in touch with American friends without ceasing to value the free-wheeling accomplishments of Cambridge and the English tradition.

By the early 1970s, when I was attempting to get a programme of research up and running, there were already economists who saw the value of control theory methods, and were adapting them to economic systems. Among these pioneers were Jan Tinbergen[3] (1952), A.W. Phillips[4] (1954), Herbert Simon[5] (1956) and Henri Theil[6] (1958).

Another pioneer was Gregory Chow[7], who, in 1975, had produced an early systematic textbook for economics graduate students. (Gregory, incidentally, is a US citizen, but he was born in south China, not too many miles from my birthplace; we discovered we had been born in the same year, 1930, the Chinese 'Year of the Horse'. Horses, he told me, are hardworking and willing – which certainly applies to Gregory. Gregory has had very extensive influence in China over the past two to three decades: his influential textbook, regularly updated, is the basis of a competitive examination for Chinese economics students, with the winners of the scholarships being funded to undergo further graduate study in the USA. This in no small part explains the Chinese attitude to economic liberalisation.)

David Livesey, a research student in Dick Stone's team in Cambridge, with an engineering background, was meanwhile completing a remarkable Ph.D. thesis, giving the first optimal control solutions of an empirical model of the UK economy[8]. His thesis was so massive he had to ask Mervyn King, who shared with him an office for research students in the Cambridge Department of Applied Economics, to help him submit it in two bicycle loads! That was probably enough to put Mervyn off optimising

---

[3] Tinbergen, Jan (1952) *On the Theory of Economic Policy* Amsterdam: North Holland
[4] Phillips, A.W. (1954) 'Stabilisation Policy in a Closed Economy' London: *Economic Journal* 54, 290-323
[5] Simon, Herbert (1956). 'Dynamic Programming Under Uncertainty with a Quadratic Criterion Function' *Econometrica* 24 (1) 74-81
[6] Theil, Henri (1958) *Economic Forecasts and Policy,* Amsterdam: North Holland
[7] Chow, Gregory C. (1975) *Analysis and Control of Dynamic Systems* New York: Wiley
[8] Livesey, David (1971) in the *Economic Journal* London

models for life. Inconsiderately and stupidly I criticised Livesey at the time for making his problem more difficult than it need have been (by working with a non-linear economic model with continuous variables, instead of linearising the model, and working with discrete time series data). I should have known that all pioneering work is messy, and pioneers are best advised to stick together and support each other. (David Livesey is now – in 2002 – the Secretary General of the Faculties of the University of Cambridge, and Mervyn King is the Deputy Governor of the Bank of England, and destined to become Governor.)

So the time was ripe for a systematic attempt here in Britain to apply control theory to the management of the national economy, to test how decisions about handling the economy can be optimised. The problems of measurement in the economy are formidable, as are problems of predicting the outcomes of making changes using the instruments available (for example, interest rates, taxation, and government expenditure). But the consequences of governments persisting in making off-the-cuff decisions to suit political expediency or to fight bush fires were painfully obvious.

Economics: the make-or-break issue for governments

Throughout the post-war period the British economy had been experiencing wide swings in growth and inflation, and apparently inviting stop-go policies to deal with them. Problems tended to be tackled in succession as and when they became intolerable: first inflation, next unemployment, then the balance of payments, then the exchange rate and then inflation again. The way instruments were being changed - interest rates, taxes, government expenditure and so on - was obviously contributing to the instabilities.

As a politician I wanted guidance not only about the future (that is, forecasts based on present trends), but also guidance on how to shape that future. What we needed was a method for keeping a balance, not merely for a particular variable, like inflation or growth, but between the different objectives. Forecasting by existing models gave extremely uncertain results with wide error margins, whether measured by average past forecast errors, or from statistical measures of estimated errors. The errors were too big for economic advisers to say to policy makers, 'If you do this, that will happen', but that did not prevent many pundits from saying precisely that.

Economic management is the make-or-break issue for governments. Harold Wilson's reputation never recovered from the devastating effects of devaluation, and Labour lost the 1970 election.

Edward Heath, Prime Minister from 1970-74, saw himself as a moderniser, with an interest in the machinery of government. While he subscribed to the post-war consensus of full employment and social peace, he believed too that what the economy needed was a 'cold douche'. Entry into the European Common Market would reinvigorate the British economy. But by 1974 he was facing crises on many fronts: Northern Ireland; the miners' strike and the rancour caused by the government's industrial relations legislation; inflation and incomes policy; rising prices for international commodities, and especially, after the Yom Kippur War of 1973-74, soaring energy prices.

The Tories were narrowly defeated in the 1974 February election ('Who governs Britain?' was the prime issue). Harold Wilson returned to No 10.

But it was a lack lustre premiership – Wilson, always a tactician rather than a strategist, seemed to have run out of ideas and the will to govern. He ignored the most pressing problem – the economy – while inflation soared to an all-time high of 26.5%. In 1974 he was succeeded by James Callaghan.

Launching PROPE (Programme for Research into Optimal Policy Evaluation)

It was against this background that Maurice Peston (of Queen Mary College), John Westcott (of Imperial College) and I had set up a research unit to investigate optimisation in early 1971. This, perhaps fortunately, was before 'rational expectations' and the 'time inconsistency of optimal plans' had been raised as a problem by Lucas[9] (1976), Kydland[10] and Prescott (1977), Lucas[11] and Sargent (1978). So initially we did not need to cope with these complications.

We originally called our research project the Programme for Research into Econometric Methods (PREM). When we moved from Queen Mary

---

[9] Lucas, Robert E. Jr. (1976) 'Econometric Policy Evaluation: a Critique' in *The Phillips Curve and Labour Markets*, ed. K. Brunner and A.H. Meltzer. Amsterdam: North Holland
[10] Kydland, Finn E. and Prescott, Edward C. (1977) 'Rules rather than Discretion: The Inconsistency of Optimal Plans' *J. Pol.Econ.* 85,3
[11] Lucas, Robert E. and Sargent, Thomas J. (1978) 'After Keynesian Macroeconomics' in *After the Phillips Curve: Persistence of High Inflation and High Unemployment* Federal Reserve Bank of Boston Conference Series 19. This and the papers by Lucas (1976), and Kydland and Prescott (1977) were republished in Lucas and Sargent eds.(1981) *Rational Expectations and Econometric Practice*, London: Allen & Unwin.

College, London, to Imperial College, the project was more aptly named the Programme for Research into Optimal Policy Evaluation (PROPE).

The economists and control theorists who worked in PREM or PROPE included Kent Wall, Alan Preston, Sean Holly, Elias Karakitsos, Berc Rustem, Martin Zarrop, Robin Becker and B. Dwolatzky. All have prospered and carved out distinguished careers, many ending up as professors in highly respected institutions.

I had stimulating contact with American economists like Lawrence Klein, the Nobel prize winner; Gregory Chow, David Kendrick and Mike Athans, through the conferences of the Society of Economic Dynamics and Control; and Peter Tinsley at the Federal Reserve Board.

Then there were also my own research assistants in the 1980s – Sam Lovick, Ganesh Nana, and, in the 1990s Paul Walker, Andre Kuleshov and Ali Enis Uysal. Together we produced a series of research papers[12], some in conjunction with Peter Westaway. I discuss their contribution, and my debt to them, in greater detail in Chapter 14 where I outline the opening up of access to the Treasury Model.

Flourishing and floundering

PROPE flourished. Not so the governments.

As early as 1974, when Labour returned to government, PROPE had made sufficient progress with the use of optimisation methods on economic models to make it possible to produce practical guidance to the economic policy makers. Furthermore, there was no very obvious alternative.

---

[12] Bray, Jeremy and Nana, Ganesh (1989a) 'International economic coordination in the G7 as a dynamic Nash game' *Proceedings of 6th IFAC/SED Symposium on Dynamic Modelling and Control of National Economies*, London: IFAC

Bray, Jeremy and Nana, Ganesh (1989b) 'Policy Optimisation in democratic political processes'. *Proceedings of 6th IFAC/SED Symposium on Dynamic Modelling and Control of National Economies*, London: IFAC

Bray, Jeremy, and Kuleshov, A., Uysal, A.E., and Walker, P. (1993) *Balance Achieving Policies: a comparative policy optimisation study on four UK models*, Warwick: ESRC Macromeconomic Modelling Bureau, University of Warwick

Bray, J., Hall, S., Kuleshov, A., Nixon, J. and Westaway, P. (1995) 'The Interfaces between Policy Makers, Markets and Modellers in the Design of Economic Policy - and Intermodel Comparison' *The Economic Journal* Policy Forum July 1995

Wilson had inherited a very dicey economic situation from Ted Heath's defeated Tory government in 1974. From the start the Wilson and Callaghan governments of 1974-1979 were floundering with the narrowest of majorities in parliament. The oil price cartel – OPEC – had driven up oil prices, and the world economy was in recessions. The 1944 Bretton Woods system of fixed but adjustable exchange rates had collapsed. Labour was struggling, unsuccessfully, to impose an incomes policy to control the rate of inflation.

By 1976, with Callaghan now at No.10, the government was in the throes of yet another sterling crisis, and negotiating a humiliating IMF (International Monetary Fund) loan, with its stringent conditions.

By now the SSRC (Social Sciences Research Council) funded PROPE was producing optimal policy methods, and these had already been installed on the Treasury, LBS (London Business School), and NIESR (National Institute of Economic & Social Research) models. These offered governments an alternative to crude monetary targetry. The Chancellor of the Exchequer, Denis Healey, knew something about the kinds of policy optimisation that we had developed. But he never seriously considered it before or after adopting, perforce, IMF style targetry in 1976. No doubt he was influenced by the Treasury's hostile attitude manifested in its response to my successful amendment to the 1975 Industry Bill (of which more in the next chapter).

The Bank of England was also using optimal policy methods in its model. I had kept Treasury officials informed of developments, and Gordon Richardson, Governor of the Bank of England, invited the Labour backbench Treasury Group along to the Bank. I had a long chat with him and said I thought the Bank ought to beef up its research effort: this advice was acted upon.

As will become apparent, my involvement with PROPE and broader issues concerning the economy were to continue for over twenty years.

The economy - a complex abstraction of human behaviour

You can view the economy – that complex abstraction of human behaviour – as rather like a moving landscape, subject to erosion and seismic shocks. The most important property of an economy is that it is made up of human beings, as its active agents. That makes it unique. But that does not stop economic modellers learning from the behaviour of other systems. And the economy (and models of it) can always develop or learn new ramifications as human behaviour changes or is described more fully.

As we in PROPE were to find out, this demanded mathematics able to handle the 200-dimensional space of five policy instruments over 40 quarters (ten years). By the mid-1970s there was sufficient computer power to handle the quasi-Newtonian algorithms developed and applied by Berc Rustem, Elias Karakitsos, Martin Zarrop and Robin Becker and others as they actually worked on the large messy, practical, empirical working models that were – and are – the best the economists can offer of how the economy functions.

A criticism made of us policy optimisers is that we are applying mechanistic rules to reduce unpredictable and intractable political, human and social problems to the Procrustean bed of a computer model. In fact the mental and verbal models and pictures used by my political colleagues to describe how the economy works were – and are – crude, rigid, static and naïve by comparison.

As economics has become more complex, technical, specialised and mathematical, the political world – politicians, journalists and officials – has had increasing difficulty in coping.

Now jumbo jets and television receivers are complex objects, but you don't need to understand them to ride in them or watch them. You can ride in and watch the economy too. But whereas the jumbo will usually get you to New York quickly and safely if that is where the airline says it is going, and the television will show you the football match you wanted to watch, the economy will take you for a ride to an uncertain destination, and involve you and countless others in games you could not have anticipated. And the more you struggle to cope with its behaviour, and seek the help of the experts, the more mathematical does the argument become.

For me, as the argument became more mathematical, it became clearer. Many economists, old and young, have criticised this trend and avoided it in their own work. But on the whole, the greatest long term impact has been made by those who have used mathematical forms where they can help in the argument. Such economic research has become the prime intellectual source of new economics, percolating into the economics profession, mainly by the teaching of later year undergraduates and graduates.

Unfortunately, at the leading edge, the economic argument is often not accessible to, or read by, the average competent business economist or economic journalist, let alone the politician. Even academic economists often have only a partial understanding of each other's work. Small wonder my parliamentary colleagues mocked my interest. But I enjoyed the work we did in PROPE which was, in its time, leading edge – enjoyed its intellectual rigour, and the stimulus of working with outstanding practitioners.

However, by the end of my parliamentary career, in the late 1990s, developments had taken it beyond my comprehension, and I could only applaud from the sidelines.

The uses and limitations of models

Economics had started off by describing relationships, such as that of income and expenditure, in verbal terms, illustrated by graphs. That is by and large where it has stopped in daily political and journalistic usage. However economics did not stop there because it was found to raise more questions than it answered, and left a lot of questions unresolved.

Although from the early days in the 1950s it was clear that models could provide useful answers to some macroeconomic problems, they were by no means infallible – and there were always good economists who had no close association with a particular model: indeed such practitioners saw professional advantages in remaining free.

Now economic forecasts (like weather forecasts) may err. But (like weather forecasts) they have become more reliable. Despite errors, they often usefully indicate the general direction of policy needed. Models offer a way of systematically reviewing future prospects, and looking at the probable effects of alternative future policies, which is a lot more subtle and realistic than the rhetoric of much political discourse and journalism.

Distinguishing between actual economic behaviour, and the accidental effects of particular constraints on the modelling process, is one of the interpretative skills practitioners need to learn. But it is not a fudge that discredits the whole process: results have to be judged against the background of other models, and of economics generally.

While macroeconomic model building was a popular and fashionable research activity up until the 1970s, the poor performance of large-scale models in the wake of the two oil shocks in the 1970s, and the destructive stage of rational expectations, led to much criticism in the '70s and '80s.

Since then new types of model have necessarily been developed, and while there has been a continuing stream of criticism, they have settled down to roles underpinning finance ministries, central banks, and international organisations.

My concerns in economics have been practical ones: how to achieve stable prices and the growth which yields full employment. The constraints and objectives under which I have worked have been the politics of a free society. I have not had to bear the additional burdens of an academic economist, nor gained the benefits of the disciplines of passing examinations, using particular analytical tools, and enjoying the stimulus of teaching students. I was never really a member of that elite club. But it was a privilege to work with – and learn from – leading economists engaged in trying to sort out some of the more intractable problems closest to the heart of government. Inevitably, those who pioneer advances in methodology are soon forgotten. If unhelpful, their work is discarded; if productive (and PROPE was productive), it lies buried in the foundations of more advanced work.

A unique contribution that I, as a parliamentarian, could make, however, was to force the government to open up access to the Treasury model. For this is what my amendment to the Labour government's Industry Act 1975 was to achieve. I turn to this next.

10

Open Government & the Industry Act
1975

In the 1974-79 Labour government, proposals for major expansion of public enterprise were shelved. The discredited National Plan was quietly dropped. But Tony Benn, as Secretary of State for Industry (the successor department to the Ministry of Technology), was still trying to launch a system of 'Planning Agreements' between government and individual companies. The disclosure of companies' future plans was intended to provide the information base for a new industrial policy, to work by agreement between government and major firms, on lines that had just been proposed by Stuart Holland in *The Socialist Challenge*[1].

The 1975 Industry Bill was to create the necessary rights and powers for the proposed industry policy. The making of an Agreement was to be voluntary, but industrialists feared that government would put pressure on firms to participate in an agreement.

My amendment to the Industry Bill 1975

I argued that if firms were to be expected to disclose their plans, government should too. So I drafted an amendment which required the publication of Treasury forecasts, access to the Treasury model, and a statement of policy priorities by the Treasury.

The text of my amendment in Committee was set out in a new schedule to the House of Commons Industry Bill 1975[2].

The text, which I have printed out in full on the next page (opposite), read as follows:

---

[1] Holland, Stuart (1975) *The Socialist Challenge* London: Quartet Books
[2] House of Commons (1975) Industry Bill 1975 Standing Committee E, Official Report 12 June col. 2300, London: HMSO

DISCLOSURE OF INFORMATION BY GOVERNMENT

1. The Treasury shall maintain a macro-economic model demonstrating the effect of alternative government policies and alternative assumptions about external factors on the economy of the United Kingdom. It shall describe the expected level of gross domestic product, unemployment, the balance of payments, the retail price index, the index of average earnings and other economic variables in successive quarter years and years, and in each quarter year the Treasury shall publish such forecasts on alternative assumptions on policy and external factors. The Treasury shall provide access to the model for other Government departments and for any other person to make forecasts on alternative assumptions. The Treasury shall publish regularly after the events forecast an analysis of the forecasting errors that would have been made had the assumptions on policy and external factors been made correctly, and shall publish the estimated standard errors of current forecasts and of the effect of changes in policy instruments.

2. Any Minister of the Crown who makes a planning agreement with an undertaking shall have constructed and made available to the undertaking a sub-model which demonstrates the dependence of the undertaking, its markets, suppliers and sources of manpower on the national economy, as described by the Treasury macro-economic model, if any such dependence can be demonstrated.

3. The Treasury shall state on behalf of all Ministers of the Crown, the priorities in quantitative terms which the Government attaches to a marginal improvement in each macro-economic variable, indicating thereby the trade offs the Government will in future seek to make in adjusting the level of policy instruments.

My amendment was a common sense initiative in the cause of open government. The last requirement, stated in rather technical jargon, was that the Treasury should state its priorities, in the form of an objective function for use in a policy optimisation exercise.

While my amendment was under consideration in Committee, Tony Benn's industrial policy was causing political embarrassment to the Prime Minister, Harold Wilson.

I remember Harold coming into dinner in the members' dining room one evening, obviously well pleased with himself. He told the table in general, and me in particular, that he had spent the afternoon drafting amendments to meet the Confederation of British Industry's objections to the Industry Bill. These would make the clauses of the Bill about disclosure of information by firms virtually inoperable.

Matters soon came to a head when Harold swapped Tony Benn, the Secretary of State for Industry and the prime architect of the policy, with Eric Varley, the Secretary of State for Energy. He was putting Eric in specifically to emasculate the Industry Bill. The political upset was minimised because Tony and Eric, his successor, were both regarded as on the left. Tony Benn, who was not prepared to resign, was after all being given responsibility for North Sea Oil, with John Smith as his junior minister. John was expected to keep an eye on Benn. It was a stitch up: effectively the end of Labour's planning agreements approach to industrial policy. And the move was made despite diligent efforts to find willing industrial partners in planning agreements by the very able civil servant responsible, Ron Dearing, who later proved so useful to other governments in other roles on accounting standards and in education policy.

The Committee stage of the Bill in the Commons ended in some confusion. Asked by the Chairman of the Committee if I wished to move formally the new Schedule to the Bill (my amendment), I replied, 'Yes, Mrs Butler.' Those three words were enough. There was no further debate. The Committee divided. The Government had been arm-twisting the Labour members to ensure a 'No' vote. But the amendment won the support not only of Labour backbench members of the Standing Committee but also of the Tories, if only as a tactical move to defeat the government. I had been lobbying.

When my amendment came before the whole House a large backbench Labour revolt, supported by the Conservative opposition, supported it. I had been lobbying assiduously behind the scenes. All the Committee members – Labour, Tory and Liberal – voted for it except for Labour ministers, their parliamentary private secretaries, and the Labour whips.

Seldom is a government so comprehensively overruled in Committee, stripped of all external support. However had I been able to explain policy optimisation to the House of Commons on that occasion, I doubt if it would have reduced the time Britain has taken painfully to edge towards viable principles of economic policy[3].

The most visible and lasting legacy of my amendment has been the twice yearly Statement by the Chancellor, usually in April, in connection with the budget, and again in the autumn at the time of the announcement of the Public Spending Review.

Policy Optimisation and the Ball Committee

My original version of the Schedule contained a third paragraph, which I have already quoted (page 127), instructing the Treasury to specify priorities that could be used in policy optimisation. This was more than Treasury ministers could stomach, and Edmund Dell, the Paymaster General, was deputed to do a deal with me. Had I refused, Treasury ministers would have dug in and thrown out the amendment altogether.

The Treasury were no doubt opposed to the idea of policy optimisation for technical and political reasons. Technically there would have to be a good deal of trial and error testing in finding an optimisation criterion which would reasonably reflect the political priorities of the Chancellor of the Exchequer, given the economic practicalities. (Remember, this was in 1975, when we were staggering from one economic crisis to another.) And politically it would be difficult to avoid presenting the expected economic outcome as a firm forecast. My attitude was that economic policy makers and market operators would only learn the nature of the uncertainties by seeing how to make positive use of them in a coherent policy optimisation process, which recognised the difference between the wishes of the Chancellor and the economic practicalities.

It is certainly true that the House of Commons will usually mock at ideas they do not at first understand. But the House of Commons is prepared to learn from those who have a serious lesson to pass on.

The House of Lords did at least have a debate (28 July 1975). Richard Kahn thought my amendment was a Conservative initiative to discredit the Bill or expose the Treasury to public ridicule! That was mild compared with Thomas Balogh's expletives in the lobby: fortunately he was gagged in the debate itself because he was a minister at the time. It was more than an elder statesman of the left economic establishment could stomach. But then, you can't teach an old dog new tricks, as Nicky Kaldor once told me.

---

[3] For a fuller account see Holly, Sean (Ed.) (1994) *Money, Inflation and Employment : essays in honour of James Ball*, Aldershot: Edward Elgar, to which I contributed Chapter 1 (pp. 3-25).

Under pressure from Edmund Dell I had agreed to the omission of paragraph 3 from the revised Schedule moved by the Government in the Lords, in return for the setting up of a Committee on Policy Optimisation under the Chairmanship of Professor R J Ball.

Jim Ball was the natural choice for Chairman, when Edmund Dell put it to me. Following Ball's earlier work with Klein, he had initiated the LBS (London Business School) model as the first macroeconomic model to produce regular forecasts of the UK economy.

I urged that the Committee on Policy Optimisation should include economists and control theorists with actual knowledge and experience of policy optimisation on economic models, and recommended specifically Gregory Chow and David Kendrick from the USA, and Karl Astrom from Sweden. But the Treasury was too chauvinist to accept foreigners.

Of the Committee appointed, only David Livesey had any experience of policy optimisation on an empirical macroeconomic model. But it was a strong committee of theoretical and applied economists and econometricians, the other members being Tony Bispham, Gwylim Jenkins, James Mirrlees, Michael Posner, Denis Sargan and David Worswick. Gwylim Jenkins, with George Box, had made a major contribution to empirical time series analysis (which had proved very useful to me in my ICI days), but this was in fields other than economics, and before the days of vector autoregressive analysis. Jim Mirrlees was to be awarded a Nobel prize for his work on optimal taxation, and Denis Sargan was an accomplished econometrician.

The Committee conscientiously sought evidence, and Ball and Livesey met most of those working in the field on a visit to the United States. But it did not grasp where the problem lay. The final conclusion of the Ball Committee, which reported in 1978, was that 'an optimal control framework would push in the direction of encouraging a more coherent approach to economic policy-making and its public presentation'.

The Ball Committee on Policy Optimisation in its report[4] anticipated that the technical problems of policy optimisation would not be difficult to overcome, and so it proved. Given the technology of the time – the late 1970s – to install such a framework would have required perhaps a doubling of the size of the economic modelling teams, and strong leadership. Since then there has been a formidable development of

---

[4] Ball Committee on Policy Optimisation (1978) *Report of the Committee on Policy Optimisation* London: HMSO Cmnd. 7148

economic and econometric theory and methods, in policy design and analysis, and available computer power.

The Treasury and the Ball Committee did however miss an opportunity to establish economic policy-making methods at a political and technical level which might well have saved Britain from major policy mistakes in the years that followed.

Open government

The interest of my 1975 Industry Act amendment is not in its present application to economic policy, though it pointed to the modern way of setting policy according to the priorities of government. Its real political interest however lies rather in giving parliament and people some degree of ownership of economic policy.

No pressure group, political party organisation, think tank, company, or learned society seems to have taken advantage of the full possibilities opened up by the amendment. When Don Cruickshank was Director General of OFTEL, the Office of Telecommunications maintained a model of the telecoms market. I asked Don if they made it available to outsiders. He said they had never been asked. Yet that was in a market which was to yield more than £20 billion in license revenue in the next generation of technology – and disastrous losses in world-wide telecommunications markets. There is a void in the public debate when anyone asks how two numbers fit together.

The Thatcher government repealed Labour's 1975 Industry Act – but, interestingly, not the clauses relating to disclosure of information by firms. The amendment had had Tory support during its passage. Nigel Lawson, the future Tory Chancellor of the Exchequer, had been particularly supportive: possibly an opportunist rather than a principled stance. Lawson came to regard Treasury forecasts as a 'self-inflicted wound'[5].

The amendment continues to exert its influence on the use of models in the consideration of economic policy to this day.

In 1975 no individual or MP had the capacity to access the Treasury model: personal computers were not yet available. I had to wait nearly a decade before I was myself able to carry out policy optimisation exercises on the Treasury model on a desktop computer.

---

[5] Lawson, Nigel (992) *The View from No. 11* London: Bantam Press

11

The IMF loan & the abandonment of Keynsian demand management
1976

I was concerned in a minor episode in the International Monetary Fund (IMF) loan negotiations in November 1976. I mention this mainly because it opens up the question of the appropriateness (or otherwise) of the criteria used by the IMF to set conditions on loans. This is an important and recurring issue since inappropriate loan conditions can do immense harm to struggling economies, particularly in the Third World.

The incident also sheds some light on the attitude of Denis Healey, the Chancellor of the Exchequer, to international monetary questions.

Denis was, in my view, at his best in the area for which he never had Cabinet responsibility – foreign affairs. I sometimes found him in the Strangers' Cafeteria when the Members' Cafeteria was closed: it was fun to get him going on some obscure twist in the Beijing leadership of the Chinese Communist Party. My first recollection of his mastery of the minutiae of foreign policy was in 1950 when, as International Secretary of the Labour Party, he came to speak at the annual Student Christian Movement conference at Swanwick. The impression he gave then was one of competence and confidence which was encouraging to me as a student developing an interest in politics.

But to return to more serious matters ....

By 1976 we were – yet again – plunging into a very serious economic crisis. Indeed, this was, of all the crises that beset the ill-fated Callaghan administration, the most serious.

With the floating of the dollar, sterling and other major currencies in the early 1970s, the post-war Bretton Woods system of fixed but adjustable exchange rates had come to an end. The surge in oil prices, which had quadrupled between the beginning of 1973 and the first quarter of 1974,

11 : The IMF loan 1976

had led to a world-wide acceleration in inflation. In the UK, inflation under the 1970-74 Heath government had been between 7% and 9.4%. With the oil shock, it soared to16% in 1974, and then 24% the following year under the Labour government. By 1976, the value of the pound was falling rapidly, with an exchange rate of $2.0 to the pound at the beginning of the year dropping to $1.65 by the end. For the newly formed Callaghan government (Wilson had recently retired) disaster loomed. James Callaghan announced, at the Labour Party Conference in October 1976, the abandonment of Keynesian demand management, in a famous paragraph, drafted by his son-in-law, Peter Jay[1].

An IMF loan – a loan from the International Monetary Fund – was a humiliating but urgent necessity.

However, the US was in the throes of a presidential election, with Carter the democratic candidate and strongly tipped to win. The election would take place on 2 November.

In so far as the existing US administration was giving attention to any international monetary issues at the time, the priority was Mexico. Anxiety mounted. And the Treasury and Denis Healey were unable to contact any one in the Carter team – the incoming administration (if the polls were to be believed) – to seek support for the pound. However I was in touch with Carter's chief economic adviser in the economic campaign, Professor Lawrence Klein, of the Wharton School in the University of Pennsylvania. Klein was no enthusiast for Friedmanite money supply targeting (nor, later, for rational expectations).

Negotiations on the IMF loan : a side show

When I heard of the difficulties in contacting Carter, I wrote to Denis Healey on 2 August, and offered to see if I could open a line of communication with Klein. Denis told me to go ahead.

I had visited Klein in Philadephia recently – we had a common interest in economic policy optimisation. Klein indeed was *the* pioneer of econometric modelling, for which he won the Nobel Prize. He had been very helpful to me, not least in refereeing a Social Science Research Council grant application for PREM (see Chapter 9).

Klein was unable to talk during the election campaign, but he invited me to come to Philadelphia the weekend after polling day if Carter won.

---
[1] Callaghan, James (1976) in *Labour Party 1976 Report of the Annual Conference* London: Labour Party

Before going I met the Chancellor, Denis Healey, to hear his view of the situation, and of Britain's interests. I told him what I thought would be the advice of Klein to the UK and the IMF. Healey recommended Charlie Coombs' recently published book *The Arena of International Finance*[2] to me: 'It'll give you a good description of how international monetary negotiations are carried out,' he said. Charlie Coombs had handled US interventions in money markets in the New York Fed for many years, and attended Bank for International Settlements (BIS) meetings: he highlighted the drama and the politics rather than the economic arguments in international finance.

Carter won the election on 2 November. I met Klein in Philadelphia on the following Saturday. I had told Denis Healey I would like to have somebody from the Treasury present, so that he (Healey) could have an independent report of what Klein said. Simon Broadbent, an economist from the Treasury team in Washington, came with me: his record of the meeting and mine are on the file in the Churchill archive in Cambridge. I flew to Washington on 4 November (paying my own fare because Denis Healey said the only way the Treasury could pay was on the security services vote! That must be rubbish.)

On 5 November I met Jan Polak, the economist at the IMF, who had designed the IMF conditions for loans, and Andrew Crockett, seconded from the Bank of England to the IMF, to see if they had any flexibility towards more modern loan conditions based not on monetary principles but on optimal policy ideas. They were totally negative – as I had expected. Andrew Crockett said that even if there were a well proven model available he would be against its use in setting policy because that would reduce the number of people able to understand the arguments! What are all those well paid bankers for? And he is now General Manager of the Bank for International Settlements.

Our meeting with Klein lasted four hours from mid-morning and over lunch to mid-afternoon. I started by saying that I represented nobody but myself, and Klein said likewise. For the US the main international problem was still Mexico. The timetable of the UK negotiations with the IMF would probably mean that they would be over before Carter's Inauguration on 20 January 1977, and the President elect would make no commitments on US policy before that. (In the event Healey's Letter of Intent to the IMF accepting loan conditions was sent on 15 December 1976.)

---

[2] Coombs, Charles A. (1976) *The Arena of International Finance* New York: Wiley

11 : The IMF loan 1976 ♦ 135

For the longer term it might be different. Klein said he hoped the incoming US administration would seek to base IMF conditionality on the performance of the real economy – for the UK, on investment and productivity. But he added that he did not expect to serve in the US administration because his early membership of the Communist Party as a student in California in the 1930s would be dragged up in congressional hearings, and had indeed been raised in the campaign. (He had joined the Communist Party in California as a student because it gave him an opportunity to present a paper, which would have been on Keynesian lines!) However he said he would be glad to do what he could to help establish relations with the new team, including an early visit to the UK. I returned straight to London on 6 November.

Larry and Sonny Klein (his wife) visited London on 26-28 November as guests of the Treasury, and stayed at the Intercontinental Hotel. I met them on the evening of Friday 26 November. On Saturday they were invited to lunch by Denis Healey at 11 Downing Street, a lunch to which I too was invited. Edna Healey told me it was one of the very few occasions when she had entertained Treasury guests at Number 11, and rather fun. Larry stayed on afterwards for talks with the Chancellor and his officials, who had joined us for lunch: Douglas Wass, the Permanent Secretary; Derek Mitchell, Second Permanent Secretary (Overseas Finance); and Geoffrey Maynard, the Deputy Chief Economic Adviser. Larry told me afterwards that the main message that Denis wanted to give was that Britain was credit worthy and had always repaid its debts on time. It sounded to me like a well rehearsed line Denis had been giving to the Republican Under Secretary to the US Treasury who had been visiting London during the IMF negotiations.

Harold Lever, who was a Treasury minister, gave a convivial dinner in his luxurious Eaton Square flat for Larry that evening with wives. It was one of those intimate occasions when the exquisite Fabergé eggs were left on display. (They were safely locked away when the Levers entertained larger gatherings.) Fellow guests were Michael Posner, David Worswick of NIESR (the National Institute of Economic and Social Research), and David Lea of the TUC: three economists invited at my suggestion.

I had hoped that the optimal policy methods favoured by Klein, which we too had been developing with PROPE (the Programme of Research in Optimal Policy Evaluation), might offer governments an alternative to monetary targetry favoured by the IMF – a straight jacket that damaged, in my view, not only the British economy but also that of many a developing country. It was not to be. And my hopes that my good offices might earn me a place back in the government got nowhere.

The acquiescence to monetary targeting

The moral of this tale – if there is one – is that inappropriate conditions set on international loans can do immense harm to economies. The sad fact is that it is struggling economies in the Third World that have been most damaged by our arrogance in this respect.

The IMF loan negotiations were important for Britain not only for their immediate content, but because accepting the loan committed the British government to adopting targetry for the money supply. I shall be discussing the unfortunate results of adopting money targetry in the next three chapters. It is with some justice that Nigel Lawson later recalled that 'the setting of an annual target had already been inaugurated by Denis Healey, Chancellor in the previous Labour Government, essentially to propitiate the IMF and the financial markets'[3].

Some years later, when he had ceased to be Prime Minister, Jim Callaghan, in a conversation again in the Members dining room, said to me, in waspish tones and quite out of context, 'You disagreed with us on economic policy'. I suspect his 'us' included Harold Wilson, from whom Jim had inherited a distrust, and Denis Healey. Yet many other Labour members and, indeed, ministers disagreed with the government's economic policy. But they kept quiet. And, as events would prove, there was an alternative.

The Labour government stumbled on for another couple of years. It had been elected without a working majority, and only held power this long through Liberal support. It was in April 1979, after the 'winter of discontent' that the Prime Minister, James Callaghan, went to the country.

On 3 May 1979 Mrs Thatcher swept into power with reforming zeal, pledged to 'restore the balance in our economy'.

---

[3] Lawson, Nigel (1992) *The View from No 11* London: Bantam Press

12

Monetary policy:
the Treasury Select Committee Report
1981

The General Election of 1979 was a crushing defeat for Labour, as the Conservatives swept into power with an overall majority of forty four.

From the beginning of its term in office, the new Thatcher Government emphasised the importance of monetary control. In his 1979 Budget Statement, the incoming Chancellor, Sir Geoffrey Howe, said:

> It is crucially important to re-establish sound money. We intend to achieve this through firm monetary discipline and fiscal policies consistent with that, including strict control over public expenditure. ... We are committed to the progressive reduction to the rate of growth of the money supply.

'Monetary policy', as he was to confirm a year later, in evidence to the Treasury Select Committee,

> has an essential role to play in the defeat of inflation ... Inflation cannot persist in the long run unless it is accommodated by an excessive expansion of money and credit. That is at the heart of what 'monetarism' means in practice.

On coming into office in May 1979, the Government had inherited a difficult position from the crisis-ridden Labour government. The IMF loan negotiated in late 1976 had been conditional on Government policies which included deflationary economic measures and the adoption of limits for Domestic Credit Expansion (which implied targets for growth of the money supply as measured by £M3). Such money targets formed an increasingly important part of economic management, first for Denis Healey, as Labour Chancellor of the Exchequer, and even more for Geoffrey Howe, Mrs Thatcher's first Chancellor. Monetarism was espoused by both the Prime Minister and by her Chancellor as an article of faith. 'Any suggestion of a reversal [of the policy] would take us into horrendous areas of outer space so to speak,' Sir Geoffrey was to affirm in his evidence to the Treasury and Civil Service Select Committee, in 1980.

The Thatcher government was making a major departure in the principles of economic policy, and the new principles needed to be critically examined. A parliamentary debate is a poor vehicle for a rigorous, well-researched, evidence-based critique.

Fortunately Norman St.John-Stevas, the new Leader of the House of Commons, was in a position to create a system of new departmental select committees, and the Treasury and Civil Service Committee in particular. These offered a new forum to examine the fundamentals of policy.

The launch of the Treasury Select Committee

The accepted wisdom (as expressed by people like Richard Crossman[1] and Edmund Dell[2]) was that select committees 'might provide occupation for frustrated backbenchers'. That may be so, but they do at least offer a means for someone in parliament to think more fundamentally than ministers have time to do. Otto Clarke, our permanent secretary in the Ministry of Technology in the 1960s, used to say, 'Ministers don't have time to think. That is their job in opposition.' Very few do even then.

Select Committees give backbench MPs, of both government and opposition parties, the opportunity of access to thinkers and specialists, supported by professional staffing by House of Commons clerks. Ministers may invite in experts for lunch or half an hour's chat, but all that they get from that is a small smattering of jargon. That is no substitute for digesting serious argument. Because Select Committees choose their own subjects and lines of inquiry, they have the opportunity to investigate matters before they become topics for hot political debate. In my experience that has been their best work, keeping one step ahead of the game.

I asked the Whips to put me on the list for the new Treasury Committee. I was enraged when Denis Healey, now Shadow Chancellor, thereupon moved to veto my nomination. I told the Whips I would move at the PLP (Parliamentary Labour Party) meeting that the list of party

---

[1] Crossman, Richard (1970) *Inside View: Three Lectures in Prime Ministerial Government*, London, Jonathan Cape

[2] Dell, Edmund (1973) *Political Responsibility and Industry*, London: George Allen & Unwin

12 : Monetary Policy : the Treasury Select Committee Report 1981 ♦ 139

nominees to all select committees should be approved by the PLP as a whole, rather than be selected by the Whips and front bench.

The Whips accepted that perforce, but required that the list would be voted on without amendment. That was good enough for me. The result was that I was put on the Treasury Committee. The practice of whips and ministers (or shadow minister) picking and choosing members of select committees is, in my view, deplorable.

The new Treasury Committee had opportunities – and a chairman, Edward du Cann, who was determined to make it succeed. He was in a strong political position. He was Chairman of the 1922 Committee (the body representing Tory backbenchers), and a former Treasury minister; and he had undoubted abilities despite his colourful City background and rather oily charm. The members of the Treasury Committee were all interested in the subject, and none of them were exactly Whips' Office lobby fodder. The Tory members were Kenneth Baker, Anthony Beaumont-Dark, Timothy Eggar, Terence Higgins, and Richard Shepherd; Michael English, Robert Sheldon, Ken Woolmer, and I were Labour; and Richard Wainwright, the Liberal. We represented the balance of parties in the House.

I argued from the start that we should tackle the mainstream economic policy of the government – the government's monetary policy which lay at the heart of their economic management – and do that with evidence from prime researchers, not from pundits and expositors (either academic or journalistic). We would not rely just on ministers and officials. That Edward du Cann endorsed strongly, and the committee agreed.

I spoke to John Flemming, who was chief economic adviser at the Bank of England, and sought his advice. We agreed that, on their records, the obvious advisers for this particular inquiry were Professors Marcus Miller of Warwick University, and Director of the Parliamentary Policy Unit; David Hendry, editor of the *Economic Journal*, and shortly to become a Fellow of Nuffield College, Oxford and Professor of Economics at Oxford; and Willem Buiter, who was soon to become Cassel Professor of Economics at the London School of Economics (LSE). I knew their record in the field well, through our work over the previous ten years in the Programme of Research into Optimal Policy Evaluation and its precursor.

David Hubback, our clerk, was an unusual appointment, as he was seconded from the Treasury. But he went along admirably with the spirit of the inquiry.

While inviting witnesses to give such evidence as they thought relevant, we also asked them to reply to a questionnaire on the principles of monetary policy, the evidence for them, and the practice. I suggested such a questionnaire because my experience of select committees was that if such a questionnaire were done fairly, it produced a much more coherent and probing body of evidence, without biasing replies. Otherwise the evidence submitted is pitched at a level broadsheet newspaper readers can digest over breakfast. That is scarcely able to cope with the level of argument in Federal Reserve Board working papers and articles in the economic journals. This was particularly important with monetary policy in the phase it was in, in 1980.

Monetary policy and the Lucas critique

First, a few words on the technical background.

Mrs Thatcher's mentor, Milton Friedman, and Anna Schwartz had published in 1963 *A Monetary History of the United States*[3]. This had left a lasting impression on American economists of the importance of the money supply.

To this the idea of rational expectations was to give a cutting edge in its policy implications. In 1976, Robert Lucas at the University of Chicago had published a paper 'Econometric Policy Evaluation: A Critique'[4]. This was followed up in 1978 by a paper by F.E. Kydland and E.C. Prescott, 'Rules Rather than Discretion: the Inconsistency of Optimal Plans'[5]. A couple of years later a requiem on Keynes, *After Keynesian Macroeconomics*[6], by Robert E. Lucas and Thomas J. Sargent, appeared.

The problem, identified by Lucas, is 'time inconsistency'.

That is not merely a matter of 'ensuring that the government actually has an incentive to achieve the goals in the future, which it says now, it

---

[3] Friedman, Milton and Schwartz, Anna (1963), *A Monetary History of the United States 1867-1960*, USA: Princeton

[4] Lucas, Robert E. Jr. (1976) 'Econometric Policy Evaluation: a Critique' in *The Phillips Curve and Labour Markets,* ed. K. Brunner and A.H. Meltzer. Amsterdam: North Holland

[5] Kydland, Finn E. and Prescott, Edward C. (1977) 'Rules rather than Discretion: The Inconsistency of Optimal Plans' *J. Pol.Econ.*

[6] Lucas, Robert E. and Sargent, Thomas J. (1978) 'After Keynesian Macroeconomics' in *After the Phillips Curve: Persistence of High Inflation and High Unemployment* Federal Reserve Bank of Boston Conference Series 19. This and the papers by Lucas (1976), and Kydland and Prescott (1977) were republished in:

Lucas, Robert and Sargent, Thomas J. (Eds.) (1981)*Rational Expectations and Econometric Practice,* London: Allen & Unwin

wants to achieve in the future,' as Edward Balls[7], Gordon Brown's economic adviser, was to define it rather neatly in 1998.

As Kydland and Prescott had observed,

> Even if there is an agreed-upon, fixed social objective function and policymakers know the timing and magnitude of the effects of their actions, discretionary policy, namely, the selection of that decision which is best, given the current situation and a correct evaluation of the end-of-period position, does not result in the social objective function being maximised.

The problem is that people base their decisions partly on what the government says it is going to do next year. The passage of time means that when it comes to next year, the government's fixed social objective function may still be sought and with the same priorities, but it is over a shorter period, and the calculation of what that implies has changed. Hence the *time inconsistency* of its action.

If you have not understood that, you are not alone. If you want to try understand it, put a big block of ice on your head, and read the first 6 pages of Kydland and Prescott's paper[8]. (To give you a hint, it is Lagrange multipliers that they use on page 4.)

Kydland and Prescott went on to remark, 'Reliance on policies such as constant growth in the money supply and constant tax rates constitute a safer course of action.' In 1980, everyone understood that. So that is what the Thatcher government set out to do, with disastrous results: the exchange rate soared and put out of action great swathes of British industry as the intermediate target of the growth of money supply was pursued and the exchange rate was neglected. Labour's taunt of Mrs Thatcher was that, as a result of ignoring the exchange rate, she had knocked out more of British industry than Hitler had done. (Unfortunately, Gordon Brown was to repeat this mistake when Labour returned to office in 1997.)

The scope of the Select Committee's work

In 1980, if the Select Committee were to do serious work it needed to do several things. It needed to recognise the difficulties that had been raised in monetary economics, to look at the analysis that had been done,

---

[7] Balls, Ed (1998) 'Open macroeconomics in an Open Economy', *Scottish J. Pol. Econ.* Vol. 45, No. 2, May
[8] Kydland, Finn E. and Prescott, Edward C. (1977) 'Rules rather than Discretion: The Inconsistency of Optimal Plans' *J. Pol.Econ.*

and to adapt it to the British circumstances of a much more open economy. (Britain has more than twice the American share of exports and imports in GDP.) Our Select Committee could not itself hope to do the research and development work needed, but it could point out its direction and suggest possible solutions among those being canvassed.

The time inconsistency problem had led immediately to much work in the US on three lines.

The first line stemmed from the initial solution proposed by Kydland and Prescott that policy planners should pick *ex ante* settings for *intermediate targets* for central banks, which should then stick to them. Candidates for use as intermediate targets included the money supply, money GDP (Gross Domestic Product), commodity prices, and the nominal exchange rate. The money supply was tried out as an intermediate target by all major central banks, and subsequently abandoned by them all as firm targets. The nominal exchange rate has been tried by a number of medium sized economies, particularly through the European Exchange Rate Mechanism which, before the introduction of the Euro, was sustained in the form of the short lived EMU; this however is not relevant for the US.

A second line of research explored the many ways in which *time inconsistency* can be exploited by monetary or fiscal policy makers, to renege on past *ex ante* policy announcements.

A third, time consistent, line of work has considered the design of *constant-parameter feedback policies*. Feedback rules have been used by the staff of the Fed (the US Federal Reserve Fund) to explore possible responses to alternative policies since the mid-1970s[9]. But using feedback rules as guidelines for monetary policy only became respectable in the late 1990s. Of which, more anon[10].

The Treasury Select Committee's working methods

That sets out sufficient of the background of previous and subsequent events to provide a context within which to describe, and to judge, our work on the House of Commons Treasury Select Committee in 1979-83 on monetary policy[11].

---

[9] Kalchbrenner, J. and Tinsley, P. (1976) 'On the use of Feedback Control in the Design of Aggregate Monetary Policy,' *Am. Econ. Rev.*, May, 349-355
[10] See Chapter 15, pp 173 *ff*
[11] House of Commons (1981), Treasury and Civil Service Committee, Third Report on *Monetary Policy*, (HC 163-I) London: HMSO

12 : Monetary Policy : the Treasury Select Committee Report 1981   ♦   143

It was clear at the time we were working on our Report that the economy was in difficulty, despite the Tories' much heralded panacea of monetarism.

As our Report was to point out, in his 1979 Budget, Geoffrey Howe had cut income tax but increased VAT (Value Added Tax) with dire results. The increase in VAT, combined with higher nationalised industry prices, caused inflation to soar from the 10.6% the government had inherited from Labour to 21.5% in early 1980. Unemployment – the price paid by ordinary working people – shot up from 1.3 million in 1979 to 2 million by the end of 1980 ('a price worth paying' according to its Tory defenders).

Even the sacred money supply growth rate doubled! The annual growth rate of the money supply, as measured by £M3, had increased from 10.3% (June 1979) to 22.2% (March 1980).

Was there a causal relationship?

The Select Committee sent out a questionnaire to 32 individuals, economists with a wide range of views, including such notables as Milton Friedman, Rudi Dornbusch of MIT, James Tobin of Yale, David Laidler and Nicholas Kaldor; and institutions, including the Treasury and the Bank of England, the US Federal Reserve System, the Bundesbank and other central banks. Our questionaire sought evidence and views on the principal objectives of economic policy, the intermediate targets, and the instruments and effects of policy. In particular it asked questions on money supply, interest rates and the PSBR (the Public Sector Borrowing Requirement); on money and the exchange rate; on money, output and inflation; and on monetary control. It asked for econometric evidence, for economic models, their track records, and methods of estimation. We offered to have their models run for policy design, testing and comparison purposes, at Imperial College.

Even the despatch of such a questionnaire was too much for the *Economist*, which had not been invited to submit evidence. It responded with a six page article under the headline 'The cheekiest examination'[12]. But fortunately that was not the response of our 32 invited witnesses, 29 of whom replied, all helpfully.

The replies of witnesses to Select Committees are published in full along with the Committee's Report. They make fascinating reading.

The witnesses' replies made it possible in our report broadly to distinguish four major schools of thought: the *New Classical*, represented in

---

12 *Economist* (1980) May 24 'The cheekiest examination', London

the UK by Patrick Minford; the *Gradualists*, represented by David Laidler, and among whom might broadly be included Milton Friedman and the UK government of Mrs Thatcher and her Chancellor of the Exchequer, Geoffrey Howe; the *Pragmatists*, among whom might be included James Tobin and the Bundesbank; and the *Anti-Monetarists*, including Nicholas Kaldor.

Each school took a different view on money and interest rates, the PSBR, the exchange rate, output and inflation. These views the Committee discussed in the light of the evidence available such as it was.

The Treasury, which used formal econometric models for forecasting and policy analysis for some purposes, might have been expected to be the principal source of econometric evidence. But the evidence the Treasury at first submitted, and the questioning of the Chancellor and Treasury officials, yielded no empirical evidence in support of government policy.

I repeat, the Treasury's evidence yielded *no empirical support* of government policy. Indeed the memorandum submitted by the Treasury in response to the Committee's questionnaire did not contain a single number. But the Treasury then submitted two further papers containing useful empirical evidence, though this evidence was not necessarily supportive of the government position.

The Committee's conclusions

In its conclusions the Committee welcomed the readiness of the Government to announce medium and longer term objectives which express its policy intentions. But we noted that events had shown that the Medium-Term Financial Strategy of aiming to keep the rate of growth of sterling M3 within a declining band was not soundly based. It was over-ambitious in the first year and in setting specific targets for a four year period. A combination of influences had reinforced the effect of tight money in pushing up the exchange rate, where the government should keep under review methods of influencing it. The practical way forward appeared to be to take some account of both the money supply and the exchange rate as well as final objectives in setting the instruments of monetary policy.

The final chapter of the report made recommendations on the development of policy, including the testing and comparison of models. It included an Annex on the optimisation of economic and monetary policy by myself, discussing the evidence of the PROPE group at Imperial College.

Press comment on the Monetary Policy Report

The immediate press reaction to the report itself was mixed, dividing on party lines.

Peter Kellner, in *The New Statesman*[13], said,

> The committee's report is quite the most important to have been published by any select committee for more than a decade. The report methodically, and at times ruthlessly, exposes the Government's economic strategy as devoid of any basis in plausible theory or any nation's experience. The importance of the report lies not only in the competence of its arguments. The committee obtained evidence from almost anyone with anything to say on the subject, from monetarists like Milton Friedman to anti-monetarists like Lord Kaldor. It penetrated the inner economic calculations of the Treasury. It received advice from the central banks of Germany, Switzerland, Austria and the US – all of which have had more experience, and generally much more success, in linking monetary with other economic policies. The committee was chaired by Edward du Cann, a Conservative who does not normally inhabit the wetter regions of present day Toryism. A majority of MPs on the committee are Tories. And at the end of its operation the committee's report was agreed unanimously.

Unlike most of the commentators, Kellner went on to report the contents and not merely the politics and personalities of the report.

The Guardian[14] leader said,

> If Treasury ministers seem more than usually concussed over the next few days, do not put it down to the state of the economy, or even to the complications of the impending budget. The likely cause will be the all-party Commons select committee on the Treasury and the Civil Service, which has delivered itself of a report on the Government's monetary policy that can only be described as a bomb-shell, or perhaps a land mine. This authoritative effort has taken the MPs – six Conservatives, four Labour members and one Liberal – the better part of a year. They have sent out detailed questionnaires to numerous organisations, including foreign central banks, and have taken evidence from some very distinguished and some not so distinguished academics. Their report itself runs to a

---

[13] Kellner, Peter (1981) *New Statesman* 6 March 1981
[14] *Guardian*, (1981) Leader, 6 March 1981

mere 127 pages, but the mountain of accessory evidence, memoranda and appendices fill another four volumes with the approximate bulk of the Manhattan telephone directory. This report's findings demolished the very foundations of the Government's policy.

The critical comment was led by Samuel Brittan[15] in *The Financial Times*, under the headline 'Mr. Du Cann's bogus science'.

> When someone grabs you by the arm and tells you how good, kind, musical, well-read, religious or well travelled he is, it is wise to be suspicious. People of really great accomplishments usually leave these accomplishments to speak for themselves.
>
> The same applies when people say how scientific they are. The unifying theme of the du Cann Committee Report on Monetary Policy was the need to be scientific. Government policies were criticised for not being formulated and tested in the most rigorous possible way. It was from this high pedestal that the Medium Term Financial Strategy and the monetary approach to inflation were condemned.
>
> The running in all this was clearly made by Dr. Jeremy Bray, who took committee members for a very big ride in persuading them that certain highly tendentious conclusions represented hard science....

Brittan's fiercest criticism was of the Committee's condemnation of the Medium Term Financial Strategy (a strategy doomed to be discarded within a few years). The members of the Select Committee, he said, had 'all signed out of a mistaken desire for unanimity.' He concluded that the committee urgently needed new leadership. Sam Brittan was, of course, the elder brother of Leon Brittan, who was appointed Chief Secretary to the Treasury, with a seat in the Cabinet, in Mrs Thatcher's next reshuffle.

The only journalist who picked up the relevance of my 1975 Industry Act amendment was David Smith, writing in *Now!* Magazine[16], who wrote,

> But on the Labour side is the MP who has really been the prime mover in the committee – Dr. Jeremy Bray, who has staged a long and lonely battle to get the Treasury to open up and to change its methods of putting economic policy into practice. It was he who pushed through an amendment to the 1975 Industry Act which requires the Treasury to make its economic model available to outsiders and to publish certain elements of its forecasts.

---

[15] Brittan, Samuel (1981) 'Mr. Du Cann's bogus science' *The Financial Times*, 9 March 1981
[16] Smith, David (1981) *Now!* London, 27 March 1981

12 : Monetary Policy : the Treasury Select Committee Report 1981

Was the judgement of the Committee broadly correct?

The criteria for judging retrospectively the value of any Report is whether the balance and judgement of the report has proved broadly correct; and second, whether the report helped or hindered successful changes in economic policy.

In my view, the report has stood the passage of time well, and its style of argument and conclusions seem relevant twenty years later, in 2002, and after several changes of economic strategy.

The role of the money supply as the appropriate sole intermediate target has long since been rejected not only in the UK, but in every major country. Indeed in the UK before the end of the inquiry it was relegated to the role of one among other indicators to be watched.

Our select committee report on *Monetary Policy* in 1981 raised a good deal of interest in macroeconomic policy research in the UK. The recommendations we made for diverse model-based research and inter-model testing and comparison made it possible for Michael Posner, as chairman of the Economic and Social Research Council (ESRC), to organise a consortium of the Treasury, the Bank of England and the ESRC to finance a macroeconomic modelling research programme which ran for sixteen years as the largest single ESRC research programme.

Twenty years later policy optimisation still seems a useful tool in designing policy. I note that the particular optimisation programme used even now in the Treasury is CRECY, an extension of its AMODEL model solution programme; it is used both for the derivation of optimal policy instrument settings, and for the derivation of optimal coefficients in feedback rules. This programme was in fact written by the PROPE group at Imperial College – the group of which I was a founding member. PROPE's optimisation methods or similar methods were adopted by all the main UK modelling teams. The Economic and Social Research Council set up a consortium with the Treasury and the Bank of England to finance research by the principal economic model teams, and it set up the macro-economic modelling bureau at Warwick University to test and compare the models; it ran for sixteen years.

All these developments have been the result of the work of many economists, some very distinguished. I never aspired to counting myself as an economist. Any role I have had has been in seeing and encouraging developments and applications in the work of others. It is a role I believe I personally was the better able to pursue from within parliament, facing practical political problems. That did not necessarily help my political career – nor my standing with economists, where, as a politician, I was rather suspect. But it enabled me to see and to feel the nature of the problems, and to remain dissatisfied by solutions that did not address the real problems in effective ways.

And the future?

By now (2002) the use of policy optimisation has won general acceptance in the form used by Taylor for the calculation of a reasonable rule for interest rates, with the time inconsistency of rational expectations avoided by the simple device of keeping the rule fixed. (I shall be discussing what is known as the 'Taylor Rule' in Chapter 15).

The recent Performance and Innovation Unit report, *Adding It Up: improving analysis and modelling in central government*[17], issued in January 2000, unfortunately excluded macroeconomic modelling and policy in the Treasury from its scope, though it noted that the ESRC's macroeconomic modelling research programme 'is widely regarded as having pushed the UK to the forefront of technical modelling'.

True this may be.

But the UK will not maintain this primacy for long unless something is done to offer younger home-grown economists good career prospects in economic research. By now – the start of the twenty first century – I am told the economic departments in top universities are averaging less than two new British PhD students a year. In the London School of Economics, for example, with probably the strongest and most sought after economics post-graduate programme in the UK, British applicants are a rarity. It does not bode well.

---

[17] Performance and Innovation Unit (2000) Report *Adding It Up: improving analysis and modelling in central government* London: The Cabinet Office, HMSO

13

International Monetary Arrangements The Treasury Committee Reports
1982-1983

The Treasury Select Committee planned to follow up our Report on *Monetary Policy*, published in 1981, with two hard-hitting Reports, one on *International Monetary Arrangements: International Lending by Banks*[1] and the other on the linked subject, *International Monetary Arrangements*[2]. The exchange rate problem obviously was central to both. In preparation for this, I visited the United States again. I was well aware of the fact that economic policy-making was being influenced by research in leading American universities and institutes.

The Prime Minister, on coming into office, had proclaimed that Britain was in a state of total political and economic collapse. Her cure was to be a strong dose of radical economic liberalism, along the lines advocated by, among others, her gurus Milton Friedman and Adam Walters, both Americans.

So, to keep in touch with new developments, I made a round of visits to give seminars on our *Monetary Policy* Report in some of the foremost US research universities including Princeton, Pennsylvania State, Chicago and Stanford. Monetarism, linked with the theory of rational expectations, was rapidly becoming the new orthodoxy among academic and government economists' thinking. How agents learn and form their expectations was an outstanding problem for the theory of rational expectations.

---

[1] House of Commons, Treasury Select Committee [4th Report] 1982-83 *International Monetary Arrangements: International Lending by Banks*, 4 volumes, London: HMSO
[2] House of Commons, Treasury Select Committee 1983 *International Monetary Arrangements*, London: HMSO

Learning rational expectations

When I arrived in Chicago I found myself the object of unexpected interest from Bob Lucas, who had collaborated with Thomas Sargent in work on rational expectations. I was flattered. But then I found his interest arose not because of the Treasury Select Committee's criticism of money supply targeting, but because his students had told him that I was the father of Margaret Bray, by then a young professor at Stanford who was making a name for herself!

Margaret was clearly far more expert than her father in this field. In her very interesting Oxford DPhil thesis, and subsequent publications[3], she had raised – and solved – some of the key problems about learning, estimation and the stability of rational expectations of economic agents.

In the view of Lucas, Sargent and their school, rational expectations rendered any government's policy ineffective, particularly policy based on Keynesian demand management. 'We conclude,' Kydland and Prescott[4] had said, 'there is *no* way control theory can be made applicable to economic planning when expectations are rational'. If true, this was the death knell to my work on policy optimisation.

The truth about rational expectations however was more complicated.

Some years later *Evolving Rationality of Rational Expectations: An Assessment of Thomas Sargent's Achievements*[5], by Esther-Mirjam Sent, appeared. I found Margaret's views on this revealing. In her review[6] of Sent's book, she comments:

> The framework of analysis used in this book is inspired by the increased interest of science studies scholars in scientific culture and practice, where culture is defined as a heterogeneous multiplicity of skills, tools, social relations, concepts, model theories and so on ...

She continues, recalling her experience in publishing her DPhil thesis:

> The problem [of how agents might come to have rational expectations] is a difficult one, both conceptually and technically ...

---

[3] Bray, Margaret (1982) 'Learning, Estimation, and Stability of Rational Expectations', *Journal of Econ.Theory*, 26:318-39

Bray, Margaret (1983) Convergence to Rational Expectations Equilibrium' in Frydman, Roman and Phelps, Edmond (eds.), *Individual Forecasts and Aggregate Outcomes*, Cambridge

[4] Kydland, Finn E. and Edward C. Prescott (1977) 'Rules rather than Discretion: The Inconsistency of Optimal Plans' *J. Pol.Econ.* 85,3

[5] Sent, Esther-Mirjam (1998) *The Evolving Rationality of Rational Expectations: An Assessment of Thomas Sargent's Achievements* Cambridge: Cambridge University Press

[6] Bray, Margaret (1999) review of Sent (1998)

Perhaps only a Ph.D. student would be naïve enough to persist with it. My own interest in the learning problem stemmed from complete disbelief of the stories told by Sargent and others of how agents might come to have rational expectations. I wrote a paper for a conference in New York in December 1981 in which I made what I thought was an aggressive attack on Sargent's argument. I modelled agents as naïve econometricians, making inappropriate use of ordinary least squares. Perhaps I was too English for the aggression to be obvious. Tom Sargent, whom I did not know personally, was both courteous and interested. Nevertheless, I was very surprised when papers by Marcet and Sargent landed on my desk for refereeing. These papers took my approach and generalised my results by using results due to Ljung in the engineering literature.

Margaret's review points out that Sent's book

.... says very little about Sargent's political views and their relationship with his research, apart from quoting an interview where he said, 'When I came out of Berkeley and Harvard I had a really naïve view of what the government could accomplish ... I distanced my self from that'. Sargent cited his experience of serving in the Pentagon as one reason for his change in perspective, but his story has to be part of the story of the generation that came to adulthood in the Vietnam years; Sargent obtained his PhD in 1968. The relationship between academic economics and public policy making is uneasy, but at times intense, as economists move back and forth between government and academia. I for one would like to know something of the political views of an economist who is best known for a proposition on policy ineffectiveness.

How right she is. Politicians need to understand the general import and limitations of technical economic arguments, and economists need to set out any political considerations that may have influenced the assumptions and conclusions of their work.

The Committee's Reports on International Monetary Arrangements

An immediate problem that remained in 1981 – and which still remains today – is the achievement of reasonably stable exchange rates. It was particularly acute at this time, and a natural subject for the Treasury Committee's final inquiries of the 1979-83 parliament.

The Treasury Committee had again sent out a questionnaire and collected evidence, written and oral, in the UK and the US, which formed the basis of our first report on this important topic: a substantial four volume report entitled *International Monetary Arrangements: International Lending by Banks*[7]. This was published in March 1983.

We had intended to follow this up with a second, even more probing Report on the core topic: international monetary arrangements themselves. But, although an election was not due until 1984, rumours were flying. The Labour opposition, under Michael Foot, was in total disarray. The papers were ecstatic about the emergence of the Social Democrats. And Margaret Thatcher, having triumphed in the Falklands War, was weighing up her chances ...

We on the Treasury Select Committee knew we probably did not have the time before the dissolution of parliament to produce a major report on international monetary arrangements generally.

However, work proceeded on the production of the Chairman's Draft Report. This, as is usual, was drafted by the clerk with the help of our specialist advisers, reflecting the general tenor of the evidence and the attitude taken by the Committee. Our advisers were Professor Willem Buiter again, Professor Brian Tew of the Loughborough University of Technology, and Professor John Williamson of Fred Bergsten's Institute for International Economics in Washington.

I had picked up on the grapevine that the Tory Whips, having been stung by the impact of our earlier report on Monetary Policy, were going to neuter the Committee in the next parliament by moving out our Tory chairman, Edward du Cann, and putting in their backwoodsmen. The effect would have been (and indeed was) to dilute not so much the conclusions as the standard of our evidence and proceedings. This would make it impossible for me to operate, with advisers and witnesses, as I had been doing at a reasonably technical level. That, I judged, would bring to an end my usefulness on the Committee.

So I had to conclude anything I wanted to say on monetary policy through the Committee in that Parliament.

The Chairman's draft was produced. However, no formal proceedings had begun. However, we felt confident that we would be able to get it out if the election were delayed until the autumn.

---

[7] House of Commons, Treasury Select Committee [4th Report] 1982-83 *International Monetary Arrangements: International Lending by banks*, 4 volumes, London: HMSO

13 : *International Monetary Arrangements* ♦ 153

Scuppered?

As events turned out, our final Select Committee *Report on International Monetary Arrangements* was nearly scuppered by the calling of the 1983 General Election by a triumphalist Margaret Thatcher. She was exuberant after her remarkable victory in the Falklands War: the defining moment of her premiership. She was determined to capitalise on it.

Shortly after the announcement of the date of the election, Edward du Cann, the Chairman, and I had a hurried consultation in a House of Commons lift. The Report existed in draft. We did not have time to complete the process. We had two options: abandon the almost completed Report – or publish in draft. We decided to recommend publication. Other select committee members agreed.

The Chairman's draft

As the Chairman observed in his Draft Report (published as a draft):

> This Report naturally reflects the major developments in the world economy since we reported in February 1981 [the Committee's first *Report on Monetary Policy* (1981)[8]] – the welcome reduction in inflation, and the unwelcome recession accompanied by a debt crisis. Those developments are related. In our Report on Monetary Policy we warned that inflation posed an intractable problem that would not subside painlessly in response to announcements about monetary policy, no matter how credible. The severe recession that resulted from *inter alia* the determined use of monetary policy to bring inflation under control has confirmed our forebodings.

> The recession has been the deepest for half a century. It has raised unemployment in the OECD to some 32 million and in Britain to over three million. This together with persistently misaligned exchange rates has provoked increasing resort to 'beggar-my-neighbour' remedies for unemployment, especially import restrictions.

The Chairman's Draft noted that in our 1980-81 *Monetary Policy Report*[9] we had said:

---

[8] *Op. cit*
[9] See Chapter 12

The practical way forward appears to be to take some account of both the money supply and the exchange rate as well as final objectives in setting the instruments of monetary policy ... (para 1.5)

We therefore [the Draft continued] favour what we term a joint exchange rate/monetary policy regime. (para 4.20).

We argued for the adoption of a joint exchange rate/monetary policy regime, as one element of what would ideally be a comprehensive programme for the balanced pursuit of the objectives of economic policy. This leaves undefined the method of choosing and combining numerical targets, the strength of the policy adjustments to be made in pursuit of such targets, the circumstances in which the targets may be changed, and the role of international cooperation in defining or pursuing targets. (para 4.36)

In principle, however, such policy design falls squarely within the field of dynamic optimal control theory. We therefore sought evidence on the progress of the large econometric models which are needed to give an empirical base to policy design, and on the development of policy optimisation techniques. (para 4.37)

In this connection we received evidence from Professor Artis and Dr Karakitsos about the application of policy optimisation methods to compare monetary target and mixed monetary-cum-exchange rate target regimes on the London Business School and National Institute of Economic and Social Research models. Similar work has been undertaken by Treasury officials on the Treasury model. We also discussed the technical feasibility of such work with Dr Enzler and Dr Tinsley of the Research Division and Dr Henderson and Dr Hooper of the International Finance Division of the Federal Reserve Board in Washington. We enquired into the state of the main systems of linked national economy models maintained in public agencies, specifically the OECD, the Federal Reserve Board, and the Japanese Economic Planning Agency. (para.4.38)

The progress that has been made in developing these techniques is impressive. (para 4.39)

However the Chairman's Draft failed to go on from there to recommend a combined real exchange rate and anti-inflation objective, and the practical steps needed to use policy optimisation in the support of such a strategy.

Instead the Chairman's Draft was side-tracked into discussing some of the bugs reported, honestly enough, by Artis and Karakitsos in the use of the UK macroeconomic models. He concluded that the models were not yet in a state where one could, with reasonable assurance, use the estimated optimal trajectories as policy objectives.

To practical policy makers that implied – in my view, mistakenly – that the methods were unusable. None of our three specialist advisers (Willem Buiter, Brian Tew and John Williamson) had had extensive experience on policy optimisation using large scale empirical macroeconomic models. Having myself worked with optimisation of such models for ten years I recognised the sort of bugs to which Artis and Karakitsos referred, but I had good reason to believe that they could be dealt with easily enough with well-directed research and application programmes in the near future. (In this events proved that I was not mistaken.) David Hendry commented helpfully.

In one of the final meetings of the Select Committee in 1983, I tabled an amendment to the Chairman's Draft proposing an alternative draft, taking a more positive line towards policy optimisation. I should have expected the roughing up that provoked from our advisers: the cut and thrust of their robust academic argument somewhat perplexed my colleagues who could be forgiven if they concluded I must be a twit: after all, I was only an MP, and here were professional economists giving their unprejudiced advice. (In the long term, my judgement was to prove correct. But that lay in the future[10].)

The Report attracted some headlines. It was comprehensively rubbished by the Tory high command, but it was soon overtaken by the razzmatazz of electioneering.

The Prime Minister had a rather cavalier way with facts. Peter Hennessey[11] recounts how the Iron Lady found a Central Policy Review Staff report on unemployment unacceptable. Professor John Ashworth, the government's Chief Scientist, who was a member of the CPRS team objected: 'But Prime Minister, it is based on the facts.' The famous withering, slightly manic gaze was turned on. 'The facts,' she blazed. 'I have been elected to *change* the facts!'

---

[10] See Chapter 15.
[11] Hennessey, Peter, (2000) *The Prime Ministers* London: Penguin 2000

14

Opening up access to the Treasury Model
1984-1993

An important effect of my amendment to the Industry Act 1975 was that the Treasury Model was opened up for public use by academia, by city analysts, by commentators on the economy in the media, and by Members of Parliament. This, however, was in the infancy of computing. Some sort of intermediary was necessary. So before personal computers were commonly available I had arranged for the House of Commons to finance the setting up of a Parliamentary Unit which, working alongside the ESRC Macroeconomic Modelling Bureau at Warwick University, would provide MPs with access to the Treasury model.

Meanwhile Michael Posner's initiation of the Consortium of the Treasury, the Bank of England and the Economic and Social Research Council to finance a programme of research on macroeconomic modelling provided a continuity of effort for sixteen years. The Consortium financed the Warwick Bureau, the London Business School and the National Institute models, and the Programme of Research into Optimal Policy Evaluation (PROPE[1]), by now based in Imperial College.

The ESRC Macroeconomic Modelling Bureau at Warwick University

Unfortunately, MPs were denied access to the Treasury model through the Bureau: Ken Wallis, the Director of the Bureau, took the bizarre view that the Bureau itself could not properly do work for individual MPs, although the Bureau owed its existence to the recommendation of a House of Commons Treasury Select Committee in the first place, and the House of Commons was funding the Bureau.

---

[1] See Chapter 9, pp 116-125.

Moreover the Warwick implementation of the Treasury model on their own software was such that they were never even able to run the Treasury model as it needed to be run, with rational expectations for the exchange rate and long term interest rates. (When, later, I began to run the Treasury model on my own computer, I had no such problems, because I used the Treasury programmes which were written by PROPE.)

Later Professor Marcus Miller took on the Directorship of the Parliamentary Unit. Over the years the unit hosted a number of seminal workshops – the ESRC Macroeconomic Modelling Seminars – at Warwick. The published proceedings (to which I and my team were regular contributors) were influential. But when I asked Marcus for specific work to be done, he said he would not work as my research assistant. This rather defeated the point of giving MPs the access. The Bureau's Directors probably saw the Parliamentary Unit more as a resource for their own research than a research facility for the use of MPs.

However, my luck was to change.

Running the Treasury Model on a desktop computer

With the advent of reasonably powerful personal computers in the mid-1980s I was myself able to run policy optimisation exercises on the Treasury model. By about 1983 the MPs' office allowance had increased sufficiently for me to save up to buy one of the (hugely expensive) early desktop personal computers. By this date too I was Opposition frontbench Spokesman on science and technology – of this, more later[2] – and I supplemented my allocation of 'Short Money' (paid to opposition frontbench spokespersons to employ research staff) from my own salary.

Readers may have reservations about my use of the 'Short Money' not only to fund research on science policy but also to continue working on the management of economic policy, using the new power that desktop computers gave to individual researchers and small teams. Often scientists would see economics as distinct from 'real' science. They are prepared to look at the claims of economics to be a science, but they tend to get frustrated by all the difficulties.

Many scientists, even those heading big projects, tend to see science policy as comprising simply the determination of the science budget, that is to say, the public funding of research. This budget includes funding for special topics like global warming, and the research which underpins public

---

[2] See Chapters 16-19

policy for particular departments like the Department of the Environment, Food and Rural Affairs or the Department of Health, as well as funding channelled through the research councils and so on.

But to me economic policy and science policy were linked.

First, I was, and remain, convinced that economic policy should not give up the ambition of building an empirical data-based scientific approach for its methodology. That is needed not only on economic policy, but increasingly in the administration of social security, education, employment, health, transport and other departments. So the struggle for a scientific basis for economic policy is needed for such services too. But it is not a struggle to be undertaken as a confrontation. It must be fought with all the understanding, intelligence, finesse and subtlety of which, at their best, politicians, officials and all who are concerned with policy are capable.

Secondly the resources required and the scale of action needed in the special topics of science policy may be a major factor in economic policy, and make them interdependent. Without a reasonably successful economy, science is starved of resources. The success of the economy in its turn is increasingly based on the success of science and technology.

So, as Opposition Spokesman on science and technology (1983-1992) I had no qualms in undertaking further research in economic modelling and policy optimisation. I was able to employ, on a very part-time basis, a series of invaluable young research assistants. I will discuss later, in Chapter 16, the contribution my research assistants made directly to the formulation of science policy. Here I simply wish to acknowledge my indebtedness to those who worked with me on the application of the methods of science to the building of economic models.

All my research assistants have prospered since they left my employ.

One of the first was Sam Lovick, a young medical student turned computer expert, who worked in the early 1980s both on science policy and on the application of computers to model building, an immensely time consuming and difficult task, given the primitive state of computers. Sam mounted the Treasury model and programmes in the MS-DOS operating system of my BBC Acorn computer – a feat in itself. Later on he joined the faculty of the London Business School. He is now head of the Network Economics Consulting Group, Melbourne, Australia.

Sam was succeeded by Ganesh Nana, a very bright New Zealander, who was only too glad to leave his boring job of in-putting data in the NHS – all he could get – for a full-time job in my office. Ganesh did a brilliant job working on Nash games (named after the Nobel prize winning mathematician, John Nash, the subject of the book and film *A Beautiful Mind*). Together we produced a series of useful papers[3]. Ganesh now holds a senior post in economics at the Victoria University, New Zealand.

Finally in the 1990s I took on as part-timers three post-graduate student economists recommended to me by the London School of Economics: Paul Walker, Andrey Kuleshov and Ali Enis Uysal. Again, we worked collaboratively, producing important papers[4].

Paul was a South African with a very pretty, and highly intelligent, wife. His ANC connections, and his marriage across the racial boundaries, clearly marked him in South Africa as politically subversive. The South African security service's hostile reports (we were still in the days of apartheid) gave endless headaches to the Common's conscientious security vetting system. Until he got his pass Paul had to be escorted around parliamentary buildings for some months by another member of my staff.

Parliamentary security clearance for my Russian assistant, Andrey, however gave no problems at all. Andrey was descended from generations of high ranking Soviet army officers, who were of course entirely respectable according to the KGB. He was given a clean bill of health by the Russian security services, and promptly given a parliamentary pass. It was only later I was to learn that Andrey's compulsory military service during the Cold War era had been rather secret and mysteriously linked computer services and nuclear missiles. Andrey, with whom I have kept in touch, is now a Senior Researcher at the Institute of Mathematical Modelling in Moscow, after working for several years for a United Nations agency.

---

[3] Bray, Jeremy (1988) 'Policies for exchange rate stabilisation on the UK Treasury model', *Economic Modelling*, January. *ESRC Macroeconomic Modelling Seminar*, Warwick: University of Warwick, 5 July
Bray, Jeremy and Nana, Ganesh (1989a) 'International economic coordination in the G7 as a dynamic Nash game'. *Proceedings of 6th IFAC/SED Symposium on Dynamic Modelling and Control of National Economies*, London: IFAC
Bray, Jeremy and Nana, Ganesh (1989b) 'Policy Optimisation in democratic political processes'. (!989a and 1989b) both published in *Proceedings of 6th IFAC/SED Symposium on Dynamic Modelling and Control of National Economies*, London: IFAC

[4] Bray, Jeremy, Andrey Kuleshov, Ali Enis Uysal, and Paul Walker (1993) 'Balance Achieving Policies: a comparative policy optimisation study on four UK models', ESRC Macromeconomic Modelling Bureau, University of Warwick
Bray, J., Hall, S., Kuleshov, A., Nixon, J. and Westaway, P. (1995) 'The Interfaces between Policy Makers, Markets and Modellers in the Design of Economic Policy - and Intermodel Comparison' *The Economic Journal* Policy Forum July

Ali Enis Uysal was the third member of my team. I had a lot of problems with the Home Office's Immigration Department about employing Enis, who came from Turkey, though his employment was, like that of the others, part-time, and related to his course work at LSE.

Making sense of policy optimisation

To satisfy myself that it was possible to get good sense out of policy optimisation of a well constructed model using rational expectations, and despite time inconsistency considerations, from about 1986 onwards we – I and my research assistants under my guidance – carried out the exercises on the Treasury model. For example, we compared the outturn with successively updated alternative policies; we ran a G-7 multi-country game on the IMF (International Monetary Fund) model. We eventually set up a series of comparative exercises on the Treasury model, London Business School model and the National Institute of Economic and Social Research UK models[5][6]. This, in its time, was groundbreaking stuff.

By 1987 it had become practicable for a single person with a desktop computer to run non-linear policy optimisation algorithms with rational expectations on large data-based macroeconomic models. I published and circulated my results on the Treasury model for a several years to successive Chancellors of the Exchequer, to the Treasury and to others including Labour spokesmen. My published policy optimisation exercises on the Treasury model produced policy recommendations which in retrospect look as if they would have been less de-stabilising than the policies pursued. These can be compared with the record and the very readable account by Nigel Lawson[7], the Chancellor at the time, of the considerations behind economic policy making during this period.

Lawson was preoccupied to the point of obsession with the fallibility of forecasts, econometrics, models and all their uses, sometimes with some justification. Immediately after the 1979 election, according to his autobiography *The View from No. 11*[8], he tried to persuade Geoffrey Howe, then Chancellor of the Exchequer, to repeal my 1975 Industry Act amendment (for which he had voted!). According to Lawson, the move to repeal this clause was defeated by Treasury officials who argued

---

[5] Bray, J.; Kuleshov, A; Uysal, A.E & Walker, P (1993) *Balance Achieving Policies:* [Op.cit]
[6] Bray, J., Hall, S., Kuleshov, A., Nixon, J. and Westaway, P. (1995) 'The Interfaces etc. [Op.cit] *The Economic Journal* Policy Forum July 1995.
[7] Lawson, Nigel (1992) *The View from No 11* London: Bantam Press
[8] Lawson, [Op.cit]

successfully that once Parliament had been provided with 'so-called' information (Lawson's words), that entitlement could not be withdrawn. There would, moreover, be a stink if the right to the information was withdrawn when the economy was in deep trouble – or so a leak suggested.

Lawson succeeded Howe as Chancellor, presiding during his term of office (1984-1989) over a rollercoaster period of inflationary boom and bust. Lawson acknowledged that he did not foresee the full extent of the boom that began to develop. Moreover, he adds, 'I was not helped by the Treasury's economic forecasts, which despite being castigated by Labour as ludicrously optimistic, in fact seriously and consistently underestimated the strength of the outturn'.

However, as my studies at that time showed, the Treasury model, reasonably used, was warning at the time about balance of payments difficulties and the need for corrective action, long before Lawson was alerted by what he calls the 'staggering 1988 August trade figures' and the consequent rise in base rates which marked the turning point in his Chancellorship.

Among other things, Lawson highlights the Treasury's misguided over-reaction to the 1987 stock market crash as one of the 'origins' of the inflationary boom of 1988[9]. Yet I had written to him personally, within days of this event, warning against any over-reaction, and enclosing a paper, based on runs using the Treasury model, which I subsequently sent to the Treasury Select Committee (of which I was no longer a member)[10].

What secured these policy optimisation results I was getting was not better short-term forecasts than anyone else's, important though accuracy is, but the balancing of short and longer term responses against constraints, systemically secured by judicious use of policy optimisation on the model. The optimal policy studies did not call consistently for soft options, nor were they consistently pessimistic. They warned about the risks to the exchange rate, but they were not alarmist over the 1987 fall in the stock market. They were persistently better balanced and more timely than the policy pursued.

Readers who would like to follow the arguments in detail will find a fuller account of my work in the first chapter of *Money, Inflation and*

---

[9] Lawson, Nigel (1992) *The View from No 11* London: Bantam Press
[10] Bray, Jeremy (1987) *The appropriate response to the fall in the stock market* [Paper submitted to House of Commons Treasury and Civil Service Committee, and others, 21 October]

Employment: Essays in Honour of James Ball[11], where I summarise and analyse the papers I published throughout the 1980s.

I continued to publish after the 1992 General Election, though I found myself less and less able to handle the ever changing technology of economic modelling and optimisation. I was by now in my sixties, and had recently undergone major heart surgery.

Do we still need the Treasury model?

No other MP ever used the Treasury Model seriously, the Parliamentary Unit lapsed, and eventually in 1999, the Warwick Bureau itself lost its Economic and Social Research Council (ESRC) grant when the whole Macroeconomic Modelling Programme fell victim to jealousies from softer social sciences within the ESRC. The work it had supported was left to fish with little success in the general pool of ESRC research funds.

I urged Bob May, as Chief Scientific Adviser (and now President of the Royal Society) to remonstrate with Terry Burns, who had become Permanent Secretary of the Treasury. I believe he did so, but to no avail.

When Gordon Brown wanted an audit of Treasury forecasts, he did not turn to the ESRC and the Warwick Bureau. Instead he turned to the much less expert General Accounting Office. But the staff of the GAO had not even attended the relevant conferences and workshops. So they had to depend on advice from the Treasury officials – officials of the very department whose work the General Accounting Office was meant to be auditing.

There is currently a rather trendy view that forecasting (one of the key activities of the Treasury model team) can be dismissed as at best a minor and subsidiary activity. This seems to be the position of David Lipsey, as expressed in his fascinating *The Secret Treasury – How Britain's Economy is really run*[12]. Treasury forecasts, he says, now 'matter less'. What has changed over the years, he says, 'is not the accuracy of the forecasts. It is their importance.' I would disagree: the accuracy of forecasts has improved markedly. And forecasts still matter, however unfashionable it may be to acknowledge this.

Lipsey goes on to give this brief (and misleading) summary of the history of attitudes to forecasting:

---

[11] Holly, Sean (Ed.) (1994) *Money, Inflation and Employment: Essays in honour of James Ball*, Aldershot: Edward Elgar, pp. 3-25.
[12] Lipsey, David *The Secret Treasury – How Britain's Economy is really run* London: Viking 2000

14: Opening up access to the Treasury Model 1984-1993 ♦ 163

At Keynesianism's height, the forecaster was king. In the 1960s, for example, when Harold Wilson's government was fiddling around with experiments in planning, forecasts were central to the project....

Britain in the 1960s and 1970s was still prisoner to a Keynesian orthodoxy which said that government, through fiscal policy, could 'fine-tune' the economy to ensure growth. Britain in the 1980s and 1990s was a prisoner to an alternative post-Keynesian orthodoxy which said it could do no such thing. But of course if it was powerless to fine-tune, the forecasts that told it how to fine-tune were powerless also.

So why do it? The question gets asked in the Treasury every couple of years. Kenneth Clarke in particular as chancellor asked it. A well-known and public sceptic about forecasts, he insisted that the Treasury consider 'outsourcing' ...

This reads a little like *1066 and All That*!

The so-called 'forecasts' used by the early Wilson governments in the 1960s were indeed wildly inaccurate. This is not surprising. They were back-of-an-envelope jobs based on unreliable and inadequate statistical evidence, which predate the statistical reforms introduced in the second Wilson government 1966-70. (Readers will recall that these reforms were introduced on the recommendation of a Select Committee I had chaired in the mid-1960s[13].) Moreover, there was *no* Treasury model in the 1960s. It was only conceived in about 1969[14], had a long gestation period, and only gradually came to maturity in the late 1970s and early 80s. Over the past thirty years the accuracy and usefulness of forecasts has improved significantly, as I hope I have shown.

Lord Lipsey may be reflecting current views within the Treasury and among outside observers. If so, it indicates how easy it is for recent history to be rubbished, and the modest disclaimers of experienced forecasters to be taken at face value. Even Lipsey concedes,

> The Treasury could hardly do without any forecasting capacity. It has to be able to give the chancellor a view of what would happen to the economy if he (say) doubled taxes or halved spending. For this it needs some numbers. But in principle that is not decisive. For it requires only the most exiguous capacity: a personal computer, a secondary model, a routine mathematical exercise...

---

[13] See Chapter 4, pp 58-60, 64-65.
[14] See Chapter 5, pp 74-76.

So the question has to be whether the Treasury should retain its role as a primary forecaster on a substantial scale. The Fundamental Expenditure Review considered the case in some detail – and concluded that it should. ...

... There is no doubt that forecasting is a highly imprecise and uncertain business; indeed no one is more aware of the uncertainties involved than the forecasters themselves.

However, we regard it as completely implausible that the Treasury would want (or be allowed by Parliament and the public) to eschew completely any attempt to predict the likely path of the economy over the period ahead. Forward economic projections and assumptions are clearly essential to the tasks of planning public expenditure, determining appropriate interest rates and so on. Indeed, the treasury would not be able to carry out any of its core macroeconomic responsibilities if it had no view of what was likely to happen to the economy in the future.

I would agree with at least on that last point: without the model the Treasury could not carry out its core macro-economic responsibilities.

The Treasury model: a tribute

Since I left the House in 1997 no MP or peer has used the Treasury model seriously, which was a shame because it was – and, I very much hope, still is – easily the best UK model.

The reasons for its excellence are first the superb AMODEL Fortran software that David Rampton wrote and maintained; and second, the tender loving care which Rod Whittaker has given the model over many years. Both of these dedicated civil servants maintained the highest professional standards, as did other first rate economists who worked on the model. These are the unsung heroes who kept British economic policy at least on nodding terms with the rails, if not always on them.

The Treasury Model furthermore underlies a number of other forecasts regularly made by bodies such as Item Club run by city analysts Ernst and Young. Without this public critique economic debate would be even poorer than it is. But their work is so briefly reported in the broadsheet press and the media that it has little impact on debate in the chamber of the House of Commons, including the debates on the autumn statement and the budget, or on the work of Treasury and other Select Committees. It remains however available for use.

15

New Labour's macroeconomic policy as it emerged
1992-1997

In 1996, during the run-up to the election, I carried out a series of exercises on the Treasury model on my desktop model, and wrote up the results as a paper for the incoming Labour government. I entitled this, *Labour's Options for Economic Policy: an appraisal of medium term prospects using the Treasury Model*. I circulated it to both Tony Blair and Gordon Brown, and other spokesmen, but did not publish it.

Here is part of what I said:

> Using the Treasury model, as of May 1996, the policy design problem which is a serious concern for the medium term is that whatever the rate of economic growth, public borrowing will not fall to sustainable levels under present tax rates and expenditure plans.
>
> If however in 1997 tax and spending plans are changed to correct this deficit, it should be possible to sustain a growth rate of GDP at around 3% from 1998 through to 2002 with unemployment falling to 2.5%, the current balance going into modest surplus, with modest tax reductions and public borrowing less than 2.5% of GDP, with sustained real increases in public spending and a reduction in the rates of tax. Inflation should remain less than 2.5% throughout.
>
> There is a long term constraint on the rate of growth after 2002, indicated by the rate of unemployment falling to levels which under present skill distributions would reflect a shortage of skills. There is however time to address such structural constraints if sufficient steps are taken in 1997.

That does not compare badly with the outcome, except for the deterioration in the balance of payments, caused partly by the uncompetitive exchange rate which made it easier to hold inflation down and to allow real disposable income to grow within the monetary constraints, for a while.

The run-up to 1997: Lessons from America

Soon after Tony Blair succeeded John Smith as Leader of the Opposition, Blair and Brown went off to Washington. This was in January 1993. They planned to meet some of the team that the newly elected President Clinton was taking into office. In particular, Gordon wished to meet Lawrence Summers, professor of economics at Harvard, and destined to become US Treasury Secretary. Summers, a broad brush economist, is the nephew of two Nobel prize winners in economics. Gordon Brown was introduced by Edward Balls, a Financial Times journalist, and a former student of Lawrence Summers.

At that time the US was enjoying a period of unparalleled growth and seemed to provide a good model. Indeed, 1987 to 2000 was the longest peacetime continuous expansion in American history. There were useful lessons to be learned. The performance of the US economy was a painful contrast to Britain's experience. Just cast your mind back to this period – the massive unemployment of the Thatcher years, the Lawson boom and bust, our humiliating exit from the ERM on Black Wednesday...

Was Gordon Brown wise to rely so heavily on US experience? Yes – and no.

US macroeconomic policy-making

The US economy, and the problems and challenges of macroeconomic policy-making in the US, differ in some important respects from that of the UK. The federal constitution of the US, and the separation of powers between the President, Congress, and the Supreme Court, make fiscal policy, and the interaction of fiscal and monetary policy, not only much more complicated, but also much more difficult to handle politically, than in the UK. On the other hand, the continental size of the US economy makes the exchange rate less important than it is for us. Britain also has a far more open economy, with exports and imports more than twice those of the US when measured as percentages of GDP. For the UK and other economies with an important foreign sector, the exchange rate has to be taken into consideration.

In no small part, the improved performance and stability of the USA economy owed much to the scores of economists, econometricians and control engineers who have been hard at work since the 1970s. They have greatly improved our understanding and the quality of economic management, often at a very practical level, as will become clearer when I discuss later on in this chapter one product of this research – the so-called Taylor rule[1].

The independent, high-powered, competing schools of economists in academia in the US have no inhibitions on the use of technical mathematical methods or the scope of analysis. The Federal Reserve Board is responsible for a relatively self-contained area of policy (monetary policy – setting interest rates). The Fed engages in high-powered research on its own account, and participates fully in an on-going dialogue with academia.

Powers of taxation and expenditure, and exchange rate policy, rest with the President, the US Treasury and Congress. These have no comparable research effort (and, from the perspective of 2002, the lack of expertise shows now as the US economy slows ominously).

The role of the Federal Reserve Board

The Federal Reserve Board, a US federal agency, was created by Congress after a panic in 1907. Since then the Fed has been very careful to observe and to ensure accountability for its actions to Congress, and not to the Administration. It is helped in this by the Humphrey-Hawkins legislation that requires semi-annual reports to Congress on the state of the economy, and explanations of policy. In many ways the Fed is quite open and responsive, if one does not get overly anxious about rules and targets.

The main policy instruments of the Federal Reserve Board are the setting of short-term interest rates, and intervention in money markets. The rate of interest is decided by the Federal Open Market Committee, which is made up of members of the Board and of the Federal Reserve Banks from different parts of the US. They are in touch with business conditions throughout the US, and they use their own judgement in deciding how to vote on policy issues. They are supported by briefing, models and expert analysis from the research staff of the Federal Reserve Board in Washington, and of the discrete Federal Reserve Banks.

The Federal Reserve Board was clearly a model which Gordon Brown had in mind as he considered the role of the Bank of England.

---

[1] See later in this this chapter, page 173 *ff*

President Clinton's advisers ... and Gordon Brown's

You will recall that on his visit to the USA in 1993, Gordon met Lawrence Summers, soon to be appointed US Treasury Secretary. On Summers' recommendation, Gordon recruited Edward Balls, a fluent and very able *Financial Times* journalist, as his economic adviser. It was a long term commitment: by now, May 2002, Balls is virtually second-in-command at the Treasury. So his opinions and attitudes matter.

However, it was with some disquiet that, in February 1994, I read Ed Balls' tirade against models in his final contributions to the *Financial Times*[2], published the day before Balls became full time economics adviser to Gordon Brown, then shadow Chancellor.

Balls' article was headlined: 'The Markets: No advantage in pseudo-scientific futurology'. He declared:

> The willingness of newspapers to report the outpourings of model-based forecasters gives economists a terribly bad name. If manipulating giant and complex statistical models of the world economy delivered reliable results then all would be fine. But the recent record of the UK Treasury, the IMF or the OECD has been miserable. ...
>
> Economics is just not suited to the kind of pseudo-scientific futurology that these models purport to deliver. ...

Most of the best UK City economists, he claimed, eschew large-scale models. They were successful, he said, 'precisely because they continually doubt whether the future will be like the past. Their value lies in their analysis, although it is their forecasts which make the headlines.'

Now of course, this was written in February 1994. Just cast your eye back over the events of the previous fifteen years: see-sawing interest rates, soaring unemployment, exchange rate problems, inflationary booms, and most recently the mortifying exit from the ERM (the European Exchange Rate Mechanism) on Black Wednesday, 16 September 1992 ... But these were hardly the result of Prime Ministers Thatcher and Major, and their succession of Chancellors, interesting themselves on the Treasury model. Indeed, the opposite was the truth.

Ed Balls' article no doubt reflected his own view at the time. But it also positioned him comfortably between his boss at the time, Sam Brittan, the Editor of the *FT*, and his mentor, Lawrence Summers. It reminded me of a

---

[2] Balls, Ed (1994) 'The Markets: No advantage in pseudo-scientific futurology' *Financial Times* 21 February

15 : New Labour's macroeconomic policy as it emerged 1992-97 ♦ 169

bit of fun Sam had had back in 1981 when he was roundly attacking what he called the 'bogus science' of a Treasury Select Committee Report[3] which was critical of Thatcherite monetary policy.

Summers' position had been well set out in his paper, 'The Scientific Illusion in Empirical Macroeconomics'[4], published the previous year, 1991. After a swingeing attack on macroeconomic modelling he strongly stated his preference for

> verbal characterisations of how causal relations might operate rather than explicit mathematical models, and the skilful use of carefully chosen natural experiments rather than sophisticated statistical technique to achieve identification.

'Surely,' he argues,

> Friedman and Schwartz *A Monetary History of the United States 1867-1960* (1963)[5] had a greater impact in highlighting the role of money than any particular econometric study or combination of studies. It was not based on a formal economic model, no structural parameters were estimated, and no sophisticated statistical techniques were employed. Instead, data were presented in a straightforward way, to buttress verbal theoretical arguments, and emphasis was placed on natural experiments in assessing directions of causality.

Friedman and Schwartz, you will recall, were the master-minds behind Thatcher's disastrous experiment with monetarism.

My worry is that, if Balls still holds that modelling is 'pseudo-scientific futurology', the previous very high quality of research in the Treasury, and the long careful tending of the Treasury model, may be in danger of being neglected. I have already note with concern that, according to David Lipsey (whom I quoted in the previous chapter), 'crystal ball gazing' in the Treasury is treated with scepticism and possibly derision[6]. I hope this is not an indication of Balls' continuing attitude.

True, the Bank of England now carries the can for monetary policy (setting interest rates), and fortunately the Bank has long maintained its own models of the economy.[7] (The Bank of England models of the

---

[3] See Chapter 12, page 146.
[4] Summers, Lawrence (1991) *Scand. J. of Economics 93(2)*, 129-148.
[5] Friedman, Milton and Schwartz, Anna (1963), *A Monetary History of the United States 1867-1960*, Princeton
[6] See Chapter 14, pp. 162-164
[7] See *Economic Models at the Bank of England* (1999) Published by the Bank of England.

economy, incidentally, have long used the programmes written by PROPE; the Bank of England indeed supported and funded the development of PROPE)[8].

But it is the Chancellor who is responsible for fiscal policies (taxation, expenditure). He needs high quality evidence-based data and forecasts. In particular, he needs good forecasts to make his 'Golden Rule' viable. I can only applaud Gordon's adoption of the 'Golden Rule'. But its introduction to the general public could have been better managed.

The 'Golden Rule'

I remember, before the 1997 election, asking Gordon about New Labour's economic policies. End STOP-GO, he said, and TAX-and-SPEND. Fair enough. But that has been the policy of every Chancellor for the past forty years. Their problem was not the intent, but the achievement.

Of course, Gordon, who is very bright, had cards up his sleeve, cards which he was very reluctant to display. But he was not an economist, and, like every Chancellor of the Exchequer before him has done, he has had to learn on the job. (Whether there is a less expensive way to train Chancellors is a different question).

Regrettably the Brown-Blair method of policy-making by what has been called 'briefing and bounce' – with speeches perfunctorily cleared with Shadow colleagues on the eve of delivery, only to be hastily corrected if indefeasible – could sometime land Gordon in trouble.

In the run-up to the 1997 General Election, the only way for colleagues to make even drafting corrections was to catch the policy on the first bounce. This is a somewhat shambolic way to make economic policy. For example, Gordon Brown's 'Golden Rule' – his key fiscal policy rule – emerged into the light of day while he was still Shadow Chancellor.

Here is the correct (or rather, the corrected) version:

> We will enforce the 'golden rule' of public spending – over the economic cycle, we will only borrow to invest and not to fund current expenditure.
>
> We will ensure that – over the economic cycle – public debt as a proportion of national income is at a stable and prudent level.

However, when the 'Golden Rule' was leaked to, or by, the *Guardian*, the qualification 'over the economic cycle' appeared only once. To avoid an

---

[8] See Chapter 9 for my involvement with the development of PROPE.

unintended arithmetical stranglehold, it was needed twice, to operate independently on both borrowing and debt. As soon as I spotted this, I took a letter round to Gordon's office, with a copy for Ed Balls, his assistant, by mid morning. They immediately revised the 'Golden Rule' scrupulously, if inelegantly.

It remains a touchstone of New Labour fiscal policy – and a rather successful one.

New Labour at the helm: the Bank of England

When Labour swept into power in 1997, its first act was put the Bank of England (like the Fed) in charge of monetary policy. The Bank was instructed to use interest rates to hold inflation within a narrow band. To give credit where credit is due, this by and large has been a very successful policy decision.

Viewed simply, greater flexibility can be achieved by having fiscal policy (using instruments such as taxes and government expenditure) and monetary policy (using interest rates) at the disposal of a single authority which has all the information and powers available. This was the state of affairs in the pre-1997 UK Treasury.

The Chancellor, Gordon Brown, by dividing the powers, was in effect acknowledging that Chancellors of the Exchequer, as politicians, cannot be trusted with the combined powers; or, from the point of view of the Chancellor, that he will be more trusted if he chooses to delegate his monetary policy decisions to the Bank of England.

The move was timely. The digestion and development of economic policy-making ideas and methods at this period was proving fruitful in application.

The Golden Rule in practice

The 'Golden Rule' is actually a prudent re-statement of neo-Keynesian economics, and in many ways it has served New Labour well. Fortune smiled on the incoming Labour government as the century drew to a close and the US economy powered onwards. Commendably, significant repayments were made of the national debt, thus reducing interest charges. Here at last was a safe pair of hands: a competent Labour Chancellor, whom the electorate felt could be trusted.

However by now – I am writing in April 2002 – the US economy is in recession and a risky and very expensive war in the Middle East is threatening. President Bush's irresponsible tax-cutting economic policies seem to me to be unlikely to lead to stable, sustainable growth.

The Chancellor will find his critics sharpening their pens if the British economy falters. The current stock market's collapse (April 2002) is probably unimportant except insofar as it has seriously damaged final salary and other pension funds. It will recover, if slowly. But my guess is there will almost certainly be occasions when the Treasury forecasts of growth, and revenue, will have to be revised, and revised downwards. With serious instability in the global economy, such errors are inevitable. Now is the time in the economic cycle, according to the 'Golden Rule', to pump money into the economy to counter the cyclical downturn. There will inevitably be criticism. I hope the Chancellor will stand his ground. However, it may be a bumpy ride.

Large increases in investment in public services were announced in the 2002 budget. However, this stop-go regime – the 'prudent' adherence to Tory spending plans for the first years of the New Labour government, followed by fairly massive increases more recently – makes delivery extremely difficult. Fluctuating investment in public services is counter-productive. Public services require steady investment supported by careful consultation and planning, a balance between competing priorities, and agreed long-term goals.

Unfortunately, the Blair style is all about setting targets, often plucked from the air. Such targets get headlines, but can become a political encumbrance, particularly if there is no empirical evidence that they are deliverable. They often have unintended consequences, and distort delivery of other equally desirable outcomes. They are no substitute for sound long-term planning based on adequate statistical data and competent analysis and modelling.

The Public Private Finance Initiative

This leads on to a cause for concern for me: the Public Finance Initiative (the PFI) or the Public Private Initiative (PPI). I will not rehearse the many well known reservations that many Labour MPs and trades unionists have, shared by commentators and economists.

My particular concern is how the PFI or PPI is dealt with in the Treasury model, and also in other models. We are told that the funding for these schemes does not count as public borrowing. This has obvious attractions for the government, but it appears to me to be – how shall I put it? – economical with the truth. It is our future that is being mortgaged: these are debts that must be repaid.

Unfortunately, I am no longer able to run the Treasury model on my desktop computer. It is not that the model is unavailable to a *bona fide* private individual. It is available. But I no longer have the skills and concentration. In my last years in parliament I found modelling a struggle even with the assistance of my research team. Now, with serious health problems, and a limited life expectancy, I do not have the time, the skills and the energy required.

I hope however that competent research teams will still be checking the Treasury model and reporting any inconsistencies.

The emergence of the 'Taylor rule'

Unlike the UK, the US abandoned fixed intermediate targets (such as the money supply, favoured by the Thatcher governments) as early as 1982. Since that date, the Federal Reserve Fund's interest rate has been set in response to a wide variety of factors and forecasts, latterly with widespread attention to macroeconomic policy rules and the evidence from its own models of the economy and the models of the top academic research teams.

The prolonged, steady boom of the 1990s owed not a little to an underlying stability which this method of working engendered.

Alan Greenspan[9], Chairman of the Federal Reserve Board, speaking in 1997 at the 15th Anniversary Conference of the Centre for Economic Policy Research at Stanford University, reviewed these developments. He concluded:

> Another type of rule using readings on output and prices to help guide monetary policy, such as John Taylor's, has attracted widening interest in recent years in the financial markets, the academic community, and at central banks. ...
>
> [The rules] have a number of attractive features. They assume that central banks can appropriately pay attention simultaneously to developments in both output and inflation, provided their reactions

---

[9] Greenspan, Alan, (1997) Chairman of the Federal Reserve Board, 15th Anniversary Conference of the Centre for Economic Policy Research at Stanford University, September 5.

occur within the context of a longer-run goal of price stability and that they recognise that activity is limited by the economy's sustainable potential.

The Taylor rule provides a guideline for setting interest rates to target the rate of inflation, and the percentage deviation of real GDP from potential GDP. It was named after Professor John Taylor of Stanford, but many economists contributed to its formulation and development, its testing in sophisticated models and in analysis and research.

When Taylor[10] presented his multi-country model in 1993, complete with its estimation methods, applications in the development of national macroeconomic policy guidelines, and their testing, it was acclaimed by economists as diverse as Bob Lucas, the father of rational expectations, and Ralph Bryant, formerly Director of the Division of International Finance of the Federal Reserve Board.

Professor Taylor[11] later reported that

> Research on monetary policy rules has mushroomed since the early 1990s and is now being conducted at many universities, central banks, research institutes and private financial firms. In a relatively short span of time, an enormous amount of information has been generated by this research effort. This heightened interest in policy evaluation has enabled researchers to examine the robustness of proposed policy rules with much more depth and rigour than ever before.

So what had Taylor done?

A rather remarkable feat.

Taylor[12] had demonstrated the effect of five different policy rules simulated on nine different models, including the large Fed (Federal Reserve Fund) model, and his own large multi-country model, treating separately each of the seven G7 members. You need a lot of computing power, and powerful software, to achieve this.

The Taylor rules give guidance on the short-term nominal interest rate required, given the target and actual inflation rates, and the percentage

---

[10] Taylor, John B. (1993) *Macroeconomic Policy in a World Economy: from econometric design to practical operation.* New York: Norton

[11] Taylor, John B. (1999) 'The Robustness and Efficiency of Monetary Policy Rules as Guidelines for Interest Rate Setting by the European Central Bank,' *Journal of Monetary Economics*, 43, June, 655-79

[12] Taylor, John B. (1993) *Op. cit.* New York:: Norton

deviation of real GDP from potential GDP. The Lucas critique of time consistency is avoided by inspecting the performance of the rule with different values of its coefficients and selecting a set of fixed coefficients which perform reasonably. The rule is then applied at all times in the relevant period, and not revised for each successive initial time. Policy optimisation may be used in an initial exploratory stage to choose the constant parameter values in a fixed rule. There is then very little lost in choosing constant parameter values, which will probably lie well within the standard errors of estimates of the optimal rule parameters.

Targeting forecast-inflation in the UK (a Taylor-type rule)

Gordon Brown's first act as Chancellor, as you recall, had been to hand over monetary policy to the Bank of England. American research supported this move, and provided policy rules for fixing interest rates. In the UK it is popularly understood that the Bank of England's job is to set interest rates so that inflation is held in a relatively narrow band, neither too high nor too low. This judgement is based on the deliberations of the Bank's monetary committee, their advisers, and evidence from the Bank's own model of the economy.

Now changing the Bank's interest rate does not necessarily have an immediate effect on inflation. Indeed there are considerable lags following any change in the Bank's base rate of interest, which you can track on a model. A change may impact on inflation perhaps as much as two years ahead, through the effect it has on investment, borrowing, mortgages, pensions funds, the stock market, exchange rates, and so on. So it is vitally important that the Bank's own forecasts for inflation are based on good evidence and careful modelling[13].

There is, mathematically speaking, no difference between forecast-inflation targeting (as in the UK since 1997), and an interest rate feedback rule, such as the Taylor-type rule defined above – no difference, if the model of the economy is known and well-based.

Targeting forecast-inflation is in fact a popularly explicable, 'arm chair' version, of a rule. The 'arm chair' version is easier for finance ministers and central bankers to pontificate about to lay audiences, who will not ask awkward questions about how forecasts are made.

---

[13] *Economic Models in the Bank of England* (1999) London: Bank of England
See also the Bank's Internet pages at *http://www.bankofengland.co.uk*

In practice forecast-inflation targeting is likely to use more information than the simple feedback rules generally used, with small reductions in standard deviations but some loss in robustness and transparency. Targets for inflation have been explicitly stated in Canada, New Zealand, Sweden and the UK and implicitly in the US and Germany since 1998 or earlier.

The Bank of England, like all other central banks, does not use fixed parameter feedback rules actually to set policy. But many central banks find empirical feedback rules provide useful benchmark tests of policy over time. And for private agents, feedback rules, including both the inflation target and the expected response to deviations from target, are used by agents to forecast future policy changes.

The exchange rate again – and the balance of trade

A worry in the UK is still, in 2002 as in 1981, the exchange rate. The exchange rate has been giving trouble since 1999, as trade deficits mount up. But this has rarely been remarked upon. The loss of competitiveness of the pound has aggravated the difficulties of those industries which were experiencing problems due to the recent trade recession: Vauxhall and Rover, for example in the motor industry, have folded; Llanwern in the steel industry has gone; Motorola in mobile telephones and much of the textile industry has more or less disappeared. Enterprises in some industries are committed to long-term investments in assets (such as plant and machinery), which cannot easily be sold. So they are vulnerable to variations in the exchange rate which can make their costs uncompetitive. A consequence of an unstable exchange rate is that the whole of technologically advanced manufacturing is in danger of becoming too risky.

Making the exchange rate an intermediate target would amount to pegging the exchange rate. That has the effect of making the home interest rate a noisy replica of the foreign interest rate, importing the interest rate consequences of monetary policy in, for example, the US or Europe.

The accepted view is that inflation targeting is a better policy than exchange rate targeting. This is not however an either/or choice. It is possible to put some weight on each, and explore the sensitivities, as was proposed to us on the Treasury Select Committee in 1983 by Artis and Karakitsos[14], and frequently reported by myself and my team as we began to use the Treasury model on desktop computers in the late 1980s and early

---

[14] See Chapter 13, pages 154-155.

1990s[15]. I would hope that it is still being carefully monitored by today's research teams.

This could be met by extending Greenspan's description of the Taylor Rule referred to earlier in this chapter to read:

> The rule assumes that central banks can appropriately pay attention simultaneously to developments in output, inflation and the exchange rate, provided their reactions occur within the context of a longer-run goal of price stability and that they recognise that activity is limited by the economy's sustainable potential.

The rule would have to provide for the difference between the exchange rate and the fundamental equilibrium exchange rate to play the same role as the difference between GDP and productive potential does today.

From my perspective, writing in April 2002, I think the trade deficit needs to be watched. If the deficit in goods and services continues to mount, pulling in imports, it could in time become very damaging to the real economy. It could also generate an instability in the value of the pound which would make it difficult for the Bank of England to meet its inflation target.

Of course, the situation may change overnight – for better or for worse. But that is in the nature of the international monetary system.

---

[15] See footnote, Chapter 14, page 159.

Part Four

SPOKESMAN FOR SCIENCE & TECHNOLOGY

Jeremy with Neil Kinnock in 1984
Reproduced with kind permission of J R Smith, Chorlton, Manchester.

Introduction to Part Four

SPOKESMAN FOR SCIENCE & TECHNOLOGY

In the mid-1980s I changed my focus when Neil Kinnock, on becoming leader of the Labour Party, offered me the welcome opportunity to serve as Labour Science spokesperson. I was thrilled by the offer of the science job, and felt privileged to return to the front bench after fourteen years' absence.

There are, I believe three good reasons for seeking a successful science policy: the intellectual success of science in exploring the world in which we live; the usefulness of technologies which can address our needs and aspirations; and the power of science as a source of ideas.

Unfortunately, despite the success and centrality of science and technology, parliament (and the media) has by and large consigned science policy to the margins of politics. Most politicians – and most journalists – lack a scientific background, and find the issues unfamiliar and (in career terms) unprofitable. Yet science and technology are our future.

As Labour science spokesman from 1983 to 1992 I was able, with the encouragement and support of Neil Kinnock, to argue the case for the key role of science and technology in every aspect of government policy.

Few politicians, and probably even fewer reporters on the parliamentary scene, appreciate the extent to which science shapes the way our economy develops, and that science, technology and innovation are the key to industrial success. The machinery of government is in urgent need of an institutional framework to harness this latent power. But this requires vision. Parliament is ill-equipped to hold ministers to account, or to engage in serious debate on scientific issues. This is in no small part due to the fact that a parliamentary career offers few opportunities and rewards to practising scientists. And the fact that scientists ignore the possible long-term gains of building up a good working relationship with their local MP.

Introduction to Part Four

During Neil Kinnock's time as Leader of the Opposition (and mine as Opposition Spokesman for Science and Technology), Labour's manifesto pledges in the 1987 and 1992 General Elections took science policy seriously. I was responsible for framing our commitments on science and technology. These, if implemented, would have set science policy on a new course. Had Labour won in 1992 I had good reason to hope that I might have played a key part. But Labour was narrowly defeated. To be fair, Prime Minister John Major did take over our proposals for an Office of Science and Technology. It did not survive as a significant ministerial post and machine for growth in the cabinet reshuffles which followed.

Science policy remains in limbo despite – or more probably because of – New Labour's victories in 1997 and 2001.

To give credit where credit is due, since 1997 the Chancellor, Gordon Brown, has consistently given higher priority to the funding of research and development than his predecessors. Apart from this, however, decisions lack coherence. There is no evidence of a wider interpretation of science policy. By and large ministers (and the media) have a blind spot here. Few if any New Labour cabinet ministers have a grounding in science. Blair has initiated a number of major constitutional changes, often in a rather piecemeal and opportunist fashion. But he has failed to address the fundamental questions about the role of science and technology, and its place in the machinery of government. This is a grave defect. It limits our ability to handle vital questions. I am deeply disappointed.

The responsibility for this dire state of affairs however rests not only on government, parliament and the media, but also on scientists themselves.

As Labour Spokesman for Science and Technology I was constantly amazed by the way that high-minded scientists who spent weeks, or in some cases, months, of their precious time in making grant applications yet felt it was beneath them to invite their own MP to visit their lab annually on a regular basis. Why? Apathy? Ignorance? Arrogance?

I would urge scientists at all levels to build up and maintain contacts with MPs, to share not only their problems but also their understanding of the challenges that lie ahead and the very real contribution science can make in so many fields, including fields related to core political concerns.

I stepped down from the front bench after the 1992 election, and the death of John Smith. But I continued to work on economic policy, and, through the Select Committee on Science and Technology, on questions as diverse as global warming, AIDS and the human genome, until I retired from parliament in 1997.

PART FOUR

SPOKESMAN FOR SCIENCE & TECHNOLOGY

16   **OPPOSITION SPOKESMAN FOR SCIENCE AND**   184
      TECHNOLOGY 1983-1992

      Meeting and listening to scientists ~ Government's failure to support Research and Development ~ Parliament as a science policy forum ~ Arguing the case for basic funding for R&D ~ Research and development as a factor in economic growth ~ The public understanding of science ~ The useful role of special institutions ~ Formulating and proposing science policies

17   **SCIENCE POLICY AS AN ELECTION ISSUE IN 1987 AND**   194
      1992

      Science policy as an issue in the 1987 General Election ~ Science policy as an election issue in the 1992 General Election ~ The argument on technological competitiveness ~ Targets for R&D proposed by Labour ~ Did Labour's proposals on R&D funding have any effect? ~ Science at the heart of the government: machinery of government ~ The launch of Labour Party Science and Technology Policy Proposals ~ The 1992 campaign – and the outcome ~ After the 1992 election: the Conservative government ~ and the Opposition

Introduction to Part Four ♦ 183

18 **THE SCIENCE AND TECHNOLOGY SELECT** 204
    COMMITTEE 1992-1997

   Lobbying to launch a Select Committee on Science and
   Technology 1992 ~ The work of the Science and
   Technology Select Committee 1993-1997 ~ The Select
   Committee Report on Human Genetics ~ Dolly the
   sheep – and Blair's response ~ The strengths and
   limitations of the Science Select Committee

19 **SCIENCE IN PARLIAMENT AND IN GOVERNMENT** 211

   Handling epidemics: BSE (1996) and Foot and Mouth
   (2001) ~ New Labour's style of handling evidence ~
   Science policy in parliament and government under New
   Labour ~ Joined up government ~ The place of science
   in the machinery of government ~ The Haldane Report
   on the machinery of government ~ Science at the heart
   of government

20 **FAREWELL TO PARLIAMENT 1997** 221

   I bid farewell to parliament ~ Farewell to my
   constituency ~ Farewell to Ravenscraig ~ Retirement

16

Opposition Spokesman for Science and Technology
1983-1992

My own responsibility for Labour Party science policy began shortly after the 1983 General Election and lasted nine years until after the 1992 general election.

I felt I had done all that I could do in the forum offered by the Treasury and Civil Service Select Committee on the broad front of economic policy before the 1983 election, and welcomed the freedom to return to science and technology when Neil Kinnock, newly elected as Leader of the Labour Party, offered me the spokesperson role. I had supported Neil in his election as leader, and I think it was John Smith who suggested I should do the science job: we had worked together on various constituency industry matters as Lanarkshire MPs. I confess I was glad to return to the front bench after an absence of fourteen years, a long exile.

It was an exciting challenge. There are, I believe, some powerful reasons for seeking a successful science policy.

Science has been brilliantly successful in exploring the world in which we live. Its technologies have proved extraordinarily useful in addressing our needs and aspirations. Thirdly, science and technology offer us a source of ideas – patterns, strategies, models – which help us better to describe and react to those practical social and political problems we need to cope with.

However, in practice, politicians and governments are primarily interested in science as an instrument for addressing our needs and aspirations. But (I believe) science policy cannot function without due attention to the other two aspects – the success of science in exploring our world, and science as a source of ideas: patterns, strategies and models.

Meeting and listening to scientists

An immediate bonus of my new job was the access it gave to scientists. The motives which guide individual scientists in their personal choice of occupations, of interests and of research projects often influence or shape outcomes. And to secure particular outcomes we have to start with the motivation of scientists who are the agents to bring it about.

My first impression on taking up political responsibility for Labour Party concerns in this field was the extraordinary health and fecundity of science and technology.

Over the next decade I was to meet scientists working in industry, research institutes, and universities the length and breadth of Britain. Every one was keen to talk. I enjoyed listening to them on the bench and in their offices describing their work, understanding their enthusiasm, sharing their excitements and disappointments, seeing how their research fitted into or departed from the business of the firm or the work of their faculty colleagues. I appreciated their concerns and confidences, and could at least offer them my own continuing interest through the ups and downs of work at the frontiers. There were young scientists full of enthusiasm, seeking their first post-doc appointment; others looking in vain for a permanent appointment; directors of industrial research looking for resources to open up a new technology; and the heads of research councils matching the resources they were getting against the objectives their political masters were keen to set.

I remember asking one group of science undergraduates why they were doing science. Was it to benefit the community? Or to make a living? To win a Nobel Prize? Or to build a new business? For most it was none of these. It was because they were good at science, and found it the most fascinating thing they could do: a healthy reply. But it did seem to me that the enthusiasm of young scientists was being unfairly exploited by a system which failed to outline the longer-term prospects. The insecurity of funding, and the temporary nature of almost all post-doctoral posts, is extremely worrying. So too is the brain drain – symptomatic of a short-termism due, in no small part, to a failure in government policy-making. Vague government promises or schemes are not enough. There has to be a set of values, objectives and practices which people can make their own.

Most MPs are much influenced by personal contacts, especially with their own constituents who come to them with their problems and aspirations. Of particular interest to MPs are the many ways in which the results of research are brought to the service of the public. Scientists are not alone in sometimes failing to capitalise on this when they themselves seek to engage their MP's support. Unfortunately, many scientists, even those who depend on public funding and goodwill, regard politics as an alien activity. And they do little to disguise their lack of respect for politics.

However, scientists in all fields would be well advised to invite their own constituency MPs to their laboratories on a regular basis – ideally at least once a year (that is to say, four times in the course of a parliament) – to explain the significance, the relevance and potential, and the excitement of the work they do, as well as the constraints, whether they are lack of funding, problems with public understanding, or regulations. I myself learnt an immense amount from scientists, and many of my parliamentary colleagues would benefit from such encounters.

Government's failure to support R&D (Research and Development)

From my own contacts with scientists, and from a study of national statistics, it was clear that all was not well in the science field.

In the 1980s the Institute of Fiscal Studies kept a watching brief on the situation – and still does[1]. By the mid 1980s their findings signalled the re-emergence of disturbing indications that Britain was falling behind in the global technology race.

Figures published in the early 1980s in Department of Trade and Industry's surveys, had been showing a marked expansion in research and development in industry both in terms of resources and manpower. This had been reassuring.

However, the sharp deterioration in our economy, leading to balance of trade crises, exchange rate problems, and, in the 1980s, massive unemployment, was sapping resources for R&D just at the time when they were most needed.

Moreover, reductions in public expenditure – a key principle of the Thatcher government – had cut the budget of the Department of Education and Science substantially. The dual system of funding, and the cuts in university budgets, had effectively sharply reduced research activity. The strains showed in the poor prospects for postdoctoral research assistants after their first two temporary posts.

A really worrying fact was that the proportion of GDP (the Gross Domestic Product) devoted to R&D (Research and Development) fell

---

[1] http://www.ifs.org.uk/innovation/randdcredit.shtml

during the 1980s (see below). By contrast the R&D intensity of our main competitors had risen. This fact could not be explained simply by the rapid contraction of the UK manufacturing sector since the ratio of manufacturing R&D to value added also fell during the 1980s.

Table: Industrial R&D/GDP in G7 Countries			
Country	*1981*	*1985*	*1990*
Canada	1.21	1.38	1.29
France	1.18	1.33	1.49
Germany	1.69	1.99	2.02
Japan	1.44	1.85	2.17
UK	**1.61**	**1.53**	**1.47**
US	1.76	2.13	1.93
Sources: OECD and Cabinet Office, various years			

You will note that in 1981 we had been among the leaders. By 1990 we were almost at the bottom of the league. This macroeconomic picture was all the more worrying because economic growth theory current at the time (and indeed still valid) emphasised the importance of R&D.

The figures confirm that throughout the 1980s – the Thatcher years – the UK science base was being relentlessly eroded.

Parliament as a science policy forum

Obviously, as the Opposition Spokesman for Science and Technology I very much wanted to raise in parliament issues like this worrying drop in R&D.

Fortunately, from 1983, Sir Keith Joseph, by then Secretary of State for Education and Science, was ready to debate the issues with me, and we established a pattern of annual debates in the House on science policy. An annual debate actually represented a huge improvement on the previous provision of effectively no debates at all on science policy.

Keith Joseph, who was probably at the time Margaret Thatcher's closest ally, had been Secretary of State for Industry 1979-81. So he knew the field well. Contrary to parliamentary protocol, as a senior Secretary of State Keith was quite ready to lead the debates with myself, although I was not even a member of the shadow cabinet: he was interested in the subject, and

I was too. I was by that time a long-serving MP, and we had known each other for twenty years.

There was a broad consensus in the science community about the shape needed for science policy during the 1980s and indeed the 1990s, and the importance of R&D. But the Tory government was, in principle, opposed to public expenditure. However, the government was forced to accept that basic research still had to be funded by the state. Credit for that view was in large part due to Duncan Davies, whom I had known since we were colleagues in ICI. He had since become Chief Engineer and Scientist in the Department of Industry. It was a title he invented for himself, to underline the importance of application as well as basic research, and to boost the status of engineering. He had persuaded his Secretary of State for Industry, Keith Joseph, and through him Mrs Thatcher. She was herself a graduate in chemistry. But that was by no means a guarantee that she would support funding, any funding, for science. The case had to be made on first principles. It was a constant battle.

Unfortunately, from my point of view, at the time of the 1987 General Election, Sir Keith stood down (and was created a life peer).

Thereafter, the continuing responsibility for science policy rested with a succession of junior ministers in the Department of Education and Science. Not all were adequately equipped for the job. Few MPs have a science background. Some lacked the energy, the commitment and the competence required to tackle day-to-day issues or longer-term policy decisions. Others, notably George Walden, tried to think for themselves, but it cannot have been easy: George Walden had the extension of Britain's membership of CERN to deal with, where the particle physicists sought a disproportionate share of the science budget. They sought to strengthen support for their science by deploying the national champions' arguments against American domination, while I certainly wanted to see cooperation with the Americans in the construction of the Large Hadron Collider at CERN.

Arguing the case for basic funding for R&D

As I have already indicated, the continuation of government support for R&D was under constant attack from senior ministers.

Market incentives were central to Tory principles. But for market incentives to work, entrepreneurs must be able to appropriate sufficient of the benefit of research to give them an incentive to finance the research. The further research was away from application, and the more basic the research, the greater is the need for public funding. But a modern industrial country, particularly a country such as the UK which had a strong tradition in a wide range of basic and applied science, needed to maintain a balanced research effort, from basic to applied, in different core disciplines, and in defence and civil research, depending on costs, and on defence and foreign policy. At the same time a medium-sized industrial economy such as Britain could not do everything.

I argued we needed a framework of accounting for the sources and the uses of funds for different purposes, and then to keep them in balance. Such accounts hardly existed in 1983. Significant sources and agents included the government, research charities, business, and foreign sources; and each source of funding and type of agency could be sub-divided by industry and technology. In making international comparisons of research resources, it was necessary to sub-divide sources, to see where the real strength of a country lay. Thus in Japan, business was a heavy funder, and in the United States, defence. Britain was strong in pharmaceuticals, but not in engineering.

Given appropriate incentives and resources, the direction of the research must be left to the basic and applied scientists expert in the field.

But what were the appropriate resources? We did not have the figures to answer this question.

Research and development as a factor in economic growth

There had been a growing interest in research and development as a factor in economic growth. The theoretical work, and the best quality data on business R&D, was to be found in the US. So it was necessary to look in that direction[2]. But there was useful and important work in the UK, by Dasgupta, Stoneman, Van Reenen and others. I also looked at the position and practices in France, Germany, Japan, Australia and Canada. OECD was a useful and improving source of international comparisons of R&D expenditure. These comparisons, particularly those on basic research funding, were monitored and improved upon by SPRU (the Science Policy Research Unit) at Sussex University.

The UK had a fine record on basic research, but was weak on applied research and development. Bearing in mind the big differences between

---

[2] Hall, Bronwyn (1993) 'R&D Tax Policy during the 1980s: Success or Failure?' in Poterba, James, ed. *Tax Policy and the Economy* vol 7 Cambridge, Mass.: MIT Press

firms, I put forward proposals to encourage all companies to improve their technological competitiveness in ways appropriate to them.

The public understanding of science policy

Resources and machinery are important in the management of science policy. But so are public attitudes. Worryingly, the public's hostility to science has increased over the past forty years. There is much activity in the general area of the public understanding of science, but there the assumption is often that the problem lies in the public's understanding of science and not in what the scientists do. Unfortunately, reporters, leader writers and presenters of programmes such as the BBC 4 *Today* programme by and large have contributed little to a serious public understanding of science and science policy, and their alarmist or credulous reporting has contributed much to public anxiety.

As Opposition Spokesman for Science and Technology, I found it very hard to establish and maintain in parliament a serious interest in science policy, and almost impossible to be get an invitation to comment on science policy issues on air or in the media. There was a curious assumption by the media that, unlike policy in other fields such as economics, industry, education and so on, science policy is in some way a-political, and that opposition politicians had no alternative policies or strategies.

The few parliamentary debates I managed to get (usually only one or two a year) were sparsely attended and were never reported in the press or broadcasts. Sometimes this neglect was a relief: I remember two or three occasions when the minister replying in a science-orientated debate was either so little a master of his brief, or so well lubricated, that his half hour at the despatch box was a farce. The bizarre performance of a Secretary of State for Industry who had succeeded Sir Keith (and who shall be nameless) sticks in my mind.

The useful role of special institutions

Yet, though there are relatively few MPs with a science background, there was a well established Parliamentary and Scientific Committee, the first of the modern style interest groups wishing to inform and lobby government. It had a membership of MPs, peers and outside membership organisations like professional institutions, learned societies, universities, firms, trade associations and trade unions: I felt it should be non-party, with back bench officers.

The more recently founded Parliamentary Office of Science and Technology (POST) was modelled on the congressional Office of Technology Assessment in Washington, which it survived. POST was staffed by professional scientists and produced well-researched reports and briefing notes on current scientific issues. It was funded initially by a few mainly Tory members of parliament pooling their research allowances, with a few grants from firms, but it is now financed from the House of Commons Vote. It does an invaluable job.

Outside parliament, Save British Science was a straightforward and very effective lobby, particularly well-supported by senior academic scientists. Its main area of concern was the diminishing science budget, and it put up a powerful case. Professor Denis Noble was one of the founding fathers.

There were also other bodies that were not engaged in parliamentary lobbying as such. These included a number of university and academic research institutes which concentrated on or contributed to science policy. The Science Policy Research Unit (Christopher Freeman) at the University of Sussex was one such. Also noteworthy were the Programme of Policy Research into Engineering Science and Technology (PREST) at Manchester University (Michael Gibbons), the Science Policy Support Group (John Ziman).

Bodies such as the Royal Society, the Royal Institution and the Royal Academy of Engineering have developed well-informed and influential science policy activities, and were increasingly aware of the need to contribute their expertise. The Royal Society, founded under royal charter in the 1680s, has a long and distinguished history of giving independent and well-researched advice to government. Its institutional links with parliament are weaker.

In a serious attempt to bridge the gap between science, government and parliament, several important and influential journals have been launched. MPs would be well advised to read these.

Most valuable and notable are *Science and Public Affairs*, published jointly by the Royal Society and the British Association for the Advancement of Science; *Science in Parliament*, published by the invaluable Parliamentary and Scientific Committee; and briefings from the increasingly influential Parliamentary Office of Science and Technology (POST) which are addressed to MPs. I would hope that these, which can be regularly mailed to interested Members of Parliament, land up on the desks of all such MPs not in their waste paper baskets.

A problem for all such bodies was the lack of a Cabinet minister with well defined responsibilities for science and technology – and an opposition frontbencher with the same kudos. (The status of an opposition spokesman is determined by that of the minister he or she shadows.) However over the course of years I personally attended various occasions including conferences organised by the Royal Society, and through it met many distinguished scientists. It also gave me the welcome opportunity to renew links with my Cambridge contemporary, by now President of the Royal Society, Sir Michael Atiyah.

The Royal Institution complements the activities of the Royal Society, and I got to know its director, Professor John Meurig Thomas, well.

All these were valuable contributors to science policy, but they were not in the mainstream of politics, and thus were not involved in the parliamentary decision-making.

Formulating and proposing science policies

In parliamentary terms, an opposition spokesperson has a responsibility not only for shadowing a government minister and his or her department (a reactive role), but also for the development of alternative strategies and policies (a proactive role). It is the job – and the privilege – of front bench spokesmen to formulate and propose policies, and to clear them with colleagues, in preparation for the election manifesto. This offers a distillation of many years' work, and a public declaration of principles.

As Opposition Spokesman for Science and Technology I had a problem: there was no department in Whitehall with specific responsibility for science policy and technology policy. These concerns were dispersed between various departments. Science policy scarcely merited any parliamentary scrutiny or media attention. It is one of the great ironies of the age in which we live – an age in which, for better and for worse, science and technology are transforming our world – that even now in the twenty first century, the great majority of our political leaders, MPs, senior civil servants and journalists, are almost proud of the fact that they know nothing and care less.

So there was a great deal of background work to be done. I was meeting regularly with scientists and scientist spokesmen, but I needed to put together a small team to help me formulate arguments and policies.

16 : Opposition Spokesman for Science & Technology 1983-1992 ♦ 193

I was fortunate in being able to trawl for help in the universities for advice and indeed for research assistants to work with me in the formulation of science policy and its propagation. For a couple of years, beginning in 1983, Andrew Barry worked with me on science policy. Andrew was then a graduate student at the University of Sussex Science Policy Research Unit. He is now Lecturer at Goldsmiths College, University of London, and author of a recent book *Political Machines*[3].

At more or less the same time Joycelin Hobman assisted me very ably in producing a pamphlet advocating the formulation of a Labour policy on food[4]. This was well ahead of its time and owed not a little to my eighty year old father-in-law, Dr Hugh Trowell, a pioneer nutritionist who was, with his colleague Denis Burkitt FRS, publishing ground-breaking research on the connection between nutrition and health.

Andrew Barry was succeeded by Sam Lovick, a young medical student turned computer expert, who worked both on science policy and the application of computers to model building[5].

Later I was to employ Tim Walker, a former Education Officer of the National Union of Students, whose political experience was very useful in the formulation of science policy, in selling the proposals to my parliamentary colleagues and then to the science community. Tim did an excellent job in the handling of science as an election issue in the 1992 election. After he left my employ he was appointed Public Relations Manager for the Royal Academy of Engineering, and later became Special Adviser to Jack Cunningham when he was a minister.

For a couple of years Bryan Sykes, now a professor at Oxford and editor of *The Human Inheritance: genes, language and evolution*[6], came in regularly very much on a voluntary part-time basis, to give a hand. I felt honoured by the help of such a distinguished scientist and valued his insights and friendship. Would that there were more scientists able and willing to involve themselves in the hurly-burly of politics as it touches on science issues.

Policy proposals are eventually put to the test in the heat of general elections. Science policy does not generally feature in manifestos. However, it was to become such an issue in 1987 and 1992.

---

[3] Barry, Andrew (2001) *Political Machines: Governing a Technological Society* London: Athlone Press
[4] Labour Party (1985) *Food Policy – a priority for Labour* London: Labour Party pamphlet
[5] See also Chapter 14, page 158.
[6] Sykes, Bryan (1999) *The Human Inheritance: genes, language and evolution* Oxford: Oxford University Press

17

Science Policy as an election issue in 1987 & 1992

Science is rarely an election issue. But, encouraged by Neil Kinnock, my proposals would feature in the 1987 and 1992 elections. Had we won the 1992 General Election – which the polls, briefly, suggested we might achieve – it would (I have reason to believe) have fallen to me to implement these policies as a minister.

Science policy as an issue in the 1987 General Election

At the time of the 1987 General Election, the Labour Party included in an official policy document proposals I had been advocating. In *New Industrial Strength for Britain – Labour's Programme for National Renewal*[1] we proposed a radical scheme of financial incentives to increase expenditure on civil research and development. The aim was to help reduce the widening gap between research expenditure in Britain and other industrialised countries, which we saw as one of the main causes of Britain's inability to compete successfully in world high-technology markets. The scheme would have been accompanied by restructuring of defence research, a renewal of the science base, and changes in the machinery of government to give science a stronger voice in national affairs. We planned to increase expenditure on the universities, to appoint a Minister for Science and Technology, and to establish both a Council of Science and Technology to advise on strategy together with an Office of Technology Assessment. Finance for the scheme would have been provided by an increase in corporation tax.

John Maddox, the energetic and imaginative editor of *Nature*, the premier science journal, organised what he hoped would be a series of pre-

---

[1] Labour Party (1987) *New Industrial Strength for Britain - Labour's Programme for National Renewal* London: The Labour Party

election meetings with the spokespersons from the main parties. In the event, I was the only spokesman to take up the challenge. Kenneth Baker, who had succeeded Keith Joseph as Secretary of State for Education and Science in 1986, did not deign to participate, and science and R&D merited only the briefest of mentions in the Tory manifesto. Whoever spoke on science matters for what was then the SDP/Liberal Alliance also declined the invitation.

I presented Labour's proposals at a lively meeting in the Inner Temple before five distinguished interlocutors – Dr Geoffrey Cooper (director, Technical Change Centre), Professor Martin Rees (Cambridge), Professor Denis Noble (Oxford), Peter Rigby (National Institute of Medical Research) Professor Sir Hans Kornberg (Cambridge) – and an audience of eighty which included many eminent scientists. The meeting was reported at some length in *Nature* 2 April 1987[2].

With the encouragement of the invaluable Kay Andrews, from Neil Kinnock's office, a number of very senior scientists endorsed our proposals. Among them I remember in particular Professor Steven Rose, of the Open University, and Professor Denis Noble, from Oxford. A half page advertisement in the Guardian, paid for by donations from these fifty scientists, was launched. And we held a fairly well attended press conference at the Labour Headquarters in Smith Square, although science as an election issue did not catch fire. My research assistant, Sam Lovick (and earlier, Andrew Barry) contributed usefully.

In the event, the Conservatives won the 1987 election with a somewhat reduced majority. I continued as the Opposition Spokesman for Science and Technology throughout the 1987-1992 parliament.

Science policy as an election issue in the 1992 General Election

In the run up to the 1992 General Election, Labour party's policy statement on industry, *Modern Manufacturing Strength*[3], had been masterminded by Gordon Brown (then shadowing the Department of Industry). So the science document which I drafted, *Pushing Back the Frontiers: Labour's policy statement on science in the service of society and industry*[4], was concerned mainly with how Labour intended to make use of our growing scientific

---

[2] *Nature* 2 April 1987 London
[3] Labour Party (1991) *Modern Manufacturing Strength: Labour's industrial policy* London: The Labour Party
[4] Labour Party (1992) *Pushing Back the Frontiers: Labour's policy statement on science in the service of society and industry* (20 July).London: The Labour Party

knowledge so that it would serve our society, our culture and our economy more effectively.

In *Pushing Back the Frontiers* I argued that we were living at a time of great discovery and fertility in science: remarkable advances were taking place in medicine, physics, astronomy, chemistry, mathematics and biology. Economic and social research was contributing to understanding the responses needed to the massive changes in society. There was growing recognition of the benefits science can bring to improving the quality of our lives. But I recognised the exploitation of particular technologies could also be damaging, and that we needed scientists to enable us to make intelligent, well informed and human choices. Science and technology had a key role in every aspect of government policy: science shapes the way our economy develops, and science, technology and innovation are the key to industrial success.

The statement argued firstly for good-quality science, well taught and widely understood. This required strengthening science in schools, raising people's understanding of science, and improving the channels for funding for research in higher education, and supporting the science base. This is self evident, and I will not recapitulate the arguments here.

Secondly I argued that we must ensure that science and technology were well linked to applications, sustaining innovation and enhancing economic performance. This called for improved links between higher education, the research councils, and industry; an increase in the level of R&D in industry, and incentives for improvement; greater innovation and the use of competitive technology through technology transfer and other support. I will be discussing this below.

I also, with Neil Kinnock's backing, proposed the establishment of a new Office of Science and Technology at the heart of government in the Cabinet Office. It would have been headed by a Minister of State for Science and Technology. This proposal was hardened up in the run up to the 1992 general election, and became a manifesto pledge.

A priority for the proposed Office of Science and Technology would have been to ensure that we have the knowledge and capability to anticipate and respond to the challenges for the future. The challenges that I foresaw at that time – 1991 – included assessing the impact of humankind on the global environment; re-examining the relationship between civil and military R&D in the light of changing global political circumstances; strengthening collaborative links with other countries on major research projects; and providing better information and better assessment of the impact of science and technology to the public and to policy makers.

The argument on technological competitiveness

There is good evidence to show that R&D generates economic growth.

Britain's trade deficit, its declining share of the world market for high technology products, and its falling share of USA patents, were all signs that Britain's pace of innovation and its output from R&D were falling behind.

This was directly related to the decline in our R&D effort.

International comparisons confirmed that the UK was lagging behind other countries in the level of civil R&D (see below: Figure 1). Indeed, by 1989 it had been overtaken by its leading competitors. Twenty five years earlier, in 1964, the UK had been second only to the US in its spending on R&D. By 1989 (the latest year for which there were figures) it was spending less (as a percentage of GDP) on R&D than it had in 1964.

Fig. 1 R&D expenditure as a percentage of GDP

	France	Germany	Japan	USA	**UK**
1964					
Civil R&D	1.2	1.3	1.3	1.5	1.5
Defence R&D	0.4	0.1	0.0	1.4	0.8
All R&D	**1.6**	**1.4**	**1.3**	**2.9**	**2.3**
1979					
Civil R&D	1.54	2.30	2.10	1.81	1.67
Defence R&D	0.27	0.10	0.00	0.57	0.53
All R&D	**1.81**	**2.40**	**2.10**	**2.38**	**2.20**
1989					
Civil R&D	1.90	2.67	2.90	2.00	1.77
Defence R&D	0.43	0.18	0.02	0.80	0.42
All R&D	**2.33**	**2.85**	**2.92**	**2.80**	**2.19**

Worryingly, a careful analysis of the 1989 figures – the most recent then available – showed disturbing trends, as the table over leaf (Figure 2) clearly shows.

Fig. 2 R&D expenditure as a percentage of GDP (1989) with breakdown of sources of funding

	France	Germany	Japan	USA	UK
1989					
Civil R&D	1.90	2.67	2.90	2.00	1.77
Defence R&D	0.43	0.18	0.02	0.80	0.42
All R&D	**2.33**	**2.85**	**2.92**	**2.80**	**2.19**
of which (latest figures)					
Industry funded Civil R&D	1.15	1.92	2.29	1.42	1.20
Gov. funded Civil R&D	0.75	0.75	0.61	0.58	0.57
Gov. funded Defence R&D	0.43	0.18	0.02	0.80	0.42
Gov. funded R&D total	**1.18**	**0.93**	**0.63**	**1.38**	**0.99**
of which academic & academically related	*0.44*	*0.49*	*0.25*	*0.31*	***0.38***

As this table shows, UK government funded R&D amounted to under 1% of our GDP of which nearly half was spent on Defence R&D. This compared unfavourably with the total government funded R&D in USA (1.38%) and France (1.8%), and indeed with Germany and Japan too if their lower expenditure on defence R&D is taken into account.

Targets for R&D proposed by Labour

A reasonable target I set for Labour in the 1991 Labour Party policy paper *Pushing Back the Frontiers*[5] – and reiterated in Labour policy documents at the time of the 1992 General Election – was to use tax incentives to increase civil R&D from the 1989 level of 1.77% of GDP, to 2.5% of GDP in the course of a parliament. This would put us ahead of France (1.9% in 1989) and the USA (2.0% in 1989). But we would still be lagging behind Germany (2.67 in 1989) and Japan (2.9% in 1989).

Within that total of 2.5% I proposed there should be increases in civil R&D carried out in industry. This would generate faster economic growth.

To set the process going there would have been a R&D tax incentive scheme giving a 25% tax credit to companies for increases in their R&D expenditure over a base year, in addition to the existing 100% tax allowance for R&D. The scheme would have given those foreign companies that paid

---

[5] Labour Party Policy document (1991) *Pushing Back the Frontiers* London: the Labour Party

sufficient corporation tax to benefit, an incentive to conduct R&D and not just product assembly in this country, while avoiding the opposite extreme of intensive UK R&D with no associated production. This was designed to come within the experience in different respects of the US and Australia, and was allowed under EU rules. Using the best US data on the productivity and timing of R&D pay offs, I argued the scheme should pay its own way without reducing tax yields.

Out of the increase in GDP, there were to have been increases in funding of the science base through the research councils and universities; an increase in R&D on the environment, transport, services, non-nuclear energies, and technologies for developing countries; and a diversion of resources no longer required for defence R&D to civil R&D.

However, in my view the dual system of basic research funding – through the research councils, and through the universities – also needed attention: there were issues of the division between subjects, particularly in rapidly expanding biological fields, and a need to review not so much the responsibilities of the research councils, as government responsibility for them, and for the channel of funding through the universities.

Did Labour's policy proposals on R&D funding have any effect?

The Tory government, returned to power in 1992, was opposed to selective tax credits and allowances of the kind I had proposed, and did not consider there to be a case for general tax incentives for spending on R&D. This was confirmed in a policy paper, *Realising our potential*, written by William Waldegrave, when John Major appointed him as Science Minister.

Tory science policy, though having much in common with Labour policies, failed the challenge to find adequate resources and incentives to increase R&D activity overall. Tory forward plans always showed a reduction in the Science Budget in later years. However, the budget was actually maintained as a fixed proportion of GDP. Overall Waldegrave's *Realising our potential* reads like a departmental bid without Treasury participation in the drafting of the strategy proposed.

Since 1997, the Chancellor Gordon Brown has introduced R&D tax credits for small, new firms, but there was no reason to believe small firms are more efficient in R&D than larger firms: it looked like a means of sounding modern and efficient. Gordon avoided giving tax credits to large, profitable multinational pharmaceutical companies which would have been

---

[6] Waldegrave, W (1993) *Realising our potential*, London: HMSO Cm 2250

economically efficient, but politically unpopular. That issue has been grasped in 2001, with the Chancellor's proposal in the Budget to introduce R&D tax credits for companies of all sizes in 2002: a welcome move.

Science at the heart of government: machinery of government

Incentives and resources, I argued in 1992, were in themselves insufficient. We needed the appropriate machinery in government to deliver. So, with the support of Neil Kinnock, I put forward the argument for the creation of a Minister and an Office for Science, Technology, Research and Statistics in the Cabinet Office. This would have had the effect of a major re-balancing of priorities and responsibilities.

Under my proposals, which, in the 1992 manifesto, became party policy:

- The Science Minister, based in the Cabinet Office, would have been responsible for the Science Budget, for the Research Councils, and for the Meteorological Office which works with the Research Councils on climate change.
  The Science Minister would also have been responsible for a reformed Government Statistical Service, and for an Office of Policy Research providing services to Statistics and Policy Research Units within other Departments.

- A Ministerial Cabinet Committee would have been charged with reviewing science and technology policy on a regular basis.

- The Science Minister would have represented Britain on science policy in European Community and other international science and research councils, with Education, Trade and Industry, Transport and other ministers taking a lead in their respective areas of responsibility.

- The Technology Minister, based in the Department of Trade and Industry, would have had primary responsibility for programmes for the support of industrial R&D and technology transfer, including fiscal R&D incentives.

- The Department of Education would have developed with the Higher Education Funding Council new ways of supporting basic research required to maintain the essential plurality of channels of support for research.

Bill Stewart, Chief Scientific Adviser at the time, was in favour of these arrangements for science, and before the 1992 election I had had a meeting with Robin Butler, Secretary of the Cabinet, and Bill Stewart, going over the principles.

I will be discussing the question of the machinery of government in greater depth in Chapter 19, since it is still a relevant issue.

The launch of Labour Party Science & Technology Policy Proposals

The launch took place in the august setting of the Royal Institution, and for once, with Neil Kinnock present, we had a good attendance from the press, not only the science press, such as the *New Scientist* and *Nature*, but also from the broadsheets. This was in some sense a reward, for science policy by and large usually gets very poor coverage from the media, including broadcasting, although science scare stories get massive, though often sensation-seeking and ill-informed, reporting.

The Opposition Spokesman for Science and Technology at the pre-election launch of Labour's Science & Technology Policy Proposals at the Royal Institute. Note the red roses! Photo: Phil Maxwell.

The 1992 campaign – and the outcome

In the run up to the 1992 election, during the campaign, and immediately after it, Tim Walker, my then research assistant, proved a great asset. A computer scientist, and former officer of the National Union of Students, he knew his way about, and had good press contacts. We organised a press conference and photo opportunity for Kinnock in Cambridge, with leading scientists, but this was overtaken by the row over 'Jennifer's ear', which the press deemed of greater importance.

During the campaign there was a brief period when it looked as if Labour might win. For front benchers this is a moment of heady excitement, as senior civil servants begin to make contact and discuss manifesto pledges with potential ministers.

Had Labour won the 1992 election, I knew Neil Kinnock planned to make me Minister for Science, despite the fact that in 1991 I had undergone a triple coronary by-pass. Would this, I had wondered, affect my chances? But Neil Kinnock encouraged me to continue as spokesman: he told me his father had undergone similar surgery, and, fifteen years on, was still in good heart[7].

It was the nearest I ever got to holding high office. But that is democracy for you ...

After the 1992 election: the Conservative government

My proposal of an Office of Science and Technology was (briefly) implemented by John Major when the Tories won the election although it was not in their pre-election policy. William Waldegrave was given ministerial charge as Chancellor of the Duchy of Lancaster. I had a long meeting with William in his first few days of office, and was encouraged to find he had much the same conception of the job as I had had, though he was in the event not able to implement it all.

The appointment of Professor Robert May to head up the Office of Science and Technology was an excellent choice, and one which, had I been minister, I would have welcomed. An Australian by birth with an

---

[7] *Editor's note:* Neil Kinnock, writing to me after Jeremy's death, wrote:
'There were obviously many reasons for wanting to win in 1992. One of them was to install Science and Technology understanding and policy firmly in the mainstream of government for the first time. Jeremy would have given exactly the right enthusiasm and wisdom to that. In this as in many other innovations, the country lost when we lost.'   *Elizabeth Bray*

international reputation, he was by this time a Royal Society Research Professor. He had been Chairman of the University Research Board since 1977. He was very much on the same wavelength as myself, with extensive experience in using mathematical tools to model systems, from ecosystems, the epidemiology of infection diseases, and chaos theory. Robert May – now Lord May PRS – served for five years with distinction. It is unfortunate that, with the ups and downs of cabinet reshuffles, the OST was never able to realise its potential at the heart of government.

After the 1992 election: the Opposition

I continued briefly as Science and Technology Spokesperson for the Labour Party after the 1992 election. But I could not expect to be a senior minister after next election, probably in 1997, by which time I would be sixty seven. So I told John Smith, who had succeeded Neil Kinnock as Leader of the Opposition, that I would like to give a younger member a chance to pick up the background of science policy before becoming science minister: there would be plenty of time before the election for John Smith to groom a successor.

Throughout my time as Opposition Spokesman for Science and Technology, I had had excellent contacts with Neil Kinnock, the Labour leader. He had a good grasp of the essentials of my proposals and their implications, and he supported them generously and with considerable insight.

I also knew John Smith well. We met quite frequently, for he was my near neighbour as MP for nearby Monklands East. A Scotsman with a keen intelligence, John appreciated the importance of science and technology. Both Neil Kinnock and then John Smith relied a good deal on the invaluable Kay Andrews, who worked in the office of the Leader of the Opposition. She had a good scientific background and acted as a vital line of communication on scientific or science policy matters.

On John Smith's sudden death, Tony Blair became Leader of the Opposition. I shall be discussing his handling of science issues in greater detail in Chapter 19.

I confess that I was glad that I had already relinquished the job of shadow Spokesman for Science and Technology, and opted to serve on the new Select Committee on science and technology, before Blair became leader.

18

The Science & Technology Select Committee
1992-1997

The present Commons Select Committee on Science and Technology owes its existence to a short-lived change in cabinet responsibilities, instituted by Prime Minister John Major immediately after winning the 1992 General Election – and some very vigorous lobbying on my own part.

There was in 1992 no Science and Technology Select Committee in the Commons. It had ceased to exist in 1980. Before that date there had been effective Select Committees on science in both the House of Commons and the House of Lords. However, the modern system of Commons Departmental Select Committees (set up in 1980 at the outset of the Thatcher government[1]) had led to the abolition of non-departmental select committees. No Department of Science and Technology meant that there could be no Commons Select Committee on Science and Technology.

The Lords Committee had continued, of course, doing good work, with the comparative advantage over the Commons of being able to nominate among its membership recognised scientists of distinction. Reading the Commons and Lords Select Committee reports does not however suggest a great difference in style because the drafting process does not record individual authorship, and both committees draw evidence from similar and often the same sources and authorities.

The demise in 1980 of the Commons Select Committee for science had the unfortunate result of effectively removing science from the mainstream parliamentary agenda. The Select Committees for departments such as Education, and Trade and Industry, concentrated on the core business of such departments. They largely overlooked the fact that the Department of Education was responsible for science research in the universities and the

---

[1] See Chapter 12, page 138.

research councils, and that the DTI (Department of Industry) was responsible for the applied sciences, technology and industry (I simplify somewhat).

The position changed after 1992 when John Major created the Office of Science and Technology (OST): that, I argued, now constituted a 'Department', and it was demonstrably the main responsibility of a cabinet minister, William Waldegrave. (The OST had been a key proposal in the Labour manifesto. Rubbished in the election campaign by the Tories, it re-emerged as Conservative policy with the first cabinet appointments.)

William Waldegrave, the Science Minister, told me privately that he was in favour of a science and technology committee. And the fact that the Chief Scientific Adviser (Robert May) was directly responsible to the Prime Minister added weight to the argument.

Lobbying to launch a Select Committee on Science and Technology 1992

I drafted an EDM (Early Day Motion) calling for a Select Committee on Science. An Early Day Motion calls for a debate in parliament on a topic; there is not the slightest chance of such a debate being called. However, the EDM has become a means whereby backbenchers can express an opinion, and the more signatories you can get, the greater the strength of opinion.

I wrote personally to every single Labour MP (apart from the shadow spokesmen, who do not sign EDMs) urging them to sign this Early Day Motion. And I had a quiet word with Tories who campaigned on science issues, encouraging them to do likewise. An Early Day Motion which receives more than 100 signatures is considered by the Cabinet. My EDM received many more than that.

The move was successful and a Commons Departmental Select Committee on Science and Technology was appointed. In the course of the 1992-97 parliament we were to issue a number of important reports about significant topics.

Interestingly, the Commons Select Committee survived the relapse of the Office of Science and Technology, while still under the Tories, into the Department of Trade and Industry where science was again relegated to the care of a junior minister. The departmental position was not changed by Labour after 1997. By then the Select Committee on Science and Technology had proved so useful it continues to function to this day.

The work of the Science and Technology Select Committee 1993-1997

The Select Committee on Science and Technology seemed to me a way of opening up the debate so I sought nomination to it. The carve up of select committee chairs meant that the chair of the Science and Technology Committee had to be a Tory, Sir Giles Shaw. I served as deputy chairman.

It was necessary first of all to establish the competence and *bona fides* of the Committee, and so our first act was to produce a general report on technological competitiveness which was given the clumsy title *The routes through which the science base is translated into innovative and competitive technology*[2]. The title was chosen to propitiate the well established Trade and Industry Select Committee, which reasonably enough considered industrial competitiveness their territory.

This was quickly followed by other reports. Important as some of them were, I will confine myself here to one – that on human genetics – since that topic is still very much a live issue, and it illustrates well how a Select Committee works and its lines of inquiry.

The Select Committee Report on Human Genetics

The Select Committee were well aware of the hazards in undertaking our enquiry into human genetics. Human genetics was a rapidly developing field of research of great importance on which public attitudes had not crystallised. It had not, as yet, attracted popular disapproval and media hype ('breakthrough', 'catastrophe') – something I wished to avoid if possible. Its potential for good or evil, and its importance for the future of the human race, were undeniable. Attitudes in the UK seemed likely to have a worldwide influence, because US attitudes were suspected by some countries, and the UK was strong in genetics and in the bio-sciences generally.

We had decided we would not get a serious scientific discussion going if we were diverted by important side issues, such as abortion, or genetic modification, which were already being debated elsewhere. We avoided these by saying we would work on the assumption that the present abortion law and practice continued, and we would not examine the genetic manipulation of plants in agriculture (a separate issue). That is not to say the ethical and other dimensions of genetics were unimportant, or should

---

[2] House of Commons (1993-94) Science and Technology Committee *The routes through which the science base is translated into innovative and competitive technology* (HC 74, 1993-94) London: HMSO

be ignored in parliament. But in this our first major report we were anxious to get to grips with the science.

In the event we got excellent evidence in Britain and the US. We were well served by our science advisers: Professor David Porteous, of the Medical Research Council Human Genetics Unit in Edinburgh, and Dr (later Professor) Bryan Sykes, of the Institute of Molecular Medicine in Oxford, and a leading authority in this area[3]. Our report was well received both by the researchers and by those concerned with the ethical, legal and social issues.

The Committee's report was wide ranging. We aimed at clear statements that were understandable by lay people. We were ready to venture into philosophical, ethical, legal and social issues; to reach clear conclusions where we considered these possible, and to provide for thorough consideration as research progressed in a rapidly moving field where they were not possible.

We reached practical conclusions and made recommendations on research in the science, genetic screening, somatic cell therapy, germ-line manipulation, the provision of genetic services, the regulation of medical genetics, industrial research in genetics, the patenting of genes and its utility, genetic discrimination and privacy, medical confidentiality, employment, insurance, public understanding, and international regulation.

Finally, because research in genetics is developing so rapidly, we recommended the appointment of a standing Human Genetics Commission.

Re-reading the Report now, five years after its publication, I still think it reads well, but there are undoubtedly respects in which it needs updating.

The report was warmly commended by *Nature*[4]:

> The Mother of Parliaments ... has been well served by the House of Commons Select Committee on Science and Technology, whose report on human genetics is published this week. The committee's conclusions are panic-free, the arguments by which it reaches them are intelligent, its findings are plainly based on a huge amount of work and it repeatedly emphasises that its capacity to foretell the

---

[3] Sykes, Bryan (1999) *The Human Inheritance: genes, language and evolution* Oxford: Oxford University Press. See too Sykes, Brian e-mail enquiries @oxfordancestors.com
[4] *Nature* 376, 200-202, 20 July 1995

future is hampered by the speed with which knowledge of human genetics is being enlarged.

In three respects, the committee goes further than others have recently done. On the patenting of genes, ... , employment, and insurance. ...

On regulation, the committee's chief proposal is that there should be a statutory Human Genetics Commission. ...

Against its instincts, the government should listen.

The Committee Report was issued in July 1995. The Conservative Government, well aware that there was an election in the offing, did not listen. It declined to create a Commission. Instead it sent a patronising reply.

The Committee reconvened some key witnesses, and checked and reiterated its proposal. This time the government moved half way and appointed a Human Genetics Advisory Commission. Four years later the Labour government claimed credit for creating a Human Genetics Commission without of course acknowledgement of its belated response to the Select Committee.

This has often happened with good select committee reports: the recommendations of supposedly half-witted MPs are rejected by wise all-knowing ministers, only for the ministers to propose them as their own ideas a few years later. This is not due to the frailty and injustice of particular ministers, but to the political tradition within which they are functioning.

The overall response of public attitudes and opinions to human genetics has remained strongly positive, and I think the Select Committee contributed to that. It showed that the accepted ways of seeking to interest and inform the public are worthwhile. But are they sufficient? It depends on what role you aim at, what objectives you set, for science policy.

Dolly the sheep – and Blair's response

Genetics was a subject which I thought government and politics as at present conducted could find difficulty in handling. That was borne in on me flying down from Inverness after the Scottish Labour Party conference shortly before the 1997 election. I found myself sitting in the row behind Tony Blair and his No. 10 assistants, Alastair Campbell and Anji Hunter. Tony had just launched Labour's proposal for a Food Standards Agency.

The Select Committee had reacted very fast, and was by this date finalising its report on *The cloning of animals from adult cells*[5] which we were able to complete very quickly after the cloning of Dolly the sheep because we had done most of the background work for our earlier report on *Human genetics*[6].

Dolly was headline news: she featured as the cover story in *Time Magazine*, in *Newsweek* and in *The Economist* that week, following Ian Wilmut's announcement in *Nature* the week before. *Newsweek*'s headline was 'Can we clone humans?' President Clinton had asked a Commission to report to him within three months. Tony Blair had said nothing about it that day although Dolly and the Roslin Institute were just down the road from him in Scotland, and he was talking about food and agriculture.

I passed the magazines to Anji saying I thought it would be wise for Labour at least to have a statement in draft in case it came up in the election: there were electoral hazards on abortion and genetically modified organisms. Anji leafed through them and passed them on to Alastair who did the same, and returned them to me. Nothing was said to Blair. Tony evidently did not need to know. I did draft a statement and sent it to him after the weekend. As it happened Dolly was not raised by Labour or Tory spokesman or by any journalist during the 1997 campaign: if Tony was slow in the uptake, so was the political system and the media!

The strengths and limitations of the Science Select Committee

Select Committees decide upon the course of their own inquiries.

Having decided on a topic, the Science and Technology Select Committee will engage distinguished scientists as advisers, and invite witnesses who are probably leading researchers or authorities in their own area. All being well, it will, after months of inquiry, be in the position to produce a well-researched and authoritative report. This report will be debated in parliament, and the government should make a response. If the findings are controversial, the committee's report, the debate, and the government's response will probably get a mention in the broadsheet press. The Report will certainly be covered in more detail in specialist journals. It may have a long term influence on the formation of opinion and public attitudes, and shape government policies possibly over a period of years.

---

[5] House of Commons, Science and Technology Committee 1996-97 *The cloning of animals from adult cells* London: HMSO

[6] House of Commons, Science and Technology Committee 1994-95 *Human genetics* London: HMSO

Select committees have the limitations of their strengths. Select Committee members can develop considerable expertise within their own field of interest. But that does not mean they can be relied upon to carry out particular professional tasks like audit, modelling and analysis. There may simply be nobody on the committee who is interested in such technical questions. And there are always other, perhaps more pressing, questions to be pursued within the competence of the committee.

The most important requirement for the proper exercise of their role is that select committees should be free and independent of government or party instruction. That means that the government should not attempt to manipulate the membership of select committees, nor the choice of chair. The government should not seek the subjects of their inquiries, or to control their terms of reference. It should not interfere with witnesses. It should not attempt to prejudice the course or outcomes of inquiries undertaken by the committee, nor the way the proceedings are written up, nor the form of conclusions and recommendations. (These things do happen – but they should be strongly opposed: committee chairmen have been known successfully to take up the cudgels on behalf of their committee.)

The Select Committee system opens important channels of communication with and between parliamentarians and the public. In the case of the Science Select Committee, for example, it opens two-way channels of communication between parliament and scientists. It will call on expert witnesses in the universities and research institutes; in the professions; in business, finance and industry (including researchers and technologists); in the media (including professional science journals) and among the general public. Many science and technology questions affect human relations, society at large and our relationship with our planet and perhaps the destiny of mankind. So a Select Committee may be wise to seek the advice of thinkers in the fields of religion, philosophy, law, ethics and the social sciences and economics.

The Select Committee on Science and Technology has, I believe, served parliament and the nation well. It has improved the quality of public debate and debate in the House, and the ability of parliament to monitor and criticise government policy and performance in this vital field. We should not underestimate the power for good of influential, well-argued and well-informed Select Committee Reports dealing with topical and major issues. But in the end, back bench committees cannot move mountains.

19

Science in parliament and in government

The need for a better understanding of science issues by parliament, by parliamentarians and by governments is often painfully obvious. This raises issues of competence and of trust.

The basis of a polity lies in the establishment and maintenance of that trust. And (as I shall argue later in Chapter 25) the role of trust in politics (trust in systems) and of trust in politicians (trust in persons) are both crucial. They are moreover to a significant degree interdependent. It is extremely difficult for a minister (or Prime Minister) to deliver on promises if the systems are not robust and reliable; and conversely reliable systems tend, in time, to produce a breed of politicians who have the experience and understanding to respond and to deliver in a trustworthy and competent fashion.

When, on John Smith's sudden death, Tony Blair became Leader of the Opposition, he had nobody in his office who had a scientific background and who could act as a line of communication on scientific or science policy matters, in the way that Kay Andrews had done very usefully for Neil Kinnock and John Smith. Blair had never shown any interest in science or science policy. It was difficult to get him to focus on the issues, or even to go through the formal motions of Prime Ministers and party leaders in communicating with the leaders of the scientific community. For all his considerable flair and charismatic qualities in his honeymoon period with the electorate, his lack of understanding of scientific evidence served him ill when he was called upon to deliver in some crucial areas.

Let me give just a couple of examples from his early years.

Handling epidemics: BSE (1996) and Foot-and-mouth (2001)

The inadequate grip of parliamentarians on science issues was painfully obvious when the BSE (Bovine Spongiform Encephalopathy, popularly known as 'Mad Cow Disease') story broke in March 1996.

Stephen Dorrell as Minister of Health announced to parliament the possible effect of BSE jumping the species barrier from bovine spongiform encephalitis into human CJD. He was careful not to go beyond the advice he had had from the scientists, because he had earlier allowed himself to be pressured too far by Jonathan Dimbleby, who had asked, 'So there is, you are saying, no conceivable risk from what is now in the food chain; that's the position?' Dorrell had confirmed that that was 'the position'. Dorrell later told the BSE Inquiry that he regretted that answer because it went further than the words of his Chief Medical Officer.

So Dorrell was careful in a parliamentary reply on Wednesday 20 March not to go beyond his advice. These are his words:

> There is at present no age sensitivity, and the scientific evidence for the risks of developing CJD in those who eat meat in childhood has not changed as a result of the new findings. However parents will be concerned about the implications for their children, and I have asked the advisory committee to provide specific advice on that issue following its next meeting this weekend.

The next day, Tony Blair was asking the Prime Minister:

> I assume from what the Health Secretary said yesterday that the scientific advice that the Government have received is absolutely clear that it is entirely safe to carry on feeding beef and beef burgers to children. May we have a categorical statement that the Rt Hon Gentleman's scientific advice does indeed say that? The clearer and better the statements, the sooner public concern will be allayed – Conservative members should realise that.

'Absolutely clear'? 'Entirely safe'? Dorrell (on the advice of the Chief Medical Officer) had said no such thing. Blair's fighting talk is typical of a barrister's approach, and of an opposition parliamentarian with a barrister's training. It was plainly not possible to make such 'categorical' statements, still less after only a weekend's research. A scientist would handle the newly disclosed evidence far more cautiously, with various caveats. This style may not suit politicians concerned with point scoring in debate and in electoral battles. I urged Tony to talk to the scientific experts, which he did. Somewhat better informed, he developed a rather sounder line of questioning. But he was never at home with the issue.

Unfortunately, even with the previous experience of BSE the Blair government proved itself incapable of getting to grips with the epidemiology of its own food and agriculture related disaster: the foot-and-mouth epidemic of 2001. Politics – the desire to hold and win an early election – was given precedence over the analysis of the epidemic and the modelling (very belatedly employed) of how it was likely to spread and how it might be contained. The price to the tax payer was huge. This is now forgotten. And Blair won the 2001 election with ease. But has he, I wonder, learned anything?

Blair's use of a lawyer's casuistry in arguing a case for the prosecution or defence is likely to land him in trouble if he is in a tight corner. Playing politics with science issues like this does not auger well at a time when we may be facing the use of chemical or biological weapons by terrorists[1].

New Labour's style of handling evidence

I confess I am uncomfortable with the style of politics adopted by New Labour in Britain. It does science, and the truth, no favours. Were it only the style, that could be put right by some tactical changes in the rhetoric or, if necessary, the leaders of the party. But it is so plainly damaging, as policy making born out of sound bites 'by briefing and bounce', threatens to give way to paralysis and indecision, to be followed by excess. And the substitution of manipulable focus groups for House of Commons policy debate and select committee inquiry, neglects the accumulated wisdom and cultural resources of the British constitution.

But the problem may lie deeper: and it can lead to a loss of confidence in the rationality of politics. Is that irreversible? We had developed a way of allowing or enabling individuals and the state to address particular problems with particular instruments; these could be seen, the effects measured and choices made. The affinities between science and the objectives of predicting and responding to nature and to human behaviour constitute one of the technological successes of science. This provides in the long run a way of justifying and legitimating a form of politics confined to actions directed by practical, instrumentally attainable goals.

Under New Labour however there has been a proliferation of public service agreements, schemes and targets. But no amount of election pledges, pilot schemes or target setting will win support for politicians if they lose their credibility and are not able even to test whether their chosen instruments – targets – have sufficient leverage to achieve the results sought.

---

[1] This is a prescient observation. Jeremy, who died in May 2002, did not live to see the government's publication of the September 2002 dossier with its allegations about Saddam's ability to launch weapons of mass destruction at 45 minutes' notice.

Science policy in parliament and government under New Labour

Personal competence and trustworthiness, I have been arguing, are dependent on the trustworthiness of systems. Unfortunately Blair seems to have given little attention to systemic questions in relation to science and technology.

Although there are now more members in parliament than ever with a science background, this experience is not necessarily seen as an asset. An interest in science and technology issues, and science policy, should be seen as a launch pad for election to parliament in a safe seat, and to be capable of leading thereafter to a serious parliamentary and ministerial career. But is it?

Throughout Blair's time as Leader of the Opposition (1993-97), he appointed a succession of relatively minor spokespersons to act as shadows to ministers of science – the lowly parliamentary under-secretaries in Major's government in the relevant departments of education (where responsibility for research in the research councils and universities is situated) and industry (which has responsibility for the application of science and technology). If Blair was aware of the problems with duality, he seems to have regarded it as an issue of little importance.

As Prime Minister Tony Blair's appointments followed much the same pattern, though he was now in a position to address the problem of the split up of science issues as between the Department of Education and Skills (the DES) and the Department of Trade and Industry (the DTI); and to raise the profile of science posts by appointing an experienced senior figure as a Minister of State for Science. He has not done so.

In Blair's governments the Minister of State for Lifelong Learning and Higher Education in DES (the Department for Education and Skills) has, among his or her many responsibilities, responsibility for 'research and innovation and relations with the DTI' as well as for the universities and colleges of further education, students and adult life-long learning, and much else. The minister with responsibility for science issues in the DTI is Lord Sainsbury, the Parliamentary Under-Secretary of State for Science and Innovations (the bottom rung of the ministerial ladder). He is responsible for the Office of Science and Technology, which survives in an emasculated form. But he is safely out of reach in the Lords. There is no serious accountability to the Commons on science issues.

I hope that my erstwhile colleagues now holding ministerial office with science responsibilities will forgive me my calling them 'relatively minor figures'; but that, despite their commitment and ability, is how they appear to rank in the eyes of the political 'village', including their parliamentary colleagues and the media. The message is, science doesn't matter.

Joined up government

Ministerial Cabinet Committees – the twenty four cross-departmental committees of ministers and a score of sub-committees – are supposed to ensure 'joined-up government'. They range from four heavy-weight committees on Constitutional Reform to ones on the Wembley Stadium, Animal Rights Activists and the Millennium Dome. The Science Policy Committee is clearly rather lowly in rank order. And rank order is, as any cabinet insider will tell you, considered of great importance by ministers. These things are judged by the seniority of the Chair and the ministers on the committee, the size of the committee itself, the frequency of meeting, and the number of its sub-committees (just one for science, the Biotechnology Sub-Committee – genetic engineering to you and me).

Why, we should be asking, is there no Science Sub-Committee focused on Climate Change? Global warming is clearly the most serious long term issue facing this and future governments, and one which crucially depends on the scientific evidence. Lord Sainsbury, the 'Science Minister' is neither on the Environment Committee nor its Green Sub-Committee, which perhaps considers climate change. However, the Parliamentary Under-Secretary at the Ministry of Defence, currently Dr Lewis Moonie, is. I hope he is there because his defence responsibilities include the Meteorological Office, the lead body on modelling climate change. But I doubt it.

Until science is put at the heart of government – in systemic terms – the culture and norms of parliamentary debate and of government policy-making will remain suspect, and a parliamentarian's interest in the issues will continue to be an impediment to hopes of front bench responsibilities within government or in opposition.

The place of science in the machinery of government

You will recall that during the 1992 General Election Labour published a policy document *Pushing Back the Frontiers* in which I had argued the case for a radical overhaul of the machinery of government, and an increased role for research in government in the development and evaluation of policy, and in their delivery and effectiveness[2].

---

[2] See Chapter 17, pages 200-201.

To refresh your memory, I summarise below my main proposals made in 1991, which then became part of the Labour Party Manifesto in 1992.

LABOUR'S PROPOSALS FOR THE CREATION OF A MINISTER AND AN OFFICE FOR SCIENCE, TECHNOLOGY, RESEARCH AND STATISTICS IN THE CABINET OFFICE AS PROPOSED IN THE 1992 LABOUR PARTY MANIFESTO

Under these proposals:

- The Science Minister, based in the Cabinet Office, would be responsible for the Science Budget, for the Research Councils, and for the Meteorological Office which works with the Research Councils on climate change and global warming.

- The Science Minister would also be responsible for a reformed Government Statistical Service, and for an Office of Policy Research providing services to Statistics and Policy Research Units in other Departments.

- The Science Minister would coordinate science and technology issues and policies across government.

- A cabinet committee would review science and technology policy on a regular basis.

- The Science Minister would represent Britain on science policy in European Community and other international science and research councils, with Education, Trade and Industry, Transport and other ministers taking a lead in their respective areas of responsibility.

- The Technology Minister, based in the Department of Trade and Industry, would have primary responsibility for programmes for the support of industrial R&D and technology transfer, including fiscal R&D incentives.

- The Department of Education would have developed with the Higher Education Funding Council new ways of supporting basic research required to maintain the essential plurality of channels of support for research.

No such machinery has been proposed, let alone implemented, by the Labour governments elected in 1997 and 2001.

You may consider that, in my case, such proposals were simply the opportunist scheming of a would-be minister. I admit that I would have considered it an honour and a challenge if, had the 1992 General Election result been different, I had been called upon to serve in such a capacity. But my proposals were more serious. And they still have relevance, for they are grounded on the conviction that it is important to put science at the heart of government.

My conviction was supported by my research, and especially my reading of the Haldane Report of 1918 – probably the most farsighted and influential report on the machinery of government in the last hundred years.

The Haldane Report on the machinery of government

The *Report of the Machinery of Government Committee of the Ministry of Reconstruction*[3] (known as the Haldane Report) was produced at the end of World War 1 (1914-18). The machinery of government proposed by the Haldane Committee was adopted by the then government, and (with an important exception, which I will discuss below) has endured more or less intact to this day.

The three MPs and two permanent secretaries on the Haldane committee seem to have left Beatrice Webb and Lord Haldane to draft the report, reflecting their own shared interests, notably on research and the role of women. On the evidence of Beatrice Webb's diaries they got on famously.

The Report set out the principles which, by and large, were to underlie the machinery of government for the next century:
- First, the Report proposed a structure of 'Administrative Departments' for services provided (such as health and education and defence), rather than for groups of people served (such as children and the elderly), and
- Secondly, Haldane proposed research councils in different fields, where the councils would be largely responsible for choosing their own subjects for research.

---

[3] Haldane, Lord (1918) Chairman, *Report of the Machinery of Government Committee*, HMSO Ministry of Reconstruction,: London

Experience during the 1914-18 war had demonstrated that research undertaken by 'general use' organisations could have wider application. Such organisations, Haldane and Webb argued, did not, and should not, replace research organisations for particular departments, but would 'strengthen the hands of all the Administrative Departments concerned with subjects which are departmentally distinct but scientifically related'.

Lord Haldane recommended three 'general use' organisations:

- the Government Actuary (this proposal was immediately accepted);
- the Medical Research Committee (which survives to this day, now known as the Medical Research Council, and became a model for the other Research Councils); and
- a Department of Scientific and Industrial Research, also sometimes described in the Report as the Department of Intelligence and Research.

So what happened to the Department of Scientific and Industrial Research?

The Haldane Committee did not propose the creation of such a Department *de novo* to challenge the Administrative Departments. The Report argued rather that a Department of Scientific and Industrial Research should evolve, as the appreciation of the value of its work grew, from an existing (war-time) Committee of the Privy Council on Intelligence and Research. (Remember, this was in 1918, *before* the end of the war.)

The Committee's Report strongly commended the setting up of a Department of Scientific and Industrial Research (we would now describe such a body as a 'Department of Science and Technology') in the following terms:

> 64. Lastly it will be to the positive advantage of the administrative Departments to encourage the development of Intelligence and Research work for general use to the fullest extent which is practicable. Science ignores departmental as well as geographical boundaries. The harvest of results is won for the benefit of the Administrative Departments as a whole, and increases with the expansion of the territory which is assigned to the general Research organisations. Success or failure in a particular field of enquiry will, indeed, often depend upon the presence or absence of a fertilising contact with another field. A generous conception of the scope to be assigned to Intelligence and Research work for general use will strengthen the hands of all the administrative Departments

concerned with subjects which are departmentally distinct but scientifically related. ...

74. It may, therefore, not be premature to anticipate that the distinctive character of the organisation of Intelligence and Research for general use; the proper scope of such an organisation ... could thenceforth all be maintained by a Minister specifically appointed on the ground of his suitability to preside over a separate Department of Intelligence and Research, which would no longer act under a Committee of the Privy Council, and would take its place among the most important Departments of Government.

It had seemed so blindingly obvious to Haldane and Webb.

The trouble was that the proposed 'Department of Intelligence and Research ... for general use' failed to evolve. Science grew enormously, and its application. The science base contributed decisively to victory in WW2 (1939-45) with, among other things, radar and the atomic bomb. But the structure to integrate the lessons of science with the processes of government had little impact outside the defence field.

The contributions of scientific research, applied science and technology were acknowledged to be of increasing importance to our competitiveness and prosperity through trade and industry. But links between departments responsible for these areas (Education, and Trade and Industry) remained tenuous. The dual system of basic research funding – through the research councils, and through the universities – likewise grew enormously, but were poorly accommodated within the machinery of government.

The application of the strategies and patterns of science to government (for which I have argued earlier) was not realised by Major in 1992. Nor by Blair in 1997 and 2001. But that does not mean they are irrelevant.

I happen to believe, with Haldane, that there was and is a role for research more widely in government, and that it needs to win general acceptance by demonstrating its usefulness. I had seen the difficulties the Ministry of Technology encountered in being created from scratch as a full government department. My proposals did not lead in that direction.

Science at the heart of government

The Labour manifesto of 1992 would have placed the Minister for State with responsibility for Science and Technology firmly in the Cabinet Office, the Prime Minister's own coordinating office at the heart of government.

From this base the Minister of Science and Technology would have drawn together (using a ministerial cabinet committee) present activities within the Department of Education and Science (responsible for the research councils and university research), and the Department of Trade and Industry (responsible for the application of science and technology), thus ending an unproductive dichotomy.

Other, more recent, policy areas also demand attention. Climate change and global warming, as I have already observed, is undoubtedly the most pressing and problematic area of concern, and I will be returning to these issues in Chapters 23 and 24. A Minister for Science and Technology, with a department based in the Cabinet Office, would, I hope, be better able to co-ordinate scientific research and to develop and implement appropriate policy responses across all departments than is the case at the moment. What is not widely appreciated is that by establishing a ministerial department you build up the necessary foundations for policy making and implementation: civil servants specialising in this area, and scientific advisers. This is a long-term investment in human resources, a repository of wisdom and expertise: in short, an investment that outlives ministerial changes and governments. We shall need this.

The case for a senior, co-ordinating minister and department is overwhelming in the case of climate change. So many other departments are involved. For example, the Meteorological Office models weather and climate, and is the prime source for evidence on climate change; yet the Met, for historic reasons, is positioned in the Ministry of Defence. The Department for Environment is responsible for sustainable development, climate change and other environmental issues, but also for its core concerns of food and rural affairs. A Treasury minister has responsibility for using tax and other economic instruments, such as the climate change levy, to counter global warming, and is responsible for Treasury involvement in funding science, research and development. But for the Treasury these long term considerations are not a priority. The same is true for the Foreign Office. Global warming may be a world-wide issue. But our chief ally, the US, is the most intransigent polluter. President Bush's sights are fixed on the so-called War on Terror. He disputes the evidence for global warming. There are no easy answers. But burying these issues is not a sensible course.

I would hope that at some time in the not too distant future an incoming Prime Minister will have the vision to bring science into the heart of government.

20
Farewell to parliament

Farewell to Madam Speaker – Betty Boothroyd (now Lady Boothroyd)
This is not the standard practice, just a bit of fun between two old friends!
Photograph courtesy of the Methodist Recorder.

Farewell to parliament

After the 1992 General Election I had moved to the backbenches. I had decided that I would retire at the end of that parliament. If the parliament ran the full five year term – from 1992 to 1997 – I would be nearly sixty seven. Despite my successful coronary by-pass, I was aware that I had a long standing health problem. (I had had a heart murmur since childhood.)

It was a wrench to retire from parliament in May 1997. It had been my workplace for most of my adult life: a vocation as well as a career and a job.

Looking back on my parliamentary life, which had covered over three decades, I would claim three modest but lasting successes that, in a sense, epitomise the central concerns of my parliamentary career, and still provide a launch pad for the work of my successors.

My amendment to the Industry Act of 1975 has opened up access to the Treasury model, an indispensable tool; the amendment also required a twice-yearly detailed statement to parliament from the Chancellor. (This now takes the form of the autumn economic statement and the spring budget statement.) Optimisation programs I developed with collaborators and colleagues are now embedded in the Treasury model and many other models of the economy and, wisely used, can do much to contribute to our economic prosperity and stability.

Secondly, the present Select Committee on Science and Technology, which serves parliament so well, owes its existence indirectly to policy proposals I caused to be written into Labour's 1992 election manifesto, and directly to my energetic lobbying following the 1992 General Election.

Thirdly, the Office of Science and Technology, proposed in the Labour Party 1992 election manifesto, survives, though in an emasculated form. I would hope that one day it may become the foundation for a Department of State along the lines I have just outlined.

I would miss parliament. It is very much a community, with its own conventions (some arcane) and a social life based on the Chamber and committee rooms, fortified by the numerous dining rooms and convivial bars. It offers companionship and nurtures some long-standing friendships.

It is a challenge to your core values. Its judgements are sometimes severe, but it can also be very supportive. The unsung heroes of our great institution of parliament are those many honourable members who fight the good fight, doing the best job they can for their constituents and for our country. They do not make the headlines – but they make parliament.

When you leave parliament you leave all this behind. You clear your office, pack up you belongings, surrender you parliamentary pass. Farewells are brief: your colleagues, some of them friends of many years standing, are busily hurrying away to fight an election.

In 1997 I knew we were on the brink of a Labour victory – how big I could not guess. And I would not be there to make any contribution.

My wife, Elizabeth, looked forward to our retirement, though she too had some regrets at leaving. She had supported me throughout my political life, from the first time I stood for parliament in the 1959 General Election until my retirement in 1997: a period of close on forty years.

For the last fourteen years of my parliamentary career, since retiring from a career in teaching, Elizabeth had run my busy office in Westminster. We had many mutual friends. Working in the Palace of Westminster, she had joined the T&GWU, the trade union to which (for some obscure reasons) Labour Members' staff belonged. She had represented their interests in a joint committee with the Parliamentary Labour Party; she insisted that the Fees Office should refuse to pay the salaries of Members' staff where there was no contract of employment (to the surprise of many MPs, who seemed to be unaware that this was a legal requirement), and drafted a model contract of employment which was adopted; she had concerned herself with staff entitlements to pensions; she had given evidence to a Select Committee on information technology in parliament … and had been my friend and confidant.

Farewell to my constituency

There were other farewells to be said.

I had served Motherwell and Wishaw as their member for twenty three years. That is a great privilege. You say your goodbyes. There are parties and reminiscences, visits to be made, thanks offered. I had known and worked with many local party members, local councillors and community leaders, doctors, teachers, shop stewards and works managers, priests and ministers of religion, for nearly a quarter of a century. I had formed many close friendships; I knew people's grannies and had seen youngsters grow up, marry and produce a new generation. My wife and I had enjoyed living in the constituency. My good wishes went to my successor, Frank Roy.

Farewell to Ravenscraig

You may recall that Ravenscraig had finally been closed in June 1992, ending bulk steelmaking in Scotland after 120 years. For the next five years the giant tower continued to dominate the skyline.

In 1997, just after I had retired as MP, Elizabeth and I travelled up to see Ravenscraig for the last time. Charges had been laid ringing the foot of each of the huge cooling towers. The watching crowed included some hundreds of former workers, many of them known to me personally. Among them were Tommy Brennan, the chairman of shop stewards, and Frank Roy, formerly my election agent and now my successor as MP for Motherwell and Wishaw.

We waited, reminiscing. A helicopter buzzed overhead, with journalists and TV cameramen at the ready.

Then a hush fell. There were some little pops, like distant shots; then a few puffs of smoke. Then a low grumbling roar. The massive towers crumpled in a spectacular cloud of dust.

The first puffs of smoke. Photograph: Jim Donnelly, Wishaw Press.

20 : Farewell to Parliament 1997

The collapsing towers. Photograph courtesy of Jim Donnelly, Wishaw Press

The size of the towers can be gauged by the large trees near the towers, and the three storey building in the foreground, right.

JEREMY & ELIZABETH ~ THE ALTERNATIVE CV
as set out in a party invitation July 2000

Come & celebrate with us

our **70** *th birthdays and*

the **50** *th anniversary of our first meeting*

Sunday
9 July 2000

---

140 Birthdays - 138 Christmases
First 8 years in China (him)
& 18 years in Africa (her)
4 beloved Daughters - 5 Grandchildren
Assorted Dogs, Hamsters & Gerbils
Untold Nights under Canvas
(now best forgotten)
1 By Election Victory in 1962
9 General Elections
32 years working
in the Shadow of Big Ben (him)
& 14 years working there (her)
1,001 Late Night Sittings (him)
About 35 Computers from 1953 to 2000
More 3 Line Whips than Free Lunches
Up to 200 Letters a week for years
Several Models (him) (of the Economy)
5 Books - 3 Boats (2 made from kits)
Some Glorious Memories of Sea Voyages
(and several Near Disasters)
573 Toothbrushes
11½ pairs of Socks (him)
3 Years Retirement & still counting ....

20 : *Farewell to Parliament 1997*

Retirement

Elizabeth and I could now look forward to a happy retirement in Linton, a village about ten miles south of Cambridge. On the whole it is best not to retire to your constituency: it now belongs to your successor.

Cambridge was an obvious choice. We had met as students in Cambridge nearly half a century before, and began our married life together in Cambridge. We still had family ties with the area, and long standing friendships. We looked forward too to enjoying more time with our friends and our large extended family. And most of all we looked forward to having more time to spend with our four daughters and their families: Margaret and Michael Akam, and their sons, Thomas and Simon; Bridget and Gary Davies, and their two youngsters, Sam and Alice; Tess and her daughter, Stella; and Beatrice, who, unpaid, had put in a lot of work in my office in my last term in parliament working on difficult social issues relating to one of the All Party Committees I had chaired.

We planned to travel abroad, visit China and Hong Kong again, make more time for music and the theatre, entertaining friends, visiting libraries.

And of course, I was going to write a book.

PART FIVE

ON TRUST

Man's capacity for justice
makes democracy possible;
man's incapacity for justice
makes it necessary.

Reinhold Niebuhr

Introduction to Part Five
ON TRUST

Why, you may ask, did I devote so much of my political life to these concerns – to the science underlying tools and strategies for optimising our economic performance and the management of the economy, and to science and technology policy? These are hardly the headline-grabbing topics to which an ambitious politician should devote his or her energies. My answer would be, because they mattered. The potential of science for good – and yes, for evil – is great. But the proper milieu for exploring, developing and using science for good in the service of humanity is an open, liberal, democratic society. Like so many MPs I entered politics because I hoped and prayed I might be able to change things for the better. And I continued in this hope until the end of my political career.

As a committed socialist and committed Christian, I believed passionately in certain causes. These included not only improving the management of the economy and Britain's economic performance, but also the good that might flow from this.

Let me give two or three examples. I believed in, and worked towards, the alleviation of poverty in the Third World not just by charitable giving but also through improved trade and political actions by the international community. This was why I was glad to serve as unpaid Deputy Chairman of Christian Aid from 1972 to 1984. I stood down at that date as I had joined the front bench. But my interest and support continued.

I also took up various causes of justice and opportunity for the disadvantaged. For example, throughout my last parliament (1992-97) I was heavily involved, as Chair of the All Party Parliamentary Mental Health Group, in promoting the case for helping people with mental illness gain a better quality of life. Mental health is not a subject which will win you plaudits from the press or preferment from the front bench. Yet the debates in the House, some of which I initiated, were outstanding in the quality and compassion of the speakers from all sides of the House, and the lack of political point scoring. The media coverage was nil.

Throughout my parliamentary career I enjoyed my constituency work, and took my responsibilities to my constituents very seriously. I found this rewarding. As the years went by my respect for my constituents grew. Many showed great courage in difficult circumstances; many worked selflessly for the good of their communities. Problem cases would sometimes show up sharply failures in legislation, in administration, in foresight in government. An MP's surgeries and postbag are important and instructive.

Creating better opportunities for my constituents and their communities, and bringing social justice both to lives impoverished within our own communities and in the Third World, depend not only on good will and high ideals, but also on the practical means to effect change. And that means promoting the sound management of our own economy and developing a coherent science policy.

Most politicians aspire to ministerial office, and most are disappointed, as I was, by a failure to make progress in this respect. I spent over thirty years in parliament. Throughout most of that time, including my last eighteen years, I was on the opposition benches. While I might well have achieved high office if Labour had won in 1992, by 1997, and with Tony Blair as leader, I was both too old, and, given my heart condition, too frail, to hold office. The democratic process comes with a price. But these were not wasted years. Free-lancing within a parliamentary framework, I was able to take the long view. Unfettered by a hunger for office or celebrity or lucrative employment outside parliament, I was free to pursue my interests in science and technology and economics.

Beyond science

Now there is undoubtedly more to life than science, even if, in the broadest sense, science may be the key to managing the economy and public policy competently, efficiently and effectively. In itself science is not enough. It also raises many questions which take us beyond science.

Science affects how we think of ourselves as individuals, as communities, as a nation, and in global terms: What are we for? How do we know? We have to ask, Does science enhance or detract from our respect for other people and ourselves?

PART FIVE

ON TRUST

21 GROUND ON WHICH TO STAND   236

An open and liberal society ~ Science: Daedalus or Icarus? ~ Science and the transformation of contemporary democracy ~ Ezrahi's bleak conclusions ~ No easy answers ~ Can the pursuit of politics generate a relevant body of science? ~ The Mertonian norms for the behaviour of scientists ~ The Common Thread ~ Could we establish better political norms?

22 POLITICS, SCIENCE AND CRYSTAL BALLS   249

Problems and opportunities ~ Epistemology: How do we know? ~ The evidence from science ~ But is science 'rational' or 'objective'? ~ Can science's 'customers' skew outcomes? ~ The preservation of integrity ~ Real science ~ Models for decision: How do we make sense of the evidence? ~ The way forward ~ Norms for policy decisions ~ Guidelines for present practice in policy modelling

Introduction to Part Five ♦ 235

23 THE ETHOS OF A COVENANT 266

A breakdown in the moral and ethical foundations of our society? ~ The 'covenantal' relationship ~ Cooperation and collaboration ~ Multi-cultural cooperation and collaboration ~ Stewardship ~ The stewardship of our biosphere: global warming ~ Global warming: the response from governments ~ Has the concept of covenantal commitment a place in politics?

24 THE MORAL AND ETHICAL FOUNDATIONS OF SOCIETY 277

Terrorism: the moral issues ~ Defeating global warming: the moral issues ~ The common good? ~ 'Social capital' ~ Where do our moral and ethical codes come from? ~ Where do we turn for guidance? ~ The dialogue between science and religion ~ Science, religious faith and politics – a Bermuda triangle ~ Science and religion have been punching below their weight

25 A CLIMATE OF TRUST 287

Trust in systems – trust in persons ~ Covenant and redemption ~ Openness of mind ~ We can venture confidently ~ Action as fellowship ~ A valediction

21

Ground on which to stand

'The form of life in which we make our scientific knowledge will stand or fall with the way we order our affairs in the state.'

This arresting conclusion offered a foothold in my search for some ground on which to stand to map the shifting sands of politics, science and faith as they work today – and as I experienced them myself in a lifetime in parliament. It was during that time that people began to speak of what was widely called 'the collapse of the Enlightenment project'. By that portentous phrase was meant the demonstrated incapacity of modern society to achieve a rational, realistic, just and secure polity, despite the advances of science, politics and religion since the launch of the Enlightenment some three centuries ago.

The lessons of history cannot be learned simply by acting in previously successful ways. But with politicians, scientists and believers now struggling to rebuild public attitudes and participation in their respective spheres, it is instructive to look at a successful solution of an earlier date when crises were occurring simultaneously in all three areas. The Enlightenment still seems so obvious to most people, including myself, that it may still have something to teach us.

I found this vantage point, linking science and the affairs of state unexpectedly in Steven Shapin and Simon Schaffer *Leviathan and the Air-Pump: Hobbes, Boyle and the Experimental Life*[1]. This is not the place to discuss their case study – a prolonged disputation between Robert Boyle (1627-1691 – a prominent member of the recently founded Royal Society) and Thomas Hobbes (1588-1679). What interested me was the part that science, politics and religion together played in launching the

---

[1] Shapin, Steven and Schaffer, Simon (1985) *Leviathan and the Air-Pump: Hobbes, Boyle and the Experimental Life*, Princeton University Press.

Enlightenment. Science in the Seventeenth Century was not as powerful a factor in the physical and human environment as it is today, but it was seen very clearly as a political factor. The foundation of the Royal Society was indicative: the world's premier such foundation, it still today, over three centuries later, commands world-wide respect and offers high quality advice to government, a function it has performed since its foundation. Science, the science of the Enlightenment, was used to legitimate the constitution – the restoration of a monarchy more constrained than in the past, a monarchy licensed (it was claimed) to rule not by an arbitrary disorderly God, but by a law-making, law-abiding God whose work was discoverable and demonstrable in science.

The three things Shapin and Schaffer wanted to connect were the polity of the intellectual community; the solution to the practical problem of making and justifying knowledge; and the polity of the wider society. 'We have made three connections,' they conclude:

> We have attempted to show
>
> (1) that the solution to the problem of knowledge is political; it is predicated upon laying down rules and conventions of relations between men in the intellectual polity;
>
> (2) that the knowledge thus produced and authenticated becomes an element in political action in the wider polity; it is impossible that we should come to understand the nature of political action in the state without referring to the products of the intellectual polity;
>
> (3) that the contest among alternative forms of life and their characteristic forms of intellectual product depends upon the political success of the various candidates in insinuating themselves into the activities of other institutions and other interest groups. He who has the most, and the most powerful, allies wins.

An open and liberal society

This leads us to ask, 'What sort of society is able to sustain, legitimate and authenticate science? What contribution does scientific knowledge make to the maintenance of liberal society?'

Shapin and Schaffer say the answer given since the seventeenth century was unambiguous: an open and liberal society was the natural habitat of science. Such science, in turn, constituted one of the sureties for the continuance of an open and liberal society. Interfere with one, and you will erode the other.

But now, say Shapin and Schaffer, we live in a less certain age. Scientific journals are in our public libraries, but they are incomprehensible to the citizenry. Traditional statements about the connections between our society and our knowledge are not taken for granted any longer. We realise it is ourselves and not reality that is responsible for what we now know. Knowledge, as much as the state, say Shapin and Schaffer, is a product of a human polity.

It is not within the scope of this book, nor within my competence, to trace the development of the Enlightenment. Nor am I able to explore the impact on politics and faith in major scientific advances such as Darwinism (which, very significantly, coincided with the emergence of a parliamentary democracy in the turbulent politics of the nineteenth century).

As significant is the influence of the Twentieth Century's extraordinary explosion of scientific knowledge. This is the century which encompassed Einstein's formulation of the fundamental laws of physics in the early 1900s and the unravelling of the human genome which was reaching completion in the closing decade of the century.

The impact on what Shapin and Shaffer call the intellectual polity – on the general culture, and on politics and government – has been profound. But with the Enlightenment project now being widely thought to have broken down, we can try widening the post-modern political debate.

A major casualty in the collapse of the Enlightenment project in our day has been the decline in the public esteem of science, despite an acknowledgement of its importance as an almost overwhelming economic and social force. We have our fears: fears of epidemics from modern life styles from obesity and diabetes to flu-like pandemics spread by air travellers; fears of the cornucopia of modern technology undermining employment as the basis of social organisation, and of emerging instabilities rooted in the complexity and confusions of modern society; fears of natural disasters stemming from the effects of global warming; fears of global terrorism, of weapons of mass destruction … These are nightmare mixes of (often pseudo) science and dark forces. Should we take them seriously?

Science: Daedalus or Icarus?

Soon after the first World War, J.B.S. Haldane's *Daedalus, or Science and the Future*[2] appeared. Haldane used the Greek myth of the father and son duo who, using birds' feathers stuck to their arms for wings, aspired to fly

---

[2] Haldane, J.B.S. (1924) *Daedalus, or Science and the Future*

to escape captivity. The son, Icarus, flew so close to the sun that the wax melted; the wiser Daedalus, his father, and a master craftsman, survived.

Daedalus captured the prevailing mood of confidence in the affinity between science and the political and social objectives of predicting, guiding and ameliorating human behaviour. (The author, J.B.S. Haldane, incidentally, was a nephew of Lord Haldane, who produced the Haldane Report[3] on the machinery of government, which I have discussed earlier[4].)

In *Daedalus* the author presented what he supposed was a progressive view of human conquests ranging from space, time and matter to the 'dark and evil elements' in the human soul. But it encompassed science fiction proposals such as covering the country with rows of metallic windmills; artificially evolved nitrogen fixing; the alteration of character through drugs, eugenics, and the artificial development of human embryos outside the body.

Aldous Huxley borrowed extensively from these ideas in his novel *Brave New World*[5].

J.B.S. Haldane (unlike his uncle) had nothing to say about down-to-earth objectives like unemployment, growth and income distribution. So it is not surprising that *Daedalus* did not take root as a clarion call for a scientific socialism.

The philosopher Bertrand Russell, in a response entitled *Icarus, or the Future of Science*[6], immediately took issue with J.B.S. Haldane: 'I fear that the same fate may overtake the populations whom modern men of science have taught to fly,' he trumpeted. 'Science is not a substitute for virtue. ...Technical scientific knowledge does not make men sensible in their aims ... Science has not given man more self-control, more kindliness or more power of discounting their passions.'

J.B.S. Haldane had overstated his case in his desire to shock with the consequences of the implications of the latest biological research. And it had dire consequences in distracting attention from the need to build sound foundations across all areas of scientific research, and for the relationship between science, politics and society. Socialists and the left were encouraged to think it was all too easy.

---

[3] Haldane, Lord (1918) Chairman, *Report of the Machinery of Government Committee*, Ministry of Reconstruction, London: HMSO
[4] See my Chapter 19, pages 216-220, for a discussion of the implications of the Haldane Report.
[5] Huxley, Aldous *O Brave new World!*
[6] Russell, Bertrand (1924) *Icarus, or the Future of Science*

Science and the transformation of contemporary democracy?

Writing towards the end of the Twentieth Century and with the experience of the Reagan presidency, Yaron Ezrahi took up the theme in *The Descent of Icarus: Science and the Transformation of Contemporary Democracy*[7]. Ezrahi saw Russell's pessimism about the effect of science as more in tune with the sensibilities of our age than Haldane's optimism.

According to Ezrahi, an 'instrumental concept of politics' had encouraged receptivity to scientific and technological paradigms of public action, most notably in America, and some other liberal democracies. This concept, in his view, had had wide acceptance for almost a century, from the 1880s until the late 1960s. But, he claimed, it has become increasingly suspect more recently, with profound consequences for the role of science and technology in states that would still claim to be modern liberal democratic state.

Ezrahi entitles his concluding chapter, 'Postmodern Science and Postmodern Politics'. He got there by tracing the political functions of science in that archetypal liberal democratic state, the USA. Although *The Descent of Icarus* was published in 1990, in reaction to the Reagan era, his criticisms are even more trenchant today.

Ezrahi's interest in the relations between science and politics had been motivated by his desire to understand how scientific knowledge can render the actions of democratic governments more rational and more effective. He was also interested in exploring the ways in which the integration of science and technology into the making and implementing of government decisions could be reconciled with liberal-democratic values and practices.

Ezrahi's bleak conclusions

However, as Ezrahi admits, he became increasingly convinced that the story of the relations of science and politics in the modern democratic state was not an account of the progressive and benign rationalization of politics.

He came to see it, rather, as a process through which liberal-democratic ideology and politics selectively appropriated and adapted science and technology in order to construct or maintain political authority and legitimating the exercise of political power. If scientific knowledge did occasionally rationalise politics, this was merely an unintended or secondary

---

[7] Ezrahi, Yaron (1990) *The Descent of Icarus: Science and the Transformation of Contemporary Democracy* Cambridge, Mass. & London: Harvard University Press

consequence of its primary uses as political resources[8]. (There are echoes here of the controversy between Boyle and Hobbes.)

What emerges from Ezrahi is, therefore, not another account of how the attempts to realise the Enlightenment visions of politics, rationalised by science, have either succeeded or been dashed by the forces of unreason, nor of how public policies can still be guided by functionally relevant knowledge. It is a much bleaker view of the conscription of science, for specifically political and ideological purposes, into the role of upholding the state's conceptions of action, authority and accountability.

The point, says Ezrahi, is not that scientific instrumentalism has not affected modern liberal-democratic politics, nor that competence or technical integrity has not become and does not remain a relevant standard for judging political actors, along, and at times competitively, with moral and ideological standards. It is rather that a sceptical attitude towards an instrumental-scientific conception of public actions, which was confined earlier to counter-enlightenment circles, has now become a nearly universal state of mind.

Ezrahi's pessimistic perception was that at best science and technology have been used instrumentally – as tools – for constructing political authority and legitimating the exercise of political power; and at worst he sees science and technology as mere resources used to prop up the culture of 'gesture politics'.

I have to say that watching the political style of the present New Labour government I grow increasingly cynical every time I hear ministers using 'the science' to uphold their authority.

No easy answers

Science may, however, have a more healthily politically subversive role. We would be deluding ourselves if we supposed that there are easy answers to the questions politics, science and technology throw up.

Consider these words from a book by Nowotny, Scott and Gibbons[9]:

> Even in the case of 'wealth creation', to which all are assumed to subscribe, contradictions abound. There are complex debates in both a technical and an ethical sense, about the need for re-

---

[8] Jeremy did not live to witness Blair's use of 'intelligence' in making the case for the Iraq war.
[9] Nowotny, Helga, Scott, Peggy, and Gibbons, Michael (2001) *Re-Thinking Science: Knowledge and the Public in an Age of Uncertainty* Cambridge: Polity Press. pp. 181-3

distribution, about social justice and economic equity, about strategies to protect vulnerable members, and classes, of society from the harsh forces of economic globalisation. Instead of simple answers there are only partial solutions, temporary accommodations between different material interests, social values and ethical visions. Despite science's potential for innovation, the path from present predicaments to viable policy solutions remains long, tortuous and full of unanticipated consequences.

The twenty-first century view of science is the culmination of the continuous success of science and technology. Not only has science literally transformed the world, in both material and conceptual terms; it has also made a key contribution to generating social cohesion and maintaining socio-political consensus, at any rate in democratic capitalist societies, which has often been overlooked; science and technology have fuelled, or seemed to fuel, sustained economic growth and continuous improvement in the standard of living and quality of life. If Western society has enjoyed exceptional stability in the past half-century, this is largely due to its material success, a record which few other forms of society have been able to match; this success, in turn appears to have been intimately linked to scientific and technological innovation. This triumphant calculus ... has far exceeded the most ambitious claims and predictions of the Enlightenment. However, amid this success ...decisive breaks have taken place. ...

The first break has been produced by ...the unparalleled success of science and technology in stimulating novelty. Novelty is challenging - and disturbing. It creates uncertainty by challenging, [and] changing established ways of doing - [and] also of seeing things, experiencing the world cognitively, conceiving of meanings, deeply radicalising. In industry and business uncertainties proliferate. ...

Most important of all, the uncertainties generated by novelty and innovation may threaten our sense of self and personhood. Who am I in a transformed world?

Can the pursuit of politics generate a relevant body of science?

I would like to suggest we should stand Ezrahi's argument on its head. He concluded that at best science and technology have been used instrumentally for constructing political authority and legitimating political power; and at worst science and technology are used merely to prop up the culture of 'gesture politics'.

I would argue that science should not be pursued in the hope that it will achieve the Enlightenment visions of a politics rationalised by science. It is rather that the *serious* pursuit of politics could, I believe, generate a relevant body of science.

The opinion formers, policy makers and implementers – scientists, parliamentarians, ministers and civil servants, and the media – need to involve themselves seriously in the business of science policy if they are to be competent politically. By 'science policy' I mean not just the responsibilities of a Minister for Science. I mean the whole gamut of science issues as they affect the government and governance of our nation and, in so far as they are our business, the science issues which affect the peoples of this world.

This, I hope and believe, is not a utopian dream but a straightforward extension of present practice – the pursuit of the accepted norms of scientific research. These norms have been accepted most widely within the science community involved in pure science. They were originally put forward by Robert Merton sixty years ago.

We have here, I suggest, in the scientific norms a pattern or model for the evolution, development and adoption of behavioural norms in other fields and communities and cultures. In particular I have in mind the pressing need for norms in the political world where the issues of trust and trustworthiness are of crucial importance.

The current norms for political behaviour both derive from the way the political community works *and* shape the way the political community works. It is a chicken and egg situation. That does not mean it is immutable. Which is why we may have something we can learn from the Mertonian norms.

The Mertonian norms for the behaviour of scientists

It was in 1942 that Robert Merton, a scientist (and a Quaker) put forward the idea of norms for the behaviour of scientists in two seminal papers[10][11]. These influential papers have recently been updated by

---

[10] Merton, Robert (1942) 'Science and Society in a Democratic Order' in *J.Legal and Political Sociology* 115-262.
[11] Merton, Robert (1942) 'The Normative Structure of Science' in *The Sociology of Science: Theoretical and Empirical Investigations,* ed. Storer, N.W. Chicago: University of Chicago Press

Professor John Ziman[12], a distinguished physicist and a long-established veteran of science policy studies (his Science Policy Support Group was for many years funded by the UK research councils). He comments:

> The Mertonian norms [of behaviour for scientists] are not just unattainable personal attitudes. They are embodied in innumerable social conventions and mundane practices. These define and constrain our conduct as scientists. Publish or perish. Face up to the demands of peer review. Cite generously and meticulously. Reward originality and priority of discovery. Present your work impersonally. Exclude *ad hominem* jibes. And so on.
>
> These requirements are often irksome. We may sometimes be tempted to keep profitable ideas secret, skimp on measurements, fudge data, pirate the work of others, ignore criticism, boost ourselves or vilify our opponents. But our good name is at stake. Without personal credibility, our research would be disregarded, and jobs would no longer come our way. So we strive to perform as expected, and as we expect from our colleagues. The logic of life forces us to think and act scientifically, until it becomes second nature.

Ziman describes the Mertonian norms as elements of the scientific ethos in the republic of learning. I would urge anyone interested in this area to read Ziman's *Real Science: What it is, and what it means*[13]. However, here in brief are the five 'norms' he identifies:

> *Communalism* makes the fruits of academic science 'public knowledge', requiring publication to other scientists and to the world in general.
>
> *Universalism* requires that there should be no discrimination in admission to the science academy between scientists on the grounds of their gender, race, religion, or any personal characteristic.
>
> *Disinterestedness* requires that scientists should not allow their own personal financial or career interest to influence their reporting of results.
>
> *Originality* requires a clear distinction between the ideas or results of other scientists, with acknowledgement of their source, and the work of the scientist himself.

---

[12] Ziman, John (1999) *Nature*, Vol 400, 721 (19 August 1999)
[13] Ziman, John (2000) *Real Science: What it is, and what it means.* Cambridge University Press

21 : Ground on which to stand ♦ 245

Scepticism requires that new results should be critically examined to ensure that they are well-founded.

These norms were not laid down by any requirement of a scientific academy or by an authority of any kind. Rather, Ziman (and Merton) argue, they gradually emerged within the culture we know as the Enlightenment, as a way of describing the attributes of scientific work and behaviour that commanded the attention, respect and acceptance of other scientists, and by the scientific academy as a whole.

Scientists who ignored the norms or whose behaviour breached them lost their credibility. The application and further development of these norms led to the emergence of complex patterns of organisation and behaviour.

While there is much that is virtuous in these norms, their emergence was not an indication that scientists were necessarily more honourable than the princes, politicians or tycoons who have not – or have not yet – developed such norms. The scientific norms were the result of trial and error. They evolved. They work. And they had their threatening aspects.

Nevertheless they may offer some experience for application in other fields, and they emerged in particular cultures.

It is worth quoting Ziman at some length. He writes:

> Merton's novel insight was that science – he meant 'pure' science, for industrial research and technology work differently – is not just the activity of a community of like-minded individuals. It is a distinctive institution, with a distinctive culture. Its everyday practices dovetail into a compelling social framework. This framework supports a 'method', an attitude of mind, a profession, a body of knowledge. He made us realise that science is driven, shaped and honed as much by its internal sociology as by its philosophy or psychology.
>
> In 50 years, the sociology of science has grown into an established academic discipline. Unfortunately, the focus of this discipline has shifted. Sociology seems almost against science as it strives to put it into its place. Well, of course, science is not the only pebble on the social beach, and scientists like traffic wardens and airline pilots, are ordinary folk too. These are realities that we should all humbly accept.
>
> Yet science remains a peculiar institution, with its own way of doing things. Love it or loathe it, we need to understand just what

makes it tick. Is extreme specialisation, for example, an essential cog in the social machine? What winds the clockwork - social imperatives, co-ordinated curiosity or competitive ambition? How can we tell anybody whether it is working properly? Whose hands are on the lever for adjusting its output?

What is more, science is no longer what it was when Merton first wrote about it. The bureaucratic engine of policy is shattering the traditional normative frame. Big science has become a novel way of life, with its own conventions and practices. What price now those noble norms? Tied without tenure into a system of projects and proposals, budgets and assessments, how open, how disinterested, how self-critical, how riskily original can one afford to be?

There is no going back to the world we have lost. Anyway science has never had it so good as in this past half-century, and is still going great guns. But soon it will be offered a new contract with society. To renegotiate that contract with its eyes open, on even terms, science will need to understand itself much better. That understanding is going to require, not adherence to an obsolete ethos, but a sharp but sympathetic sociological self-analysis. That is the unfinished business that Merton's little paper began.

Ziman has now carried out himself just such a 'sharp but sympathetic sociological self-analysis' in *Real Science: what it is and what it means*[14]. At the same time he has edited an interesting book of papers on *Technological Innovation as an Evolutionary Process*[15]. It is not a companion volume offering a formal epistemology of technology, but it does collect together ideas for what he described as a pragmatic *habitus* of technology. I make use of these books later in the light of my own experience.

The Common Thread

One of the most compelling witnesses to the Mertonian norms is Sir John Sulston, the Nobel prize winner. I had visited the Sanger Centre in Cambridge on several occasions, meeting Sir John, the Director, and members of his team, part of the international team selected to map the entire human DNA sequence. One, Richard Durbin, Deputy Director, is

---

[14] Ziman, John (2000) *Real Science: What it is, and what it means*. Cambridge University Press
[15] Ziman, John (2000) ed. *Technological Innovation as an Evolutionary Process*. Cambridge University Press

now my next door neighbour. I was impressed by the brilliance and persistence of John Sulston's research, and the way he led his team – but also by his very human warmth and modesty.

John Sulston's autobiography *The Common Thread: A Story of Science, Politics, Ethics and the Human Genome*[16] is a gripping account of this most exciting research breakthrough, and of the setbacks and the intense competition that threatened its success.

But it is much more than that. As the boundaries between science and big business increasingly blur, and researchers race to patent medical discoveries, John was battling to make the strongest possible case for the international community to find a common protocol for the protection of wider human interest. In this case, there was particularly ferocious competition from the free-wheeling American entrepreneur, Craig Venter of Venter Celera Genomics. This (as John saw it) threatened to undermine the international community's attempts to make the map of the genome sequence freely available to everyone.

John argues that the quest for profits must not be allowed to restrict research or unreasonably limit access to treatment. It is a noble ideal, but one with which many more worldly-wise entrepreneurs and applied scientists would disagree. For them intellectual property rights are their most precious and tradable asset.

However, Sulston makes a powerful case for the backing of endeavours such as the genome project by public money, and trust funds such as the Wellcome Foundation which was totally committed to funding this project.

The debate will continue. It is my earnest hope that at least in pure science the Mertonian norms will prevail, while adapting, as they sometimes must, to new developments.

Could we establish better political norms?

The contrast between the Mertonian norms for scientists (at their best) with the norms of behaviour in politics (on a bad day) could hardly be greater. A scientist who laced his presentations with the abuse of other scientists and claims as to his own veracity would be listened to only as an eccentric curiosity, and not for his science. The norms of scientific presentation would make such presentations counter-productive. This is

---

[16] Sulston, John & Ferry, Georgina (2002) *The Common Thread: A Story of Science, Politics, Ethics and the Human Genome* London: Transworld Publishers (Random)

not because scientists are necessarily more virtuous or less vain than politicians, but because of the way the scientific community works.

The cardinal political sin is to lie to parliament. It is right that this should be treated with extreme gravity. But there is room for casuistry and semantics in parliament, and at a deeper level, self-delusion, self-interest and dishonesty. Politicians are 'economical' with the truth, yet throw around claims to 'absolute certainty'. They give 'categorical assurances' about what they call 'facts' or even 'the science' with a startling disregard for uncertainties of evidence and the caveats that any sensible scientist or economist would make about predictions.

Yet I believe that political cultural norms could change, and change for the better, if policy makers, implementers, evaluators and opinion formers – parliamentarians, ministers, civil servants and the media and indeed the electorate – based their arguments and actions not on point scoring or spin, not on short-term opportunism or theatrical performances, but on the evidential basis, on the science base. And science would prosper too.

It sounds simple. But it is not. How do we tackle complex problems? How do we know? It is to these questions I now turn.

22

Politics, Science & Crystal Balls

In today's uncertain world we face a set of interacting problems, challenges and opportunities, not only in Britain but also elsewhere in the world. I would argue that sound political policy decisions should be based, in so far as it is possible, not on political expediency or opportunism, but on knowledge interpreted in the light of experience.

This is not a very revolutionary concept. Take what has been happening in medicine over the past one hundred and fifty years. In the pre-scientific age medicinal diagnosis and treatment was very much a hit and miss affair. Since the middle of the nineteenth century, and with increasing speed and vigour over the past sixty or seventy years, medical science has made astonishing advances. There is still much to be understood. But undoubtedly, medical science has transformed not only our knowledge of diagnosis, prognosis and treatment for individuals, but also, through epidemiological studies and the studies of environmental factors, our understanding of causation and prevention, risk and costs, and the efficacy of treatments and procedures. The tools used here are statistical analysis and modelling.

The art of politics is, like medicine, very ancient. But politicians are far more sceptical about using the tools of science to improve the reliability of decision-making than are doctors. And their reliance is often on a very superficial level. The Blair government, for example, makes repeated appeals to 'the science' as justification for taking a course of action. Is this to be taken seriously, or is it (as Ezrahi suggests[1]) simply the appropriation of science to legitimise political action?

In this chapter I shall be attempting to explore, from the political view point, whether politicians should take science as a resource more seriously. In 'science' I include statistical analysis and modelling of both the problems

---

[1] See Chapter 21, page 240.

and the possible solutions, but also a more profound understanding of the mind-set behind science.

Problems and opportunities

We have to ask, What is the extent of our information on the challenges – the opportunities and the problems – which confront us? How can we improve on our knowledge? How do we distinguish between good or poor evidence? Between probabilities and possibilities? How do we handle causal links and hypotheses? How do we tackle these challenges? What tools can we use to model the problem and possible solutions? How can we predict the probability of outcomes? How, given the uncertainty of our world, do we make responsible policy decisions – decisions which may shape lives and futures?

The challenges we face are not the sort of problems that have general solutions: each initiative will have its costs, and will be of limited effectiveness. And problems do not occur simply or singly. The onset of AIDS in sub-Saharan Africa, for example, altered the terms of trade and the incentives to research into diseases in both industrial and developing countries. Global warming may be playing havoc not only with our weather but may affect water resources, food production and much else throughout the world. The terrorist attack of 9/11 has precipitated a war in Afghanistan, a recession in the US and the global economy, rising oil prices, further terror attacks, and the alienation of much of the Muslim world. As I write[2] there are ominous signs that we are likely to be involved in a second Gulf War.

At best our policy decisions, decisions that will shape that future, are made on very partial knowledge. We are none of us the sole agent and architect of even our own destiny. Indeed, at any and every time, there are many possible futures. These possible futures are the outcome of random events, and of decisions and indecision, of deliberate choices (often with unforeseen consequences) and of acquiescence to the choices of others. The agents are not only political leaders but also individuals, families and kinship groups, communities and nations, multi-nationals and despots, scientists and bankers, voters and even those denied the vote, thinkers, mystics and religious leaders. Some of the most influential choices were made years or even generations ago.

---

[2] The author died in May 2002, by which time there were clear indications of an impending war in Iraq. *Ed.*

But that does not absolve politics from the inescapable duty of taking action and changing lives. True, policy decisions are made on the basis of very partial knowledge. There are huge uncertainties. But the world we live in is not a solely deterministic one. Our actions count. And you are more likely to make good decisions, or, at least, more likely not to make very bad decisions, if you are prepared to listen to what science (and history) has to say, and to learn how to use and evaluate the available evidence and structures.

Inevitably there will be diverse opinions, and deep disagreements about diagnosis and appropriate political responses. But in almost all cases, we will need to ask, How can we know? What is the evidence? Is the evidence credible? What is the probability of this analysis being correct? Are there likely to be harmful unintended consequences as a result of a course of proposed action, and if so, what can be done to alleviate this? What are the risks – and what is the cost/benefit of proposed solutions?

Unfortunately, politicians are strongly motivated to play the game only for the short term: How do we win the next election? – or even, How do we spin the story for tomorrow's headlines? Of course, gaining and maintaining power are relevant. It is when you are in power that you make and implement decisions. But if you are in politics for long-term considerations – if you believe you have a duty to work towards making the world a better place – you need vision, a vision of the future. To an important (though limited) extent, the decisions made by parliaments and governments will, for better and for worse, for richer for poorer, shape that future. This is a solemn trust.

Epistemology: How do we know?

The answers to the questions I have raised above depend on knowing – depend, that is, on evidence interpreted by our best judgements in the light of our experience.

Epistemology is an arcane word for this basic concept: 'the theory of the method or grounds of knowledge' (as the Oxford English Dictionary defines it). Epistemology is the tool needed to answer the question, 'How do you know?'

It was Karl Popper who determined the direction of post-World War II scientific method of answering this question in his book, *The Logic of*

Scientific Discovery[3]. Kuhn's *The Structure of Scientific Revolutions*[4] and Lakatos' *Proofs and Refutations: the logic of mathematical discovery*[5] followed. The scientists' repeated cycle of tentative conclusion – tentative, limited action – revised conclusion or hypothesis – further tentative testing and action – has proved an extraordinarily tough working method.

The evidence from science

The questions 'How do we know?' and 'What is the evidence?' must be taken seriously – very seriously in the case of politics. It is not a problem in established areas of scientific knowledge: blood circulates; the sky does not fall. But our farmers did not know that it was dangerous to feed cow offal to cows. We do not know why the Euro exchange rate with the pound is currently low. Understanding the underlying causes of terrorism, and how we should respond, is even more problematic.

Yet confident statements are made by journalists, gurus and politicians in and out of government about such matters in the same tone of voice as if they were pronouncing on generally accepted truth. The subtle gradations of evidence are not allowed for; indeed, they are probably not even understood.

However, if you, as a politician, want an explanation of the nature of many problems, it is usually the scientists (the scientists in the broadest sense, including mathematicians, statisticians, modellers and economists) who can offer at least part of the essential evidence, and probably useful analysis. And you should respect their caveats, the gradations of certainty. But you may have to act on uncertain, not fully understood, evidence. Such is life.

Science may have little to say on some highly political issues – for example, the reform of the House of Lords, or the disestablishment of the Church of England. But even difficult constitutional issues, such as devolution, or whether we should join the Euro, science and economics can illuminate the economic and structural parameters.

Scientists can also often offer the most helpful analysis of what realistically can be done remedially about problems as various as global

---

[3] Popper Karl R. (1934) *Logik der Forschung* Vienna. Translated into English as *The Logic of Scientific Discovery* (1959) London: Hutchinson
[4] Kuhn, Thomas F. (1970) *The Structure of Scientific Revolutions*, Chicago University Press
[5] Lakatos, Imre (1976) *Proofs and Refutations: the logic of mathematical discovery* Cambridge: Cambridge University Press

warming or rescuing the rail network; scientific analysis may well offer useful models of how to sort out pensions or safeguard declining fish stocks, how to deal with epidemics both human and animal, how to feed a hungry world or cope with the threat of terrorists using chemical or biological weapons. The advice may sometimes be unpalatable, but political leaders who go against it for short term political gains risk our future.

But is science 'rational' or 'objective'?

Social scientists in Europe and America have questioned whether science is in fact 'rational' or 'objective'. Does science really offer an objective picture of reality? Or does the story also depend on the social behaviour of the researcher, dictated by vested interests, whether professional, corporate, intellectual or financial (including sources of funding)?

These critics have argued that the prevailing theories of scientific method were all variants of the 'representation paradigm', the idea, developed in the Enlightenment, that knowledge consists basically in making and using maps of the world. These theories, they argue, have all left out the observer, the map maker. Scientists would, however, claim that they do give close attention to defining the position and role of observers.

Ziman judiciously balances the arguments of the scientists and their critics in *Real Science: what it is and what it means*[6]. He acknowledges that –

> Contrary to the Legend, science is not a uniquely privileged way of understanding things, superior to all others. It is not based on firmer or deeper foundations than any other mode of human cognition. Scientific knowledge is not a universal 'metanarrative' from which one might eventually expect to be able to deduce a reliable answer to every meaningful question about the world. It is not objective but reflexive: the interaction between the knower and what is to be known is an essential element of the knowledge. And like any other human product, it is not value-free, but permeated with social interests.
>
> ..... science needs a new affirmative philosophy more in keeping with its actual capabilities.

What Ziman seeks to outline in his book is

---

[6] Ziman, John (2000) *Real Science: What it is, and what it means.* Cambridge: Cambridge University Press

a naturalistic epistemology that is consistent with the way that scientific knowledge is actually produced and used. In effect we have inverted the metascientific tradition. Instead of trying to justify scientific practice from a prior set of idealized philosophical principles, we have derived a more realistic account of its cognitive methods and values out of an analysis of the social institution where they operate. By first building up a sociological model of science, we have been able to explicate its real philosophy.

…..The best way now to defend the research culture is not to try to patch up the Legend but to depict science honestly as a systematic, rational human activity performed by ordinary people on common-sense lines. Instead of trying to deduce familiar scientific working methods such as 'observation', 'theory', 'discovery', 'induction', 'model', 'explanation', etc. from more abstract principles, it is better to show how essentially reasonable these methods are, and how well adapted they can often be to the logic of the situations where they are employed. This approach also encourages both researchers and their 'customers' to estimate much more realistically the quality of goods they are exchanging - the actual strengths and weaknesses of the knowledge that society gets from science. By renouncing all transcendental pretensions to authority, and presenting science as an epistemic institution trading publicly in credibility and criticism, we establish a stable place for it in our culture.

Can science's 'customers' skew outcomes?

The questions of 'knowing' may be challenging for science and scientists. It is vastly more problematic for science's 'customers'.

Let me give but five rather extreme (though not uncommon) examples of the way 'customers' may distort, or seek to distort, the results of research.

Firstly, governments are capable of misunderstanding, misrepresenting or sometimes deliberately distorting scientific evidence. President George W. Bush's refusal to sign the Kyoto convention is a case in point. The great weight of scientific evidence is there. The World Climate Programme was established as long ago as 1979, following the World Climate Conference convened in Geneva by the World Meteorological Organization and the United Nations Environmental Programme. By 1988 global climate had become a major public and political issue. Further World Climate conferences followed. The Rio de Janiro Climate Agreement was signed in

1992, Kyoto a few years later. In the cautious words of key scientists who prepared the working papers for the Kyoto agreement:

The balance of evidence suggests that there is a discernible human influence on global climate[7].

Yet the President's short term political self interest, and the influence of his entourage of oil men, dictates that he takes a line that 'the scientific evidence is not there'.

Secondly, the great majority of politicians (including Bush and Blair) have a very superficial understanding of science and the way science works. The Blair government's handing of the Foot and Mouth epidemic, for example, is a case in point. Blair, on the brink of the 2001 General Election, had his eyes fixed on how the crisis would affect the timing and the outcome of the vote. For a crucial early period he listened only to spin doctors, appeased only lobbyists. He was filmed, looking handsome but concerned, talking to army officers. Yet at the same time he was ignoring scientific evidence on the possible implications of the epidemic, ignoring scientific advice on probability and risk, refusing to consider possible science-based solutions, including the application of various models of the spread of the disease and the options for containment. The cost-benefit implications, and the economic consequences for various sectors, were not taken seriously. We have here an example of a government preoccupied by the politics of the crisis and simply using 'science' in the furtherance of 'gesture politics'. The management of public opinion, the placating of the farming lobby, and the timing of a general election, took precedence over a management of the crisis. This example is by no means unique.

Thirdly, ideologies or belief systems may put a skew on scientific results or endeavours. Scientists working in the communist Soviet Union and facing imprisonment for producing suspect theories often had to suppress or distort results. Capitalism may have short-term objectives that warp scientific research. In the previous chapter I drew attention to John Sulston's remarkable book, *The Common Thread: A Story of Science, Politics, Ethics and the Human Genome*[8], and the prolonged battle over whether his team's publicly funded research into the human genome could be patented

---

[7] Intergovernmental Panel on Climate Change, Ed: Houghton, J.T, Meira Filho, L.G., Callander, B.A., Kattenburg, A., & Maskell, K. (1996) *Climate change 1995: The Science of Climate Change.* Cambridge: Cambridge University Press
[8] Sulston, John & Ferry, Georgina (2002) *The Common Thread* London: Transworld Publishers (Random). See also Chapter 21, page 246.

and exploited by the American entrepreneur, Craig Venter. There was big money involved, and crucial matters of principle.

Fourthly, the media's hunger for sensational news may lead to distortions. These, oft repeated, can have a major impact on public opinion. Reporters get hold of science stories appearing in learned journals. There is nothing wrong in that. The damage occurs when the journalist spins the story, presenting it as a 'miracle cure', a 'scientific breakthrough' or 'a threat' or 'doomsday scenario'. Controversy sells papers, and wins celebrity for the reporter. A celebrity presenter like John Humphrys in Radio 4's *Today* programme will, under the guise of presenting a 'balanced' report, set up a confrontation between the researcher and an articulate protester. In order to liven up such an interview, even respected reporters and presenters ignore the convention of peer review used by all reputable scientific journals and instead invite criticism not from a serious scientist but a maverick self-styled 'expert'.

Finally, campaigning organisations like Greenpeace, Friends of the Earth and animal rights groups are constantly on the look out for new issues to keep the pot boiling. Their staff and supporters in the country are undoubtedly moved by genuine concern about important issues, and may have a useful role in raising ethical concerns. But so have many of the scientists whose research they are attacking. The staff of these campaigning organisations may also have career and financial interests; they, and the demonstrators they have enlisted, have often invested hugely in emotional terms in the issues to which they have committed themselves. So it is better to look at the scientific basis of what they actually say and do.

The preservation of integrity

The greatest prize is the preservation of integrity: the test of a good system is that more people seek and find that prize, and that it becomes more nearly the social norm. That is how norms develop.

However, the advice of the sociologists of science is that it is not particular cases but overall effects that matter. Harry Collins and Trevor Pinch have collected together accounts of what in their opinion are significant papers in the sociology of science in *The Golem at Large*[9]. In their conclusion, they say,

---

[9] Collins, Harry and Pinch, Trevor (1998) *The Golem at Large: what you should know about technology* Cambridge: Cambridge University Press

> It is vital that the disillusion that follows such episodes [as BSE] does not become so widespread that science and technology are no longer valued; there is nowhere else to turn if our society is not to fall back into a dark age. Neither science nor technology are the kind of 'higher superstitions' or quasi-religions, that many 'scientific fundamentalists' take them to be. The case studies in this book are meant to help to avoid the catastrophic flight from reason that could follow from an accumulation of incidents like the BSE debacle.

Yet in the case study of which I know most (economic modelling), Collins and Pinch fail even to mention, let alone to trace, the devious twists of the history of currently the most thoroughgoing and successful of applications of modelling, the control of inflation in the 1990s in the US and Britain which I have earlier described.

An aspect of the feared flight from reason not mentioned by Collins and Pinch is the loss of any world view, religious or cultural, that sees a coherence and consistency in our experience of the world. That is why due attention must be given to developing a working epistemology that people, scientists and lay people, politicians and voters, philosophers and priests, believers and unbelievers, can use and feel at home with. That is a challenge equally to the politician and the journalist, the believer and the unbeliever, the scientist and the lay person.

Real science

Ziman in *Real Science: What it is and what it means*[10] sets out to clarify the meaning of 'science'.

What dominates all other forms of science is science in the *instrumental mode* – research undertaken by the individual scientist or in partnership with a small number of colleagues to solve problems, an activity recognised by the term 'project'. There is not a single distinctive method, and a wide range of techniques is used. The societal function of science is thought of primarily in terms of the practical human needs that it might serve - needs in health, wealth, welfare and warfare. Projects are typical instruments of science policy. Such research is the use of science in the instrumental mode. The results of a research project cannot be guaranteed, but generally

---

[10] Ziman, John (2000) *Real Science: What it is, and what it means.* Cambridge: Cambridge University Press

they are thought to follow from the research, flowing from the research in what is commonly called the 'linear model' of technological innovation.

This is obviously over-simplified, but it underlies what most politicians, business people, civil servants and journalists say and believe about science: it is all about discovery leading to applications.

But in effect pure science is more easily recognised as, or associated with, *academic science*. Pure science, he says, is a complex way of life that has evolved in a group of people with 'shared traditions which are transmitted and reinforced by members of the group'.

Ziman himself, in a contemporaneous collection of papers from the Epistemology Group[11], has edited a many-sided review of the ways in which technological innovation seems to follow similar processes to evolutionary biological innovation. Applied to populations of discrete entities among which there are variations and selection, there is a wider range of dynamical systems than those used in biology. Ziman and his co-authors consider the appropriateness of evolutionary models for describing technological innovation, and cultural innovation generally.

The basic analogy between biological and cultural evolution has often been remarked from the middle of the nineteenth century onwards. Among authors who have done so are William Whewell, Karl Marx, Thomas Henry Huxley, Ernst Mach, William James, George Simmel, Jean Piaget, Konrad Lorenz, Donald Campbell, Karl Popper and Jacques Monod.

The distinction and diversity of these authors encouraged Ziman and his colleagues to consider the possibility of transforming the notion of 'technological evolution' from an evocative metaphor into a well-formed model. Ziman notes technological analogues of what an evolutionary theorist would term diversification, speciation, convergence, stasis, evolutionary drift, satisficing fitness (that is, good enough to work), developmental lock, vestiges, niche competition, punctuated equilibrium, emergence, extinctions, co-evolutionary stable strategies, arms races, ecological interdependence, increasing complexity, self-organisation, unpredictability, path dependence, irreversibility and progress.

People were making similar cross-cultural lists comparing terms being taken up by economists and engineers in the early 1970s – estimation, expectation, variance, feedback, adaptation, learning and optimisation. The development of these ideas and strategies in engineering automation have

---

[11] Ziman, John Ed. (2000) ed. *Technological Innovation as an Evolutionary Process*. Cambridge: Cambridge University Press

influenced government economic policy design – with ideas becoming sufficiently familiar to start playing a part in policy making in the 1990s – a cultural lag of twenty years.

There is now enough solid substance in multi-cultural, interdisciplinary fields to make it worthwhile looking for practical applications of cross-disciplinary ideas. There is on the one hand a need to maintain a continuing critical appraisal of new ideas, and at the same time to have an open mind towards them.

Models for decision: How do we make sense of the evidence?

Scientists are used to modelling the phenomena closest to the matter they are investigating. As scientists we produce policies for governments, which, if they follow them, will probably optimise the use of resources in that particular field. But sometimes as scientists we get it wrong, and often we are not able to identify parameters. And when we put the particular models and solutions in neighbouring fields together, they do not always fit, nor do they give an illuminating or acceptable view of the whole.

The reaction in the west over recent years has been to forsake an optimised overall model of the economy, relying on competition between different agents or companies to do the optimisation for us in the market place. The result has been brilliant economic and technological success in market areas, which is spreading yet further and faster as it takes off in developing countries and increasing trade.

However, non-market areas suffer, and the achievement of stable growth is still uncertain: the market place may be a stimulating environment in times of expansion, but when the market is itself distorted and depressed by recession, reliance on market forces may endanger the whole economy. Over the past two or three years the stock market has fallen significantly, producing, among other things, a crisis in the pension provisions for millions of people.

I have already drawn attention to the contradictory and complex ethical and social debate surrounding the aims and outcomes of wealth creation[12]. We cannot rely on markets to sort out these problems. If mainstream politics does not deal with the issues, reaction and opposition build up from society in general and from single issue pressure groups.

---

[12] Chapter 21, page 241, for quote from Nowotny, Helga, Scott, Peggy, and Gibbons, Michael (2001) *Re-Thinking Science: Knowledge and the Public in an Age of Uncertainty* Cambridge: Polity Press

Governments and mainstream political organisations have to go on, if only for electoral reasons, struggling to maintain full employment, stable prices, steady growth, and an acceptable standard of welfare – objectives on which their political survival depend, but which the market does not necessarily optimise.

The Blair government's problems with what are widely seen as failing services (education, health, transport, pensions ... the list could be prolonged) and the well documented increasing gap between the rich and poor are clear evidence that the market is not a universal solution.

In an age which prides itself on its new information handling technology you would expect that industrial organisation would be discussed predominantly in terms of the flow of information – the flow into, within, and from government – about its main activities.

Modelling is no panacea. But by seeking explanations of behaviour and basing such theories on the empirical evidence, it may bring out considerations which are productive if sometimes politically unpopular. These logical and mathematical problems and presentations may be rejected by politicians who would prefer an easy escape into gesture politics. But properly handled, the intelligent use of models does enable politics and politicians to see more clearly the real issues, and to offer more reliable ways of dealing with them.

The way forward

There is now evidence that in Britain the government is moving in that direction. The Cabinet Office Performance and Innovation Unit report *Adding it up: improving analysis & modelling in central government*[13], was published in January 2000. While welcoming this, I was disappointed that such a report had not been published earlier, shortly after the 1997 election, as an essential part of the mobilisation for modernisation under a new government. Early publication would have followed a precedent set in 1964 when, in anticipation of the forthcoming General Election (and at my prompting) the UK Computer Council, the British Computer Society and the Operational Research Society organised a conference on Computable Models in Decision Making[14].

---

[13] Performance and Innovation Unit Report (2000) *Adding It Up: improving analysis and modelling in central government* London: HMSO, Cabinet Office
[14] See Chapter 4, pages 59-60.

A difference between *Adding it Up* in 2000, and in *Models for Decision*[15] in 1964 (to which I contributed) is that surprisingly *Adding It Up* excluded from consideration macroeconomic modelling in the Treasury, and macroeconomic models in the private sector. That is a pity because this is the area where most progress has been made in terms of technique, and from which there is most to be learned. The reason for the exclusion of macroeconomic models may well be the hostility to modelling of some in the Treasury, probably including Ed Balls[16], who is closest to Chancellor Gordon Brown, and the indifference of the top tier of officialdom[17].

Another lesson which *Adding It Up* could have learned was the importance of inter-model comparisons. The interest lies not simply competition between models but also between the different theories of behaviour that underlie the design of the models, and the priorities of different model-builders (and their political masters).

The flavour of some case studies in *Adding It Up* is given by the story of tax/benefit modelling (Box 3.2)

> The Inter Governmental Tax Benefit Model (IGOTM) was originally launched collaboratively as an interdepartmental model. But DSS has preferred to rely on its own Policy Simulation Model (PSM) and not to adopt IGOTM. Similarly, difficulties agreeing changes to the Family Expenditure Survey (FES) with other users and with the Office of National Statistics (ONS) led to a decision by DSS to go it alone and set up the Family Resources Survey (FRS). The FRS provides a much better basis for modelling DSS policies. Similarly PSM is better geared than IGOTM to DSS priorities. But in both cases, the outcome involves a degree of overlap and duplication of effort. It was certainly not consciously chosen by government as a whole as the best overall way forward. Despite this overlap, efforts have been made by both departments to co-operate.

This nightmare hotchpotch inevitably gives modelling a bad name. Small wonder that policy is in a mess, in the politically sensitive and complicated world of tax and benefits systems, and pension policy, when even the modelling of the systems is so clumsily and imperfectly treated. A result is the ludicrous complexity of means testing of benefits – a practice which consumes so much time and resources, makes administering benefits so

---

[15] Berners-Lee, C.M. (Editor) (1965) *Models for Decision* London: English University Press
[16] See Chapter 15, pages 168-169.
[17] See Chapter 14, pages 162-164.

costly to the taxpayer, and humiliates and estranges legitimate benefit claimants.

What is also lost is the impact of policies on the individual, who is dehumanised by the benefits system machine.

It is, however, now within the capacity of such computer systems as the Fujitsu Parallel Computing Centre at Imperial College, London, to mount the complete historical record of individual tax and benefit payments that have ever been made, and to simulate the computer operations by which they were processed. So it is possible – though not necessarily desirable – to simulate hypothetical policy regimes on the records of individual persons, simultaneously with managing them. This would make it possible to overcome the problem of samples too small to describe accurately the situation of minorities. But clearly we will need the guidance of well formulated principles. There are issues of privacy. Will it pin-point individuals? Is that necessarily right – or wrong? Or does each individual have a unique value and unique circumstances, to which systems should respond rather than shoe-horning disabled persons (for example) into rigid categories? If so, is it possible to accord that, or those individuals, a unique value without denying such consideration to others? Or do you end up with the classical circular gaps in welfare economics?

Other case studies included in *Adding It Up* included:

Household Formation Model	Restructuring Social Rents Model
Population Projection Model	Long Term Care Cost Model
Civil Legal Aid Spending Model	Pensions Policy and Model
Labour Market Policy	Hospital Admissions Waiting Times Model
Air Quality Strategy	Formulation of Public Service Agreements
Property Crime Model	Electronic Delivery of Government Services
Impact of Tobacco Smuggling	National Road Traffic Forecasting Model

This is a wide range of policies and models. Inevitably comments made were about stimulating the demand for good analysis, integrating analysis with policy making, recruitment and retention of good analysts, how to get more and better data, and making better use of the external world.

Norms for policy decisions

It is important that the government constructs and uses models where appropriate in reaching policy decisions. But it is equally important that the construction and operation of at least one model in each field should be independent of the government.

Secondly, we must recognise the necessity of the testing and comparison, or what is popularly called the audit, of models. With the computer power that is now available, such testing and comparison can readily be provided by the public availability on floppy discs or Internet of the models and of the data. However until the practice and skills of modelling are more widespread, government will have to finance independent institutions, probably in academia, to do the testing thoroughly. The importance of such testing and presentation was demonstrated embarrassingly in September 2000 by the blank incomprehension which greeted Gordon Brown's politically inept response to the public discontent with state pension arrangements.

The underlying theoretical observations on welfare are those made by Kenneth Arrow and Amartya Sen. Arrow's General Possibility Theorem[18] states that

> If we exclude the possibility of interpersonal comparisons of utility, then the only methods of passing from individual tastes to social preferences which will be satisfactory and which will be defined for a wide range of sets of individual orderings are either imposed or dictatorial.

However, Arrow and Sen continue,

> If we wish to make social welfare judgements which depend on the values of individuals, i.e., which are not imposed or dictatorial, then we must relax some of the conditions made.

They devote the remaining part of this essay to an examination of the possibilities. In the final paragraph the authors sum up the argument thus:

> Collective rationality in the social choice mechanism [in the sense formally defined by Arrow] is not then merely an illegitimate transfer from the individual to society, but an important attribute of a genuinely democratic system capable of full adaptation to varying environments.

It was this that gave neo-classical economists the clues to designing practical democratic systems.

Amartya Sen[19], concentrating attention years later on the act of choice, says:

---

[18] Arrow, Kenneth and Sen, Amartya (1951) *Social Choice and Individual Values* Yale University Press (pp 59, 60 & 120)

[19] Sen, Amartya (1997) 'Maximization and the act of choice' *Econometrica*, 65, 4, 745-779

> The classical framework of optimization used in standard choice theory can be expressed as choosing, among the feasible options, a 'best' alternative. The general discipline of maximization differs from the special case of optimization in taking an alternative as choosable when it is not known to be worse than any other (whether or not it is also seen to be as good as any other)......
>
> ...... the important and influential concept of 'satisficing' developed by Herbert Simon[20] ...... relates to his larger focus on 'bounded rationality' ......which has transformed in many ways, our understanding of what it is to be rational in a world of limited epistemic, cognitive, and analytical opportunities.

'Satisficing' is a useful concept. You do not have to demonstrate that your proposed policy is the 'best' policy in some hypothetical space containing all possible policies. You simply have to show that it is better than any alternative that has as yet been put forward.

Amartya Sen, a Nobel laureate and the Master of Trinity College, Cambridge, has a Third World background. He has drawn attention to the fact to date that famines do not occur in democracies, for governments have to pay attention to their electorate. Whether democracies will be able to cope with drought-induced famines which are the product of rapid climate change is more problematic. It may be that short-term electoral considerations in, say, the US (where President George W. Bush has refused to conform with the Kyoto agreement) will outweigh the wishes of voters in India.

There is undoubtedly a case for deploying modern information systems at the strategic level in the private sector as well as in the public sector. And new generations of models will be developed and tested before they are implemented. So there is enormous scope for research and its application in the social as well as the natural sciences.

Taking together experience with the Mertonian norms for scientific research generally, and the development of modern information systems, it is possible to foresee their development and application as norms for the conduct and application of policy generally.

However, they will only be implemented if they are generally acceptable inside and outside government – and meet a public demand.

---

[20] Simon, Herbert (1957) *Models of Man*, New York: Wiley
Simon, Herbert (1982) *Models of bounded Rationality*, Vols 1 and 2, Cambridge, Mass: MIT Press

Guidelines for present practice in policy modelling

Drawing together these observations on present practice and problems in policy modelling, I would suggest the following guidelines for the future practice of government:

- All policy departments will cause to be built and maintained user friendly models representing their present policies and possible alternatives. At least one of these models will be publicly available and intended for public use in the monitoring and debate of public policies.

- Each department will consult with the Treasury and with other departments with whose policies it interacts on the structure and facilities that will usefully be provided.

- The useful life of a model is limited. When a model is commissioned arrangements need to be made for the development of its successor. Departmental models may be maintained in-house or contracted out to a university, research institute, or consultant firm. Departments will arrange for one outside organisation to test and compare the performance of every model which it offers publicly.

- The Economic and Social Research Council will oversee the operation of the guidelines and of the model system as a whole, and will be responsible for the training of the professional modellers required.

Clearly the usefulness and accessibility of such a system would be enhanced if there were an Office for Science and Technology located at the heart of government in the Cabinet Office, as earlier proposed[21].

---

[21] See Chapter 19, page 215-217.

23

The ethos of a covenant

Alasdair MacIntyre[1] opens *After Virtue* with an intriguing 'thought experiment'. He imagines a series of environmental disasters being blamed by the general public on the scientists. Riots occur, laboratories are burnt down, physicists are lynched, books and instruments are destroyed. Finally a Know-Nothing political movement takes power and successfully abolishes science teaching in schools and universities. Eventually a reaction sets in, and enlightened people try to revive science from the fragments that are left although they have largely forgotten what it was. All that they possess are fragments: a knowledge of the theoretical context which gave them significance, parts of theories unrelated either to other bits and pieces of theory with which they possess, or to experiment.

A breakdown in the moral and ethical foundations of our society?

Now consider, MacIntyre argues, what would occur if the moral and ethical foundations of society were similarly abolished by the cultural arbitrators – our political, religious and business leaders, the judiciary and forces of law enforcement, schools, colleges and universities, and perhaps most pervasively, the media and the entertainment industries (newspapers, books and journals, and the entire output of radio and televisions and cultural events).

MacIntyre suggests that in the world we inhabit, the language of morality today is in the same grave danger as the language of science would be in his 'thought experiment'. He searches for a way out in a return to the thought of Thomas Aquinas and Aristotle. On his way, MacIntyre says:

> In defining the particular pre-modern concept of the virtues ... it has become necessary to say something of the concomitant concept of selfhood, a concept of a self whose unity resides in the unity of a

---

[1] MacIntyre, Alasdair (1981) *After Virtue: a study in moral theory* London: Duckworth

narrative which links birth to life to death as a narrative beginning to middle to end. ...

Just because [a conception of self] has played a key part in the cultures which are historically predecessors of our own, it would not be surprising if it turned out to be still an unacknowledged presence in many of our ways of thinking and acting. Hence it is not inappropriate to begin by scrutinising some of our most taken-for-granted, but clearly correct conceptual insights about human actions and selfhood in order to show how natural it is to think of the self in a narrative mode.....

We cannot ... characterise behaviour independently of intentions, and we cannot characterise intentions independently of the settings which make those intentions intelligible both to agents themselves and to others.....

And what would be utterly doomed to failure would be the project of a science of, say *political* behaviour, detached from a study of intentions, beliefs and settings.

This detachment, and this loss of authority, was well described by Kenneth Arrow[2], the Nobel Laureate in economics and originator of modern general equilibrium theory in competitive market economies. Arrow's formulation of the neo-classical foundations of the market economy, and his contributions to the developments of economic theory, especially perhaps in its more mathematical and abstruse manifestations, have borne much fruit, as I showed in Part Three of this book[3].

In his slim volume *The Limits of Organization*, however, he is writing from the point of view of the young faculty member at Berkeley in 1968, at the time of the Vietnam War. It is, he says, much easier to undermine authority and trust than to re-build it once it had been lost. He addresses the tension that his contemporaries felt between the claims of individual self-fulfilment and those of social conscience and action. Quoting Rabbi Hillel, he asks:

If I am not for myself, then who is for me? And if I am not for others, then who am I? And if not now, when?

Arrow takes this further, addressing the basis of individual and social rationality, the limits of organisation in the handling of information, and the acquisition, loss and recovery of authority and responsibility.

---

[2] Arrow, Kenneth (1974) *The Limits of Organization* New York: Norton
[3] See Chapters 9-15, pp 116-177.

The 'covenantal relationship'

We need some well tested foundation of trust linking scientists and politicians, and the common people.

The greatest challenge in both science and politics is posed on the issue of trust and trustworthiness. Within religion, this challenge is addressed most seriously in the concept of the promised covenant: a covenant into which both parties enter voluntarily but in seriousness and commitment; a covenant which, though it is sometimes be breached, is capable of repair and renewal. Politics too has a shadow of this idea of a covenantal relationship between people and governments.

Thus, in democratic electoral politics, a commonly used concept in the relationship between government and electorate is the manifesto commitment. But a covenant goes a good deal wider than a manifesto commitment. In secular terms, a covenant is a transaction, an agreement or contract between two (or more) parties, by which relations between the two are regulated, and by which a certain status is established and 'goods' (in the widest sense) exchanged. The relationship of covenant helps to define and explain the nature of the parties between which the covenant exists.

The idea of covenant is at the heart of the collection of books that we know as the Bible's Old and New Testaments (or Covenants – for both 'testament' and covenant' are translations of a single word in the original). I shall return to the religious dimensions in my closing chapter.

Covenant offers a useful concept in tackling our modern problem, whether as individuals or as a community. Our problem is not merely the world as presented in today's newspapers, tabloid or broadsheet. It involves all the endeavours and achievements, all the failures and sins, covered by all the years we have lived, all our precious investment of learning and experience. The living past survives into the present as a deep stratum in our own minds. Our responsibilities as human beings, as citizens and as those offering political or communal leadership, are not only to the age in which we live but also to the legacy we have inherited from our forebears, a legacy which in due course we will bequeath to future generations.

The covenant we are building is founded and safeguarded by cultural norms. We do not need to understand fully what a covenant means, nor do we need to agree precisely on the nature of the parties between whom the covenant is made. Some will see it broadly as a covenant between us as individuals and the community. Some will want to be more specific, and will see it as the relationship between an electorate and its political leaders.

Some will wish to see it as a part of an over-arching covenant between God and mankind. We are asked simply to follow the norms.

Success in politics in the short term is measured, for the political party, in winning elections, and for individual politicians in preferment. For the record, I could not claim much success in either respect. But in ideas, success is manifest in their becoming and remaining a feature of the way politics is conducted. Measuring such success is problematic because there are always other contributory factors. The real test there is whether the ideas continue in use, either visibly, or as part of a large edifice.

To explore the concept of covenant fully would take a far wiser and deeper thinker than myself. So I will confine myself to just two aspects of covenant that should, I believe, play a more important part in our political culture: the ideas of cooperation and of stewardship. Both these have religious overtones, and rightly so. But in this chapter I will restrict myself to the contribution which science can make to polity.

Cooperation and collaboration

Cooperation and collaboration are, I believe, implied in covenantal relationships. In seeking to work with peoples from different cultures and political systems we – the West – are called upon to understand problems from others' point of view, not simply to expect their cooperation on projects important to ourselves. Our attitude can be arrogant, patronising, judgemental. Democracies can all too easily assume that *we* wage 'just' wars, *they* are terrorists. A covenantal relationship cannot be made to work without respect, social justice and some measure of altruism.

That said, there are many fields in which science policy may be able to contribute internationally to the well-being of the global community:

Cooperation on trade and access to markets
- international monetary relations (e.g. determining exchange rates)
- commodities and resources: including oil and energy; water for irrigation, industrial uses and human consumption
- sharing technological know-how: licensing and access
- promoting scientific education and training
- collaborating in research and development
- reducing barriers to trade (e.g. agricultural subsidies)

Cooperation in the care of the global environment
- prevention of global warming: coping skills, stabilisation, reversal

- famine and disaster relief: emergency aid and long-term development aid to tackle causes
- promoting food production, irrigation, flood control
- coping with epidemics, human (e.g. AIDS) and animal (e.g. BSE)

Collaboration on safeguarding human rights, justice and freedom
- tackling root causes of economic migration, including poverty, exploitation and political persecution
- tacking human rights abuse: slavery, persecution of minorities
- preventing the abuse, trafficking, enslavement and prostitution of women and children

Cooperation in reducing the threat of war, international crime and terrorism
- reducing the production and trafficking in narcotics
- controlling the production and trafficking of small arms, guns, landmines etc. to unstable and/or war-torn areas
- controlling the supply and stockpiling of weapons and fissile material
- controlling biological, chemical and nuclear weapons
- countering international terrorism, and the causes of international terrorism

Multi-cultural co-operation and collaboration

These issues will impinge strongly on India, China and South East Asia which have faster rates of growth and of the absorption of new ideas than the industrial countries of the west. This will make the East probably the more dynamic area for the next fifty years, in contrast to sub-Saharan Africa, where there are such acute problems including AIDS, failing governments, civil and tribal wars, poverty, drought and famine.

The reason for the west taking account of developments in the rest of the world is not primarily market competition: that is used by right wing lobbies in the west as justification for the reintroduction of exploitative colonial labour regimes at home. Nor is it to enable us to ring fence our prosperous economies and societies against alien influences. That, frankly, is not possible. No, the reason is rather that the diffusion of new ideas and cultural influences is inevitable.

Cultural influences spread with extraordinary rapidity – look at football, Coca Cola or religious fundamentalism. Electronics has taken root in Asia; genetic engineering will follow. The Web is literally a world wide web.

We should not be unduly pessimistic. A fruitful source of new ideas in science (and indeed in the development of democratic ideals) has always been the adaptation of methods that have proved successful in other fields. For example, Darwinism has influenced economic theory, and conversely. Similarly feedback, optimisation, learning and expectations in engineering automation have influenced government economic policy design, while statistical mechanics has influenced the mathematics of financial futures markets.

The ideas and methods never translate exactly, and different situations require different configurations of theory and technology. That is so in the natural sciences and it is even more true in the social and political sciences. It is particularly dangerous to base high-level political and populist generalisations on loose analogies.

Francis Fukuyama[4] traces the sources of the strengths and weaknesses of societies in Asia by comparison with Europe and America to different religious traditions. Confrontation with the technological and social prowess of the West forced Asian societies to drop many key elements of their traditional cultures. China had to eliminate 'political Confucianism', the entire imperial system with its class of gentleman-scholars. Japan and Korea had to do away with their traditional class divisions, and the former had to redirect the samurai warrior ethic.

China, Japan, Korea, Taiwan, Hong Kong and Singapore went different ways as they reacted and absorbed political and economic lessons from the West, but none of them accepted a self-sustaining political and social liberalism. They maintained aspects of their traditional cultures similar to those which Adam Smith found in his *Theory of Moral Sentiments*, which provided the basis for community organisation to appear. Social capital is the social organisation and habits which creates ways of functioning which are not based merely on individual interest.

In the modern world, India, China and South East Asia are also making major contributions in new ideas. Look at the names of authors of new papers in scientific journals; ask the staff teaching and supervising postgraduate students at LSE and Imperial College, and the conclusion is inescapable that the greatest national share of the research capacity of the

---

[4] Fukuyama, Francis (1995) *Trust: the social virtues and the creation of prosperity* London: Hamish Hamilton

next generation of researchers will be from Chinese and Indian families, or of Chinese and Indian origin.

At an international conference in 1999 in Beijing on the contribution of science and education to economic development, I argued the value of encouraging greater political interest and participation by scientists and engineers in political leadership. I was not alone in this view.

We need to hear the assertion of values and objectives by scientists participating democratically in government, as well as advising from outside. And we need to develop a greater competence on the part of society in the industrial and developing world in following through those objectives into harmonious policies. Scientists and engineers must learn to work with the economists and social scientists, and with the political process in their own countries.

Stewardship

Our stewardship includes a responsibility for our social capital: our cultural heritage and social bonds; the way our traditions and our history, particularly our social history, has shaped our way of life both as individuals and as members of families and communities; and our generation's contribution to the way forward for generations yet to come.

In many cultures, people see themselves as guardians and stewards, entrusted for a brief lifetime with responsibility for the world they bequeath to future generations. Many Christians would acknowledge that the commandment to love our neighbour as ourselves extends to loving 'neighbours' who are culturally different and to generations as yet unborn.

This is a huge and diverse subject. I would like here however to deal with only one aspect of stewardship – our responsibility for the biosphere – for here science can give great insight, and it is perhaps the major responsibility of our generation.

The stewardship of our biosphere: global warming

The realisation that the biosphere is finite and affected by human activity is but the first step in realising that the environment reaches into the workings of our very being. It has come as a sobering shock that the scientists working on the Intergovernmental Panel on Climate Change[5]

---

[5] Intergovernmental Panel on Climate Change *First, Second and Third Reports* 1990, 1995, 2001 Cambridge: Cambridge University Press

reached over a series of high-level conferences backed by years of research the sombre conclusion that the balance of evidence suggests that there is a 'discernible human influence on global climate'.

The evidence[6] given draws not only on a wide range of physical causes but also on a wide range of scientific methods needed to investigate them. These investigations have included studies of the radiative forcing of climate change from the atmosphere, the sun and space; observations on climate change from measurement of CO_2 and other gases; data from drilling cores from sediments and ice sheets; models and anomalies of sources, sinks and inventories; climate processes; the construction and evaluation of coupled climate models comprising the atmosphere, ocean, and land surfaces; projections of future climate, changes of sea level, detection of climate change and attribution of causes, terrestrial and marine biotic responses, and feedbacks to climate.

I visited the Meteorological Office throughout my parliamentary career, beginning in the 1960s when I had asked James Lighthill to check the case, put to us in the Ministry of Technology by John Mason of the Met Office, for a big American computer to model the atmosphere for weather forecasting purposes. (I supported the case.) Later, as Opposition Spokesman on Science and Technology I was a regular visitor.

In 1990 John Houghton, the Director General of the Met Office, invited me to the first meeting of Working Group 1, on the scientific assessment of the Intergovernmental Panel on Climate Change. He was the Chair, and edited the Panel's Report. I was impressed by the international composition of the group, its informality, and its scientific competence. Their report *Climate Change: The IPCC Scientific Assessment, 1990* was well received in the scientific community. It carefully balanced its examination of the evidence and its conclusions. Scientists are careful people. The Panel judged, *inter alia*, that

> The unequivocal detection of the enhanced greenhouse effect from observations is not likely for a decade or more.

Political leaders cope poorly with such probabilities and caveats. When it came to the 1995 IPCC assessment I urged on John Houghton the

---

[6] Intergovernmental Panel on Climate Change (1995) *The Science of Climate Change, Contribution of Working Group I to the Second Assessment Report of the Intergovernmental Panel on Climate change* Cambridge: Cambridge University Press

importance of stating conclusions in a way which would register with politicians and governments.

The complexity and sophistication of the analysis had grown by the time of the third assessment due in 2000. It was not possible to reach agreement in time and the publication of the full report, and *Climate Change 2001* was delayed until June 2001. It was the work of three working groups, with writing teams of 100-200 lead authors, dozens of review editors and hundreds of peer reviewers from scores of countries which produce assessments for about 100 governments.

The IPCC assessment report published in January 2001 projected a rise between 1.47 and 5.87° C by 2100 over all 108 cases considered. There are uncertainties, but the cumulative message of these series of models gives a much better feel for the policy questions that face governments.

The modelling and policy design problem for policy on climate change is far more difficult than for the economy alone, if only because the economy is one element in the global climate. But whereas there are other ways of treating the economy, there is no alternative way of exploring global climate change, other than by the use of global climate models. The problems of economic modelling cannot be ignored, but the treatment of climate as an endogenous part of the global system changes the nature of the problems, not least in requiring longer horizons.

The nature of the global policy design negotiation will be a game with greenhouse gas emissions as global and national instruments, and global average temperature the objective.

Nor will general theories about capitalism and the superiority of a market economy have very much help to offer on avoiding runaway climate instabilities that have been allowed to gather momentum despite the warnings of climatologists. By all means use market mechanisms, but do not suppose that they can be used blind.

Global warming: the response from governments

The political community is only slowly coming to terms with the realisation of what it means when experts tell us that the environment reaches into the workings of our very being. This is true not only of our global physical climate, but also of the global cultural climate, with its impact on the way we humans think of ourselves. We are not just individuals with a set of preferences seeking instantaneous 'satisficing' but agents created by a long history and dependent on each other over distant horizons. The threat of global warming challenges the way the community thinks about human affairs.

Taking action to safeguard the global environment will not be easy. It will entail fundamental changes not just in technology but in our cultural, economic and political climate if we accept that a responsibility rests on each generation to look after the global climate and the environment not just its own enjoyment and welfare, but for and on behalf of future generations. It is summed up in the word 'stewardship'.

Is this a politically viable concept? President George W. Bush, from the very beginning of his presidency, has rejected the Kyoto policies on the reduction of carbon dioxide from the combustion of carbon fuels in pursuit of US economic interests. This bodes ill for the future.

Stewardship calls for political vision and political and economic sacrifices. Our horizons are not the next election, not even the welfare of our grandchildren. We are being called upon to defer satisfying our needs and our wants to safeguard unborn generations that we will never see in our own lifetimes. This poses questions about who we are and what we are here for – ideas to which I will return in my final chapter.

Has the concept of covenantal commitment a place in politics?

In parliamentary democracies, as I have already observed, a commonly used concept in the relationship between government and electorate is the manifesto commitment. Governments are held to account as to whether they have fulfilled their electoral promises.

I was very much aware of this in the run up to the 1987 General Election and even more the 1992 General Election when, as Opposition Spokesman for Science and Technology, I was primarily responsible for formulating policies for science and technology that would have become government policy had Labour been elected.

By convention, in Britain the House of Lords may act as a revising chamber when it considers legislation which enshrines manifesto commitments. It can amend, and return a bill to the Commons. But ultimately it cannot block enactment of a manifesto commitment. So, theoretically, a government should be able to deliver on all its election promises. If the government consistently fails to deliver on matters of crucial importance to the voters (and governments always fail to a greater or lesser extent) the ultimate penalty for that government is electoral defeat.

Manifesto commitments can thus be seen as a bargain or contract between a government, its MPs, parliament and the electorate. But it is very short term commitment: it lasts for only four or five years.

Now consider again the gains that might be made if society were to turn away from the current craze for undermining the moral and ethical foundations of our society. (I include in 'society' parliament and people, our cultural and religious institutions, and, very importantly, the media which shapes and echoes back to us our norms and *mores*.) What would happen if instead society gave serious consideration to the potential for a covenantal relationship between parliament and people? Is it too daring to suppose this might gradually change the norms for political behaviour?

For many MPs there is already an underlying sense of commitment, which I think could be described as 'covenantal'. As I came to know my parliamentary colleagues, I found that those whom I most respected had entered politics very often for idealistic reasons, reasons about which they seldom spoke. The best quietly held on to an ideal of public service, despite the hurly-burly of parliamentary life, the corruptions of power, the numerous disappointments of political careers. The rewards are few. Parliamentarians who conform to norms of civilized parliamentary behaviour rarely attract attention or plaudits. The media prefers to portray parliamentarians as rowdy exhibitionists, venal, self-seeking, hypocritical and untrustworthy. Idealism is often lampooned.

Similarly, political parties and party loyalty are often derided. Yet idealism plays an important part in many MPs' choice of party – whether Labour, Conservative, Liberal or another. Yes, parties can be fallible, wrong-headed, misguided and misled. But party politics is essential in a healthy parliamentary democracy. Party allegiance – potentially a covenantal relationship – need not be self-serving or subservient or uncritical.

Interestingly, opinion polls consistently show that the public by and large regard politicians as untrustworthy, yet the majority believe that their own MP is a good constituency MP! In my experience, this latter view is often well-founded. Many MPs, particularly long-serving MPs, have a genuine and heart-felt commitment to their constituents and constituency. It goes well beyond the mere need to be re-elected.

I am not saying that parliamentarians are saints. They are fallible human beings doing a difficult job. But if their job were seen in a different light (and more fairly reported) we might be on our way to developing political norms that would serve our country and the world better.

24

The moral and ethical foundations of society

I began the previous chapter with a discussion of Alasdair MacIntyre's *After Virtue*[1]. MacIntrye is concerned at the erosion of the moral and ethical foundations of our society if we lose the language of morality as a means of discussing life. In this chapter I wish to explore this concern.

It is a serious concern, widely held. If true, it threatens the basis of our polity and governance.

We face in our own generation two major threats, two moral dilemmas. At present they are discrete. If we fail to act, they may come together with devastating results. One threat is that arising from world-wide terrorism. The second threat arises from global warming, an equally intractable, politically fraught and pressing problem. If we fail here, the long-term effects may well threaten the future well-being of humanity and the globe.

Both these concerns raise serious moral issues. In both cases – countering world-wide terrorism and countering global warming – we (the Western liberal democracies) are in business of changing human behaviour, by force (it would appear) in the case of terrorism; by the power of argument in the case of global warming.

Terrorism: the moral issues

Man has a terrible propensity to a self-belief that justifies inhumanity. 'Enemies' are dehumanised or demonised. Fear fuels revenge. We justify exploitation; justify enslaving, subjugating, abusing, and oppressing the 'other'. Remember the holocaust? Hiroshima? Rwanda? Other atrocities? The horror is that though we are sometimes victims, in *some* cases these things were done in our name, some we applauded, and some we ignored.

---

[1] MacIntyre, Alasdair (1981) *After Virtue: a study in moral theory* London: Duckworth

The future is bleak if we cannot find ways to contain and then de-escalate dangerous situations. It may take years. It calls for great self-discipline to master our terror, our vengefulness. The threat of terrorism is real. Yet tangled up with our fears, our anger, our sense of injustice and outrage, are our ideals of justice and peace, respect and tolerance, equity and compassion. We must cling to these. In the present crisis we shall need all our statesmanship if we are to avoid inflaming moderate Islamic opinion, respected religious leaders, governments and peoples.

We have to ask, will our superior firepower in the so-called 'War on Terrorism' actually change the mind-sets of terrorists? The difficult part for the superpowers is not winning a war: it will be winning the peace. That is the business of politics, of diplomacy, of peace-makers, of community and religious leaders. It is a moral issue.

Defeating global warming: the moral issues

War may, or may not, defeat terrorism (a threat that could kill tens or hundreds of thousands). But what about the more serious threat, that of global warming, which may kill millions? Here we are forced back on to the power of the scientific evidence, of political argument and of moral persuasion. It is inconceivable that we should bomb the US into submission to the Kyoto protocols on global warming!

Yet unless we take the necessary steps to reverse the global warming, for which there is ample scientific evidence, we will not simply destabilise our own climate and economy but that of the whole world.

The combination of a continuing 'war on terrorism' and the foreseeable consequence of global warming could be lethal: the collapse of fragile economies, new epidemics, desertification, famine, wars over food and water resources, flooding, massive population movements from devastated areas to countries such as Britain that are less vulnerable to climate change.

Political action on global warming is not easy. Present trends in global warming will only become fully apparent to ordinary people in the next fifty to one hundred years. We ourselves will not live to see the worst effects of our thoughtlessness, and that of our forbears.

This is indeed a moral issue. Never before have we been asked to take a decision of this magnitude with no benefits, and some very real costs, to ourselves. Yet if we refuse to act, the effects may become irreversible and the penalties for future generations severe. Are we willing to obey the call to safeguard generations we will never know and populations that are beyond our national boundaries or indeed our continent? This conflicts with many of our immediate goals, and our tendency to a short-term hedonistic self-absorption and indulgence.

If the moral and ethical foundations of our society have crumbled, as feared, we and our leaders may well refuse the sacrifice. That is currently the position of the Bush government. Smart politics. But a profoundly corrupt policy decision.

The stakes are very high. Will our political system, our political and social culture, our media, our Prime Minister, have the courage, the vision, the resilience, the integrity and the altruism to rise to the challenge?

The common good?

We feel very puny in the face of these global threats. Yet there are ways in which we, as individuals, as communities, can join in repairing the damage. Take democracy, one of our proudest boasts. Do we just pay lip-service to this concept, or can we renew and enlarge our political institutions and democratic traditions to meet these new challenges?

After Virtue is a complex and densely argued book, but let me just pick out one or two pointers. Early on MacIntyre discusses the seminal concept of democracy as it was evolving in Athens in Aristotle's time (384-322 BCE). Democracy – a rule based on the *demos* (the people) – was, according to Aristotle, the sharing of all in the 'common project of creating and sustaining the life of the city' – the *polis*.

But have we lost this insight? MacIntyre writes:

> The notion of the political community as a common project is alien to the modern liberal individualist world. This is how we sometimes at least think of schools, hospitals or philanthropic organizations; but we have no conception of such a form of community concerned, as Aristotle says the *polis* is concerned, with the whole of life, not with this or that good, but with man's good as such.

Democracy, MacIntyre argues, even in our own generation, should rediscover its core value, 'good as such', in the 'common project of creating and sustaining the life of the community'. I agree.

Furthermore, I would argue, the community – the *polis* – is no longer a small city state but for some purposes (including global warming and global terrorism) the whole global *polis*, the global village. All of us, and particularly those of us who have the good fortune to live in a democracy, have a right and a duty to be involved in this 'common project', a project which extends across continents and seas, across races, political systems, states and generations, and embraces all mankind.

Later in his book MacIntyre argues in favour of 'the unity of human life'. 'Virtue' (he argues) is an underlying and unifying characteristic displayed to a greater or lesser extent in all the roles we play:

> The unity of a virtue in someone's life is intelligible only as a characteristic of a unitary life, a life that can be conceived and evaluated as a whole ... a concept of self whose unity resides in the unity of a narrative with links birth to life to death as a narrative beginning to middle to end.

I cannot do justice to this closely argued book. Here I simply wish to bring to your attention the way MacIntrye couples democracy, the 'common project of creating and sustaining the life of the *polis*', with the unitary and unifying nature of what MacIntyre calls 'virtue' for the self.

MacIntyre's position (if I read him aright) is that we need such moral and ethical foundations in our society to safeguard both our own integrity as persons and the collaborative pursuit of the common good which constitutes our polity. Lose one, and you are in danger of losing the other.

'Social capital'

The concept of 'social capital' is beginning to emerge in some recent studies. It embraces our investment (not necessarily in monetary terms) in communal and social goods, in the pursuit and enjoyment and sharing of what MacIntrye calls the 'common good'.

Robert Putman, among others, raises the issue in his *Bowling alone: the collapse and revival of American community*[2] as does Francis Fukuyama in his arresting book, *Trust: the social virtues and the creation of prosperity*[3].

Putnam, drawing on the evidence of surveys, shows how over the past twenty five years we (by which he means primarily, Americans, but by extensions all of us in the West) have become increasingly disconnected from family, friends and neighbours, and social structures, whether the PTA, church, recreation clubs, political parties or bowling leagues. He argues that our shrinking access to the 'social capital' that is the reward of communal activity and community sharing is a serious threat to our civic

---

[2] Putnam, Robert (2000) *Bowling alone: the collapse and revival of American community* New York: Simon and Schuster

[3] Fukuyama, Francis (1995) *Trust: the social virtues and the creation of prosperity* London: Hamish Hamilton

and personal health. There is, he argues, good statistical and other evidence that social bonds are the most powerful predictors of life satisfaction.

Fukuyama, in his book *Trust: the social virtues and the creation of prosperity*, comes at the question from an interesting perspective, exploring the way in which countries that share apparently similar economic systems are in fact quite different – different in their approaches to work, to social cultures, to entrepreneurship, industrial organisation and, ultimately, financial performance. A former deputy director of the US State Department's policy planning staff and now an analyst at the RAND Corporation, he asserts tendencies in some democracies will be damaging.

What is worrying is that both Putman and Fukuyama see a decline in what they call 'social capital' and, like MacIntyre, have forebodings for the future.

Where do our moral and ethical codes come from?

Edward O. Wilson, the American sociobiologist, approaches the issue somewhat differently. In his synthesis *Consilience: the Unity of Knowledge*[4] he marks the steps towards asking the key underlying questions about the purpose and meaning of human life.

Wilson argues that our intellectual mastery of the truths of our universe, originating in the ancient Greek concept of orderliness and reaching it apogee in the Age of Enlightenment, has been gradually lost in the increasing fragmentation and specialisation of the last two centuries. He argues however that the goals of the Enlightenment, with its belief in the fundamental unity of all knowledge, will surge back and are reappearing on the very frontiers of science and humanistic scholarship.

Wilson takes his title – 'consilience' (which is derived from the words for 'jumping' and 'together') – from a treatise by William Whewell, published as long ago as 1840[5]. Wilson defines 'consilience' as meaning the 'jumping together' of knowledge linking facts and fact-based theory across disciplines to create a common groundwork. Like MacIntyre, Putman and Fukuyama he is arguing for a common grounding in a shared cultural, or ethical, resource.

In the course of his discussion, Wilson distinguishes the two broad schools of thought on ethics: the Transcendentalist and the Empiricist. To the Transcendentalist, the moral code is given – handed down if you like,

---

[4] Wilson, Edward O.(1998) *Consilience: the Unity of Knowledge* London: Little, Brown.
[5] Whewell, William (1840) *The Philosophy of the Inductive Sciences*

on tablets of stone at the top of a holy mountain. To the Empiricist the code evolves. Both positions, he says, may be held whether or not you believe in God. (I am sure he is right here.) 'The argument of the religious transcendentalist,' Wilson recalls, 'is the one I first learned as a child in the Christian faith. I have reflected on it repeatedly since, and am by intellect and temperament bound to respect its ancient traditions'. But it is the argument of the Empiricist that is his own.

(Wilson came from a fundamentalist Southern Baptist background. As a young scientist learning about evolution, he rejected the fundamentalist doctrine of 'creationism' – and with it, religious belief. Unlike Wilson, but like most Christians in Britain, I have never subscribed to a belief in 'creationism', and see evolution as the way God acts in his creation.)

I would embrace both the transcendentalist and empiricist positions..

I believe with the transcendentalist that morality and ethics have their ultimate origin in the transcendent nature of good and loving God, revealed slowly to us over generations. But I also believe moral codes have evolved over the long course of human evolution and history and thus have an empirical basis.

In that sense I am optimistic. However, these moral codes are, like all human institutions, liable to degenerate and be corrupted. Constant renewal is needed. Are we facing a crisis? Where can we turn for guidance?

Where do we turn for guidance?

From my student days, now over fifty years ago, I have been reading widely in theology, not only by mainstream theologians but also authors such as the physicist Charles Coulson; the cosmologists James Jeans, Arthur Eddington, Fred Hoyle, and Herman Bondi; philosophers including Martin Heidegger, A.N. Whitehead, Bertrand Russell, Karl Popper, Imre Lakatos, Stephen Toulmin, Simone Weil and Alasdair MacIntyre; and the physiologists Charles Sherrington, C.H. Waddington, and J.Z. Young.

Whilst I was Opposition Spokesperson for Science and Technology from 1983 to 1992, the science lobby was in constant touch with me, through the learned societies and professional associations, as well as campaigning organisations like Save British Science. Scientists did not hesitate to raise such issues as abortion, bioethics and developing countries' debts. They did not hesitate to take a moral or ethical view on such issues, whether they held religious convictions or not. More recently, they have been raising forcefully issues such as global warming.

Many of the scientists whom I met were however practising Christians who acted, it seemed to me, out of much the same motives as other scientists – to try to make the world a better place, to enjoy discovery, to care for people. Those who were Christians saw this as serving God. Some held senior or very senior positions in universities or research teams. This did not cause problems to agnostics, humanists and those of other faiths. While there are exceptions, in general, scientists of whatever faith tend to be tolerant and undogmatic in their science. They do not make a parade of their personal beliefs. And because they have an openness towards the personal, and the rational beauty and the fruitfulness of the universe, they join in a common struggle; they see their theology and their faith as allied with science against a modern despair of any knowledge of reality.

Scientists who are on the record as Christians often emerge as leaders in major projects in global science. I have in mind people like John Houghton[6], who is chairman of Working Group I on the Science of Climate Change of the Intergovernmental Panel on Climate Change; Francis Collins, who is Director of the US National Centre for Human Genome Research, and involved in the human genome project; and Derek Burke[7], who was Chairman of the UK Government Advisory Committee on Novel Foods, and worked on genetically modified organisms. From my knowledge of the activities and interests of other scientists in nuclear power, information technology, material sciences and other fields, I became aware of the fact that many are active Christians.

Within Britain we have examples of scientists who have felt a vocation to become ordained priests in the Church of England and have contributed notably as theologians such as John Habgood, formerly the Archbishop of York, Arthur Peacocke, John Polkinghorne and Fraser Watts. An important objective for them has been to establish the study of science and religion as a serious element in theology and religious studies, along with subjects such as history, philosophy, politics, sociology and anthropology and comparative religion.

The dialogue between science and religion

Much of the popular dialogue about science and religion in Britain has been addressed to, or at least received by, Christians as a reassurance about their faith. For centuries religious institutions and faith systems have

---

[6] Houghton, John (1995) *The Search for God: Can Science Help?* Oxford: Lion Publishing
[7] Burke, Derek (1996) *Strategic Church Leadership* London: SPCK

(misguidedly in my view) seen science as a threat to faith. Most Christians however see science and faith as working together; if there is a tension between them, it is usually the dogmatic elements in the faith that is modified in the light of the empirical evidence.

However, as the years have gone by, I have become increasingly aware that on the central substance of science and technology and a philosophy which made it possible to act effectively on global issues, there is a gap, a blind spot, which mattered to science and to politics as well as to religion.

Science, religious faith, and politics, taken together, are perceived as a kind of 'Bermuda triangle' into which no theologian dares to venture.

Science, religious faith and politics – a Bermuda triangle?

May I give a typical example of gaps in the dialogue? John Polkinghorne's *Scientists as Theologians*[8] gives a useful overview of the dialogue between science and religion. It is well worth reading. In this he compares three 'mini-systematic theologies' produced by Barbour[9], Peacocke[10], and by himself[11]. All three expound Christian belief approached from the viewpoint of a scientist theologian. This tradition has more recently been extended and updated by the more recent books of Southgate[12], McGrath[13] and Luscombe[14].

However, Polkinghorne's book has some curious gaps. Published in 1995, we should not expect a concern about international terrorism. But global warming was already a live issue. It does not get a mention. Neither Polkinghorne's *Scientists and Theologians* nor the later books by Southgate, McGrath and Luscombe – all useful standard texts on science and religion – list any of the following in their subject indices:

> Apartheid, BSE, climate change, conservatism, debt, disability, economics, employment, family, global warming, government,

---

[8] Polkinghorne, John (1996) *Scientists as Theologians: A Comparison of the Writings of Ian Barbour, Arthur Peacocke and John Polkinghorne* London: SPCK
[9] Barbour, Ian (1990) *Religion in an Age of Science* London: SCM Press
[10] Peacocke, A.R. (1990) *Theology for a Scientific Age: Being and Becoming - Natural, Divine and Human* Oxford: Blackwell
[11] Polkinghorne, John (1994) *Science and Christian Belief Theological Reflections of a Bottom-Up Thinker* London: SPCK
[12] Southgate, Christopher et al. (1999) *God, Humanity and the Cosmos* Edinburgh: T&T Clark.
[13] McGrath, Alister E. (1998) *The Foundations of Dialogue in Science and Religion* Oxford: Blackwell
[14] Luscombe, Philip (2000) *Groundwork of Science and Religion* Peterborough: Epworth Press

growth, health, Keynes, medicine, money, parliament, pensions, politics, policy, racism, social, social choice, socialism, Thatcher, wealth, welfare, work.

Now I knew and respected Arthur Peacocke and John Polkinghorne as distinguished scientists, scholars and theologians, and personal friends. I knew they were themselves interested in these and other questions about social affairs. So why is there no attempt to engage with, or in, politics? Without engaging in politics they are inevitably incomplete in their treatment of social questions and ethical issues affected by both science and religion.

It could, of course, be claimed that the introduction of political questions just complicates the science and religion discourse. True. But this blocks off the possibility of offering a unique contribution to remedying the current loss of trust in science and trust in politics.

Barbour does treat ethics in a separate volume *Ethics in an Age of Technology*[15]. In this he considers technologies with environmental impacts in some detail, and looks to a combination of education, political action, catalytic crises, and vision, to open the way to a more just, participatory and sustainable society on planet earth. The general balance of Barbour is however perhaps more sympathetic to the protesters at the gates, than to the designers at their work stations, who need their vision too.

'Serious scholarship in the history of science', says John Hedley Brooke in his masterly analysis *Science and Religion: Some Historical Perspectives*[16],

> has revealed so extraordinarily rich and complex a relationship between science and religion in the past that general theses are difficult to sustain. The real lesson turns out to be the complexity. …. Conflicts allegedly between science and religion may turn out to be between rival scientific interests, or conversely between rival theological factions. Issues of political power, social prestige, and intellectual authority have repeatedly been at stake.

The dialogue about science and religion in Britain cannot be pursued far in isolation from the rest of the world, particularly the US. Nor, if we are concerned with the effects on people and society, can it be considered without examining the experience of Asian cultures with Christianity and other religions, as discussed, for example, from one point of view by David

---

[15] Barbour, Ian (1992) *Ethics in an Age of Technology* London: SCM Press
[16] Brooke, John Hedley (1991) *Science and Religion: Some Historical Perspectives* Cambridge: Cambridge University Press

Gosling and Ninian Smart in *Religion and Ecology in India and South East Asia*[17], and from another by Francis Fukuyama in *Trust: the social virtues and the creation of prosperity*[18].

The present condition of the dialogue is set in its context in the essay *Theology and Science: Current Issues and Future Directions*[19] by Robert Russell, Founder and Director of the Center for Theology and the Natural Sciences at Berkeley, California. Scholarly journals and books are being published and the Internet has been saturated.

Most politically impressive were the practical explorations of trust and risk at the grass roots in Northern Ireland and South Africa, where they had been so sorely tried. Duncan Forrester, in his lecture on *Trust and Risk: Christian Virtues in Politics?*[20] has explored the cost and the gains as people began to move from a theology of containment to a theology of confidence building, from a theology of liberation to a theology of nation building, from a theology of confrontation to a theology of reconciliation.

Science and religion have been punching below their weight

After a lifetime of experience dealing with science policy questions in the British parliament I do not feel defeatist or as sceptical as Ezrahi[21] about the possibility of instrumentalist social action. What I do have is a lively sense of the need for deliberate engagement with politics.

The neglect of politics by the science-and-religion debaters is a real loss. Have these experts no challenges to politicians on, say, bioethics or climate change? Or guidance on how to prioritise expenditure on, say, the control of malaria in Africa, space exploration, and subsidies to agriculture?

With the current unsettled state of world politics and world economics, it is easy to forget the real gains that science and religion have given us. But the opportunities ahead for exercise of stewardship and the building of social capital will be a major challenge to our society.

---

[17] Gosling, David L. with a foreword by Smart, Ninian (2001) *Religion and Ecology in India and South East Asia* London: Routledge

[18] Fukuyama, Francis (1995) *Trust: the social virtues and the creation of prosperity* London: Hamish Hamilton.

[19] Russell, Robert (2001) *Theology and Science: Current Issues and Future Directions* Berkeley, California: Centre for Theology and the Natural Sciences (CTNS) http://www.ctns.org

[20] Forrester, Duncan (2000) *Trust and Risk: Christian Virtues in Politics?*, Catherwood Lecture

[21] See my Chapter 21, pages 240-241.

25

A climate of trust

The basis of a polity lies in the establishment and maintenance of trust. The role of trust in politics (trust in systems) and of trust in politicians (trust in persons) are both crucially important aspects. They are to a significant degree interdependent. However, it is often impossible even for a totally trustworthy minister, to deliver personally on promises if the systems are not robust and reliable. That is why I have spent so much of this book discussing how we can build reliable systems.

In politics, and with politicians, the practical problems are not in discerning the importance of trust, but in finding how it can be won and held, in dealing with particular issues. It is a situation which is constantly on the move. What, Prime Minister Macmillan was once asked, what is the most troublesome thing to deal with in politics? 'Events, dear boy, events,' he growled.

However, the issues with which I have been concerned in this book have seldom been events of the kind that excite and transfix Downing Street, Whitehall and Westminster, and the ravenous political commentators in the media.

Integrity matters, of course: professional integrity. We are all of us imperfect human beings. But I expect from professionals – my bank manager, the journalist who writes in my daily paper, the scientists whom I have consulted – professional integrity. And in turn I would hope that politicians value their own professional integrity.

The issues that concerned me, issues which evolved over a long political career, were science, science policy, science as a provider of patterns, strategies and models in government, and in particular in the management of the economy. But if trust – trust in systems, trust in persons – cannot be maintained in these areas, the body politic will certainly suffer.

We cannot build and maintain trust – both trust in systems and trust in persons – without building and maintaining social and cultural norms. I believe – and have believed throughout my long political career – that these are built up and kept in repair by a relational God. I trust such a God. In practical matters that God works through social and cultural norms, but these need constant renewal.

We are here into the realms of theology. I will try to keep things simple. In discussing my faith, I hope readers of other faiths – or none – will join me as guests, join me in the same spirit as those to whom Professor David Ford extended his invitation to celebrate the millennium. How, he asked, in his epilogue to *The Modern Theologians*[1], how should he phrase his invitation?

> A simple yet rich answer (he replied) is by being guests and hosts. A theology under the sign of hospitality is formed through its generous welcome to others - theologies, traditions, disciplines, and spheres of life. It has the host's responsibility for homemaking, the hard work of preparation, and the vulnerability of courteously offering something while having little control of its reception. It also has the responsibility of being a guest, trying to be sensitive to strange households, learning complex codes and risking new food and drink. Ideally, habitual hospitality gives rise to trust and friendship in which exchanges can plumb the depths of similarity, difference and suffering.

Trust in systems – trust in persons

Used as we are within the western tradition to think of ourselves as persons, as individuals, we need to remember that existing solely as an 'individual' is out of the question. It is in and through the many and varied relationships which make up the life of human communities and families that our being as persons is realized. Each of us exists as a person in a complex web of relationships which predate our birth and infancy; these enduring yet ever changing relationships are the setting of the narrative of our lives, are responsible to a significant degree for our character and attitudes, our experiences, our successes and failures, and the contribution we make to society. Relationships are our present milieu and will extend into our future. They extend beyond our death, for our lives touch others'. These relationships are both personal and intimate – family relationships, and friendships – and community relationships – school, work, the place where you live, groups which you join, and so on.

---

[1] Ford, David (1997) *The Modern Theologians: An Introduction to Christian Theology in the 20th Century*, p727 Oxford: Blackwell

25 : A climate of trust

Communities too – and this includes political institutions – have this rich, deep rooted complexity. We belong to many, and to many overlapping, communities. The ones in which I have been most intimately involved was parliament and my constituencies. The one from which I have drawn most strength is the church. For, despite its weakness and divisions, the church offers the greatest accumulation of experience and wisdom that we have. It has lasted some two thousand years, outliving all political institutions, states, and empires.

What is very clear is that we need to work with others in the formation, or reformation, of structures and in building social relationships. These structures include the structures underlying politics, economics, science and religion.

Francis Fukuyama[2], Robert Putnam[3] and others have called for an increase in 'social capital'. Fukuyama defines 'social capital' as the capability that arises from the prevalence of trust in a society, and in its constituent parts, from the smallest and most basic social group, the family, to the largest groups, the nation, and international, supranational and global bodies. Such bodies or communities may be informal (science and ideas work largely without borders), or structured and political (such as the European Community or the United Nations). They include the global activities of trade and investment; and the life of faith communities – the Christian churches, the faith communities of Islam, Judaism, Buddhism, and Hinduism and so on.

Within the sphere of politics it is the duty of the politician to seek to be worthy of that trust. This is a personal responsibility for every politician. It is unfortunately true that neither the system, nor the personal qualities of the participants, can ensure the trustworthiness of our political system – or *vice versa*. Corrupt systems attract and nurture and gather strength from corrupt politicians, and from other corrupt or corruptible inhabitants in the 'political village' including lobbyists, interest groups, power-brokers, fund donors, and, very importantly, the media. Incorrupt, or relatively incorrupt, systems likewise attract and nurture kindred spirits.

Open as political parties and institutions are to corruption, their strength and purpose is that they are also wide open to constructive, benign infiltration. Getting our political institutions to work – the economy, social

---

[2] Fukuyama, Francis (1995) *Trust: the social virtues and the creation of prosperity* London: Hamish Hamilton.
[3] Putnam, Robert (2000) *Bowling Alone: the collapse and revival of American community*, New York: Simon & Schuster

services, parliament, government - calls for initiatives from academia and faith communities, and, with the headway generated by them, from our political institutions – parties, legislatures, and governments.

The faith community, the political party, the research institution or university, to which we belong and in which we play a part, cannot be the sole repository of wisdom and truth. Nor will colleagues in one sphere necessarily share our beliefs and attitudes in others. If we think they do, we delude ourselves. But we do need to recognise that the health of society depends on the participation by at least some of our colleagues across the boundaries of these communities.

Covenant and redemption

I have already spoken briefly of the being of God as a relational being. Without the concept of communion it would not be possible to speak of the being of God. That too, for the Christian, is the profound nature of the Trinity. And without the relationships of love it is not possible to conceive of the person, the individual. Incomparably the most serious and practical description and demonstration of how to build a community is given by faith communities, and in particular, the church. In many remarkable ways churches and faith communities are not merely repositories of the wisdom and experience of past generations, but also the guardians and transmitters of tradition to present and future generations, and the seedbed of new ideas and forms of living.

The historical process is subject to time and change, irreversible in direction: the past is never wholly dead, but remains part of the situation we have to face in the present. The Bible is offered to us by the Church as a revelation of God: not as an inspired encyclopaedia which can settle questions out of hand. On the contrary, it first makes us aware of the depth and range of our problem, plunging us into the stream of history in which we have to act with an incomplete understanding and knowledge of the situation.

You will recall that in Chapter 23 I discussed the concept of a relationship between government and electorate going beyond the manifesto commitment towards the idea of a 'covenant'. While this concept has its roots in the past, 'covenant' offers a useful concept in tackling our modern problem, whether as individuals or as a community. Our problem is not merely the world as it is presented in today's newspapers, tabloid or broadsheet. It involves all the endeavours and achievements, the failures and the sins, that are covered by all the years we have lived, all our precious investment of learning and experience. The living past survives into the present as a deep stratum in our own minds.

Building a successful covenant relationship depends on a set of cultural norms. These, like the Mertonian norms for scientists which I discussed in Chapter 21, are needed to enrich and support structures. No one group can lay them down unilaterally. However, I would suggest that theology might – no, should – contribute. It could extend the epistemology of science and technology to encompass moral and political issues. They would deal with truth, beauty, goodness, humility, prudence, justice, temperance and fortitude, as well as faith, hope, and love. We experience pain, suffering and sin. We are corrupted by pride, hypocrisy and selfishness. But that, and the power of redemption, is precisely the territory which the world's faiths explore so exhaustively.

Openness of mind

My own belief is that there is today an openness of mind and an opportunity for dialogue. Starting from my own territory of politics, the institutions we have inherited of freedom in a parliamentary democracy somehow allow voices to express concerns for fairness and justice, despite attempts to filter, select and censor them out. The same is true of the press, the bench, of academia and the teaching profession, and of all aspects of our life as a community of nations.

But we need to have the confidence to affirm that these are the norms, and that they work. We can, I think, draw strength from the evolutionary process that underlies not only the biology of our planet but also, I believe, evolutionary forces in human society.

The survival of the fittest does not necessarily reduce to a war in the jungle. It has produced and it is producing the highest human achievements. Nor are the entities – the individuals – in an evolutionary process mere disposable vehicles for carrying characteristics from one generation to another. Each, I believe, has a value, an 'eternal life', a being secure in the love of God. That is a huge assumption, but I do not think it is meaningless wishful thinking.

The beliefs and behaviour of mankind have developed over the centuries, even millennia. It has not been a matter of steady or even fitful progress. It would be complacent if we assumed we would progress further in the future. But there have been and there can be major changes from time to time and place to place. It is practicable and realistic to seek changes in the future. It is a cynical falsehood in politics to say, 'You cannot change human nature'. It is changing all the time: the continuing evolution of humankind is an extension of evolution in Christ.

Jesus – the Word of God – taught us that his world and our world would work best if we love God and love each other. Just what love is, and how we love God and our neighbour, challenges us at the very root of our being. Whether we are simply lay people, agnostic scientists, scientists who are Christians, or scientist theologians, we can seek to explore further the ultimate questions. Jesus showed us, for example, that there are many difficult things to learn about suffering, sin, evil and death, which each of us has to learn afresh for ourselves in our generation.

Yet God created us to triumph over evil and death.

We can venture confidently

I believe that by responding to what Christ taught us, and by the guidance of the Spirit, we can venture confidently in each generation, not only into scientific research, but also into engineering and politics. We can, indeed we must, start where we are. Whatever the process by which the church was initiated, it brought into being a renewal process by which it could be handed down and reconstituted in each generation.

I find this well summed up by Karl Rahner, a Catholic theologian who contributed much to Vatican II. He writes:

> The miracle of God's incarnation is an absolutely free act of God himself. But once it has taken place and is known by faith, it is possible to recognise that that incarnation can be brought into positive relation with the perspectives of man's knowledge of himself and the world. It is true of course, that by insertion into these contexts, the intellectual perspectives themselves are given a radically different character.
>
> We assume that there is such a thing as an evolutionary view of the world and that it is objectively well founded. This presupposes a unity of spirit and matter. The essential difference between them is not denied, but in view of the common origin of both from the same creative ground (God as the one Creator of matter and spirit), matter cannot be a reality totally different in kind from spirit.

Rahner continues,

> What is earlier and lower rises above and beyond itself into what is later and higher (higher through its greater complexity and through growing self-consciousness in the individual and therefore of the

world as a whole), and does so in virtue of the dynamism communicated to it by God's absolute being (*creatio continua*) as the innermost centre of the world (and therefore superior to it).

If this is so, then the last, highest, unsurpassable instance of such self-transcendence – under the necessary divine dynamism which in this case is called 'grace' – is the coming of this material-spiritual world into immediate relationship to God. This immediacy guarantees that God is not merely the original ground, the self-supporting dynamism of the world and its history, the ultimate goal which it always pursues, though only asymptotically. It shows that he does not merely create the world but that he himself is the perfect fulfilment of the world through his self-communication in grace and glory[4].

Action as fellowship

Finally, let me turn to a theologian who has stimulated much of the interest in activating a practical theology, Karl Barth (1886-1968). Barth sums up his views thus:

> Jesus Christ Himself allowed and commanded His disciples – even before all the other petitions which are materially so much more important and urgent – to pray also for their daily bread. And strikingly the 'signs and wonders' by which He attested the Kingdom of God come to earth were nearly all genuine aids to life in the simplest sense of the term.
>
> Indeed the Old and New Testaments generally have an extraordinary amount to say about such things as man's dwelling, food, drink and sleep, labour and rest, health and sickness, in short about his life and limitation by death; nor are all these statements incidental only, nor overshadowed by the greater and more decisive matters at issue[5].

Barth is not the easiest theologian to read. (An accessible introduction to Barth and to 'practical theology' is Duncan Forrester's *Truthful Action*[6].)

---

[4] Rahner, Karl (1975) *Encyclopaedia of Theology*, Tunbridge Wells, Burns and Oats pp 764-765, in his article on 'Jesus Christ'
[5] Barth, Karl (1936) *Church Dogmatics Vol III*, 4 p.338, (1936) English translation. Edinburgh: T&T Clark
[6] Forrester, Duncan (2000) *Truthful Action: Explorations in Practical Theology*, Edinburgh: T&T Clark

Apart from the length of this work, and his ponderous style (Barth is writing in German) for scientists one problem is Barth's dispute with Emil Brunner on natural theology, the validity of which Barth contested: he affirmed that our faith in God can only be based on God's revelation, and not on human reason. (One of the first serious theological books that I read as a schoolboy was Emil Brunner's *Revelation and Reason*[7]. I could not think what all the fuss was about, because these two reformed theologians seemed to be arguing on remarkably similar lines.)

I have found it however worth persisting with Barth. Here is how he proclaims a Christ-based epistemology:

> If the being of the Church is identical with Jesus Christ, the place from which the way of dogmatic knowledge is to be seen and understood ... can be only the present moment of the speaking and hearing of Jesus Christ Himself[8].

Theological language seems to be unavoidable. That is fine for the believer, but it does not appear to offer the unbeliever a place to stand, nor the believer a place to stand with him.

Yet in his *Romans* commentary, Barth includes among the 'righteous' not just believers but also unbelievers with others who have sought to live honestly by their own moral lights. I would stand by this. Barth declares:

> However ambiguous and questionable the position of the righteous man may be as a human position, he nevertheless performs a distinct and necessary function as a symptom of the will and action of God. ..... It is irrelevant whether [the righteous] possess and are concerned to guard Moses or John the Baptist, Plato or Socialism, or that moral perception which dwells in all its simplicity in the midst of the rough and tumble of human life. In each case there is vocation, promise, a parabolic possibility, something which is offered to men as an open road to their deepest perception. If they have been veritably entrusted with the oracles of God, their claim to peculiarity and to special attention is not necessarily presumptuous.
>
> But there is a necessity of faith, and it is as we point to this that we shall give a sound answer to the question. Faith does not stand or hover somewhere in the face of the possibility of unbelief (which is not itself a possibility but the solid actuality of sinful man). It is not

---

[7] Brunner, Emil (1947) *Revelation and Reason: the Christian doctrine of faith and knowledge* London: SCM Press

[8] Barth, Karl (1932) *Church Dogmatics Vol. I,1* p.41 English translation (1936) Edinburgh: T&T Clark

itself a mere possibility, grand and attractive but impotent and useless like all mere possibilities[9].

Barth, after struggling with the 'impossibility of faith', goes on to describe the genuinely free act of faith – 'an objective, real and ontological necessity for all men and for every man.' How this comes about with all men so drastically failing as God's 'covenant-partner', Barth has explored in earlier chapters, and sums up once again[10].

> The fact that God Himself did not become identical with the totality, or with specific beings within it, but with man when He became flesh in Jesus Christ, is the execution of His choice and His decree and the fulfilment of His covenant at the heart and as the meaning of all creaturely existence. God stands by man.

Barth is taking man with total seriousness, for all our sin and pride, and recognising our independence and responsibility. He had a long record of confronting the evils of totalitarianism in Hitler's Germany. Yet he proclaims, 'God stands by man', and his covenant with man.

A valediction

Towards the end of his life Barth, writing as an old man, looked back on a lifetime of struggle, and forward to his own death.

This now is my own position.

In writing this book I have looked back on my long parliamentary career. What lies ahead, how long my pilgrimage here will continue, I cannot know. Yet despite my limitations – limitations of understanding, of skills, of powers of persuasion, of personality, of political appeal – I trust in God. It leaves me 'at bottom a cheerful man'.

The phrase comes from Barth's discussion[11] of the act of faith, not as an arbitrary human act, but as the response of ordinary human beings, however fallible and sinful, to the Word of God. In closing, let me echo his words:

> What is it that really follows from the recognition that my right and life have been restored once and for all in the death of Jesus Christ and manifested once and for all in His resurrection? ...

---

[9] Barth, Karl (1922) The *Epistle to the Romans*, translation from German. Sixth Edition by Hoskins (1933), London: Oxford University Press

[10] Barth, Karl (1932) *Church Dogmatics* Vol. III,4 p.337 English translation (1936) Edinburgh: T&T Clark

[11] Barth, Karl (1932) *Op.cit.* p.775

I can rely on that which has taken place for me. ... I can think my few thoughts in peace, say my few words in peace, do my few works in peace. I can look forward from myself as I am, and from the things of myself as they are and as they are done. To what? Certainly not to the void of a better future, but to the fulfilment of the promise given to me in Jesus Christ. .... I can trust.

... Not an arbitrary trust, but a trust which responds to the Word of God spoken to me ... Not an indefinite trust, but a trust which is grounded in the knowledge of faith as the knowledge of Jesus Christ.

When a man knows in Jesus Christ his Saviour and that of the world, when, therefore, he is determined and stamped and enlightened by Him, this heartfelt act cannot be omitted. On this side too there is nothing more: no ultimate things, no eschatological decision. ... No one must imagine that ... the new heaven and the new earth has dawned even for himself, let alone for the Church and the world. But there can be nothing less than this confidence – a confidence on the old earth and under the old heaven but resolutely grasped.

.... When a man believes, then, in spite of all the limitations in which he still exists, in the knowledge of the restoration of his right and life as it has taken place in Jesus Christ, he will become a free man, that is, a man who is no longer a simple servant and victim of his pride, but who is called away from it to the obedience of humility, for which he is both ready and willing. As he bears that deep wound and accepts that bitter pain of penitence, he will hope for the grace of God and in that hope he will be at bottom a cheerful man.

And although on his journey from the beginning of his way to the end he will often enough be assaulted and will have to fight and he will often be thrown down, but will always rise up again and continue, yet in his relationship with God and man and himself he will be seriously and finally a peaceful man, peaceful because held by the One in whom he is already restored, in whom he is already the righteous and protected covenant-partner of God[12].

---

[12] Barth, Karl 1932 *Church Dogmatics Vol. IV,1* Extracts from pp 774-.775 775 English translation (1936) Edinburgh: T&T Clark

*This portrait of Jeremy was almost the last photo taken of him.
He is seen here with his eldest daughter, Margaret (left) and Elizabeth.*

Elizabeth writes:

Jeremy died on the evening of Friday 31 May 2002, peacefully at home, after a long illness. We both knew he did not have long to live. During the day I had agreed to edit his book. That afternoon he decided to print out part of it to assist me.

I found this chapter in his printer soon after his death. These, in a sense, are his last words: a valediction and an affirmation of his faith.

Index of names

Akam, Michael, 227
Akam, Simon, 227
Akam, Thomas, 227
Allan, Douglas, 61, 83
Allison, Jimmy, 102
Andrews, Kay, 195, 203, 211
Aristotle, 279
Arrow, Kenneth, 58, 263-264, 267
Artis, Michael John, 154/5, 176
Ashworth, John, 155
Astrom, Karl J., 85, 130
Athans, Michael, 121
Atiyah, Michael, 13, 192
Attlee, Clement, 21, 51, 57
Aylward, Ron, 73

Baker, Kenneth, 139, 195
Ball, Jim, 75, 130-131
Balls, Edward, 141, 166, 168 *ff*, 171, 261
Balogh, Tommy, 56, 67, 129
Barbour, Ian, 284-285
Barnard, George, 29
Barron, Ian, 73
Barry, Andrew, 193, 195
Barth, Karl, 9, 10, 293-296
Beaumont-Dark, Anthony, 139
Becker, Robin, 121, 123
Beeching, Dick, 28, 31, 60
Benn, Tony, 71-74, 82, 83, 126-128
Berners-Lee, C.M., 69, 260
Besicovitch, A.S., 14
Bevan, Aneurin, 51, 52
Beveridge, Lord, 8
Biffin, John, 14
Bin Laden, Osama, 278
Bispham, Tony, 130
Blackette, Patrick, 72-73

Blair, Tony, 165 *ff*, 172, 203, 208-9, 211-213, 214 *ff*, 231, 249, 255, 260, 279
Blessing, Dr., 62
Bohlin, 85
Bollabas, 16, 17
Bondi, Herman, 19, 282
Boothroyd, Betty, 221
Boreham, John, 55, 74-75
Bottomley, Arthur, 35, 36, 63
Boyle, Edward, 54, 63-64
Boyle, Robert, 236
Box, George, 29, 85, 117, 130
Braddock, Bessie, 38
Bray, Arthur, 5-8, 10, 22
Bray, Barbara, 6-8
Bray, Beatrice, 66, 90, 227
Bray, Bridget, 33, 66, 90, 227
Bray, Denis, 6-8
Bray, Eleanor, 6-8
Bray, Elizabeth, 14, 15, 22, 37, 43, 66, 85, 90, 94, 223 *ff*
    See also Trowell, Elizabeth
Bray, Margaret, 15, 20, 22, 33, 66, 90, 150, 227
Bray, Muriel, 5-8, 10, 22
Bray, Stella, 227
Bray, Teresa, 33, 66, 90, 227
Brennan, Tommy, 101-103, 224
Brittan, Leo, 146
Brittan, Sam, 14, 146, 168
Broadbent, Simon, 134
Brooke, John Hedley, 285
Brooker, Tony, 28
Brown, George, 42, 47, 52, 55-56, 61-64, 71, 72, 199, 261

INDEX OF NAMES ♦ 299

Brown, Gordon, 98-99, 141, 162, 165 *ff*, 170 *ff*, 175, 181, 195, 199, 261, 263
Brown, Pat, 75
Brown, Stanley, 54
Brunner, Emil, 294
Bryant, John, 70
Bryant, Ralph, 174
Buiter, Willem, 139, 152, 155
Burke, Derek, 283
Burkitt, Denis, 193
Burns, Terry, 75, 162
Bush, George W., 89, 112, 172, 220, 232, 254-255, 264, 275, 279
Butler, Joyce, 128
Butler, Robin, 201

Cairncross, Alec, 55, 60, 76
Callaghan, Jim, 42, 52, 56, 61, 84, 108, 112, 120, 122, 132-133, 136
Campbell, Alastair, 208-9
Campbell, Donald, 258
Campion, Harry, 64
Carlaw, Bill, 90
Castle, Barbara, 52
Carter, President Jimmy, 133, 134
Catherwood, Fred, 61
Challis, Tony, 44
Chambers, Paul, 38
Charlton, Neil, 22-23
Christ, Jesus, 292-296
Chow, Gregory, 118, 121, 130
Churchill, Winston, 55
Clark, Michael, 36
Clarke, Charles, 72, 73
Clarke, Kenneth, 163
Clarke, Percy, 37
Clarke, Richard (Otto), 72, 73, 138
Clarke, Tom, 98
Clinton, William (Bill), 166, 168, 209
Coales, John, 30, 60, 117
Collins, Francis, 283
Collins, Harry, 256-257
Collins, Ken, 98

Cook, Robin, 99
Coombs, Charles, 134
Cooper, Geoffrey, 195
Coulson, Charles, 91, 282
Cousins, Frank, 72
Crighton, Dick, 19
Crockett, Andrew, 134
Crosland, Tony, 20, 52, 58, 89
Crossman, Dick, 20, 138
Cruickshank, Don, 131

D'Agapeyeff, Alex, 73
Dalton, Hugh, 56
Dalyell, Tam, 47, 51-52, 98-99
Darwin, Charles, 238
Dasgupta, 189
Davies, Alice, 227
Davies, Duncan, 35, 188
Davies, Gareth, 227
Davies, O.L., 29
Davies, Rupert, 9-10
Davies, Sam, 227
D'Avigdor-Goldsmith, Henry, 55
Dearing, Ron, 128
Debreu, 58
Dell, Edmund, 36, 72, 73, 129-130, 138
Dewar, Donald, 98-99, 101
Diamond, Jack, 76
Dimbleley, Jonathan, 212
Dornbusch, Rudi, 143
Dorrell, Stephen, 212
Douglas-Home, Alec, 21, 57, 60
Du Cann, Edward, 139, 145, 146, 152-155
Durbin, Richard, 246
Dwolatzky, B., 121

Eddington, Arthur, 282
Eden, Anthony, 21, 60
Edwards, Ronnie, 54
Eggar, Timothy, 139
Einstein, 238
Emmwood, 80

INDEX OF NAMES

English, Michael, 139
Ennals, David, 61
Enzler, Dr, 154
Evans, Harold, 32
Ezrahi, Yaron, 240 *ff*, 242 *ff*, 249

Ferranti, Basil de, 60
Finniston, Monty, 33, 70
Fleck, Alexander, 36
Flemming, John, 139
Foley, Jim, 94
Foot, Michael, 152
Ford, David, 288
Forrester, Duncan, 286, 293
Forrester, Jay, 88-89
Freeman, Christopher, 191
Friedman, Milton, 140, 143, 144, 145, 149, 169
Fukuyama, Francis, 271, 281, 286, 289
Fulton, John, 64, 83

Gaitskell, Dora, 22
Gaitskell, Hugh, 21-22, 38, 42-43, 52-53, 57
Galbraith, J.F., 59
Garland, 81
Garrett, Edward (Ted), 36
Garrett, John, 36
Gates, Bill, 73
Gee, Ken, 25-26
Gibbons, Michael, 191
Gill, Stanley, 73
Godley, Wynn, 75
Gosling, David, 285-286
Gould, Bryan, 20
Greenspan, Alan, 173, 177

Habgood, John, 283
Haldane, J.B.S., 54, 238
Haldane, Lord, 217-219, 239
Hall, Arnold, 90
Hardy, G.H, 14-16
Hart, Judith, 98

Harvey-Jones, John, 23, 35-36
Hattersley, Roy, 36
Healey, Denis, 52, 122, 129, 132-136, 137, 138
Healey, Edna, 135
Heath, Edward, 36, 49, 84, 87, 94, 12Hebb, 19
Helsby, Lawrence, 64
Heidegger, Martin, 282
Henderson, Dr., 154
Hendry, David, 139, 155
Hennessy, Peter, 71, 155
Henry, Brian, 85
Herbison, Peggy, 98
Heyerdahl, Thor, 88
Higgins, Terence, 139
Hitchens, Ivor, 10
Hitler, Adolf, 295
Hobbs, Thomas, 236
Hobman, Joycelin, 193
Hodgeson, Maurice, 31
Holland, Stuart, 126
Holly, Sean, 121
Hooper, Dr., 154
Houghton, John, 273, 283
Howe, Geoffrey, 137, 143-144, 160, 161
Howard, W.F., 8
Hoyle, Fred, 282
Hubback, David, 139
Humphrys, John, 215, 256
Hunter, Anji, 208-209
Hutton, J.P., 85
Huxley, Aldous, 239
Huxley, T.H., 258

Ingram, Adam, 98
Iverson, Kenneth, 104

Jackson, Edward (Teddy), 59, 65
Jackson, Willis, 60
James, William, 258
Jay, Douglas, 52
Jay, Peter, 133

Jeans, James, 282
Jenkin, Patrick, 14, 36, 101
Jenkins, Gwylim, 29, 85, 117, 130
Jenkins, Roy, 20, 38, 80, 84,
Jensen, 81
Jesus Christ, 292-296
Jones, Frank, 90
Joseph, Keith, 35, 103, 187-188, 190, 195
Jouvenal, Bertrand de, 88
Judge, Edward (Ted), 34

Kaberry, Donald, 55
Kahn, Richard, 56, 129
Kalchbrenner, J., 142
Kaldor, Nickolas, 56, 129, 143, 144, 145
Kalman, Rudi, 30
Karakitsos, Elias, 121, 123, 154-5, 176
Kearton, Frank, 38
Kellner, Peter, 145
Kendrick, David, 121, 130
Kennedy, John, 60
Keynes, J.M., 8, 16, 52, 55, 56, 58, 78, 140, 285
King, Alex, 88
King, Mervyn, 118
King, Horace, 66
Kinnock, Neil, 179, 180-181, 184, 194 *ff*, 200-203, 211
Klein, Lawrence (Lawrie), 75, 121, 130-136
Klein, Sonny, 135
Kornberg, Hans, 195
Kuhn, Thomas, 252
Kuleshov, Andre, 121, 159
Kydland, Finn 120, 140-142, 150

Laidler, David, 143, 144
Lakatos, Imre, 252, 282
Lancaster, Osbert, 80
Laski, Harold, 8
Laver, Murray, 73

Lawson, George, 94-95
Lawson, Nigel, 131, 136, 160-161, 166
Lea, David, 135
Lee, Fred, 67
Lever, Harold, 70, 135
Lewis, C.S., 8
Lighthill, James, 273
Lipsey, R.G., 84
Lipsey, David, 162-164, 169
Livesey, David, 118, 130
Littlewood, J.E., 14-20
Lloyd, Selwyn, 56
Lorenz, Konrad, 258
Lovick, Sam, 121, 158, 193, 195
Lubbock, Eric, 51
Lucas, Robert (Bob), 120, 140, 150, 174, 175
Luscombe, Philip, 284

MacDougall, Donald, 55, 62, 83
McEvoy, Tommy, 98
McGahey, Mick, 102
McGrath, Alister E., 284
McGregor, Ian, 103
MacIntyre, Alasdair, 266, 277, 279-280, 281, 282
McKelvie, Willie, 98
Maddock, Euan, 72-73
Maddox, John, 89, 194
Macmillan, Harold, 9, 21, 34, 51-52, 56, 57, 60, 287
Major, John, 181, 199, 203, 204-205, 219
Marsh, Dick, 67-69, 83
Marshall, Alfred, 58
Marshall, Robert, 67
Marris, Robin, 59, 65
Marx, Karl, 258
Mason, John, 74, 273
Massé, Pierre, 59
Matthews, Robin, 116
May, Robert, 31, 162, 202-203, 205
Maynard, Geoffrey, 135

Meade, James, 55, 75
Meadows, Dennis, 88-89
Meadows, Donella, 88-89
Merton, Robert, 243 ff,
Miller, Marcus, 139, 157
Minford, Patrick, 143
Mirlees, James, 130
Mitchell, Derek, 135
Minsky, Marvin, 19
Mitchison, Dick, 54
Mitchison, Naomi, 54
Mond, Alfred, 36
Monod, Jacques, 258
Moonie, Lewis, 251
Moore, Henry, 10
Moser, Claus, 60, 65
Mugabe, Robert, 62

Nana, Ganesh, 121, 158-159
Nash, John, 159
Niebuhr, Reinhold, 229
Noble, Denis, 191, 195
Nolan, Sydney, 72
Nowotny, Helga, 241
Nugent, Dick, 55

Okita, Sabro, 88
Ozbekhan, Hasan, 88

Paley, R.E.A.C., 16, 17
Parkin, J.M., 84
Paxman, Jeremy, 215
Peacocke, Arthur, 284, 285
Pecci, Aurelio, 88
Pestel, Edouard, 88
Peston, Maurice, 116, 120
Phillips, A.W., 118
Piaget, Jean, 258
Pinch, Trevor, 256-257
Pitblado, David, 67
Polak, Jan, 134
Polkinghorne, John, 283, 284-285
Popper, Karl, 251, 258, 282
Porteous, David, 207

Posner, Michael, 67, 130, 135, 147, 156
Preston, Alan, 121
Price, David, 36
Profumo, John, 52, 57, 60
Prescott, Edward, 120, 140-142, 150
Prescott, John, 61, 104
Putman, Robert, 280-281, 289
Pyatt, Graham, 64

Quennouille, 17
Quinn, George, 100

Rahner, Karl, 292
Rampton, David, 164
Ramsey, Michael, 12
Reagan, Ronald, 240
Rees, Martin, 195
Rees, Merlyn, 61
Reid, John, 98-99
Richardson, Gordon, 122
Rigby, Peter, 195
Rivett, Patrick, 60
Robens, Alf, 54, 69
Robertson, George, 98-99
Robinson, John, 11-12
Robinson, Ruth, 12
Rodgers, Bill, 36
Roll, Eric, 61, 78
Rooke, Denis, 54
Rose, Steven, 195
Rosenbrock, Howard, 30, 117
Rowland, Chris, 62
Roy, Frank, 224
Russell, Bertrand, 16, 239, 282
Russell, Robert, 286
Rustem, Berc, 117, 121, 123

Sackett, A.B., 9
Sainsbury, David, 214, 215
St.John Stevas, Norman, 138
Sargan, Denis, 85, 130
Sargent, Thomas, 120, 140, 150, 151
Scargill, Arthur, 22

Books by Oliver Kerrigan

***

The Arcane Investigators Series
Episode 1: The Vermillion Curator

Other Series
The Zoharian Bladers
Volume 1: The Successor of Ramiel
Volume 2: The Taming of the Qliphoth
Volume 3: The Reign of the Invidia
Short Story: The Calculus of Bifrons
Short Story: The Gambit of Andras

The Arcana's Bestiary
Volume 1: The Tellier Cockatrice
Volume 2: The Gulliver's Gryphon

Sin Magic

***

The Church of the Dies Mater is the central religious authority on the western continent of a vibrant land steeped in magic. Its scholars, who are the most revered members of this historic and sacred institution, consider themselves experts when discussing the Arcane – an old term that encompasses magic and its role in the natural world – and they have outlawed Sin Magic. This corruptive force arises from the malicious thoughts and desires within the hearts of all sentient creatures. It can penetrate a person's very soul. The vigilant efforts of the Arcane Investigation Bureau assist in this unending crusade against those who would use Sin Magic for their own selfish goals. Gluttony is a vice of insatiable desire, a relentless inferno that could devour all in its path. How does one stop a soul that knows no satiety?

I - Obsidian

The Abandoned Cordovan Sewers

'I'm getting close to the truth.'

Obsidian, hiding his face under a thick hooded cloak, endeavoured to blend into a gang of thieves he had infiltrated. Despite the potent, sulphurous smell of rotting detritus, he needed to go into the sewers for the mission. To safeguard his identity as a discreet, senior Arcane Investigator, he went to great lengths to conceal his giveaway angular features. In contrast, the smugglers, confident in their invincibility, took minimal precautions to hide their faces and, as sparse moonlight filtered through holes in the stone ceiling, they revelled in their familiarity within the murky subterranean environment.

In an unwelcome gesture, a low-ranking thief patted Obsidian on the back. 'Relax.'

Obsidian, who preferred the melody of dripping water to the unnecessary banter, feigned a smile. 'Better be safe than sorry, Rust.'

Rust, whose features had been rearranged by too many punches to the face, lacked both charm and appeal, but nevertheless exuded an unfounded self-assurance. 'As long as Jasper is in charge, we'll be fine.'

The thieves' admiration for their brutish leader, Jasper, baffled Obsidian, who watched in silent horror as the thieves arranged the stolen artifacts in open crates, ready for inspection and delivery. Included in the stolen loot were marble idols, paintings, jewels, etchings on metal plates, and golden cups. Jasper, ladened with battle scars and tattoos, rubbed his hands together, salivating over his potential windfall.

Obsidian already knew the provenance of these stolen items, though needed first-hand confirmation. He coughed into his hand. 'Where did you get this loot?'

'Some old churches out in the countryside. It was too easy,' Rust boasted; the heists were not a challenge. 'We kicked down the doors and only had to deal with the odd vicar. It is ridiculous to leave so much wealth on display. It was asking to be stolen!'

Obsidian stifled his disdain for the thieves, focusing on the imminent criminal transaction.

'They've arrived, boys,' Jasper announced with a sinister grin, drawing attention to a woman navigating the sewer's foul recesses.

Walking by the bank of the flowing stream, Miss Rosewood was unaccustomed to such torrid surroundings. She much preferred to be in the refined cultural centre of a museum, pawing over precious artifacts. With her brunette hair tied up with delicate precision and her makeup applied to cover her emotions, she wore a crimson red business jacket and dress and, aware of the territory she was about to enter, flat shoes. She turned up her nose at the sight of rats scurrying passed as she chuntered under her breath. 'I need a full glass of wine when I get home.'

Jasper bowed his head. 'Miss Rosewood, we have the items you requested.'

Obsidian suppressed a smirk, pleased his source was correct.

'You have done well, Jasper.' Rosewood scrutinised the stolen haul. 'I hope you can continue to impress us. In fact—'

Obsidian shivered. He sensed a disturbance. His gaze followed Rosewood's path. A malicious presence was approaching – an aura saturated in vice and sin – and he wasn't the sole person who shivered at the primal threat. Jasper, Rust and the other thieves found themselves feeling tetchy; their spines straightened to attention. They could not explain why.

Behind Rosewood, a rotund, bordering on obese, man draped in scarlet robes, entered the scene with a palpable malevolent presence. His breathlessness did not concern him, nor did his body weight strain on his heart because he was too busy slobbering, his pudgy fingers eager to caress his prize.

'Lord Vermillion,' Rosewood implored – a vain attempt at maintaining decorum. 'Please keep your distance. This is no place for—'

At first, Obsidian couldn't believe his luck – he had the mastermind in his sights – but then he realised there was something about Vermillion which was more problematic than he expected. The strangest thing about Lord Vermillion's appearance was a splendid yet peculiar ring on his left hand with a burning ruby embedded in its structure. Obsidian felt sick; Vermillion possessed an arcane artifact that was corrupting the world around him.

'Let me through!' Vermillion boomed, fuelled by his insatiable desire for more acquisitions. 'I came to congratulate the entrepreneurial fellows who acquired such magnificent artifacts for my collection.'

Through the power of his ring, Vermillion believed the world around him must bend to his will to satisfy his desires. An indescribable madness emanated from his eyes; his bizarre scarlet pupils posed a danger that even the blackest of hearts found disconcerting. Even Jasper, a hardened criminal, was unsure how to process Vermillion's presence. 'I suppose you want your money.' Vermillion waved his hand and instructed the henchmen following in his wake to hand over their heavy sacks of golden coins, which were causing their backs to creak from the sheer weight.

A look of shock and amazement crossed Jasper's face as he counted. 'That's ... that's more than we agreed?'

As Vermillion enjoyed Jasper's surprise, the glow of his ring intensified, enticing Jasper to submit into his service. 'Consider this a loyalty reward, Jasper. I reward those who do me well. Given your recent successes, I may require your services again.'

Rosewood tapped her foot disapprovingly, and Obsidian noticed. She intrigued him and he continued to make mental notes about her body language, not least the way her gaze locked on to the ruby ring like prey trying to psyche out a stalking predator. On the other hand, Rust was too busy being enamoured by the sacks of money to notice her distaste. But Obsidian, having seen enough, slipped away, back into the shadows with silent strides unnoticed.

'A great first day, rookie,' Rust declared. 'I never got your name—' He turned to find he was alone. 'Where? ... Where did he go?'

Obsidian clambered out from the sewers at the designated extraction point and discarded his cloak, knowing no amount of washing would ever cleanse the stench. Clad in pitch-black body armour, his pale skin provided a striking contrast to his dark hair and eyes. His features possessed a glass-like quality, a subtle reflective sheen that caught people off guard when meeting him. Looking around for his getaway ride, he adjusted the sturdy volcanic-glass bracers which adorned his wrists, their resilience defying their fragile appearance, and smiled a satisfied smile when he spotted it.

Junior Arcane Investigator Gainsboro, clad in an ashen grey uniform with tied-back coppery-brown hair, was a nervous sentry of the horse-driven, black-painted wooden carriage. Equipped with a sharpened wand, she awaited Obsidian's arrival. Her relief was palpable on seeing him unscathed. 'Everything go to plan, sir?'

Obsidian, pleased with a good night's work, remained eager to get out of there. 'I learnt more than I expected. Come on. We can discuss while heading back to the cathedral.'

'Excellent. Timberwolf's waiting inside.'

They boarded the carriage, with Obsidian slamming the door shut behind Gainsboro. Adorned with the crest of the Church of the Dies Mater – a dove carrying an olive branch in its mouth – the carriage presented them as priests on official business. As the horses pulled away with a crack of the reins, it was time to debrief Timberwolf.

Inside, the team's third member, Timberwolf, eager for news, perched himself on the edge of his seat. His hair, despite his young age, was silvering and his bluish-grey uniform portrayed a readiness for action. His magical gloves, resembling claws, cooled the surrounding air, no matter the time of day or year. 'So, was my source correct? Were the artifacts there?'

Obsidian smiled. 'Your source was accurate to the letter. I even received a reward for my patience. Lord Vermillion himself appeared in person.'

'What?' Gainsboro's eyes widened. 'Isn't that dangerous?'

'I don't think he cares. He thinks he's untouchable.'

'We'll see about that.' Timberwolf embraced the challenge, punching his fist into his flat palm.

Obsidian ignored Timberwolf's lust for a fight. Instead, his thoughts grew troubled. Despite the mission's success, Vermillion's ring plagued his thoughts. 'We need to be careful. Vermillion is stronger than he looks.'

Timberwolf's immaturity slipped through. 'Why? I doubt he can run fast.'

Obsidian's unamused glare extinguished Timberwolf's bravado. 'Powerful Sin magic circles exist around him.'

'Sin Magic?' Timberwolf's spine straightened. 'How strong are we talking about?'

'I don't know.' It was rare for Obsidian to be lost for words in front of his juniors, but he was grappling with the implications of the ring's power.

Gainsboro had not seen Obsidian so perturbed. 'But we've dealt with that kind of magic before?'

'Yes, but not like this,' Obsidian folded his arms. 'I'll put in an information request once we get back to the cathedral. Scholars could find something in the archives. Until then, neither of you should approach him. Understand?' Obsidian aimed his orders at Timberwolf, in particular.

Gainsboro and Timberwolf exchanged glances and, nodding, accepted their leader's seriousness.

Obsidian recognised a public investigation involving Vermillion would draw extra unwanted scrutiny of The Church, which avoided public controversy at all costs. 'We'll get our orders in the morning. We must be careful and disciplined.'

As the carriage hurtled forwards, Obsidian's thoughts crystallised around a single ambition. 'Your criminal enterprise is over, Vermillion.'

II – Visitation from a Scholar

The Spymaster's Office, The Arcane Investigation Bureau, Cathedral of the Dies Mater in Spectra City

Obsidian fronted the presentation, flanked by Gainsboro and Timberwolf.

The audience comprised their spymaster Father Grapha, who occupied a grand chair behind an antique mahogany table, his signature cane leaning against it. The strategic positioning of torch crystals in his office mimicked candlelight and created a cold and focused atmosphere; Father Grapha, a seasoned Church agent, now managed the Arcane Investigation Bureau.

'With the information provided by Timberwolf,' Obsidian acknowledged, nodding at his younger subordinate, who reciprocated the gesture, 'I infiltrated Jasper's gang and witnessed the sale of artifacts acquired from the pillaging of provincial churches. Although I did not have time to confirm whether any were Arcane in nature, I validated the claims of Timberwolf's source because Lord Vermillion's presence at the sale confirmed his personal involvement in the theft and smuggling of these artefacts.'

'Excellent work, all of you.' Grapha commended his investigator's diligence, but now, as a seasoned strategist, he grappled with the political intricacies of confronting an influential figure like Vermillion. 'We need more evidence than eyewitness testimony. For someone as prominent as Vermillion, we require tangible evidence that eliminates even the smallest of doubts to secure a conviction.'

Grapha stood and addressed Timberwolf first. 'Your source insists on remaining anonymous, correct?'

'Yes, Father.' Timberwolf almost stumbled in his speech, taking care of protecting his source. 'They don't want to be identified.'

Grapha accepted such an inconvenience in their line of work. 'Always the way. We can't help it. Whilst I dislike sources hiding behind anonymity, we cannot compromise their trust. Your duty of care is to ensure their protection, Timberwolf.'

'Yes, Father. I will take measures to safeguard the source.'

Grapha then turned his attention to Obsidian. 'I understand you reported a ruby ring which transmits Sin Magic. Could you elaborate?'

Obsidian expressed his apprehensions. 'It is an Arcane artefact, I'm certain of it. With that ring on Vermillion's finger, he's no ordinary criminal. He's dangerous to a degree unprecedented in my years as an Arcane Investigator. You had to be close to it to understand, Father.'

Gainsboro and Timberwolf, accustomed to Obsidian's methodical and calm manner, noted the departure from his usual professional demeanour.

Grapha, recognising the potential severity of the threat of Vermillion's ring, believed further elaboration was necessary. 'You are right to be cautious, Obsidian. Caution is necessary when dealing with Vermillion, a person of distinction, to secure a conviction. His previous donations to the Church make some within these walls reluctant to pursue him.'

Obsidian sought immediate action. 'What are your orders, Father?'

Grapha scratched his early morning stubble. 'Vermillion is hosting an opening at his personal private museum on his estate. I want you to go as the Church's representative. Perhaps you could turn a casual conversation into an interrogation. Let's see how he reacts when confronted.'

'But—' Gainsboro caught her own interjection by clamping her hand over her mouth.

'Speak.'

Gainsboro stepped forward. 'Would antagonising someone like Vermillion work? He would refuse to answer, and we'd get nowhere.'

Grapha's expression broke into a mischievous smile. 'Applied pressure can be revealing. It can focus minds and force little slip-ups people make when under stress. Let me handle the Church bureaucrats. We have evidence they cannot ignore. Obsidian, read Vermillion's personal file before tonight's gala.'

Nodding, though grimacing at the thought of reading such dry texts, Obsidian agreed. 'I'll read it, Father.'

Grapha assigned tasks for his juniors; Timberwolf was eager for orders and the old spymaster admired his youthful vigour. 'Contact your source, Timberwolf. See what else they can tell us. See if you can find where Jasper's hideout is.'

He turned to Gainsboro, believing she was ready for a step-up in responsibility. 'I want you to go to Vermillion's Museum before mid-morning on behalf of the Church. They sent a request a month ago to verify a certain tome which fell into their possession. We will prepare you with a cover story. See the lay of the building. Report anything of note.'

'Yes, Father!'

'What aliases will you use?'

Obsidian chose a personal favourite. 'Arcanite.'

'And you, Gainsboro?'

Gainsboro, preferring variety, selected a new alias. 'Ashen?'

Grapha approved. 'You three have your tasks. It won't be easy. As always, I expect the utmost professionalism. Now, secure that conviction.'

'Yes, Father!' all three announced before being dismissed.

As Gainsboro and Timberwolf exited to perform their duties, Grapha sat back down. 'Obsidian, a moment.'

Obsidian waited for Timberwolf to close the door behind him. 'Yes, Father?'

'If Vermillion's ring is as dangerous as you suspect, it changes the complexion of this investigation and requires a specialist to neutralise him before making any arrest.'

Obsidian expected this scenario. 'I'm ready.'

'Good.' Grapha opened the drawer in his desk and produced an extensive file of papers. He dropped it on to the desk with a crash, then chuckled. 'I know how much you like reading, Obsidian. Have fun.'

Obsidian suppressed a sigh. 'I'll read it before tonight.'

'Splendid.' Grapha pushed the file towards the far side of his desk.

As Obsidian lifted it, surprised by its weight, he grew convinced that Grapha had gathered more information than necessary.

With a forced smile, he left.

Once Grapha's moment of amusement passed, his expression fell, his thoughts riddled with worry. 'Tread with care, you three. I foresee complications ahead.'

Obsidian's Private Office

Obsidian found himself unable to stifle a yawn. As he suspected, the pages of the hefty files did not prove riveting. When Grapha asked him, he always denied he hated reading and, if caught, would blame his yawning on the previous night's excursions taking their toll, but the truth was, he was struggling to stay awake.

Yawning now, he sat in his office, which was more modest than Grapha's, but held its own charm, including the quaint oak table at which he sat; the soft, orange glow from the luminous torch crystals he had configured offering a welcome warmth.

To stay focused, Obsidian read aloud. 'Vermillion has no recorded history of criminality. He inherited the family fortune ten years ago when his parents and siblings perished in a tragic fire. He's made sensible investments and charitable donations to the Church. On paper, he's an exemplary citizen. Nothing in here suggests he's a criminal mastermind.'

A deep yawn escaped Obsidian and the notion of a brief nap before tonight's mission was appetising.

A cup of tea materialised on his desk, right under his nose, and its fruity aromas snapped him back into the room. He blinked, dazed, and looked up to see a scholar had slipped into his office unnoticed. The man with a round face and darkening blond hair seemed similar to his bookish peers, but possessed a unique, quiet assurance in his abilities.

Embarrassed by being caught dozing, Obsidian snapped in defence. 'Who are you? And how did you get in?'

The uninvited guest sat opposite Obsidian; the tea was a ploy to get his attention. 'I'm Mauveine and you left your office door open.'

Sitting up, Obsidian paid attention. It wasn't everyday someone had the nerve to stroll into his office. Discombobulated, he glanced at the young man sitting opposite him. The odd thing about Mauveine was his striking violet eyes. They were a contradiction; he appeared younger, but his eyes betrayed an older spirit. But what fascinated Obsidian most was the thick protective glove Mauveine wore on his left hand, a glove which was so long he needed to tuck it into his sleeve. Aware he was staring, Obsidian averted his gaze.

Mauveine, long since accustomed to the attention his glove garnered, made light of such stares. 'It's a good job I'm right-handed.'

Sipping the tea Mauveine had brought him, Obsidian felt its steam revive his senses and kick-start his synapses. 'Why are you here, Mauveine?'

'You placed a research request late last night, regarding a mysterious ring. They assigned me to the case because of my expertise, considering the peculiar description you provided.'

'And what is your expertise?'

Mauveine smirked. 'Let me show you. I believe I may have found what you were asking for.'

He presented an open grimoire to Obsidian, its fibrous parchment pages filled with strange words in an obscure and odd sentence formation. 'Languages from northern continents and tundras outside the Church's jurisdiction are used in the text.'

Obsidian gasped at the detailed illustration of a glowing, red ring. 'That's it! That's the ring Vermillion was wearing.'

'I am pleased I am correct.'

Obsidian shook his head in disbelief. 'What am I looking at?'

Mauveine cleared his throat. 'According to the text, the ring is a Sin Magic conductor and amplifier.'

Obsidian's expression dropped. 'That's? ... Oh dear.'

Mauveine gave Obsidian the time required to process the hefty ramifications of his revelation before continuing his analysis. 'Indeed. If not for its malicious disposition, it would be a technological marvel worthy of further study. According to my initial translations, it draws power from the cruel and selfish thoughts and desires of the ring bearer and amplifies their ill will, creating a vicious, negative feedback loop. This ring magnifies a person's gluttony.'

Obsidian considered whether this ring explained Vermillion's behaviour as a collector whose obsession had taken a criminal turn. 'What is this ring's origin?'

'I only received your request first thing this morning. You need to give me more time to discover the exact details.' Mauveine knew how to manage the patience and expectations of his superiors. 'Given the context clues, the ring came from the northern continents before ending up in our humble realm. A collector like Vermillion is apt at finding obscure, unique treasures.'

Obsidian continued sipping his tea, struggling to make headway in deciphering the text in front of him. He appreciated Mauveine's valuable talents as vital for this case. 'Sin Magic always keeps us on our toes. It keeps manifesting in strange ways. I've never seen a Sin Magic conductor like this before.'

Mauveine, noting Obsidian's ease discussing Sin Magic, probed further. 'Sin Magic is a phrase feared by many here. Most can't distinguish between Sin and Dark Magic.'

Observing Mauveine's boldness, Obsidian believed he was being tested. 'Sin magic is associated with evil actions and deeds. Dark magic is more abstract, fuelling the processes in nature that we would prefer not to dwell on.'

Mauveine nodded. 'The unseen glue that keeps the world together. Life cannot sustain itself without death. Morality and ethics are absent in these processes.' He tapped the side of his head. 'Morals. Principles. Ethics. Those are human ideas. A product of our minds. What we perceive as evil is the fuel for Sin Magic.'

Obsidian allowed himself a smile; he appreciated Mauveine's skill at articulating the complex philosophical ideas surrounding magic. He had found someone who could hold their own in a debate. 'Anyone capable of magic is also capable of Sin Magic. You can't control human nature.'

Mauveine, amused, sought a deeper understanding of Obsidian's world view. 'So, it is natural to sin then?'

'As an Arcane Investigator, you realise everyone has malicious thoughts. No one is perfect all the time, whether awake or dreaming, but most people ignore the temptation to act on malign impulses. That said, there are some who can't.'

Respecting Obsidian's insight, Mauveine embraced his audacity. 'It's rare you meet someone who understands human nature with such clarity. If I may, I wish to attribute the ring an official codename.'

Obsidian found the request reasonable. 'What would you call it?'

'The Gula.'

Obsidian had no reason to object. 'I'll permit it.'

Mauveine closed the tome, careful not to reveal a Byzantine purple heptagram on the front cover, and stood up, ready to leave, taking the tome with him. 'I best get back to my research. I don't want to miss anything, do I? After all, I have a puzzle to solve that requires ancient Arcane knowledge. It's what gets me out of bed in the morning.'

Obsidian laughed, recognising Mauveine's passion. As the scholar departed, Obsidian contemplated the true intention of the unusual visit. Leaning back in his chair, he may have appreciated the tea, but that conversation was no accident. His thoughts raced aloud. 'Most scholars fumble over their words, but not him. He was testing me. I'm sure he concealed the true extent of his translations.'

Obsidian dismissed the notion for now; his priority was his junior investigators. He worried about their youth and inexperience – despite their talents, they were rough around the edges and prone to mistakes. 'Timberwolf's naïve lust to be the hero makes him foolhardy. Whilst Gainsboro masks it well, she has anger within her heart.' He shook his head at himself; being pessimistic was the sign of a poor leader. 'I wish you both luck. Can you step up?'

III – The Informants

Kaleidoscope Hill, Outside the Spectra City Walls

'Where is she?' Timberwolf uttered, glancing back over the city walls at the colossal clock face on the tallest tower which peered out above the old brick city walls. Impatience gnawed at him as he paced alongside a fast-flowing stream on the edge of the forest. He settled on a sizable boulder, immovable by ordinary strength. He often retreated to this spot, his chin resting on his fist, lost in contemplation.

'I got your message.' Timberwolf's secret source, Alabaster, arrived late as usual. Dressed as a humble cleric of the Church of the Dies Mater, she donned the traditional buttoned-up black and white robes that exuded an aura of chastity and civility. Except for a glimpse of platinum blonde hair peeking from beneath her habit, her form remained veiled. She laughed, embarrassed. 'I'm sorry I'm late. Prayers overran as usual.'

Timberwolf, eager for a good working relationship, did not query; after all, he believed she was the key to an early promotion. 'Don't worry. Your information about last night was accurate. Our investigations are moving at a great pace now.'

Alabaster bowed her head. Her kind smile brought warmth to Timberwolf's heart, solidifying his trust in her. 'I'm pleased and I hope you can recover and return those stolen treasures to their rightful owners. I was right to trust the Arcane Investigation Bureau with this matter ... I take it you require more information from me?'

'Yes,' Timberwolf stumbled over his words, recognising her perceptiveness. 'Do you know when Vermillion started collecting stolen artifacts?'

Alabaster, calmer, took her time. She measured each word, leaving no room for misinterpretation. 'Years now. Ever since he acquired that strange ring of his.'

Timberwolf felt shocked. 'You never mentioned the ring before?'

Alabaster blushed to admit her omission. 'I'm sorry, the whole affair sounds ludicrous and I'm taking significant risks here, telling you all of this. I'm breaking someone's confidence.'

'Of course!' Timberwolf was careful not to jeopardise his primary asset. 'I understand.'

Alabaster shook her head. 'You're sweet. People confide in me. They tell me their deepest secrets. I know I'm not supposed to divulge ... you know? ... given my oaths. I'm trusting your discretion, Timberwolf.'

'And you can trust my confidence.'

Alabaster felt a tinge of shame pulling Timberwolf into her troubles. 'I know. Forgive me. I'm nervous too. Vermillion has a power over people. Many have been hurt because of him.'

Timberwolf admired her righteous determination to bring Vermillion to justice. She was no shrinking violet and possessed a strong heart underneath the cleric's uniform. 'How do we stop him?'

Alabaster returned the question. 'That's your job, isn't it?'

'Yes ... silly me.' But Timberwolf needed concrete information; Grapha's instructions resonated in his mind. 'Since you told us about Jasper's gang, you must know more about how they operate. Any idea where I can find his hideout?'

Alabaster looked to the west. 'The Old Cinnabar Mines. Be careful, though. Going there requires courage. I don't think you could punch your way through on your own. They'll kill you if given the chance.' Her concern was palpable. She could not afford to lose Timberwolf, just as he could not afford to lose her valuable information.

'Don't worry,' Timberwolf cracked his knuckles. 'I can handle myself in a fight. Besides, I wouldn't go alone.'

'I do not doubt your strength.' Alabaster bowed her head. When she looked up again, she seemed agitated. 'Look, I must return to work now before they notice my absence. I pray for your victory and safe return. Inform me if you need more information. I'm always eager to help.'

With that prayer, Alabaster whisked herself back into town and Timberwolf turned his gaze westward to where the Cinnabar Mines awaited. A smile spread across his face as he anticipated Obsidian's and Grapha's approval. And once they approved the raid on Jasper's gang, he could showcase his excellence in the heat of the action. He relished the opportunity.

Approaching Midday, Vermillion's Private Museum

'Stay in character, Gainsboro. You're here to ask questions. Keep control of the conversation.' She finished her mantra before she took hold of the bronze lion-head doorknocker and knocked on the grand door of Vermillion's personal collection – a museum built on his expansive estate. Instead of her usual uniform, she had opted for a subtle disguise – the traditional grey work clothes that clerics wore for non-religious engagements. A chocolate brown leather satchel hung off her left shoulder, containing a mishmash of papers she hoped no-one would inspect.

Before she had a chance to knock, the door swung open and a young woman dressed in a reddish-brown suit, stood in front of her. Impatient, this woman tapped her foot – on a tight schedule, a visit from the Church of the Dies Mater was not her priority today, given the gala

Vermillion was holding tonight. She feigned a smile. 'My name is Rosewood. I'm the collection manager here. Come in.'

Gainsboro entered, overwhelmed by the sight which greeted her. 'Oh, my!'

Priceless artifacts – marble statues, exquisite oil paintings, glass cabinets filled with jewellery, exquisite ivories, pottery and religiously significant artifacts – adorned the bold, crimson foyer walls. Luminous torch crystals bathed the room in a warm yellow glow, fine-tuned to create the perfect radiance for such a grand display.

Rosewood had grown used to such reactions. 'You may wish to close your jaw. You're new, aren't you? Who are you?'

'Ashen.' Gainsboro struggled to remember her alias. 'I'm attached to Father Arcanite's taskforce in The Sacred Artifacts and Relics Office.'

Rosewood furrowed her brow. The name 'Arcanite' did not ring a bell. 'Come along, Ashen, you've seen nothing yet.'

Gainsboro regained her composure. 'This collection … It's just so impressive.'

Rosewood, already ascending the marble stairway, was not waiting around for compliments. Gainsboro, struggling to keep up, noticed the rooms off the hallway filled with priceless treasures that could inspire generations of historians and archaeologists – suits of armour and ceremonial swords to precious medallions, and icons and idols from historic religions.

She stopped and sighed.

Rosewood heard the sound, turned her head and looked down the stairs. 'What's wrong?'

Gainsboro shook her head. 'It's a shame in a way they are not on public display.'

'How dare—' Rosewood's instant fury made Gainsboro recoil. The collection manager took a deep breath, aware of the Church member she was addressing. 'You want these artifacts in public hands? Ordinary people have no concept of their value.'

The contempt and disgust Rosewood held for the average person astonished Gainsboro, but she knew better than to argue. Instead, she hurried towards the stairs and studied the woman now waiting for her; the heavy make-up could not obscure the dark rings under her eyes and, underneath the overpowering scent of sweet perfume, Gainsboro's nose picked up a peculiar scent – that of alcohol.

Rosewood continued. 'Ordinary people do not understand the artifacts' beauty. They would not care for them. Only we can do that. Only we have the facilities and the dedication to preserve such a priceless cultural heritage.'

Gainsboro remained silent, biting her tongue. Her thoughts were far from complimentary. She believed Rosewood had forgotten how real people behaved. 'This must be one expensive project.'

Rosewood found Gainsboro's naivety tiresome. 'Indeed. Vermillion converted his ancestral home to create this museum. He comes from old money, you see. Inherited wealth—' Her voice trailed off. Gainsboro had to fill in the blanks and let her imagination run wild. She suspected people considered the source of money politically incorrect today.

Rosewood's time was precious. 'Shall we move on?'

Gainsboro caught up and followed the primary route through the collection, walking passed the various displays of oil paintings of nobility from centuries past. She could identify numerous coats of arms and family crests – it would be a snub of the highest magnitude if the insignia of an important house was not present – and wondered what else he had stored hidden away from view. 'He enjoys collecting things, doesn't he? He's not an ordinary man, is he?'

'No. If it's old and has significance, he must have it. This is his genuine passion. He sees it as his legacy.'

If not for the criminal element to Vermillion's endeavours, Gainsboro could admire such dedication and passion. It was a shame such an obsession had corrupted his character. 'You said you wanted the Church to inspect something?'

Rosewood led Gainsboro to a workshop behind one of the locked doors not accessible to the public. 'Right this way.'

Inside, the worn timber beams and cracks in the walls were in stark contrast to the opulence of the museum. At her workstation, a junior curator sat polishing a golden bracelet and did not look up when they entered the room, preferring not to be disturbed. With frizzy hair and thick lenses in her spectacles, this archivist had a messy setup. Yet there was an order to her chaos, which no-one could understand even if she tried to explain it to them. Even Rosewood had given up.

The archivist sensed visitors and did not want to be disturbed. 'I'm busy! Go away!'

'Carmine! Remember your manners!' Rosewood's sharp voice brought her to attention; her glare cut deep and forced obedience.

Carmine dropped her instruments and bowed her head in penance. 'Sorry, ma'am.'

Gainsboro did not like the strict formality; it did not inspire a healthy hierarchy. 'I heard you wanted advice from the Church.'

Carmine realised who Gainsboro must be and leapt from her seat. 'Come!'

She rushed to an old encyclopaedia sitting to one side on the bookshelf, still waiting for approval to be displayed. She grabbed the old book and blew away the layer of dust. Gainsboro followed as Rosewood, not wanting to spend any longer than necessary amongst the lower-level employees, hung back by the door. As Carmine opened the book, she grabbed Gainsboro and pulled her close so Rosewood could not hear. 'Take this.'

Inside the book was a new sheet of paper, folded into quarters. Gainsboro understood the assignment. With a sleight of hand, she tucked the piece of paper into her pocket. Carmine mouthed, 'Thank you.' She then coughed and cleared her throat. 'Is this book an original? We believe it is. Does that date of publication add up?'

Gainsboro believed her answer did not matter, although for effect she gave the volume her full attention, turning through the pages and examining the parchment for authenticity. 'I believe it is.'

Rosewood, who was eager to remove Gainsboro from the premises and carry on with her preparations for that night's gala, rolled her eyes. 'I'm glad that's settled. Carmine is so devoted she works night and day to catalogue our collection.'

Gainsboro doubted the working hours and conditions were hers by choice and would not leave without letting Rosewood know of her disapproval. 'You could have brought the book to us for inspection, you know, Ms Rosewood? Church time is precious.'

Rosewood found herself stunned and Gainsboro could sense her fury. Carmine suppressed a smirk. No-one stood up to Rosewood in her own museum.

Rosewood somehow maintained the fraying ends of her patience. 'We won't take any more time from you.'

Gainsboro, revelling in her small triumph, nodded and left; she had no intention of hanging around this museum, with its dark undercurrent which gave her the creeps. As she left, Rosewood did not bother to say goodbye and slammed the doors shut behind her. The loud clank of the lock and key affirmed Gainsboro was no longer welcome.

Her carriage awaited. Once inside, the driver set the horses on their way. She ensured she pulled the curtains across and then took out the sheet of parchment from her pocket. She opened it to find a simple message – THE CELLARS.

With a smile, Gainsboro folded the paper back into her pocket, believing she had a solid lead. 'Obsidian's going to enjoy tonight, isn't he?'

IV – Provenance

That Evening, Vermillion's Private Museum

Obsidian, armed with the information Gainsboro had brought him, fidgeted with the white dog-collar around his neck, a reminder of his most hated disguise. Despite his aversion to the priestly costume, the illusion was necessary to gain entry and converse with Lord Vermillion, although the possibility of being asked to quote scripture or officiate at a wedding was intimidating. Arriving amidst a sea of other dignitaries – politicians, theologians, judges, and a selection of society's sparkling luminaries – the liveried staff ushered Obsidian into the main entrance hall from where he could marvel at the grand marble staircase.

He had only been there a few minutes when someone spotted him – Alabaster, hiding behind one of the ornate Corinthian columns, recognised him as soon as she laid eyes on him. 'What's he doing here?'

No longer dressed as a humble cleric, she was disguised in a snowy-white cocktail dress to blend in with the other socialites. Holding a glass of fizzy wine, she adjusted the string of pearls which hung around her neck, aware that an ignorant Arcane Investigator could jeopardise her cover. She could not afford for him to spot her.

A round of applause echoed around the marble hall, stifling the murmur of pleasantries and small talk. Rosewood, adorned in a striking scarlet gown, stood at the top of the ornate stairs with a glass of wine in hand. She sipped before taking a larger gulp, then cleared her throat. 'Welcome, honoured guests. Thank you for accepting our invitation. I know you're eager to see our exhibits. However, our host tonight wishes to share a few words before we continue. Please give a round of applause to the visionary who made this extraordinary collection possible, Lord Vermillion!'

Rapturous applause ensued; Obsidian and Alabaster joined in, but with less enthusiasm. Vermillion descended the staircase with an aura of invincible arrogance – he was a force of nature in his own castle. From behind the cover of a group of judges, Obsidian's eyes focused on the glowing ruby ring - The Gula – but Alabaster manoeuvred away from the crowd and positioned herself in Obsidian's blind-spot.

'Ladies and gentlemen!' Vermillion's booming voice silenced the fading applause. 'I would like to show you the first artifact I ever collected; the inspiration behind this marvellous collection.'

He raised his hand, displaying The Gula, and everyone in the audience leant in to admire the jewelled masterpiece. 'This ring started my fascination with collecting artifacts from all over the continent. People say this ring comes from the northern tundras and possesses distinct magical philosophies.'

The inflections in his voice mesmerised the gathered crowd, except for Obsidian and Alabaster, who both believed he was omitting key information about the ring. Vermillion lowered his hand. 'If you were to indulge me, ladies and gentlemen, I've always found fire captivating. Who remembers those old travelling carnivals and circuses with fire-breathers who captured our imaginations?'

An uneasy feeling settled within Obsidian; that was an odd thing to say, considering his family died in an inferno. Alabaster, perturbed, hoped Vermillion wouldn't display what she feared he might.

Vermillion enjoyed this next part. 'With this ring, I can live out my fantasies, including—' He placed his chin on the flat back of his hand, positioning the ring where his breath would pass over it. He inhaled, filling his lungs to their full capacity. Anticipation gripped the crowd as Vermillion lifted his head, exhaled, and a stream of orange fire erupted from his mouth, resembling a dragon's tongue. Rapturous applause followed; the ignorant attendees found this parlour trick mesmerising.

Obsidian tugged at his dog-collar at the sight of The Gula's power and Alabaster now realised the severity of the threat posed by the Sin Ring.

Vermillion bowed. 'Thank you, all. You are too kind. Now! Please enjoy the reception and take your time to study my artifacts.'

As the crowd, chattering amongst themselves about the miracle they had just witnessed, dispersed into different rooms, each filled with treasures that stimulated the imagination, Alabaster sighed. Time to take an executive decision. She decided to let Obsidian have his fun tonight and slipped away from the reception whilst she remained unnoticed by the Arcane Investigator.

Alone now, Obsidian watched Vermillion and Rosewood ascend the stairs to their next duty of the evening, meeting and entertaining the patrons. He followed them. With his dog-collar, people would let him through, offering respectful nods. He smiled and laughed; he had found one advantage of pretending to be a priest. His eyes fixated on Vermillion and Rosewood, his patience unwavering. In his hand, he held the glass of sparkling wine but had no intention to sip away as he waited in line, ignoring the various canapes being offered, to speak to Vermillion. As the queue moved forward, the fake laughter coming from Vermillion and Rosewood began to get on his nerves and he wished the wait would be over.

Observing the opulent lord, he found his physical appearance odd. Despite being in his mid-thirties, Vermillion appeared much older, closer to his late sixties. Obsidian glanced towards The Gula on his finger, wondering if it caused the accelerated aging.

The time had come for his audience.

'Ah!' Vermillion opened his arms. 'Good to see the Church accepted my invitation. Tell me, what is your name?'

'Arcanite, sir,' Obsidian bowed his head – his alias proved useful in such circumstances, although had no intention of shaking such sinful hands. 'Of The Sacred Artifacts and Relics Office.'

'You're rather young, aren't you, to be in such an illustrious position?' Vermillion plucked canapes from a passing tray – an easy temptation. 'New to the job, are we?'

'Yes, I am. Just promoted. Studying your work.' Obsidian had given little thought to his cover backstory; he did not intend to make long-term acquaintances tonight.

Rosewood, suspicious of new faces, was keen to scrutinise him. 'I met one of your junior researchers today. Ashen, was it? She differed from the quiet type I'm used to seeing. Quite direct.'

'Yes, young Ashen can speak her mind.' Obsidian guessed Gainsboro could not resist a pop at Rosewood and was eager to move on to more important matters. 'I must say your theatrics tonight—' He paused to wave his hand around the room. 'Are thfe talk of everybody here.'

'This old thing,' Vermillion dismissed The Gula's importance. 'It's one of the many interesting artifacts I've collected over the years.' He stuffed more hors d'oeuvre into his open mouth, not bothering to wipe away the crumbs.

Repulsed, Obsidian watched, convinced Vermillion was not even chewing. More importantly, he doubted his words; Rosewood's involuntary grimace confirmed his suspicions. 'You said the ring came from the north? How did you collect such a remarkable piece?'

'By chance. Someone gave it away for free, would you believe?'

Vermillion did not convince. Obsidian suspected nothing in Vermillion's world was ever free.

Rosewood remained on the attack. 'Does the Church disapprove of this magic? After all, northern magic used to be a taboo.'

Obsidian shrugged his shoulders. 'So long as it doesn't cause anyone any harm, the Church has no objections to parlour tricks.' He faked a smile, noting how Vermillion's hearty laughter distracted from

Rosewood's shrinking presence; it was a clear indication – to him, at least – of how terrified she was of her employer. He began his questioning. 'Remarkable collection. I hear it keeps growing day by day. You must need to keep building more infrastructure?'

'Indeed. It will never stop growing. It will be a wonder of the modern world.'

'I believe you.' Obsidian assumed that was the first full truth Vermillion had disclosed tonight. 'Enlighten me. What is your opinion on provenance? An object's provenance would intrigue someone like you?'

Vermillion never wasted an opportunity to show off. 'Of course! The value of an object is determined by people's perception, not by its monetary worth. Whether it be sentimental or religious, if it meant something important to someone, then no amount of money could ever eclipse that attachment.'

Obsidian had laid down the foundations for his line of attack. 'And what if you buy a stolen piece?'

Vermillion's smile dropped as he realised he had fallen into a trap; his scarlet eyes flashed with instant rage.

Obsidian pretended to have a sip of his wine whilst waiting for his answer. 'You seem agitated, sir?'

The light from The Gula intensified, responding to Vermillion's growing, violent urges. Unable to walk away without looking guilty, the greedy host sought comfort in more canapes. His impulsive gluttony told Obsidian everything he needed to know.

Rosewood leapt to her employer's defence. 'I know the source of every artifact. I've spent many long nights verifying each object's provenance.'

Obsidian swirled the wine in his glass, in control and knowing it. 'But could you guarantee that under oath?'

She stumbled over her words. 'I ... I would have to check my records.'

Vermillion grew suspicious. 'You're rather cynical for a Church bureaucrat, Arcanite.'

'It is my job to be.' Obsidian's expression hardened. 'There has been a spate of burglaries, targeting artifacts in provincial churches. Have you heard about them?'

Vermillion and Rosewood denied with silence.

Obsidian pressed on. 'And you, sir, would have to admit that you would be the perfect client to sell said stolen goods to and store them in ... oh, I don't know ... your cellars, perhaps?'

'We would not be willing participants of crime, Arcanite. We would be victims of fraud,' Rosewood interjected.

'I suppose so,' Obsidian conceded. 'You are quite right. I don't see you two getting your hands dirty and doing an exchange in the Cordovan Sewers or somewhere vile like that. That would be most improper.'

Vermillion and Rosewood exchanged glances.

'Look here!' Vermillion puffed out his chest. 'This is my museum! I refuse to be interrogated like a criminal!'

'Maybe you can help me then?' Obsidian changed tact, adopting a softer approach. 'You have a tremendous influence. May I request you throw your weight around your social circles and see what you can find out?'

Vermillion faked a smile. 'Of course.'

Rosewood tried to seize some sort of initiative. 'What's stopping us from filing a complaint against your department for tonight's interrogation?'

Obsidian saluted the duo. 'I would be disappointed if you didn't.'

He timed his exit so he could place his glass on a passing tray which a waiter was carrying and disappeared into the crowd.

As he left the building, he dropped his dog collar onto the floor with the full intention of it being found.

V – A Thief's Confession

Midnight, Vermillion's Office

Vermillion's roar reverberated through the chamber as he relinquished his grasp on restraint. He cast the books and papers from his opulent antique desk onto the unforgiving stone floor, heedless of their chaotic landing. The departure of his guests granted him the freedom to unleash his pent-up anger, stemming from Obsidian's humiliating interrogation. The incandescent radiance of The Gula only heightened his fury. Rosewood, who had convinced herself he could not reason with anyone, shrank into the corner; melded with the shadows. Terrified of the ring's flames, she feared he would turn the inferno onto her and burn her like the witches of old.

'How did they learn about our exchange? Were you not careful enough?' Vermillion's accusatory bark required Rosewood to come up with a scapegoat, despite the fact she had warned him not to attend the exchange in the Cordovan Sewers. He slammed his hands on the desk with resounding force. 'Answer me!'

Rosewood quivered, bargaining not only for her job but also her life. Swallowing became arduous. 'They must have been tracking Jasper, sir.'

'Cut them loose. Dispose of them. I want no evidence!'

'Yes, sir!' Rosewood retreated with haste. Her strides were long and brisk. She closed the door behind her. Mouth parched, she would find solace in a couple of drinks.

Vermillion caressed The Gula and his thoughts turned to his new enemy. He reasoned Arcanite was not an administrator. No, he told himself – he must have been something else. Believing his interrogator was a member of the Church, Vermillion entertained the logical assumption that he was an Arcane Investigator – and he had heard stories about them. They were not to be trifled with. If they got to Jasper first, he would be in danger. He stroked The Gula as if comforting the Sin Ring as a pet. 'If the worst comes and they come to take my freedom, I'll defend myself and my beautiful collection, even if it burns away my very spirit.'

Dawn, The Cinnabar Mines

'We're under attack!' The panicked wails of thieves fleeing, scrambling to save their own skin, sounded the alarm for Rust. Knights clad in gleaming armour, bearing the crest of the Church of the Dies Mater, flooded the converted caverns, subduing and arresting any thief they encountered.

Rust harboured no intention of facing arrest. Like any good thief, he had an exit strategy. In his frantic attempt to snatch anything valuable, he bundled any artefact he could lay his hands on into a worn cloth sack. He'd take anything valuable, regardless of size.

Obsidian blocked his escape. 'You're not escaping!'

Rust looked up, eyes narrowed. 'Hang on! ... You're—'

Obsidian smirked. 'You recognise me?'

'Traitor!' Rust brandished his slingshot, loading it with a small pebble. He pulled back the elastic and aligned the centre of Obsidian's forehead in his sights. When the fibres reached their maximum tension, he released the shot.

Obsidian did not move, but his volcanic glass bracers twinkled.

Rust noticed the reflective gleam of a mirror passing over Obsidian's skin. The stone shot hit its target and rebounded, striking Rust in the forehead instead. He collapsed onto the ground screaming, with blood pouring from the wound.

'Stop whinging. You're still breathing.'

Obsidian whistled. Knights under his command arrived and dragged a kicking and screaming Rust away.

'You'll pay for this!' Rust's hollow threat was not a memorable parting shot. Obsidian had learnt over the years to brush off empty threats, but at that moment another thief – this time armed with a dented dagger – was keen for revenge. He thrusted his knife into Obsidian's back, but as he did, a reflective sheen raced across Obsidian's darkened armour, shattering the knife on impact, splintering it into tiny shards against the cold rock floor.

The thief staggered back in bemusement. 'What? How did you—?'

Obsidian turned to face his foe, unfazed. 'I never let my guard down.'

Before the thief could flee, Gainsboro rushed in to assist and pointed her slender, sharpened wand at the assailant. A tremendous gust of wind erupted from its tip, knocking the thief off his feet and sending him crashing onto the ground. More knights appeared to remove the criminal, who resisted by kicking and screaming but with no actual effect.

Obsidian turned to Gainsboro. 'You didn't have to waste your magic.' Underneath the critique, an appreciative tone lingered.

'Sorry.' Gainsboro detected the thankful undertones; breaking habits always proved difficult. 'I keep forgetting how potent your Reflection Magic is.'

'The element of surprise is useful in our line of work. Has Timberwolf reached Jasper yet?'

'I believe so. Knowing him, they'll be knocking seven bells out of each other. He does like to punch first and ask questions later.'

Obsidian rolled his eyes. 'We should move. We don't want to miss the action, do we?'

The Escape Shaft

Timberwolf dispatched the last guard, cracking his knuckles and rolling his neck to celebrate his success. Now, he had Jasper cornered near the end of a tunnel. The only problem was the proximity of an escape route, a ladder leading to the surface, which was tantalisingly visible.

The light of freedom encouraged Jasper to make a break for it. 'You want a fight?'

Timberwolf knew he would not surrender at the same time he knew the official uniform of the Church did not suit dirty dishonourable tactics. He needed to think outside his usual box. 'No. I'm here to arrest you.'

Timberwolf, whose enchanted gloves constricted his fingers, did not want a fight. Instead, he focused his attention at Jasper's feet. Before Jasper could react, a thick layer of ice enveloped them; the moisture in the air freezing around his form. He tried to trudge forward but found progress impossible as if he was pushing through a blizzard. Soon, his feet became frozen to the ground, making it impossible for him to lift them, no matter his effort. And with no weapons within reach, he could not chip away at his frigid shackles. 'Using magic is cheating. Where's your pride as a fighter?'

Timberwolf crossed his arms with a contented smile. 'We're not on equal standing. There is no satisfaction in fighting thieves. Also, who claimed we would have a fistfight?'

Jasper, try as he may, could not free himself from his icy hold. He sighed and his shoulders slouched as he realised it was futile to waste energy trying to escape. His smuggling days were over, at least for now. Now was the time for patience.

Obsidian placed a congratulatory hand on Timberwolf's shoulder. 'Good work as expected.'

Timberwolf was pleased to see his efforts recognised. 'Thanks, boss.'

Gainsboro observed the icy anchors. 'You did not use brute force. You're learning.'

Timberwolf laughed. 'Why are you surprised?'

Gainsboro looked back at the three fallen, bruised guards she had just walked passed. 'You could have frozen his henchman. Still a work in progress, then.'

Timberwolf engaged in shadowboxing. 'I need to keep practicing my jabs, Gainsboro.'

Gainsboro raised a critical eyebrow. 'Your lust for fighting is going to get you into trouble one day.'

'Focus.' Obsidian reclaimed their minds. He had Jasper right where he wanted him, and he was not letting this opportunity pass until the knights handed him over to Church prosecutors.

'So, you're the boss, then?' Jasper spat; the viscous glob landed in front of Obsidian's feet.

Obsidian side-stepped. 'Did you not think there would be repercussions for stealing church property?'

Jasper lashed out. 'Churches are bricks and mortar and hold artifacts I can sell. You people are too trusting and leave them in the open, unguarded.'

Obsidian did not rise to the bait. 'Anyone else share your views, Jasper? Like Lord Vermillion, for example?'

Jasper stumbled over his words. 'I don't know … what you're … talking about.'

Obsidian knew he had broken through Jasper's defences. 'I witnessed your interaction with Vermillion in the Cordovan Sewers. I was just as surprised as you when he showed up.'

After being given time to think about his position, Jasper realised that Obsidian was offering him an olive branch. 'What do you want to know?'

Obsidian nodded, recognising Jasper understood his intentions. 'How did your arrangement work?'

'That Rosewood lady acted on his behalf. We targeted village churches and looted them. We got paid above what we would get on the black market.' Jasper, once confident in his scheme, now realised it was not foolproof as he had believed.

Gainsboro chipped in a follow-up question. 'So, Vermillion paid for exclusivity and your silence. Why?'

Jasper gritted his teeth. He hated snitches, but his freedom was worth more than his pride. 'Rosewood said that Vermillion is obsessed with any artifact, no matter its size. He just wants to collect anything he deems valuable or important. He would take every single treasure your church has ever collected if given the chance.'

Obsidian kept a level head. 'When you stood in Vermillion's presence, how did you feel?'

Jasper thought it was a strange question, but when he considered it, he understood Obsidian's tactics. 'It ... It was odd ... I don't know, but I felt compelled to answer his desires ... I was glad when he left. It felt like I had escaped a trap.'

Obsidian processed the new information. It seemed to him that The Gula's influence had ensnared not just Vermillion, but Lady Rosewood, who he guessed must know what she was doing was wrong yet could not help but obey Vermillion's commands. 'Thank you, Jasper. We will now take you away and try you for your crimes. You may remain silent. I suggest you take the option.'

Jasper's rage exploded. 'What about our deal? Don't I get a bargain?'

'Deal? Who said anything about a deal?' Obsidian had no mercy.

Jasper's whole body trembled with fury. Obsidian deceived him. It was only because of Timberwolf's ice shackles that he did not rush and attempt to rip Obsidian apart. Furious, he tried to grab Obsidian, pivoting forward like a jack-in-a-box, but he was out of reach. He screamed with frustration. 'I have friends. I'm not staying locked up for long. And when I'm free, I'll get my payback.'

Obsidian shook his head. 'They all say that, Jasper. Criminal friends are absent in times of need.'

The trio did not linger. They left the thief frozen in place, awaiting removal by the knights.

As they left him behind, Obsidian began preparing for their next move. 'I'll seek permission from Father Grapha for us to arrest Vermillion at nightfall tomorrow.'

Gainsboro and Timberwolf thought the breakneck pace of this case would never slow down. Obsidian had already planned their next steps. 'Your source came through again, Timberwolf. Let's see if they know anything about Vermillion's cellars.'

Timberwolf nodded. 'Yes, I'll meet them again.'

'Good,' Obsidian turned to Gainsboro. 'Make sure that Rosewood gets news of Jasper's capture.'

'Yes, sir.' Gainsboro could see a cunning plan forming in Obsidian's mind. And saw he was eager to set it in motion.

VI – Vice on the Heart

Kaleidoscope View, Outside the Spectra City Walls

In contrast to their previous encounters, it was Alabaster who was waiting for Timberwolf at their agreed meeting spot by the mountain stream. Dressed in her cleric's uniform, she perched on the familiar boulder where he had often waited for her. She wore a stern expression and glanced towards the giant clock tower in the city's heart which rose above the stone walls.

The sight of the cleric being early blindsided Timberwolf when he arrived.

He stopped in his tracks and noted the serious look on her face. 'Is everything alright?'

'We have to move.' Alabaster rose and grasped his forearm. 'Carmine sought my help. She wants out, now!'

'Hold on—' Timberwolf gestured for calm. 'Who's Carmine?'

Alabaster tutted. 'One of Vermillion's archivists. She's the one who reached out to me.'

'Right.' Timberwolf connected the dots. 'And you're comfortable telling me about her now? What about protecting confidences?'

Alabaster shook her head. 'She's in danger.'

Timberwolf understood. 'We'll protect her.'

'Carmine has played her part. She's been patient and provided your agent with information. Unable to resign, she's terrified for her life.'

Timberwolf crooked his eyebrow. 'Why can't she resign?'

'People who work for Vermillion don't resign, they disappear. No one has asked questions before. But once you spot the pattern, it's obvious.'

Timberwolf saw the list of Vermillion's potential crimes increase. 'We move tonight. Maybe Carmine can help?'

'She'll do anything.'

'The cellars she mentioned?'

'Rumour has it is that the cellars are a second museum underground, reserved for Vermillion's eyes only. Carmine has never entered. Only Vermillion has access.'

Timberwolf furrowed his brow. 'That's peculiar behaviour. I presume we would need a key to enter?'

Alabaster reflected and considered her options. 'I don't think she mentioned anything about a key. She may tell you when you arrive to extract her.'

Timberwolf nodded; he accepted the limits of Alabaster's knowledge. 'If I had known the identity of your contact earlier—' The more Timberwolf thought through the information that Alabaster had relayed to him, the more questions arose. 'Hold on.'

Alabaster sensed a tough line of enquiry.

'How would Carmine know about Jasper and his gang?' Timberwolf probed, watching for any changes in Alabaster's facial expression. 'Or where the exchange of stolen goods would take place?'

Alabaster caught her tongue, but her nose twitched nervously.

Timberwolf reached the only logical conclusion he could. 'You're not a cleric, are you?'

Alabaster sighed, knowing it was time to change tack.

She removed her cleric's habit and tossed it aside, revealing her platinum blond hair with a dramatic swish, relieved to no longer need to pretend to be a humble cleric. 'You're right. Vermillion has attracted a lot of attention. You're not the only ones in the Church interested in him.'

Timberwolf sat down in a huff. 'And here I am thinking you were an honest cleric, doing the right thing. I know you're not part of the Arcane Investigation Bureau, but which Church Division do you belong to?'

Alabaster considered her responses.

Trust had to be rebuilt.

'Forgive me. I needed to play the role of the innocent cleric to secure initial contact. If it helps, you were sweet and caring in your manner with me, if not a little naïve. There were times I thought you would do anything if I fluttered my eyelids at you. You'd better be careful. Someone less virtuous may try to exploit such naivety.'

Timberwolf could not believe he was receiving feedback. 'You're in no position to criticise!' He launched himself onto his feet. 'You've got some nerve. Why come to me instead of Father Grapha? Or Obsidian?'

Now it was Alabaster's turn to sit on the boulder. 'I needed to protect Carmine's identity. And ... how do I put this? Obsidian is a known entity within the Church. And so is Father Grapha. They aren't approachable individuals, unlike yourself.'

Timberwolf felt both insignificant and important at the same time, caught between not deserving respect and having the ability to contribute to the downfall of a powerful criminal.

'Listen,' Alabaster aimed to smooth things over. 'The Arcane Investigation Bureau is the most appropriate avenue the Church possesses to deal with malefactors like Vermillion. His use of Sin Magic is your area of expertise, correct?'

Timberwolf was pained to admit she was right. 'I know that. So, who are you working for then?'

Alabaster did not answer and did not break eye-contact.

Timberwolf could not stand this conversation any longer. 'OK, I'm leaving.'

'We can still work together. We both have mutual interests here and there are obvious professional benefits to our continued partnership.'

'Such as?' Timberwolf's doubt crept in.

Alabaster laughed. 'Connections are everything in our line of work and you know that. Vermillion is only one part of a grander problem. He's today's target. Your bureau will get the credit for bringing him down. And then tomorrow, another threat appears. We could end up working together for several years.'

Timberwolf found himself troubled, wondering what else was happening in the shadows. He shook his head. 'I suppose this means I must keep your identity a secret from Obsidian and Father Grapha? In exchange, we keep working together.'

Alabaster smiled. 'Please ... And thank you.'

'Fine,' Timberwolf conceded through gritted teeth. 'If Carmine wants her freedom, then she needs to help us gain access to Vermillion's Museum. Can she do that?'

Alabaster nodded. 'Yes. She can give you access via one of the staff entrances.'

'It's settled then. Let her know we're coming at nightfall.'

'Will do. Good luck, Timberwolf, and happy hunting. We'll speak again.'

Alabaster departed, leaving a confused Timberwolf.

Given his chosen career path, he knew being deceived by someone, perhaps someone he had come to trust, was an occupational hazard. He ran his fingers through his hair in a bid to clear his head. Although Alabaster may have ulterior motives, everything she had told him was correct and he had found satisfaction in being deemed trustworthy in order to aid the grander mission of the Church.

Eyes focused on the future, he gazed over the city walls at the cathedral spire and wondered how many sprawling Church Divisions the public did not know existed.

Obsidian's Private Office

The expected knock sounded on the ancient oak door, alerting Obsidian to the arrival of his scholar. He looked up from his paperwork.

'Enter!'

Mauveine strode into the room at speed and took his seat on the opposite side of the desk. 'I came as soon as your request to meet crossed my desk.' This time, instead of a cup of tea or a weighty tome, Mauveine had brought with him a compact purple chest, which he placed it in front of Obsidian.

'What is this?'

'A chest.'

Obsidian rolled his eyes. 'I know, Mauveine. Why show me a chest? Is it a special chest?'

'Of course, it is. It has a special protective lining on the interior that blocks any magic from entering or leaving the central compartment.'

Obsidian found Mauveine's answers frustrating. 'Fascinating, but why show me this particular chest? How is it relevant? I did not summon you to talk about a box you've found.'

Mauveine believed the reason was obvious. 'I brought this chest because once you retrieve The Gula from Vermillion, it will need to be placed somewhere out of harm's way. We don't want a Sin Magic amplifier tempting people to wear it, now do we? That would put us back to step one, wouldn't it?'

'I see.' Obsidian appreciated Mauveine's logic; the scholar thinking a few steps ahead of him.

'The last thing we want is our priests or bishops putting on the ring and gorging themselves on sacramental wine.' Though Mauveine enjoyed his own dark sense of humour, Obsidian did not. Mauveine recognised the scowl and stopped laughing. 'I've disappointed you, haven't I?'

Obsidian took a deep breath, resetting the conversation. 'I summoned you here because you never told me that The Gula grants the bearer the ability to cast fire magic. That is a glaring omission, don't you agree?'

'Oh?' Mauveine stretched out his bottom lip and seemed disappointed, as if someone had taken away his moment. 'Hints of such magic were present in the text, though seeing The Gula's power in action is more educational.' He dismissed Obsidian's concerns with a wave of his hand. 'Well, no harm done.'

Obsidian would not let this go. 'Anything else I should know? Does The Gula advance aging, for example?'

Mauveine crooked his eyebrow. 'An astute observation. What gave you that idea?'

'Vermillion looks like he's in his sixties, but he's only in his late thirties. And given how much he was eating at his private function, I would suggest that The Gula has changed his behaviour.'

Mauveine nodded, believing Obsidian to be correct. 'Sin Magic has negative effects on the body and the mind. The idea of The Gula placing a curse on the bearer is not an unreasonable hypothesis.'

Obsidian shook his head, becoming irritated at the lack of direct answers. 'I don't feel prepared here, Mauveine. We know too little about the ring.'

Mauveine shrugged his shoulders. 'I'm sure it's nothing someone of your reputation can't handle. After all, I hear you are capable of some potent magic yourself. Reflection magic, correct?' He paused, his fascination getting the better of him. 'How does this curious variant of Light Magic work?'

'With the help of these,' Obsidian revealed his volcanic glass bracers from underneath his sleeve.

'Those are exquisite.' Mauveine could spend hours studying them. 'How do they work?'

Obsidian rotated his right wrist clockwise whilst trying to come up with a sufficient answer. 'From my core, I feel a power inside that I can tap into. Using this magic, I can project a protective shield around me.

And with these bracers, I can increase the durability of my shield. The more focus I put into my shield, the more robust it becomes.'

Mauveine saw the immediate advantages such bracers could provide an Arcane Investigator. 'So, you must be confident you're safe when in dangerous situations. That must help increase your life expectancy.'

Obsidian would have not phrased it like that. 'I suppose so.'

'It would be interesting to see how your reflective shield would stand up against any Sin Magic coming from Vermillion.' Mauveine enjoyed contemplating such hypotheticals.

Obsidian doubted the scholar grasped the true ramifications of The Gula's essence. 'Books only tell you so much, Mauveine. Real-life combat tells you more. Do not underestimate Sin Magic.'

'I agree.' Mauveine remained undeterred. 'But you're the expert here. I am a humble scholar. I assist your endeavours by preparing you for things you have not yet considered.' He tapped the box; a secure vault to which he held the only key. 'You secure The Gula in here and I keep it safe. Deal?'

Obsidian sat forward. 'You've given this some thought. I've not seen a scholar with such practical sense before. Anything else about this ring I should know?'

Mauveine leant back in his chair and scratched his chin.

His facial expression hardened and then he stood up, looming over Obsidian. 'Tell me, do you believe you have a gluttonous heart?'

'Excuse me?' Obsidian rose to his feet and refused to be spoken to like that in his own office.

'Before securing the ring, someone must remove The Gula from Vermillion's finger and hold it in their palm.' Mauveine walked around the office while he explained their predicament. 'The ring will tempt whoever holds it. Do you think you're strong enough to resist placing The Gula on your own finger?'

Obsidian grimaced.

Mauveine was testing him. He needed to give the correct answer. 'I do not believe gluttony is my key vice.'

Mauveine paused his pacing. 'You seem to take great pride in your assertion.'

'I have many flaws, Mauveine. Gluttony is not one of them.'

'I believe you,' Mauveine came over to the desk and offered his hand. 'I hope this is the start of a fruitful partnership.'

Obsidian shook his hand and found himself surprised to be on equal terms. There was something peculiar about Mauveine that played on his mind and he couldn't help but wonder where the Church recruited someone so unique. 'You're not a normal scholar, are you?'

Mauveine accepted the compliment. 'Thank you.'

'That's not a compli— Never mind.'

Mauveine lifted his chest and turned to leave. But before he exited, he had some parting words. 'Sin magic overrides sensible conscious thought. Gluttony consumes until nothing remains. The Gula will never satisfy Vermillion's gluttony. I wish you luck, Obsidian.'

The scholar's words had a sharp clarity to them which Obsidian valued in an ally. 'I'll be careful, Mauveine.'

As the scholar left the room, Obsidian inhaled for three seconds and exhaled for five, processing the danger tonight would bring. 'Gainsboro and Timberwolf have limited experience dealing with Sin Magic. I must be the shield that protects them from Vermillion's ravenous flames.'

The Spymaster's Office

'Are you prepared?' Grapha inquired of his trio of agents who stood in front of his desk, eager to deliver Vermillion into the hands of justice.

'You three need to neutralise Vermillion before we arrest him. It would be too perilous for ordinary officers to subdue him. This mission will have its challenges. Vermillion will be a difficult foe.'

Obsidian stepped forward. 'We are ready, Father.'

Grapha nodded, noting Obsidian had taken a personal interest in this case. 'Once you give us the signal, Obsidian, I shall arrive with the scholar you've been liaising with to extract The Gula from Vermillion and secure it. Then, we will assess his collection and return any stolen property to its rightful home.'

Obsidian agreed, believing that locking away The Gula would help him sleep better.

Grapha shifted his attention to Timberwolf. 'With your source's information and co-operation, we have a way into the building. Once inside, we must protect this Carmine.'

'We will,' Gainsboro stepped forward. 'She knows me. I'll make sure she flees the scene as soon as she let us in.'

'Very good.' Grapha's focus turned to mental preparations. 'How strong are your stomachs?'

Neither Timberwolf nor Gainsboro could answer that. 'We don't know how big Vermillion's collection is. And who knows what he has locked behind closed doors? Or what tricks he will use to evade arrest and defeat us?'

Gainsboro believed they must have more stored in the cellars than was displayed in the galleries. She remembered how Carmine's hand trembled when she handed over the note and shuddered to think what was hidden. 'We won't let our fear cloud our judgement.'

'Indeed.' Timberwolf pushed his clenched fists together. 'We'll bring justice to those Vermillion has wronged.'

The spymaster turned to his protégé. 'And you, Obsidian?'

Obsidian found himself wrong-footed. 'Of course, I am ready.'

Grapha rose to his feet, supported by his cane, and made his way to the window. 'I'm allowed to be concerned. This foe is unlike any you have encountered, even with your experience. This ring you have described possesses a rare strength I have seldom encountered throughout my long career. A Sin Magic conductor poses many theological, moral and ethical dilemmas.' He gazed out of the window in the direction of Vermillion's Museum and tightened the grip on his cane. 'Be careful. I fear Vermillion may be a symptom of a wider ailment.'

Timberwolf stopped himself from relaying Alabaster's concerns. He could not betray her confidence. For now, he must remain silent. He cast a sideways glance at Gainsboro, whose expression was tight – she dreaded to ponder what other threats might be out there, hoping Grapha was being too pessimistic.

'You do not have to worry about us, Father.' Obsidian offered the old man the reassurance he believed he needed. 'You've trained us well.'

'Go. And bring Vermillion to justice.' Grapha started their mission.

The trio saluted their spymaster and exited his office to fulfil their duty.

When they had gone, Grapha glanced out of the window. 'Steel your hearts. I fear this is a crusade none of us would dare inflict on anyone else.'

VII – Infiltration

An Hour before Dusk, Vermillion's Office

'The Church has Jasper in their custody. Why would the Church send us this letter?' Vermillion ripped up the letter into minuscule fragments like a tiger tearing flesh off the bone. The Gula radiated, setting the paper ablaze in a splendid fire before reducing it to ash moments later. 'It will not be long before Jasper confesses everything!'

Rosewood dared not speak, fearing she may incur Vermillion's wrath.

'Arcanite signed this letter. He came prepared when he interrogated us. The Church is closer to catching us than we thought. He's closing in on us, Rosewood!'

Rosewood attempted a reasoned argument, though she doubted her own words. 'It would take more than a thief's confession to arrest you, sir. Remember, you have friends in high places. The Church requires substantial evidence to pursue someone of your importance.'

'I hope you're right. Even so—' He shot her a cutting stare, then rose to his feet. 'I need to think. I'm retiring to the cellars for the evening. Make sure I'm not disturbed.'

Rosewood nodded in deference.

After Vermillion departed, she allowed herself to fall apart. Tears rolled down her cheek, smudging her makeup. 'I can't take this any longer ... I just want to be free ... But I must protect him, I ... I can't help it.'

Dusk, On the Edge of Vermillion's Estate

'How much money does this guy have?' The magnitude of Vermillion's estate astounded Timberwolf as, under the cover of the diminishing light, the trio made progress across the landscaped gardens, avoiding the eyes of the guards and eluding the noses of their hounds.

'Old money,' Gainsboro wagered. 'And who knows what investments he's made since to fund his museum?'

Obsidian crouched behind a low garden wall and snapped his fingers once. 'Focus.'

Timberwolf and Gainsboro fell silent and joined him, bobbing down close to the damp grass where they could not be seen.

Warily, Obsidian peered over the wall. 'You can see the staff entrance from here. Now we wait for it to open.'

They did not have to wait long. At the agreed time, it opened, a head peeking out from within a fluorescent-lit corridor.

Obsidian spotted her first. 'Is that Carmine, Gainsboro?'

'Yes.'

From behind them came the sound of footsteps – a guard approaching, slamming a baton into his open palm, unaware anyone was lurking close by.

Obsidian signalled to Timberwolf, who understood the task at hand. Waiting until the guard had walked passed, Timberwolf leapt over the wall and rushed him, knocking him out with a single blow to the stomach before he could call for help. The guard disposed of, and Timberwolf gave the others a nod to say they were clear to move.

Nobody wanted to wait. They all dashed to the door.

As they neared, Carmine recognised Gainsboro. 'Ashen,' she called out, waving them in. After they entered, she closed the door in swift silence and let out a sign of relief.

Gainsboro respected her bravery. 'Thank you.'

Carmine's spirits soared as she realized her intuition had not let her down. 'I knew you weren't a simple clerk. But I never thought you would be—'

Gainsboro believed time was of the essence. 'Where's Vermillion?'

'He's retired to the cellars. The door you're searching for is beyond the main staircase in a restricted area. You'll need a key. Rosewood should have one.'

Obsidian had hoped to avoid unnecessary confrontation but was still prepared. 'We'll deal with her.'

'Please. Be gentle. Underneath her façade, she's a damaged woman. Working for Vermillion has changed her.'

Gainsboro's resolve hardened. 'We will, Carmine. Now go! Get out of here!'

Carmine had no intention of staying. She broke into a sprint, fleeing into the night.

'Godspeed,' Gainsboro prayed for her safety.

Obsidian had no time for sentimentality. 'Come on.'

The main staircase was their priority. In theory, Rosewood should be upstairs in her office, but to their surprise, she was standing on the staircase, swaying and out of tune with her senses, clasping an empty bottle of red wine.

'You?' Rosewood rasped, recognising both Obsidian and Gainsboro, and realising they both used false pretences to get closer to the truth. 'So, you've come for us, huh? Who are you? ... Arcanite ... Ashen ... are those even your real names?'

Gainsboro stepped forward. 'We're with the Arcane Investigation Bureau. Where's Vermillion?'

'In the cellar where he goes every evening.' Rosewood showed off her key in her hand. 'I suppose you want this key.'

'Please.' Gainsboro offered a kind hand. 'You know what's he done. He must be stopped.'

Rosewood laughed a desperate cackle. 'Stop him? You can't stop him, you silly little girl.'

Gainsboro inched forward. 'Why are you helping him?' Timberwolf made a move to protect her, but Obsidian blocked him with a single nod. He stepped back. Rosewood had become Gainsboro's responsibility. She took the first step on the marble staircase. 'You must see what he is asking you to do is wrong?'

'You do not understand.' Rosewood found her hand going into her pocket without her conscious input. 'I ... Must help him... Answer his desires ... He must be—'

Rosewood pulled out a wand, surprising the Arcane Investigators who did not know she could perform magic. Gainsboro took no risks and with discreet skill withdrew her own sharpened wand and waved it. A blade of air struck Rosewood's weapon, cutting it in half and whisking it out of her hand before she realised what was happening. Both wooden fragments landed several steps above on the staircase, out of reach.

'Huh?' Rosewood had to take a seat on the marble step. The crushing realisation of her situation hit her all at once. She wept. 'I couldn't even fight back. Look at me, a pathetic wretch.'

Gainsboro took a seat next to her and did something no-one had done for Rosewood since she entered Vermillion's employ – she gave her a hug, and the gesture made her cry even more.

Gainsboro stroked Rosewood's arm and whispered. 'There, there!'

'What happened to me?' Rosewood spoke through her tears. 'This job was supposed to make my career. Now look at me ... I'm a criminal.'

Timberwolf had to turn away. He could not bear to see a broken soul crumbling apart. Obsidian, heart steeled, pointed to the wooden grandfather clock at the bottom of the staircase; the mission was far from over, and they lacked the luxury of time.

Gainsboro mouthed back. 'I'm working on it.' She turned to Rosewood and continued to console her. 'I need that key. We need to stop Vermillion.'

Rosewood placed the key in Gainsboro's hand and closed her fingers around the cold metal. 'Take it. Be careful. The cellars are a dark place. It's where he keeps his ... private collection.' She sniffed, wanting to blow her nose.

'We'll stop him.'

'Whatever you do, get rid of that wretched ring.' Rosewood let go of Gainsboro's hand. She knew she had no choice but to acquiesce, but the tears kept coming and she felt unable to move.

Gainsboro hesitated, believing it was cruel to leave Rosewood like this.

'Come on!' Obsidian mouthed and gestured to the cellars.

Gainsboro took a deep breath. 'You can count on us!'

She stood up and walked back down the stairs, leaving Rosewood in her torment, holding a faint hope the courts might have mercy on her.

Timberwolf stepped forward. 'You alright?'

Gainsboro suppressed her feelings. 'I'll be fine.'

Obsidian gave her an encouraging nod, but he knew this was only the beginning. 'Let's keep moving.'

As a group, they moved through the hallway until they reached a door blocked by a crimson rope suspended between two golden posts. Obsidian moved them out of the way and Gainsboro moved forward to put the key into the lock. It fitted. She turned it and heard the clunk of the lock turn. With a quick glance back to the others, she opened the door.

A dark, damp, stone stairway to the cellars below welcomed them.

Gainsboro peered forwards. 'I can't see a thing.'

Timberwolf, who had been staring at a strange crystal in a glass display case to the side of the door, had a thought. Although at first, it had seemed innocuous, on closer inspection he realised what it was. 'Obsidian? Is this a torch crystal?'

Obsidian moved closer and studied it. 'It could be.'

Gainsboro's curiosity got the better of her. 'I wonder if it still works.'

Obsidian held no qualms about breaking the glass. With a smash, he grabbed the crystal, closed his eyes and placed his intent on it.

The torch crystal illuminated and shone with a dusky orange light. Warm in his hand, it did not burn to touch. Obsidian prepared to descend the first step – he was the one accepting responsibility for the torch crystal, and he would be the one to guide them into the abyss. 'Are you both ready to go down?'

'Lead the way.' Timberwolf was keen.

'No time to waste,' Gainsboro confirmed.

Obsidian stared into the darkness. 'Let's see what you're hiding down there, Vermillion.'

VIII – The Museum Below

The Cellars beneath Vermillion's Museum

'I wouldn't call these cellars,' Timberwolf remarked, breath stolen away by the scale of what he was seeing. They had descended into an intricate labyrinth of interconnected rooms, linked by tunnels stretching in all directions. Multiple torch crystals were ablaze on the walls. He and Gainsboro seized a torch crystal for themselves and used their warm forms as guides.

Gainsboro looked down the various corridors. 'Where do we go?'

Obsidian decided for them. 'We follow the illuminated crystals. Vermillion is the only one who could have activated them. Stay close. Who knows what he has down here?'

Following the trail of luminous crystals, they entered a vast chamber where an impressive array of exquisite oil paintings, originating from various corners of the continent, were on display.

Gainsboro could not help her initial reaction. 'It's a shame ... all this culture just locked away.'

Obsidian assumed there was a reason they were not on display. 'I doubt he got them legally.'

Timberwolf, more intrigued by the weaponry collection, observed an assortment of shields and armour lined up in a logical order from west to east and north to south, according to the area of the continent they came from. Swords, staffs, bows, daggers, axes and pole arms transitioned to helms, grieves, gloves and boots; centuries of military history stashed away in a single place. 'Are we sure Vermillion isn't planning to run his own private militia?'

Gainsboro did not know where to start. 'Do you think Vermillion knows where every object is located?'

Obsidian noticed a lectern bearing a hefty book at the room's edge. He opened it, flicking through the pages, noticing the column titles on the top of the page – Object name, Object Number, Date of acquisition, and Source. The more he studied the collection's provenance, the more he shook his head in disgust; it would prove easier to identify the objects Vermillion didn't get through murder or theft than those he did.

Near the lectern, there was a bookshelf, tightly packed with identical, slim volumes which caught Obsidian's interest. They appeared to be personal diaries. One particular diary, slightly askew on the shelf as if left to tease visitors, compelled him to investigate. He plucked the diary and flicked through it.

'Anything interesting?' Gainsboro went over to read.

Obsidian stopped at a certain page and read an extract aloud:

'Tonight, I had a strange encounter. At a masquerade ball, a man in a violet mask approached me. Despite my initial suspicions, he turned out to be a charming and persuasive man. I must have impressed him because he gave me a ruby ring for free. An extraordinary treasure. I think it is magical. It has stirred something inside me. My desires have never been stronger. I must appease them—'

Obsidian snapped the diary shut and placed it back on the shelf. 'That verifies Vermillion's account of how he acquired The Gula.'

Timberwolf dared to voice all their unspoken thoughts. 'Why do I think Vermillion being gifted The Gula was no accident? When was that diary written?'

Obsidian checked the date embossed on the cover. 'Ten years ago.' He looked up and around him. 'He built all of this within a decade?'

Gainsboro wondered if collecting artifacts was a family tradition that had morphed into something more disturbing. 'Maybe his family had already made a start and he's added to it ever since?'

'Speculation can wait.' Obsidian was keen to proceed. 'I'm sure Church inspectors would love pouring through these diaries. Who knows what accounts and names he has recorded? These books detail a vast criminal empire.' He paused to draw breath; he was becoming sidetracked now. 'Come on. We've got a few rooms to go, I suspect.'

Obsidian navigated through foreboding corridors illuminated by low-level crystal light, followed by Gainsboro and Timberwolf, who kept looking over their shoulders in case Vermillion was hiding in the shadows.

The next room they entered was a treasure trove of familiar artifacts.

Vermillion had collected, organised, and displayed marble statuettes, embroidered cloths and religious tapestries into a cold regimented system. He had also categorised artifacts with any hints of gold or precious metals based on their approximate weight and symbolic importance. Walking around, trying to take in the extent of the stolen hoard, the trio stewed in silent fury.

Timberwolf broke the silence. 'I think we found our missing artifacts.'

'These belong in a church. They belong to worshippers.' Gainsboro could no longer remain silent. 'How many churches have been stripped bare of their soul?'

'Too many.' Obsidian spied another lectern, this time bearing a ledger detailing the names of the churches from which these treasures had been stolen. He did not need to study it to recognise the enormity of returning these treasures to their rightful homes.

Gainsboro attempted optimism. 'We know where these items belong, at least. We can return them to their rightful homes and put them back in use once returned.'

Timberwolf pressed forward, itching for justice, and wondered how many more rooms they had to navigate until they confronted the mad, gluttonous collector. 'The sooner we apprehend Vermillion, the better it will be for everyone.'

A stale odour filled the air. The trio exchanged glances. They dreaded what else they might find and, as they ventured into the next room, Gainsboro made the mistake of tempting fate. 'We must have seen the worst?'

She was wrong.

Human skulls lined the shelves, all staring forward at anyone who dared enter their resting place – it was death they could smell, clinging to the air. Gainsboro moved closer and realised the stains and dents on some of the skulls identified the cause of death. Quickly, she withdrew.

In the centre of the room, bones from various parts of the skeletons were displayed in glass cabinets. Timberwolf shivered, 'Who invited us into a mausoleum?'

Gainsboro could not stay silent. 'I'm not going mad, am I? This isn't acceptable, is it?'

'No.' Obsidian refused to imagine the age of these skulls. It begged a question. 'How long after death before it becomes acceptable to exhibit human remains?'

'How can we answer such a question?' Gainsboro squawked. 'Who decides that?'

'Not Vermillion.' Timberwolf had unwavering clarity and certainty.

Gainsboro fought back the urge to vomit. 'This is deeply offensive. Vermillion's no better than a graverobber.'

She spotted an empty spot on one of the shelves. Gainsboro could not help herself. She went over to inspect the pre-written label and instantly regretted it. Her soul wept, reading the tag – ROSEWOOD.

Obsidian and Timberwolf went to inspect her findings. Obsidian shook his head, disappointed, but not surprised. 'Vermillion would never allow Rosewood to live with his secrets. Once she had outlived her usefulness ... well ... let's hope we've spared her that fate.'

Gainsboro was furious. The entire collection now had a far more malevolent overtone to it. 'How many skulls belonged to Vermillion's victims?'

Obsidian sensed escalating panic. 'Stay calm. We can't let Vermillion see this is getting to us. We must rise above his horrors.'

Gainsboro took a deep breath. 'I know.'

'Boss?' Timberwolf found himself concerned.

'What is it?'

Obsidian moved along the shelf to see what Timberwolf had found and leant forward to read the tag – ARCANITE.

The ink was still wet. Obsidian, as experienced as he was, was shaken. Timberwolf did not know what to say. 'You alright, boss?'

Obsidian said nothing, but moved away and silently ventured down the next corridor; that shelf would not be his fate.

Gainsboro and Timberwolf followed. They refused to stay in this morbid place.

As they reached the end of the corridor, Obsidian's senses tingled. He steadied himself. 'I feel it ... The Gula is in the next room. Brace yourselves.'

Gainsboro and Timberwolf reassured each other with a glance.

'I'll take the lead,' Obsidian instructed. Gainsboro and Timberwolf did not object. With a nod, Obsidian primed his volcanic glass bracers as he readied his heart and inner thoughts. 'Mauveine was prepping me for this moment. This will be a test of our strength of magic and soul. I end your gluttony, Vermillion, tonight.'

IX – Fires of The Gula

The Private Quarters beneath Vermillion's Museum

Vermillion's chambers sprawled with artifacts; cherished remnants gathered. A secluded desk served as his sanctum for writing private letters. A dim scarlet radiance emanating from the luminous crystals on the wall established an ominous mood as the gluttonous collector greeted the three intruders with a sinister smile. He abandoned his feather quill and placed it besides a stack of greasy plates piled high with cleaned chicken bones, rose from his seat and slid the chair across the stone floor underneath his desk. 'So, you dared to enter? Arcanite, have you come to arrest me? Kill me? Tell me, do you like what you have seen?'

Gainsboro had heard enough. 'You're sick! You've had Rosewood wrapped around your nasty little finger.'

Vermillion, devoid of remorse, eyed The Gula, its malevolent flames on the brink of ignition. 'There's the righteous anger of the Church I was expecting. Are you here to deliver your wrathful judgement on me, young lady?'

Gainsboro glowered as Vermillion laughed. 'This ring compelled Rosewood to obey my will. It demands she respond to my desires. And before tonight's end, you too shall become my servant.'

Obsidian stepped forward. 'And end up becoming a trophy in your museum? No thanks.'

Vermillion grinned as he realised Obsidian had seen his resting place. 'But you would join an illustrious company. Some of my finest employees are on display. Even some of my relatives feature in the collection.'

Timberwolf and Gainsboro paled. 'Excuse me?'

Vermillion twisted The Gula around his finger. 'As the youngest of four brothers, I dreamed of opening a museum. My father collected various pieces of art, but he lacked my vision and deemed my plans unnecessary, cutting me out of the family on a whim. But the ring stirred something inside me. I had the most wondrous dream where all the world's symbols of status, power and faith were displayed under one roof.'

Obsidian, recalling the circumstances of Vermillion's inheritance, had his next attack ready. 'Your family died. Unfortunate for most, but not for you. The fortune you inherited could fund this madness.'

'It's a shame when accidents happen, isn't it? Especially unfortunate fires,' Vermillion gloated, showcasing The Gula. 'Wondrous thing Sin Magic. I have a dark thought and it fuels the ring's power, which inspires darker ideas. Things got out of hand.'

Timberwolf and Gainsboro struggled to maintain their composure. They were facing off against an unrepentant murderer. But Obsidian stood strong against such depravity. 'Is that you talking? Or the ring?'

Vermillion acknowledged Obsidian's insight. 'This ring allowed me to fulfil my heart's burning desires, amplifying and sustaining them, threading the plot of my dreams.'

Obsidian remained brave. 'Did you fear losing it all in your nightmares?'

'The idea of my collection being divided among unworthy souls is horrifying. That cannot be reality, don't you understand? Only I can appreciate the value of this collection.'

Vermillion had tried to sound triumphant, but his voice was touched with melancholy. Obsidian shook his head, recognising that this madman needed to be stopped at all costs. It was time to act. Timberwolf pushed his two clenched fists against each other, causing the air temperature around him to dip, condensing his breath. His enchanted gloves tightened against his skin. Gainsboro stirred the air with her sharpened wand, her hair blown upwards in the draft. Obsidian readied his volcanic glass bracers. 'It's over, Vermillion. Surrender The Gula now!'

Vermillion applauded his enemies, enjoying their grandstanding. 'The Gula? Is that what you call it? What a beautiful name!' Flames erupted from the ruby ring, dancing above his finger in a perfect arc. 'Now I shall show you the power that can grant any desire!'

Obsidian – the sheen of his Reflection Magic covering his entire form – stood firm, taking the lead. 'Careful! Don't get too close until we know what he's capable of.'

Vermillion's scarlet eyes burnt with malicious intent. 'Oh? Intriguing magical armaments you've got there. I look forward to adding them to my collection ... but tell me, Arcanite, do you remember my favourite parlour trick?'

He placed his chin on the flat back of his hand and took a deep breath.

Obsidian recognised this spell. 'STAY BEHIND ME!'

Timberwolf and Gainsboro took cover behind their leader, who was ready to defend his crew. He slammed his upright forearms together and the clang of his bracers initiated its own spell; a symbol of his will and intent. He created a grey barrier of light in front of him, as if conjuring a glass wall from thin air.

Vermillion exhaled, The Gula spewing a stream of crimson flames, resembling a dragon's tongue, at his enemy. The flames lashed Obsidian's reflective shield, bowing and bending it with the pressure, almost pressing it against his skin – skin which was burning and blistering. Blood dripped from his nose.

Timberwolf was eager to support. 'You've got to hold it, boss.'

'I'm ... trying—' Obsidian regretted not projecting his shield further away from his body; he was being pushed back, feet sliding across the stones.

The fires stopped. Vermillion ceased his attack, laughing in a mocking tone. 'You're too proud of your own power. Pride will be your downfall.'

Obsidian lowered his barrier, panting, drooping, slouching forwards, dehydrated, licking his parched lips.

Gainsboro sought to check Obsidian's health. 'Are you alright?'

Obsidian shook off her concern. 'I'll be fine.'

Timberwolf spotted something more worrying. 'The floor?'

Cobbled stones on the floor were cracking, the damage deep rooted. They crumbled into dust.

'Corrosion,' Vermillion boasted. 'The Gula's fires don't just burn. They corrode everything they touch. Taking a hit head-on was foolish, despite your impressive defence.'

Obsidian wiped the sweat from his brow. He concluded Sin Magic enhanced the flames and wished Mauveine had warned him of this possibility. A suspicion formed in his mind that he kept to himself for now. He needed more evidence to be certain. 'There are limits built into any magical equipment to stop the user from overextending themselves. Would The Gula, a Sin Magic conductor, have such safeguards?'

Vermillion, too indulged in his own power to listen, hated the perceived stalling tactics. 'What will you do now?'

Gainsboro retaliated on Obsidian's behalf, waving her sharpened wand, generating blades of air that cut through Vermillion's clothes and deep into his flesh.

He bled from each wound; on the arms, upper legs, torso, and cheeks. Despite the injuries sustained, his tubby physique resisted a fall. 'Such wrathful anger.'

Timberwolf's fingers tensed, gloves constricting from the Ice Magic which manifested. He stormed forth as ice wrapped around Vermillion's body, freezing him in place. He was going to end this brawl in a single blow.

The Gula flashed once. Fire cannoned from the ruby ring towards Timberwolf, his face glowing red from the incoming inferno.

'GET DOWN!' Obsidian leapt forward, grabbing Timberwolf's shirt and pulling him to the ground. With an explosive boom, the flare stream slammed into the stone wall behind him, melting the surface into glowing, dripping slag.

Timberwolf shook, reduced to a gibbering wreck.

Obsidian got back onto his feet. 'Get your head back into the game, Timberwolf!'

The ice binding Vermillion melted from the fierce heat being given off by The Gula. Water cascaded off his opulent fire robes before evaporating away. But that was not all. Gainsboro was the first to spot something confusing happening to Vermillion. 'Obsidian? What's happening?'

Vermillion, struggling, panted. His face was sagging and contorted. His hair was thinning, greying and becoming wiry and straw-like. He did not notice at first, instead he focused on taunting Timberwolf. 'Your lust to be a hero will get you killed.'

Gainsboro struggled to describe what she was seeing. 'He's ... he's aging?'

Vermillion realised clumps of his hair were falling to the floor. Trying to keep hold of it, he found it came away in his hands.

Timberwolf stood aghast, watching Vermillion shrink, decades of aging happening within a blink of an eye. 'What's happening to him?'

Obsidian's hypothesis was being validated. 'My bracers, your wand and gloves amplify our magic, but do not risk our health because they have safeguards built in.'

Gainsboro began to understand. 'And The Gula doesn't?'

Obsidian sensed their opportunity. 'Those hellbent on using Sin Magic are less worried about their personal safety. The Gula cursed him, aging him and forcing him to have a voracious appetite to sustain himself. Now, The Gula is feasting on his very vitality.'

Vermillion touched his own face. He barely recognised it. 'I'm scarred? ... Deformed?'

Timberwolf saw his chance. 'You've got to stop now. That ring will drain you dry.'

Vermillion was on the brink of exhaustion. 'I never learnt to control The Gula's power. There was no need until now.' He paused and laughed. 'But beware, I still have enough strength to kill you three.'

Gainsboro and Timberwolf retreated behind Obsidian, who stood firm, having learnt his lesson. He raised his holy barrier again. This time, he generated the reflective shield far beyond his body, six feet in front of him.

More fire erupted from The Gula, unrestrained and erratic. Vermillion had lost control. Priceless artifacts and heirlooms which got in the way ignited and burnt with a glorious flame in their last moments. He did not care so long as the Arcane Investigators perished.

The fire crashed into Obsidian's screen. It bent under the force of the impact, but did not break. Obsidian poured all his effort into maintaining the barrier, unable to deflect the flames back at the mad lord. He staked his very pride in protecting his juniors, so they could land the winning blow. 'Prepare!'

Gainsboro and Timberwolf readied themselves.

Timberwolf's battle instincts kicked in. 'You set him up and I knock him out.' 'Got it!'

Vermillion's vision was becoming hazy; he could no longer appease The Gula's hunger for his life force. There was nothing left to give. His flames petered out. He slouched forward, exhausted; a little function remained in his muscles, but he thought nothing. Felt nothing. Forever numb.

'Now!' Obsidian lowered his barrier.

Gainsboro, swishing her wand, conjured gusts of wind that battered Vermillion, knocking him off balance. Timberwolf seized and struck with a crunching punch.

Vermillion, too weak to support his frail frame, collapsed, wheezing and drained; the scarlet from his eyes faded to reveal their original hazel hue. The Gula's menacing glow faded and cooled; a threat no more.

Obsidian hobbled over as Gainsboro supported him. They all glanced down at Vermillion, now pitiful.

'Take ... The ring,' a meek Vermillion mumbled. 'That man ... who gifted me this ring... I sold my soul to him that day. You have broken the curse. I do not ask for forgiveness. Please... Seal The Gula away ... forever.'

Defeated, but with a peaceful countenance, Vermillion closed his eyes, not in death, but with an acceptance justice had come for him. For the first time in years, his gluttony no longer held his soul captive. He would face the consequences of his deeds freed from the Ring of Gluttony.

X – Gluttony's End

Overlooking Vermillion's Estate

'Alabaster!' Carmine ran towards Alabaster with tears streaming down her cheeks. She embraced the disguised cleric, unwilling to release her; this cathartic moment crucial for her sanity.

Uncertain how to respond, Alabaster chose a gentle pat on the back. She acted the role of a caring cleric and said what was required. 'There, there, it's over now.'

Carmine squeezed her so hard she made her cough.

'Sorry,' Carmine released her grip. 'I ... I was just scared.'

Alabaster cleared her throat and regained her dignified persona. 'You've been very brave, Carmine. We must now have faith. Those brave souls you let into the building are the experts, Arcane Investigators trained to confront the magic Vermillion possessed. They'll defeat and arrest him, so the Church can secure the museum.'

'Do you believe they'll succeed?'

'Have faith.'

Alabaster spotted the Knights of the Dies Mater securing the perimeter and entering the premises. 'Carmine, your belief has paid off.'

Delighted by the prospect, Carmine gazed on from a distance, pleased her ordeal was over. 'I can sleep easy tonight.'

'Indeed.' Alabaster looked on impressed. 'Come now. We need to leave the experts to their work.'

Carmine sighed with relief. 'Maybe I can get a job in the Church's artifact division? Who knows? At least I'm free from that godforsaken place.'

Alabaster kept her counsel and led Carmine away with a silent acknowledgement of the Arcane Investigator's achievement, believing they would prove useful in the future.

The Cellars

Father Grapha arrived, leading with his cane, having navigated the labyrinthine place, pleased to see the trio unharmed. He eyed the defeated and aged Vermillion, who had slipped into a deep slumber. 'I recall him being younger?'

Obsidian stifled a yawn. 'The Gula drained him of his vitality, Father.'

'Was Vermillion a more formidable opponent than you expected?'

'You could say that, Father. The ring can cast some potent fire spells. It took more stamina to block his attacks than I thought.'

'I see.' An uneasy feeling settled in Grapha's chest as the weight of the implications sank in, but he felt a glimmer of relief knowing that The Gula was inactive. He turned his gaze towards Gainsboro and Timberwolf. Both seemed eager to leave as soon as allowed. 'I presume Timberwolf and Gainsboro gave you able help?'

'Yes. They won the day. I couldn't have done it without them.'

'Well done.' Grapha acknowledged both his young investigators with a bow of his head.

'Thank you, Father.'

Obsidian cleared his throat; he was eager to get the ring secured. 'Now where's Mauveine and his chest?'

'Out of the way!' Mauveine pushed through the gathered group of knights. He held his prize chest in his arms and nobody could stop him. 'Ah! There you are, Obsidian.'

'You could have warned me about the corrosive fire,' Obsidian sniped at the confident scholar.

Mauveine saw the stone dust and scowled. 'Yes ... Well—' He avoided dwelling on the destructive power by inserting his personal key into the chest, turning the lock and opening it. A pitch-black lining covered a deep storage space inside designed for The Gula. 'Ready to extract the ring?'

Grapha tightened his grip on his cane; this scholar's manner made him nervous, although he did not know why. But for now, he stepped forward, volunteering to do the job, unpleasant as it was. 'I will do it.'

Obsidian denied him. 'No, I'll do it.'

Grapha regarded him through narrowed eyes. 'Are you sure? You are quite tired.'

Obsidian bent down and removed the ring from Vermillion's fingers with great care. 'Gainsboro, Timberwolf ... you have permission to knock me out if I even look like I'm putting The Gula on, OK? Promise me.'

'Promise!' they said as one, although they both felt alarmed by the prospect.

Grapha, too, was nervous and stood ready with his cane, in case it was needed.

As soon as the ring was flat in his palm, Obsidian heard faint whispers, where they came from, he didn't know, but a malefic female voice sounded in his ear, and although he was unable to decipher any clear wording or meaning, he felt the urge to place the ring on his finger. 'The Gula is speaking to me.'

'What does it say?' Mauveine's eyes sparkled with curiosity.

Gainsboro had heard enough. 'Place the ring inside the box!'

Conflicted, Obsidian forced himself to cast The Gula into the chest and Mauveine snapped it shut before he had a chance to take it out again. The whispers stopped.

Obsidian sighed. 'I understand how one might succumb to wearing that ring. If I had a gluttonous heart, I don't think I could ignore her voice.'

'Her?' Grapha found the description strange.

Mauveine interrupted with applause. 'Well done! The information we've learnt today is invaluable.'

'Are you crazy?' Gainsboro screeched, catching everyone by surprise. 'Obsidian was in danger, risking his safety and you stood there ... curious.'

Obsidian had no energy left to argue. 'It's alright, Gainsboro. We got the job done.'

Seething, Gainsboro backed down, but she scowled at Mauveine.

'My apologies. If you excuse me—' Mauveine scurried away to secure the chest in the cathedral before any inquisitive scholars pestered him to study The Gula for themselves.

Grapha pigeon-holed his own observations, for now. He offered Obsidian his cane. 'You look like you need this.'

Obsidian declined with a short-lived smile. 'I'm fine. That ring is powerful. It's no simple trinket from the north.'

'Indeed.' Grapha saw the positives. 'But congratulations are in order. The bureau achieved a tremendous success. Leave the tidying up to me. Take some well-earned rest.'

'Let's go,' Obsidian said with a glance towards Gainsboro and Timberwolf. 'Our work here is done.'

Outside, in the fresh air, away from the darkened pits of Vermillion's collection, dawn was approaching. Day's first sunlight kiss was never so rewarding. Still winded, Obsidian sat on a low garden wall.

Timberwolf thought he would celebrate. 'We did well. Vermillion is in custody. He will answer for his crimes. We did a good thing. The artifacts will be returned to the Church and its communities, thanks to us.'

'Indeed,' Obsidian nodded. 'We must never forget that.'

Gainsboro gave Obsidian some water. Never had he drunk with such speed; he gulped it back so fast he was uncertain if he had swallowed. When he finished, Gainsboro, caught off-guard, quickly poured him another.

Obsidian splashed some water on his face to cool his burning skin. 'Remind me that even I have my limits.'

Laughter was a welcome relief. All three acknowledged this case's impact on their lives – it had been gruelling, but there had been satisfaction in stopping a madman.

Gainsboro was the first to stop laughing. Her thoughts had turned to the future. As she glanced back at the museum, she hoped for a reunion, longing to meet Rosewood once she had healed and was rehabilitated. Clearing her throat, Gainsboro asked what others had not dared. 'There are seven deadly sins. Do you think that are more Sin Rings out there?'

Obsidian would not entertain the idea today. 'That's tomorrow's problem. For now, we enjoy the daybreak. We achieved something important today. We stopped a mad glutton.' He paused to take in the significance of his words. 'But Sin Magic is always lurking in the shadows, looking for a new host. It always chooses the most surprising faces. We must be ready. That is our duty as Arcane Investigators.'

Extra Content I – A Spymaster's Treasure Hold

The Archives, The Cathedral

'This case ... It has a faint echo from fifty years ago.' Grapha's thoughts weighed on his heart as he waited for the discreet wooden door to be unlocked by the clerk. The door to the archives opened and the spymaster entered; the jewel at the top of his cane came to life with a brilliant flash of light, revealing its enchanted nature – his proof of identity.

Grapha entered his specialised vault alone. The jewel on top of his cane sparkled, white crystal torchlights illuminated, revealing multiple bookcases filled with files detailing case reports the Bureau had complied over the decades; his legacy stored away for select eyes only. 'The answer must lie in here.'

Unsure of what question he should ask, he looked for a file that he would have written early in his career. His encounter with Mauveine caused a name to resurface from deep within his memories, one he had not thought about for decades. 'Viorel? He'd be an old man by now, if he's not already dead. Why am I remembering him? It's been fifty years since I last encountered him.'

He accessed the Viorel file, flicked through the pages and read a report he penned. It was one of the first cases he worked on. He read aloud:

'A man – whose name could not be established – indulged in illegal, mind-altering spices to a dangerous excess, cast fire magic on anyone who dared to stop him feast. When I apprehended him, he was rabid and used a Sin Magic conductor to fuel his rampage. When I questioned him, in his frightful ecstasy, he rambled a name – Viorel.'

He closed the file with the echoes of the past reverberating. While the circumstances differed, there were clear parallels to note. The Gula, a superior amplifier, surpassed the one used by Viorel years ago, but the design principles remained.

Returning the file to its proper resting place, Grapha kept his thoughts to himself for now and decided to observe developments from afar. Years ago, Viorel orchestrated multiple incidents that defined his early career, yet what was happening now felt far larger and more significant – it had the potential to define Obsidian's career.

His enchanted cane flashed once, dimming the torchlights before their light faded. He walked out of his personal archive; the clerk bowed his head, locking the door behind him.

Extra Content II – Rosso, the Scholar

Mauveine's Study

With The Gula stowed away in a distant vault, Mauveine immersed himself in writing the intricate details of the proposals he sought to implement. Under the lavender shades emanating from his crystal torchlights, his concentration remained unbroken, not lifting his quill from the page to even take a sip of water. Countless details needed to be recorded, the pages filled with coherent thoughts – coherent to him, at least.

An errant cough interrupted his trancelike state. Mauveine's nostrils flared and his judgemental eyes rose to meet the bold soul who dared interrupt him. On the opposite side of his desk, stood Rosso, an eager scholar who held public ambitions to ascend to the role of a high theologian of the Church was tapping his fingers on Mauveine's desk.

Rosso cleared his throat. 'So, you have the ring, Mauveine? Let's have a look!'

'It's not here, Rosso. I've secured it elsewhere, away from prying eyes.' Mauveine placed his quill on his desk; he could record his plans at a different time.

He placed his gloved left hand on the desk, eager to reclaim ownership of his precious workspace; a scholar's most treasured domain of influence.

'But?' Rosso objected, only to be silenced by Mauveine's glare. 'You gave me your word.'

'In due time, Rosso.' Mauveine gestured for calm. 'I advise, once again, patience is required before accessing the ring for study. The Arcane Investigators poured considerable effort into securing The Gula. We require time for things to cool off before we consider studying it.'

Rosso tapped his fingers on Mauveine's desk. 'Not even a tiny peek?'

With his gloved hand, Mauveine swatted away Rosso's trespassing fingers. 'Pull yourself together, man. Prospective high theologians need to compose themselves.'

Rosso paced up and down in front of Mauveine's desk. 'If I'm going to become the head scholar and theologian, Mauveine, I need to understand how that ring works and answer the theological questions a Sin Magic amplifier of this magnitude poses to the bishops and the cardinals. I need to understand how that ring works!'

Mauveine played along. 'And you will. In time. You need to work with me here. Building your career won't happen in a day.'

Rosso had no time for patience. 'At least going through Vermillion's collection will yield other fascinating tomes and scholarly works worth my time. How incredibly selfish of him, hoarding all that knowledge for himself.'

Mauveine saw the silver lining. 'It's now Church property.'

'Correct!' Rosso too saw something – the obvious opportunity. 'We should have that knowledge, as we know how to handle it. The Church should be the bookkeeper of any information, not some pompous lord. If anyone wants to borrow a book, then they should come and ask us.'

'And that collection should carry on growing?' Mauveine enquired.

'If I had control, I'd amass the grandest collection in modern history.'

Mauveine saw his opening. 'Don't tell me that Vermillion's gluttony has inspired you, dear Rosso?'

Rosso stumbled over his own ambition. 'I ... I would not resort to such ... disgraceful methods.'

'Of course not.' Mauveine's sarcasm was not what Rosso wanted to hear. 'I can see The Gula at home on your finger.'

'Shut up!'

Mauveine raised his hands in self-defence. 'I jest, Rosso. I jest.' He lowered his hands and offered some consolation. 'Look, it will take a while. It's my duty to keep The Gula secure, out of the wrong hands. Once I've established an approved security arrangement, I'm sure the Church will grant your request to study it. The Church requires careful management because of conflicting and moving parts. I've requested to meet the Church Bank to secure funding for my plans to protect The Gula and similar artifacts.'

Rosso leant in. 'Are there more Sin Rings out there?'

'It would be foolish to assume this is the only one.'

'Go meet the Church Bank then.'

Mauveine raised his finger. 'It may take a while to secure that meeting. The Church cannot grasp the true nature of the situation. They're too busy trying to hide the true nature of Vermillion's criminality from the public.'

Rosso conceded. After all, Mauveine had already trapped him by turning his own ambitions against him and he was irritated that Mauveine always gained the upper hand in their conversations. 'I understand the need for patience, but Vermillion is a disgraced criminal. Why are they so worried about him? He's *persona non grata* now.'

'A *persona non grata* who used Sin Magic in his schemes which the Church is very keen for the public not to find out about.' Mauveine understood the Church's priorities even if they were frustrating to scholars such as themselves.

Rosso saw he was getting nowhere. 'Just remember, you are a scholar too, Mauveine. You're one of us. Do not forget your word, understand?'

'I won't.'

'Let me know if you need my help.' Rosso bowed his head before departing, leaving Mauveine to complete his work.

Mauveine leant back in his chair, rubbing the thumb of his left-handed glove on the middle finger. He smirked as his inner thoughts turned to the challenges facing him. 'The Arcane Investigators will take credit, as they should. But as the self-nominated custodian of the Sin Rings, I must remember there will be those within the Church curious about them and susceptible to their influence. Despite Obsidian's efforts to extinguish the flames of gluttony, there are still gluttonous hearts within these walls. I cannot afford the rings to be compromised until they are all gathered ...'

Extra Content III – The Mastermind's Diary Entry I

55 years ago

'The circumstances of birth are beyond even my control. I had the misfortune of being born to a bloodline dedicated to toppling the Church of the Dies Mater using Sin Magic, but they were not fit for purpose. They did not create nor innovate, content to rely on the inventions of the past and profit from their genius – and not their own; a slow-moving tragedy plaguing generation after generation of nitwits. Only I could see their obvious failings and recognise their naïve belief that they would succeed – a belief which would always end in stunning failure, and which drove me to abandon them. Heritage means nothing if it represents failure. I needed to create weapons of my own design and not rely on trinkets which had failed in the past to leave a lasting impact.

The truth was my family failed to understand the weight of the challenge they faced; the Church of the Dies Mater has endured so long because the institution's foundations are near impervious. They forgot the Dies Mater was an impressive woman, a warrior of light capable of performing miracles and defeating the evil mankind had let loose on the world because of their arrogance and ignorance. Her deific status was bestowed to her on her deathbed; she became a symbol of peace and harmony because people had grown exhausted of endless and brutal conflict that left the very landscape scarred.

Centuries passed and that message of peace has been forgotten by a Church that has failed to understand its purpose. Vice and sin still linger in the city as a compromise for the false sense of peace and security. Human nature cannot normally be tamed, but I can tame it with Sin Magic. With my Sin Magic conductors, I will weaponise such desires to my advantage.

Though progress will be slow, I'm a patient man and will learn from every experiment, every prototype. For I do not intend to destroy the Church, no, that would be an illogical action. Instead, I will warp it around my will using the very magic they fear ...
   Viorel'

The Next Chapter

Nightfall, The Backstreets of Spectra City

'Where are we going?' A growing sense of caution and apprehension matched Obsidian's escalating frustrations. He was acting as the bodyguard for Father Grapha, who led the way, aided by his jewel-tipped cane, keen to reach their undisclosed destination. With a vigilant gaze, he navigated through the dim backstreets where the echoes of their footsteps reverberated against the towering brick walls. Darkness had fallen, and this urban district was harsh to those who did not belong. By comparison, Grapha was carefree. 'You need to relax and learn some patience. I know these streets.'

Obsidian remained on edge, perceiving threats everywhere. Since defeating Vermillion, he believed this expedition was an unnecessary risk.

A feeble, whitish yellow crystal light emanated from a streetlamp and pierced the darkness. The volcanic glass bracers on his forearms gleamed, ready to erect a holy shield at the first sign of danger.

'You intend to protect from me from a stray rat?' Grapha jested. 'Do not fret. We're almost there.'

Obsidian growled under his breath. 'Where are we going?'

'Do you recall the name that Church investigators found when they were going through Lord Vermillion's records, a name which we found perplexing?'

Obsidian knew he was being tested. 'Goldenrod? We couldn't trace that name to anyone on record. Have you figured out who they are?'

'It's not a person,' Grapha speculated. 'It's the name of an old trade route from a time when spices were worth more than their weight in gold.'

'Spices?' Obsidian was incredulous. 'Is this a serious line of enquiry?'

Grapha, understanding Obsidian's cynicism, would not allow his professional instincts to be deterred. 'What if someone has reactivated that old trade route?'

'Then our food will taste better? I cannot see why—'

Grapha remained focused. 'Very droll, Obsidian. Spices aren't the only expensive items of interest, are they? People may want other items.'

The cogs within Obsidian's brain were churning. Grapha was pushing down a certain line of enquiry. 'You seriously think someone has reactivated the old Goldenrod route?'

Grapha nodded, pleased to see Obsidian making the connections. 'Spectra City always had a thriving black market. But in recent years, it has flourished, and I believe Vermillion must have exploited it for his own interests.'

Obsidian bemoaned the constraints the Arcane Investigation Bureau was forced to adhere to. 'We deal with crimes of an arcane nature or those which involve Sin Magic. Addressing the black market is beyond our remit unless—'

Grapha's eyes gleamed with resolve.

Obsidian recognised the look and shook his head, realising where Grapha's mind had leapt to. 'You think Sin Magic is involved somewhere, don't you?'

Grapha invited Obsidian to speculate. 'Consider the possibility ... We saw what Sin Magic did to Vermillion and how his criminal enterprise expanded. Why can't Sin Magic be at the heart of the explosion in black market activity?'

Uncertain whether Grapha was grasping at straws or whether he had deduced a genuine lead, Obsidian trusted his spymaster was right, even if his hypothesis sounded flimsy. 'Do you have any proof that they are using Sin Magic?'

'Not yet,' Grapha conceded, then grinned with mischievous intent. 'But if we find evidence of Sin Magic, we will have authority to act. Otherwise, we share our findings with the relevant authorities.'

Obsidian pinched the bridge between his nose. 'Are you sure about this?'

'Trust these old bones.'

Still unconvinced, Obsidian bowed to Grapha's seniority, believing he knew more than he had disclosed.

As they ventured through the backstreets, they came across a merchant's shop. The faint light from an orange crystal light peeked through the windows, showing it was still open for business. Obsidian read the sign – PORTOCALE'S HERBS AND SPICES.

Grapha approached the homeless man sitting in front of the shop. Weighed down by heavy, dirtied rags, the vagrant raised an empty, rusting tin, shaking it once. 'Spare a penny, Father?'

Grapha dropped two coins into the beggar's tin, eliciting a grateful shake. 'Tell me what do you know about the goings-on in this shop?'

Astonished, Obsidian watched the old spymaster show mastery in his craft.

'Portocale is in and came back in a rush. I think he's going to meet someone.' The beggar shook his tin again.

To Obsidian's surprise, Grapha produced a silver key and dropped it into the can; the clunk of metal was louder than that produced by the coins.

'Thank you, Father.' The beggar collected his things and scurried into the distance.

Obsidian's demanding gaze met Grapha's contented smile. 'Care to explain?'

'My homeless network,' Grapha boasted. 'An interconnected web that touches every part of the city. It's taken an entire career to cultivate it.'

Obsidian assumed it was a key to a Church Safehouse, a reward for his service. 'You've never mentioned such a network before.'

'A spymaster's secret.'

'I assume your homeless network does not have official recognition.'

The idea appalled Grapha. 'Of course not. I've learnt to use circumspect language when hiding it in our annual budget requests. Watch and learn, Obsidian, if you want to be a spymaster in the future.'

Laughing, Obsidian realised this was the next phase of his education. 'So, this Portocale, then … Is he a lead or an informant?'

'An old merchant, one of whom people have asked questions regarding the legitimacy of his business. If anyone knows anything about Goldenrod, he's a good bet.'

Obsidian opened the wooden door, allowing Grapha to enter the shop first. Greeted by the aroma of exotic herbs and pungent spices, the merchant Portocale glanced up from behind the counter; a portly man with a weathered face.

'Good evening,' Grapha started the conversation. 'I've been told you might be able to help me.'

Portocale's mercantile instincts kicked him. He rubbed his hands together. 'What do you wish to buy? We have a wide variety of exclusive items from all over the continent. Let me show you.'

Grapha leant on his cane. 'I'm here to buy information. Word on the street is that you are the person to ask about Goldenrod?' He looked over to Obsidian for confirmation, a critical part of his masquerade. 'It was called Goldenrod, wasn't it?'

Obsidian smiled, admiring the old spymaster performing his well-rehearsed routine. 'It was indeed, sir.'

Portocale pulled at his collar. 'Goldenrod? Never heard of it.'

'Lord Vermillion used Goldenrod to acquire stolen artifacts ... Was he one of your customers?'

Portocale avoided eye-contact. 'This is a legitimate place of business. I must ask you to leave and you'll be hearing from my lawyer!'

Grapha clocked the first slip-up. He halted his line of questioning and bowed his head. 'We look forward to hearing from them. Thank you for your time.'

Obsidian opened and closed the door, letting the spymaster leave first. They both headed down the road to a secluded spot where the streetlight struggled to reach.

'Do we wait?' Obsidian asked.

Grapha kept his sharpened eyes on the shop. 'Yes, let's see where the merchant runs to.' Ready to intercept any potential threat, Obsidian breathed in to clear the aromas tickling the back of his nose. 'You want me to be your shield if this goes wrong?'

'That's why I brought you along,' Grapha confirmed.

Obsidian laughed. 'Why not inform me at the bureau?'

'Where's the fun in that?'

A few minutes later, Portocale made his move; the urgency in his actions dispelling his supposed innocence. Leaving the shop, he inserted the iron key into the lock, turned it, and secreting the key back into his pocket, hastened away to his scheduled rendezvous.

Obsidian observed with anticipation. 'Now where are you off to?'

The thrill of the chase had begun.

Mauveine's Records

***

- **Arcane Investigation Bureau:** A division within the Church of the Dies Mater tasked with investigating arcane artifacts and incidents involving Sin Magic.
- **Arcane Investigators:** Skilled officers of the Arcane Investigation Bureau, who possess magical abilities and are trained to confront arcane threats.
- **Church of the Dies Mater:** The primary religious authority of the western part of the continent.
- **Gainsboro's Wand**: A magical conduit for Gainsboro's wind spells, ranging from gust attacks to razor-sharp air blades.
- **Grapha's Cane:** An enchanted cane wielded by the Old Spymaster of the Church of the Dies Mater.
- **Obsidian's Bracers:** Enchanted magical conduits resembling volcanic glass, capable of amplifying the power of Obsidian's reflection spells.
- **Reflection Magic:** A magical phenomenon derived from Light and Earth Magic, capable of deflecting both physical and magical assaults.
- **Sin Magic:** A primal magic derived from the malicious thoughts of the spellcaster. Often associated with villains and rogues.
- **Sin Rings:** A set of magical rings capable of creating spells using Sin Magic.
- **The Gula:** A Sin Magic Conductor in the form of a ruby ring made in the northern reaches of the continent. It harnesses the Sin of Gluttony and conjures corrosive flames.

- **Timberwolf's Gloves:** Fighting gloves invoking the image of a wolf's claws, serving as a magical conduit that amplifies the strength of his ice spells.
- **Vermillion:** The ring bearer of the Ring of Gluttony.
- **Vermillion's Cellars:** Home to the exclusive private collection concealed beneath Vermillion's old ancestral home.
- **Vermillion's Museum:** The museum built by Vermillion, which houses his amassed treasures.
- **Mauveine's Chest:** A chest with a protective inner lining. It is resistant to any magical influence from entering or leaving the central compartment.
- **Mauveine's Tome:** A tome detailing the Sin Magic rings, written in the runic languages of the north.

Spectral Index

This index details the origin and inspirations behind the character names included in this story.

Black

- Obsidian – An igneous rock and a volcanic glass formed when lava is cooled rapidly, and crystal formation is limited due to the lava's high silica content. Said to be discovered in Ethiopia by the Roman Explorer, **Obsidius**.

- Grapha – A shortening of graphite, the most thermodynamically stable allotrope of carbon in standard conditions. Name is derived from the Greek word *Graphein* meaning **to write**.

White

- Alabaster – A mineral and soft rock used for carvings and a source of plaster powder. Thought to have been first used in Ancient Egypt where ceremonial jars were made from *alabastra*, which came the **Alabastron** region.

- Arcanite – An off-white potassium sulfate mineral named after the Latin Word *arcanum*, meaning *secret*. It has been used for agriculture as a potassium source which does not affect soil pH.

Grey

- Gainsboro – An achromatic grey used in web colouring and a reference to the 17th Century English painter, Thomas Gainsborough, a founder member of the Royal Academy of Art.

- Timberwolf – A shade of grey which shares its name with the largest wolves in the Candiae family. They are often forest-dwelling wolves in North America, Europe and Asia.

- Ashen - A colour inspired by ash, the powdery remains of fire. The word is derived from the Norse and Proto-Germanic words **aska** and **askon**.

Red

- Vermillion – A red pigment made from powdered cinnabar, which has been used in both Roman Art and lacquerware in China.

- Rosewood – A shade of red named after the rich-hued hardwoods, it has a high polish and is used for luxury furniture.

- Carmine – A deep red pigment which was used by the Aztecs to dye textiles. Imported to Europe in the 16th century.

- Jasper – The red variant of this gemstone has a high iron (III) content and was used for jewellery as far back as Minoan Crete (around 1800 BC).

- Rust – A metallic red colour that resembles the iron oxide formed when iron corrodes in the presence of oxygen and water.

- Cinnabar – A mineral composed of mercury sulfide, which is associated with volcanic activity and alkaline springs, and which is also the source of the Vermillion pigment.

- Cordovan – A dark red named after the Spanish city of Cordoba where Cordovan leather has been produced since the 7th century.

- Rosso – The Italian for red derived from the Latin, *Rossius*, and used as a nickname for someone with red hair in Medieval Italy.

Violet

- Viorel – The Romanian for violet derived from the Latin **viola** and the Romanian word **viorea**, which is an alpine squill flower.

- Mauveine – One of the first mass produced chemical dyes,

discovered by accident in the 1850s. Named after **mauve** from the mallow flower and inspired the '**Mauve Decade**' in art in the 1890s.

The Zoharian Bladers Trilogy

***

***

'Zera, the Archangels demand victory from the Successor of Ramiel. It is time you earnt that title.'

Zera, a powerful angel of Heaven and wielder of the Zoharian Blade Ramiel, is thrust into the latest phase of the celestial battle that has lasted millennia. Grief stricken following the death of his wife, he must embrace divine power to save not only himself but the Earth he has sworn to protect.

And in the shadows lurks a presence. A Fallen Angel with his own Zoharian Blade.

The stage is set. Failure sparks disaster.

Available on Amazon, Smashwords, Kobo and many more.

The Arcana's Bestiary Series

***

THE TELLIER'S COCKATRICE
ARCANA'S BESTIARY PAGE 1

OLIVER KERRIGAN

THE GULLIVER'S GRYPHON
ARCANA'S BESTIARY PAGE 2

OLIVER KERRIGAN

***

'Le Bateleur, there's a monster on the loose, you must slay it.'

A halberd wielding magician, Batel, and his unusual collection of companions investigates the death of a unicorn and uncovers a dreadful and frightening monster – the Cockatrice. This abomination, half-chicken, half-dragon, is indiscriminately killing man and unicorn in a frenzy and proves immune to conventional weapons. The Cockatrice marches towards its next meal having gained a taste for human flesh. Who can stop it? Who would be bold (stupid) enough to try?

Available on Amazon, Smashwords, Kobo and many more.

Author Notes

The Vermillion Curator is the first book in my latest series, which draws on the occult detective genre, whilst maintaining my epic fantasy and action-adventure roots. It's a new venture and I hope you enjoy reading. This story was inspired by the recent debates around ancient artifact and relic ownership, following their appropriation during the colonial years, a subject which is growing in significance as the years go by.

I would like to thank everyone who has supported me. This project means a lot to me and I'm eternally appreciative of their help. If you enjoyed this book and would like to leave a review on the page where you bought the book, I'd be most grateful. Reviews really do help to spread the word, especially for independent authors.

If you wish to read more of my content, please have a look at my other series – The Zoharian Bladers Trilogy and The Arcana's Bestiary.